To Brian and Barbara Beedham

Richard Critchfield

VILLAGES

ANCHOR BOOKS
ANCHOR PRESS/DOUBLEDAY
GARDEN CITY, NEW YORK
1983

Articles about eleven of the villages have appeared in the *Christian Science Monitor*, 1973–80.

Copyright © 1981, 1983, by Richard Critchfield
Photographs by the author
All rights reserved
Printed in the United States of America
Anchor Books edition: 1983

Library of Congress Cataloging in Publication Data

Critchfield, Richard.
    Villages.

    "Articles about eleven of the villages have appeared
in the Christian science monitor, 1973–80"—Verso of t.p.
    Reprint. Originally published: Garden City, N.Y.:
Anchor Press/Doubleday, 1981.
    Includes index.
    1. Underdeveloped areas—Villages—Case studies.
I. Title.
HT421.C74   1983   307.7'2   82-22235
ISBN 0-385-18375-5

J

PREFACE TO THE NEW EDITION

Since *Villages* was published in 1981, the pace of change has quickened. The use of new hybrid, drought-resistant or nitrogen-fixing crops, and such innovations as solar pumps and drip irrigation are now accomplished fact in a few parts of the Third World. There has been such an explosion of technological, genetic and chemical knowledge and its application to farming, one cannot hope and certainly cannot claim to keep up with it.

One can now confidently say that a quiet agricultural revolution has started in the villages that is likely to have more dramatic effects on more human beings than any revolution that has gone before.

To find anything comparable in our own experience, we must go back sixty years. Before the 1920s, change in American agriculture was slow. Silent films of the time wonderfully record the dusty dirt roads, farm wagons and Model T Fords passing by, sweating threshers in bib overalls pitching bundles, and small family farms with cows, pigs and chickens. Speed and power were set by the three-mile-an-hour gait of the horse. By 1940, as highly mechanized, highly capitalized farming took over, this way of life was just a nostalgic memory. Since 1940, the number of Americans who farm has dropped from about 30 percent to 2.7 percent, and only about 1 percent produce two thirds of total output. This is perhaps the most fundamental change in modern American history. We are just beginning to face its cultural consequences.

If the 1920s and 1930s brought decisive change to American agriculture, the decade of the 1970s can now be seen, if at a much lower level of technology, as the start of a similar turning point for much of the Third World, particularly Asia. *Villages* tells the story of this decade in terms of what happened in the minds of some individual villagers.

*

The six main cultures to be found in villages are Confucian, Hindu, Islamic, Malay-Javanese, Christian (Latin American Roman Catholic) and African. (Buddhism and Judaism decide village behavior for relatively few.) Since writing *Villages*, I've toured East Asia and East Africa, stayed in villages in Sri Lanka, Mexico and Kenya, and begun a book on American rural change. This experience suggests the portrayal of African culture in *Villages* is incomplete.

Africa has a unique problem of cultural adaptation to modern farming: most food is grown by women; too few African males yet see agriculture as the key to the continent's development and their own family incomes. This apparently stems from Africa's comparative isolation until the late-nineteenth century. Periodic epidemics of disease kept population growth in check. Man was able to evolve gradually from hunter and collector into hunter, herder and primitive slash-and-burn cultivator, because population density rarely exceeded 250 persons per square mile. The Nuba and Dinka tribesmen, whose lives are described in *Villages*, represent this early stage of development, which still survives in the sparsely populated regions of Sudan.

Elsewhere, the arrival of modern medicine—first with the colonial *memsahibs* with their hygiene and Epsom salts, but most crucially with antibiotics—doomed the old way of life. The past half century has seen a mass migration toward small settled farms, or *shambas*, on ground high enough, wet enough and cold enough to grow corn. Corn has rather quickly become the main diet of black Africa. Eventually a hybrid maize belt irrigated with presently untapped rivers could transform Africa into a major food producer.

Africa needs time to culturally adapt. Elsewhere in the world, man the hunter and herder entered agriculture with draft animals thousands of years ago. In much of black Africa, the oxen-pulled plow replaced the hoe and digging stick just this past generation. Often women even do the plowing. The hunter-warrior is no more; the settled farmer is not yet. As my interpreter in Kenya, a woman, put it, "This is the problem we face here in Africa. You see those women working hard in the fields? They suffer. Their husbands may be working, drinking beer, spending their wages, enjoying themselves." In West Africa older men farm but there is a mass exodus of young males into the towns seeking jobs; few make a go of it. Visit an African game park, and in a primeval forest come upon a pride of lions, a lone rhino, or giraffes tall as dinosaurs and nibbling on the treetops, and you sense what these men have lost.

Black Africa is the last place left in the Third World where population growth rates keep going up, from 2.5 percent in the 1960s, to

2.9 percent last year. (In Kenya, where it is 3.9 percent, the current world record, the average woman has 8.3 live children.) Africa is also the only place left where food output is growing more slowly than population; the yearly growth rate in farm production has dropped from 2.3 percent in the 1960s to about 1.3 percent now. Our technological help should be concentrated in Africa, as in Latin America and the Moslem world, where cultural adaptation is coming much more slowly than in Asia.

*

Once *Villages,* somewhat unexpectedly, drew serious attention from agricultural scientists, students of development, and Washington policymakers, the necessity arose of summarizing its ideas, presented in a rather rambling and leisurely fashion in the book, in short, abbreviated form. It may help the reader if this is done at the outset:

Villages are man's oldest and most durable social institution, emerging with settled agriculture around ten thousand to fifteen thousand years ago. There are, in the Third World, about two million villages left, a third in China, a third in India-Pakistan-Bangladesh, and the rest in the other 130 or so countries of Asia, Africa and Latin America.

Man's culture, defined as a ready-made design for living handed down from father to son, is decided by how he gets his food. Villages possess a universal culture (based upon tilling land, property, and family), which varies significantly only in the realm of abstract ideas or religion. These variations explain the relative ease or difficulty in cultural adaptation to the present very rapid spread of Western agricultural science. The Confucians are roaring ahead, followed more hesitatingly by the Malay-Javanese and the Hindus. But all three purely Asian cultures are adapting more easily than Moslems, Christians or Africans.

The hope must be that a village-based agrarian civilization, with man's oldest cultures adapting to his newest scientific knowledge and expanded population, can offer an attractive and attainable future for the Third World.

Americans have a habit of looking at problems in terms of the politics of the surface, instead of the economic and cultural trends beneath the surface. This has made us slow to recognize long-term economic and cultural changes which require changes in policy. We need to picture the Third World in a new, essentially anthropological way. That is, not in terms of a devitalized fixed state peopled with dark and face-less mobs, but as a kaleidoscopic revolutionary drama in which count-less individual actors—the villagers—make choices and take actions to learn, adapt, develop and survive. Increasingly, we will take on the role of spectators while continuing to lead in the transfer of sophisti-cated agricultural and energy technology. Cultural adaptation and the survival of the village as the basic economic unit of the Third World are what we, as Americans, should be looking for, and trying if possi-ble to assist.

Not that any of them will repeat our kind of industralized agricul-ture; the 1970s exodus from the American cities suggests we may try, at last, to retreat from it ourselves. As I wrote in *Foreign Affairs* in the fall of 1982, "The villagers are not moving from their (A) to our (B). Rather we are all moving toward (C), a wholly new kind of society based upon biotechnology, electronics, new energy drawn from water and sun, and all the other new scientific advances." Our pioneer-ing quest to resolve individual freedom and community living is not over yet.

The central idea advanced in *Villages* is that village life is not only vital in itself, but is also the fundamental basis of all civilized behavior, including our own. We and the villagers exist in the same continuum stretching unbroken through time. We all seek a new economic basis to allow groups of people to live comfortably, productively and freely on the land. We stand at one end, the most technologically advanced society ever. Yet to travel in America after half a lifetime in the Third World is to discover that millions of Americans are struggling to rec-oncile the effect of ever bigger, fewer farms with emotions and values that lie deep in our past.

So let us look back, past the decaying cities, past the disappointing suburbs, past the dying small towns, past the vanished pioneer settle-ments, to the living source of all human culture: the village. As we observe how these ancient civilizations adapt to our most modern tech-niques, we just could be exploring our own way toward a more civi-lized living pattern.

R.C.
Fargo, North Dakota

ACKNOWLEDGMENTS

In a work that lasts twelve years, there are a great many who lend a hand. Let me single out the few whose help was indispensable: Norman E. Borlaug, for his own story of the Green Revolution and views on Chinese agriculture; J. George Harrar, who first gave me the idea of reporting villages; Brian Beedham and Norman Macrae of *The Economist* for their encouragement and civilized understanding; Samuel E. Bunker for steadfast belief in the work; Lowell Hardin of the Ford Foundation and Henry Romney of the Rockefeller Foundation for sustained support and interest; Richard H. Nolte, formerly of the Alicia Patterson Fund, for printing 250-page reports when he'd asked for ten-page ones; Lester R. Brown of the Worldwatch Institute for twelve years of friendly debate; Thomas C. Niblock of the Agency for International Development for imaginative and constructive help in the Philippines and Indonesia; Daniel P. Moynihan for, in his White House days, getting me to think about the nature of poverty; Sir Robert Thompson and Dennis Duncanson for their patient analysis of Marxism-Leninism; George Barrett—until his retirement, of the New York *Times*—for professional guidance and superb teaching. Special thanks to Peggy Ann Trimble of the Washington *Star,* whose kind and voluntary help in handling my business affairs the entire twelve years got us through many a cliffhanger; also to Krishanjit Singh and Nubi el Hagag for particularly gifted interpreting, good company and forbearance. For a better understanding of our own culture, the starting place, I would also mention the 1884–1927 journal of my grandparents, Dr. Hadwen and Jessie Williams, and the lifelong example of my father and mother, Dr. Ralph James and Anne Louise Critchfield, who set down their philosophy in its faithful demonstration.

There are a large number of people whose help, hospitality, information or advice were most welcome at crucial moments, most notably Howard W. Hjort of the Department of Agriculture saying, "You're right," and explaining why, just as I was about to sit down and write the book. These are, in Brazil: Daniel Johnson, Suzanne and Jim Converse, Gabriel Velazquez, Maria Elena Leme, Robert P. Bosshart, Nara Pareira, Luiz Arturo Fuenzalida, J. Jefferson Sandal, Sebastion Rodriques Pereira; in Morocco: James Hogan, Mustapha Rjik, Ouali Ahmed, Abdelouahed Bensaid, Abdelleh Benlamhidi, Amina Hachlane, Mohamed Hadj, Steve Josephson; in Sudan: Mohammed Kafi, Roland Stevenson, Ali Ahmed, John Bruce, Abdullah Mohammed Ibrahim, William J. A. Payne, Sterlyn B. Steele; in Nepal: Kesar Lall Shrestha, Ralph and Lora Redford, Douglas Heck, Desmond Doig, Tenzing Norgay, Francis J. Tatu, Birendra B. Shrestha, Tashi Sherpa, D. Namgyal; in the Philippines: Alejandro Melchor, Albert and Marjorie Ravenholt, Frank Sionel Jose, Juan T. Gatbonton, John F. Lartz, Gurdev S. Khush, Caesar Climaco; in Vietnam: Nguyen

Chanh Thi, Pham Van Dong, Edward Lansdale, Le Viet, John and Gay Dillin, Daniel Southerland, Takashi Oka, Elizabeth Pond, John Sharkey, William Tuohy, Joseph Freid, Beverly Deepe Keever, Michael Malloy, Peter Arnett, Malcolm Browne, Everett G. Martin, Frank McCullough, Father Patrick Burke, William Corson, Douglas Pike, Mark Frankland, Rose Kushner and, deceased, Marguerite Higgins, Peter Lisagor, François Sully, Henri Huet, Tran Van Huong, Tran Van Van, Jerry Rose and many, many others; in Bangladesh: Frank Wisner, Jr., Cleve Fuller, George Zeidenstein, Lincoln Chen, Pervez Ahmed, Badrul Huq; in Mexico: Claudio Zomnitz, Robert S. Drysdale, Linda Ainsworth, Haldore Hanson, Robert Havener, Bent Scovmand, Betsey Marsh, Aurelio B. Rendon; in Mauritius: Gaetan de Chazal, Octave Marie, Robert and Ada Marie, Karl Latieu, the Thug family, Julian Fromer, Malcolm de Chazal; in Iran: Eugene H. King, Odile Puesh, Jean Perrot, Elizabeth Carter, Husein Parvini, Ragat, Karim Kurd, Sherif Fawzli; in India: Chester Bowles, Ralph Cummings, Sr., M. S. Swaminathan, H. K. Jain, Raj Krishna, S. Subramaniam, Ashoka Mehta, the late Frank Moraes, Chadbourne Gilpatric, M. S. Randhawa, T. S. Sohal, Khushwant Singh, Subhash Kirpekar, Irfan Khan, M. B. Lal, Narindar K. Aggarwala, Rosanna and Minu Mohammed Ismail, Natu Samudre, Kulwant Singh Virk, B. S. Thakur, V. K. Sharma, Marcus and Vonnie Franda, Yadvendera Singh, A. M. Rosenthal, Henry Bradsher, Selig Harrison, Louis Kraar and the late Wolf Ladijinsky; in Egypt: Ahmed Hasuna, Shamsuddin Amr, Mohammed Abd el Salem, John Waterbury, Jack Foise, Walter F. Miner, Rose Risgallah, Georgette Scarzella, Richard and Dee Robarts, Marjorie Bunker, William Irelan, Jill Kamil; in Indonesia: Judy Bird Williams, Imam and Carolyn Pamoedjo, Adam Malik, Ali Sadikin, Soedjatmoko, Jon E. Rohde, Gus Papanek, Bur Rasuanto, Thomas H. Reese, Ann Soetoro, William L. Collier, Benjamin White, Enrique M. Barrau, Harriet Isom, Brent Ashabranner, Ted Smith, Richard Patten, Lee Shing-min, Terence H. Hull, Pangestu, S. Yunan, William Larson, R. Wasito, Lukas Hendrata, James G. Nemec, Jeffrey A. McNeely, Haryono Soyono, R. Rachlan, Bujung, Tjasidi, Widgna Tarma Husen, Pa Lojo and his troupe, Djuhayet; in Thailand: Rachanida Sungwanna, O-Part Nimmnop; in Pakistan: Shoaid Sultan Khan, S. M. Hussein; in Rome: A. E. Boerma, Diana Prior-Palmer de Marco; in New York: Robert Tolles, Robert Edwards, Alan Horton, Manon Spitzer, Sterling Lord, Patricia Berens, Tim McGinnis, Marie Dutton Brown, Edwin Barber, Patricia Towers; in Washington: Don Paarlberg, the late Irene Tauber, Mary Harrison, Robert S. McNamara, Orville Freeman, Walt W. Rostow, the late Walter Lippmann, Dan Rather, John Osbourne, the late Alex Campbell, Newbold Noyes, Crosby Noyes, Charles B. Seib, Burt Hoffman, Scott Smith, Philip Foise, Stephen Rosenfeld, James H. Critchfield, Erik Eckholm, Bruce Stokes, Pat Munroe, Dana G. Dalrymple; in Boston: Geoffrey Godsell, David Anable; in Los Angeles: Marshall Lumsden; in Berkeley: George M. Foster, William Critchfield, Peggy Moffett, James W. Moffett. There are many unnamed others who appeared briefly to help, but all of the above in some way walked that extra mile. Their help, encouragement or hospitality, together with the kindness of the villagers themselves, made this work possible. Among heads of government interviewed were Seewoosagur Ramgoolam, Mauritius; King Birendra, Nepal; Jawaharlal Nehru, Lal Bahadur Shastri, Indira Gandhi, Morarji Desai, India; Ayub Khan, Zulfikar Ali Bhutto, Pakistan; China's Chou En-lai, met in Pakistan; Sheikh Mujibur Rahman, Bangladesh; Anwar Sadat, Egypt; Ferdinand E. Marcos, Philippines.

Had there been a bibliography, the work of Robert Redfield would have led it; it was gratifying to discover, reading Redfield for the first time four years ago, how often our entirely different experiences with villages brought us out at the same place. Much of the research for this book, aside from the village stays themselves, was done at the library of the United Nations Center for literacy training for Latin America (CREFAL) on the former estate of Mexico's President Cárdenas in Patzcuaro, Mexico, March–August 1977. This preceded a journey, 1978–81, to revisit most of the villages with partial Rockefeller and Ford foundation support. I am also grateful to the Ford Foundation for its earlier grants, the Alicia Patterson Foundation, the American Universities Field Staff and, for the opportunity to document my findings in Java, the Agency for International Development.

I especially want to thank Hanna Papanek of the Sociology Department of Boston University for encouraging me to give more attention to the role of village women. Dr. Papanek worked with me interviewing Indonesian women in 1973. A persistent problem is that villages, except for the family households, are a man's world. My primary interest is culture and its economic basis of agriculture, which means going daily to the fields, where one's principal subjects are likely to be male. The alternative of focusing on the households behind the mud walls, I feel, while it works in urban slums, does not work in villages. Oscar Lewis, who did tend to portray women more fully than men, focused mainly on city slum dwellers and in his Mexican village study was accompanied by his wife. Village customs being what they are, I was able to use a woman interpreter in the villages only in Brazil and South Korea. Women's portraits have emerged, most notably in Ommohamed in Egypt, Surjit Kaur, whose story is told here, Husen's wife Karniti in Java, Aminah, a Sundanese prostitute in Jakarta, and so on, but always where some unusual circumstance allowed us to get around village conventions or religious restrictions—above all, the "What will people say?" kind of social pressure so powerful in villages. Ommohamed, for instance, went about telling the neighbors I was like "a son" to her; in fact, we were born the same year. In two village households, in Ghungrali in India and Shush-Daniel in Iran, the female members of the family went about with their faces covered much of the time I was there. The spunky Upper Egyptian women did allow my interpreter, Nubi, and me to sit in on some all-female activities, such as shucking maize, normally off bounds to village men. It is a problem likely to solve itself as I grow older and more decrepit (gray hair is a distinct advantage in villages). The emphasis in this book on men does not reflect any lack of interest in the women's role; indeed, as you will see, I conclude that more rights and education for women are key, perhaps *the* key, to solving many of our problems.

The village motif was designed by Richard Gerstner for "Critchfield's Villages," published in the fall 1979 issue of the Rockefeller Foundation's *RF Illustrated,* which I thank for permission to use it. The word "village," has its origin in the Latin *villa;* a farm servant was known as a *villanus.* By the Middle Ages, in England and France, a small assemblage of houses in the countryside was called a *ville.* Somehow the French word for peasant, *vilain,* evolved into the English "villain," or scoundrel. Americans tend to use small town rather than village for little communities.

I would also like to thank Luther Nichols, Doubleday's West Coast Editor, who first gave me the idea for the book; I am much indebted for his continued enthusiasm, wise advice and judicious improvements as its editor. In the copy editing of the manuscript, Kathy Casey helped greatly with her painstaking work and relentless logic, pitted against my relentless illogic.

You might ask why I became a reporter who writes about villages. I suppose it just sort of evolved naturally from earlier background and experience: a semi-rural Midwestern upbringing, journeys abroad as a soldier, student and journalist, in the early 1960s reporting the seemingly hopeless crisis of people surplus and food scarcity in India and China, and—perhaps decisive—five years of reporting the American involvement in Indochina, four on the scene and one at the White House. There were both positive and negative reasons for going off to live in villages; once started, it became totally absorbing. The specific idea was formed as a war correspondent in Vietnam; indeed, the genesis of this book was a curiosity to find out more about how village culture worked. Time and chance, the North Dakota plains, an evening in Sirmione, Calcutta's beggars during a typhoon, a Jakarta pedicab driver's cry, "Hello, mister! Where are you going?"—these had something to do with it too.

Finally, my deepest thanks to Carolina, Barek, Kuwa, Ngodup, Tonio, Karl, Octave, Prem, Rashid, Aurelio, Yahkoub, Karim, Murad, Sherif, Charan, Surjit, Pritam, Mukhtar, Shahhat, Ommohamed, Fatih, Helmi, Husen, Karniti and all the villagers themselves. They have given me the best years of my life.

RC
Berkeley and
Washington, D.C.

CONTENTS

I. PEOPLE

1	Guapira Village and Salvador, Brazil	3
2	Romanni Village, Morocco, and Paris	16
3	Neetil Village, Sudan	29
4	Tashi Palkhiel Tibetan Camp, Nepal	42
5	Tulungatung Village, Philippines	51
6	Long Phu and Kim Lien Villages, Vietnam	61
7	Joypur Village, Bangladesh	71
8	Tepoztlán and Huecorio Villages, Mexico	78
9	Grand Gaube Village, Mauritius	89
10	Shush-Daniel Village, Iran	96
11	Bhadson Village, India	110
12	Ghungrali Village, India	120
13	Berat and Sirs el Layyan Villages, Egypt	143
14	Pilangsari Village, Indonesia	162

II. IDEAS

15	Look to Suffering, Look to Joy	189
16	How Villages Came About	209
17	Village and City	225
18	Sex and Villages	235
19	Satan Is Not Dead	251
20	Nor Is God	263
21	Calcutta: It Survives	284
22	China: Revolution, Red and Green	296
23	The Great Change	321
POSTSCRIPT: Village Characteristics		341
NOTES		347
INDEX		367

And now I call upon you for a true account of your wanderings. To what parts of the inhabited world did they take you? What lovely cities did you see; what people in them? Did you meet hostile tribes and lawless savages, or did you fall in with friendly, god-fearing folk?

—King Alcinous to Ulysses,
Homer's *The Odyssey*

I. PEOPLE

GUAPIRA VILLAGE AND SALVADOR, BRAZIL

You're dancing in the street, part of a mob. All you've got on is a long burial shroud, as if in some malevolent nightmare. Drums beat, faster and faster, until thunder seems to be rising from the ground. It's a distinctly African sound, monotonous, pounding, its beats ominously interspersed with and dominated by high-pitched screamingly amplified guitars. The beat flicks you like a whip. Everybody breaks loose, eyes flashing, four limbs swinging about, defying equilibrium. Bodies are shaken from feet to head by convulsive motions that grow more violent upon reaching the shoulders. Heads wag backward and forward as if separated from decapitated bodies. You see someone lose his balance and fall; his mouth opens in a soundless scream. Nothing stops the mob, advancing, trampling, unable to stop for anything, even for breath, as if their bodies were nothing but tightly knotted muscles and nerves moving to the beat, held by the power of the drums and guitars.

Sometimes the music slows down and then the mob progresses in a sort of heavy, insistent march rather like stamping, slightly emphasized by the double swaying of the hips—steps stiff, body rigid, eyes staring and vacant. Everybody seems to be in a hypnotic state, moving slowly, always on the point of letting the beat get ahead of them, their eyes closed and yet bodies erect, swaying slightly on their toes. A black girl, all glitter and plumes, staggers forward as if half asleep, her eyes closed, as if the beat of the drums support her languid arabesques.

You gasp for breath; sweat runs into your eyes. All you see is distorted fragments. Pretty mulattoes, tripped by the long *mortalhas* which hang loosely from their shoulders, utter shrieks with heads flung back and arms thrust high in the air. Horned satyrs with sequined beards, girt with plumes, chests thrust out and shoulders back, dance with pounding, throbbing movements. Muscular blacks, biceps rippling, thump madly on kettledrums strapped to their bare shoulders; others with clenched fists, glassy-eyed and trancelike, throw out their arms in rigid cataleptic thrusts; one is tossed high in the air by his companions and lands with a whoop of drunken laughter. You see sweat-shiny Apaches, war paint glistening on brown skins; hooded, black-cloaked specters with slit-hole eyes; naked girls in g-strings and sequins, leering transvestites and pitch-black youths in bright yellow wigs. And you see these bacchants twist, shuffle and leap, sweet and savage, lewd and fun, like nothing you have ever seen before. It's a mass of bobbing heads and flailing arms, dancing joyously, panting, steaming bodies, driving each other on with laughs and cries of life. It's wild, mindless, plunging, twisting, stamping, *Walpurgisnacht*, the end of the world, all noise, light, uproar, a mob scene, get me out.

It's *Carnaval* in Salvador, Brazil, and for six straight days an entire city of a million people flies apart, everybody dancing up and down the main mile-long street, day into night. Two dozen will die, hundreds will be badly injured, but nothing can stop this saturnalia of our times, this riotous eruption and bursting free.

It starts with a doomy excitement. Night, noise, blinding lights and crowds of crazy-costumed people give the Avenida Sete de Setembro a special ambience: the old harbor city, strung along its hills encircling All Saints Bay, is eroticized; and Salvador, all gilded baroque, mosaic sidewalks, plane trees and mossy stone is obscurely, frighteningly sensual. You know you are in Bahia, the land of Brazil's old colonial capital, abandoned for Rio when the slave trade gave out, a decaying monument to the grandeur of a dying sugar civilization. Only the people were left behind, streaming in from the exhausted plantation land and from the immense and arid *sertão,* jobless and hungry but young and alive.

Somehow the dense foliage along the boulevard, the mist of blue confetti that drifts down like decadent rain from the balconies and the anonymous shrieks and laughter are tokens of a mysteriously indifferent universe; Salvador might be a reptile-infested ruin in a hallucinogenic Amazon jungle, swarming with riotous ghouls. You look around for reassurance, get pushed and jolted and see detached and psychedelic faces: pale Portuguese, dark Negro, Indian or mulatto, all grinning and glistening with paint and erotic glitter. The grins look too fixed, the laughter too self-absorbed, like performers without an audience, misshapen as if in a dream; it all seems splintered, like fear and death—death most of all, with phantoms all around you in their corpses' shrouds.

Comes a *trio elétrico,* armored with its screaming electronic amplifiers, a monstrous apparition of deafening noise and flashing naked lightbulbs, bearing a rock band high over the crowd's hysteria. As it comes, there's a rumble, a crashing and a low dull thunder; with a last trace of hostile objectivity you think, by God, I'm going to resist, I'll just stand and watch. Some try. The trio rumbles closer, its lights blind you, sparks fly in front of your eyes; then thronging and pushing and thrusting their outflung arms so violently you and the crowd press back against the trees and houses—watch out for the bubbling oil of the sidewalk vendors' pots!—come the bobbing heads and arms of dancing people.

The twanging, shrilling, piercing guitar noise seizes, shatters your mind; you are helplessly caught. Once you start dancing there's no stopping. You go on and on, one night fading into the next, a few hours of exhausted sleep, your *mortalha* sodden and stiff with sweat, downing gallons of beer to slake a steady thirst, finding, losing your friends, moving to the African samba beat, caught in the compulsive power of the music and its splintered sensual universe. The dancers bend convulsively backward and utter inarticulate cries, soundless in the scream of the amplified *trio* drums and guitars. Someone is stabbed in the back with a machete. Who did it? Who can say? The mob hesitates, then surges forward, the victim swept aside and instantly forgotten.

For a few hours each morning, the streets are silent, the spell is broken. By noon a dozen *trios* are again rumbling down Sete de Setembro and nothing can hold you back. Out in the street, the dancers incite each other to move ever more furiously, flinging out their arms and legs as if they'd fly to pieces; and it is never still. Rain falls, everyone gets soaked and riotously sings, shouting the words, never missing a beat, "Beer, Sweat and Rain!" Others break into the most popular *Carnaval* song, "Turn, turn, turn, turn, turn, turn into a wolfman!" Men dressed as women pull up their skirts and waggle large rubber phalluses. The park grass is a scene of copulating couples. Homosexual orgies take place in darkened movie theaters. Transvestites seize the steps of the governor's palace, act out sadomasochistic perversions and fight off helmeted police; a beer-guzzling crowd of thousands of onlookers roars with laughter and cheers them on. Bare-breasted girls in g-strings, straggle-haired and glassy-eyed, dance on what tables are still unbroken in improvised beer gardens. Ugly fat men with pendulous stomachs wander obscenely about in bikinis. Any passing girl is fair game for a caress or proposition. Any impulse becomes action in this fevered search for titillation, pleasure and release. A young woman is found unconscious on the beach, gang-raped by seven drunken revelers.

As the nights pass, crime sweeps the city, traffic accidents soar. Two more men are fatally stabbed, another dies after striking his head on the pavement, a boy is killed when a panicky policeman fires into a crowd, a student drowns when his gang of revelers invades the poolside bar of a big hotel and his wet *mortalha* drags him under. Some two thousand are injured from assaults, knifings, gunfire, falls, heart attacks, exhaustion or being trampled upon.

The sirens of ambulances and police cars grow frequent, street fights break out, bars are wrecked, riot police line Sete de Setembro and trucks of combat troops stand by. The secretary of public security bans six thousand young blacks dressed as Apache Indians; they resist, troops are ordered in and over a hundred Apaches are jailed. The authorities, exasperated, all patience gone, call it the most violent *Carnaval* ever.

But over it all, piercing and dominating everything, is the thrilling, coaxing music, trembling on the brink of breakdown, of the *trio elétrico*'s drums and guitars. Sweat streaming down their haggard, glistening faces, the dancers will not stop until the eastern sky above the Atlantic grows light and the full flush of dawn breaks upon Ash Wednesday. As the end nears, the laughter may flare into angry screams, flirtations and caressing hands turn violent, flailing arms provoke answering blows from broken beer bottles, bloodied victims frantically claw their way out, files of toughs heedlessly shove everybody in their path aside with howling war cries and the scream of sirens grows continuous—the gap will always quickly close. All are once more absorbed, faces exhausted, grimy, clothing stiff, legs groggy, muscles taut—but still exultant, still going, caught in the riotous dancing mob. With them, belonging to them, you become the mob, young and alive forever, unconscious of self or time or place, kicking, stamping, jumping, whirling, entangled in the steamy mass, lost but joyously lost in this frenzied bursting free.

It was left to the cardinal of Salvador, Dom Avelar Brandão Vilela, in his dawn Ash Wednesday sermon in Salvador cathedral, once the last of the revelers, grimy and spent, had entered and quieted down, to passionately attack this collapse of culture. "We must return to our traditional morality," the cardinal cried, "that acquired naturally over centuries and through belief in God."

*

I've begun this book on villages with this picture of Brazil's annual pre-Lenten carnival, experienced two years ago, because this will be a book about human culture. What happens every year in Salvador—and it is wildly fun—is the closest thing I can think of to being a metaphor for almost total, if temporary, cultural breakdown.

During the last night of *Carnaval*, I—dancing, blind drunk, beer bottle in hand—was among some fifty casualties rushed to Salvador's *Pronto Socorro*, the emergency first aid station of its big public Getulio Vargas Hospital. A high wooden bandstand, under which we happened to be dancing, suddenly collapsed from the weight of too many stamping people; dancers, drums, musicians spilled down on our heads. The scene in the cavernous, white, fluorescent-lit emergency room was like those in the street, only now with even greater delirium; there were the same girls in sequins and plumes, the same black drummers, the same revelers in shrouds, yet here everyone was battered and bleeding, their costumes ripped, dripping blood or hanging in shreds. Some of them clutched stomach wounds, others held improvised bandages to their heads, a few lay unconscious on stretchers; young interns and nurses, haggard from strain and sleeplessness after a week of such calamities, dazedly went about stitching up wounds, giving injections, wrapping on bandages, calling for blood transfusions. A young girl whose leg had been crushed kept screaming and screaming; she was told they would have to amputate. An elderly black woman went from one of the injured to the next, scraping away hair with an old barber's razor and swabbing the wounds with bright yellow disinfectant. My left leg had been torn open right up the back; it took some time before an intern came to sew it up. It was like a fantastically macabre shellshocked dream.

To me that scene, and indeed *Carnaval* itself, which I loved, came to symbolize the broken connections of our modern universe. The troubling undertones beneath the fun—and it was the wildest bursting free from all restraint imaginable—to me exemplify what Plato in his critique of reason called "an inflamed society." He contrasted it to "a simple society," of which the most universal form has always been the village.

Just look how quickly we turn away from our malaise in the modern city for a quiet weekend in the country. There seems to be a consensus that *something* ails us, whether it be the "spiritual emptiness" that Woody Allen has said was the theme of his radically moral film, *Manhattan* ("She was a kindergarten teacher, then she got into drugs and moved to San Francisco. She went to est, became a Moonie. She works for the William Morris Agency now.") or what Pauline Kael has called "the whole American screwup of recent years," when people passively accepted the counterculture view of themselves as "cynical materialists who cared for nothing but their own greed and lust." Kael calls it "a self put-down," Jimmy Carter, when he was still president, termed it "a crisis of confidence" (and it is true that confidence is the internal strength we must possess). Whatever name we give it, we feel cut off from some vital dimension of life.

One possible explanation: it may be no accident that Allen chose as his symbol of what's wrong with us our ultimate big city, New York. George Steiner once observed that the contrast between urban and rural in the works of Leo Tolstoy "may well be the center of his art." Tolstoy came to see the distinction between life on the land and life in the city as close to the primordial distinction between good and evil.

We do not have to go so far as Tolstoy did to recognize there is often a sharp contrast between the unnaturalness and inhumanness of urbanity on the one hand and the simplicity and truth of village life on the other. Raymond Chandler's 1953 description of "the big angry city" in *The Long Goodbye* could scarcely be improved upon in the 1980s:

> Far off the banshee wail of police or fire sirens rose and fell, never for very long completely silent. Twenty-four hours a day somebody is running, somebody else is trying to catch him. Out there in the night of a thousand crimes people were dying, being maimed, cut by flying glass, crushed against steering wheels or under heavy tires. People were being beaten, robbed, strangled, raped, and murdered. People were hungry, sick, bored, desperate with loneliness or remorse or fear, angry, cruel, feverish, shaken by sobs. A city no worse than others, a city rich and vigorous and full of pride, a city lost and beaten and full of emptiness.

Social critics who try to diagnose our self-devaluation and sense of loss in the flat unreality of the consumer society often end up in the same place. Take Christopher Booker, an Englishman, in 1969 and Christopher Lasch, an American, in 1979. Booker, after dismissing what he held were the phony values of the "New Britain" of the Angry Young Men, Suez, Profumo, the Beatles and such, blamed them on an urban high-technology society's vulnerability to media-fed mass fantasy (which he argued went through dream, anticipation, frustration, nightmare and death-wish stages). Then he set down what he called an "idealized portrait of human society." It was simple, based upon fixed family and community ties, close to nature and in tune with the seasons; it ended up sounding like every village I'd been in. Lasch, after analyzing the cause of our malaise (uneasiness might be a more Anglo-Saxon way of saying it)—too much self-awareness and self-indulgence and a decline of the family and moral code—does the same thing. He proposes as a remedy reviving the "traditions of localism, self-help and community action." Which also takes us back to villages.

Richard Lingeman, the author of *Small Town America,* calls the prototypical village—a cluster of families occupying a place and engaged in farming—"the primal social unit." Industrialization and the mass society, Lingeman finds, deprive a village of its sense of community, autonomy and folk traditions. He believes Americans subconsciously miss "a way of life that, for all its dumb, brutish hardship—and we are well rid of it—had an organic relationship with nature, with work, and with one's fellows that has gone from our lives."

The snag is we cannot really recapture the morality and mutual help that so typifies village life because this would demand an unacceptable return to subsistence agriculture or something close to it, the economic basis of village culture. The hippie communes of the 1960s tried it in a restriction-free, family-free fashion and they quickly fell apart. Yet we can go back partly. Norman Macrae, the deputy editor of *The Economist,* in 1975 was one of the first to observe that America's back-to-the-country movement had begun. Between 1970 and 1973, he reported, there was a population rise in America's nonmetro (i.e., rural) areas of just over 350,000 a year, "and without many people noticing it, the tide was already flowing back from both suburbia and the cities." The 1980 census was to reveal marked population declines in the cities, especially in the Northeast.

Macrae predicted, "The next crisis of lifestyles will be that of reruralization. Early in its third century America will have to create a new ex-urban lifestyle, probably again very suddenly. The crucial topic of discussion should be what it will be. At present this is not widely discussed." In his analysis, increasing wealth and technology in the rich countries allow their inhabitants to do something totally new in human society: namely, to live according to individual choice instead of in groups. This naturally means people are throwing away a lot of the old tribal restraints, religious conventions and patterns of obedience to authority that were necessary when they lived in groups.

"And then, very awkwardly," Macrae went on, "people are finding they can be happy only if they do live in groups." I take this to mean in small, village-like groups. Macrae did not suggest we can return to being ruled by the old conventions. Modern individuals have the wealth and technology so they need not completely do so and "anyway it is cramping of individual freedom to suggest that they should." But Macrae predicted that "the next twenty-five years will show whether America is going to lead the world to a totally new and exciting society."

Margaret Mead shared this thinking and in 1978, shortly before her death, proposed what she called "an elective village," to which "people move because they want to live there, not because their ancestors have always lived there." Life in such a community, she told a seminar of the Anthropological Society of Washington, would be "very different from the fragmented life of the city." Miss Mead felt that "making this choice possible is a major challenge in our contemporary world."

A free man must have an informed individual choice. An uninformed choice is hardly free. To make a wise and sensible choice about the new, much more village-like way he is going to live, I believe, he needs to know more about villages. As they are. Today about two-thirds of the people alive live in some two million villages. I have lived in a dozen of these, scattered over Asia, Africa and Latin America, during the past twelve years—some for three or four months, three for over a year. While each village has some things that are unique about it and much that is good and much that is bad, I do believe there is something generic about the way village people live and think. All villagers the world over have a lot in common. They have much in common with each other, but not much with us. This is because they all make their living in much the same way, tilling the land.

I have mentioned this will be a book about culture. The word comes from the Latin *cultura,* which means tillage, the practice of cultivation. The Latin *agri,* genitive of *ager,* for land, is how we got agriculture. In modern usage culture can also mean refinement from education. The social sciences have given the word an additional meaning which I'll be using: culture is the way of living worked out by a group of people and handed down from father to son. When we talk about a village's culture, we are talking about its design for living, a handed-down, ready-made set of solutions to problems so that each new generation does not have to start out from scratch. In great civilizations this can go on for a long time; some of village Egypt's manners and customs have been passed down at least two hundred and fifty generations.

Culture is not the same as "lifestyle," a new vogue word coined to fit rich, urban, high-technology Western man's new freedom of individual choice about how he will live; implicit is that lifestyles, like fashions, can come and go, be easily changed, tried, kept or discarded, TM and jogging this week, yoga and hang-gliding next. Culture is largely inherited, evolves very slowly and in villages changes only in response to changes in its economic basis—tillage of land (*agri* + *cultura* = agriculture). During the 1970s this has been speeded up. Villages are starting to get a bit more wealth and technology too. Yet it is notable, even in our own culture, that the funniest satirists of lifestyles, like Allen, Tom Wolfe, Garry Trudeau and Pauline Kael, are firmly rooted in traditional cultural values.

When long-held culture does change, villagers, like ourselves, face the enormous compulsion of working out new meanings and new ways and views of life for themselves. The old inherited certainties lose their coherence; things don't stick together as they should. An uneasy sense of malaise follows. In extreme cases, once a man's universe goes completely to pieces, he becomes culturally alienated, that is, estranged from his society's design for living, as a terrorist does or, as I'll try to show in the second sketch about Morocco, a criminal. Then no rules, no culture apply. For most of us, as in Salvador's week of *Carnaval,* the broken connections are only temporary. We are faced with an inability to order our experience and find meaning in it only until we have the time and means to culturally adjust. Once change is faced and we have the technical wherewithal to adapt to it, we, given time, almost always do. If energy resources stay in short supply, as they may if fusion, solar, geothermal or other alternatives don't pan out to replace fossil fuels, I think we can safely prophesy that future generations of Americans may look back on our profligate, individually styled way of life with amazement, perhaps even a bit of envy.

*

It must be no accident that Salvador's carnival is the spiritual descendant of the Saturnalia of ancient Rome, that weeklong debauch of street dancing, temporarily freed slaves, wine and rampant sex so beloved of movie makers. Look how Will Durant summed up the times in his *Caesar and Christ:*

> Moral decay contributed to the dissolution. The virile character that had been formed by arduous simplicities and a supporting faith relaxed in the sunshine of wealth and the freedom of unbelief; men had now, in the middle and upper classes, the means to yield to temptation, and only expediency to restrain them. Urban congestion multiplied contacts and frustrated surveillance; immigration brought together a hundred cultures whose differences rubbed themselves out into indifference. Moral and esthetic standards were lowered by the magnetism of the mass; and sex ran riot in freedom while political liberty decayed.

The ancient Romans called their carnival *carne vale,* "flesh farewell," and early Christians such as St. Telesphorus, Bishop of Rome in A.D. 125–136, are said to have tolerated its continuation as a burst of revelry to be followed by the forty days of fasting that became Lent. The idea of sin followed by repentance caught on, spreading from Italy to France, Spain and Portugal, and eventually to their colonies, including Brazil. It survives in Rio de Janeiro's famous carnival and our Mardi Gras, both tamed in recent times to mostly balls and parades of sumptuously costumed dancers.

Not so in Salvador, Brazil's first colonial capital (1549–1763) and a city of lost sugar wealth and present poverty. The surrounding state of Bahia has Brazil's lowest incomes and its largest concentration of West African slave descendants; Salvador preserves not only its seventeenth-century churches, palaces and forts, but also Brazil's oldest Portuguese and African traditions, such as the voodoo-like *candomblé* practices.

The "mock king" who presided over the Saturnalia was often put to death at its end. Salvador's fat, Bacchus-like King Momo goes back to his office job, but otherwise in a week of street dancing, drink, sex and temporary social dominance by the poor and the black, all in the masks, sequins, bangles, beads, wigs, streamers, confetti and shrouds of their carnival *fantasias,* the Bahians can probably challenge the Romans any time. They invented the *samba,* originally a communal dance which varies from a taut, forward stamping with only the feet and hips in motion to the most violent abandoned movement of the entire body. (This true Brazilian samba is not to be confused with the pallid, forward-backward syncopated tilting that reached North America.) Then, twenty-eight years ago, came another Bahian invention, the *trio elétrico,* a truck-mounted rock band whose guitars and drums are amplified by about thirty or forty electronic speakers; the sound is deafening, hypnotic and compulsive. If landing on an aircraft carrier can be called a controlled crash, *Carnaval* (the Bahians pronounce it cah-nah-vowel) is a just-controlled mob riot. Even in the unlikely event you stay sober, you are likely to dance all night, every night, losing all sense of self. I know I did.

One more analogy with the Romans: the Saturnalia was originally a wholesome village festival to Saturn, the god of sowing. It did not become a weeklong orgy until the triumph of rationality over mythology in the last century before Christ. By then Rome's population was swollen with rural immigrants whose family-size farms were absorbed in great slave-based estates. Salvador is so inundated by village immigrants, its population is growing at 7 percent a year. In Brazil, as in Rome, reason and logic have done much to dissolve the unquestioning Roman Catholicism and village superstitions that had buttressed the villagers' agricultural moral code. Such values as paternal authority, chastity, early marriage, divorceless monogamy and multichild marriage are being challenged in the city. Education spreads religious doubts and the old morality loses its supernatural supports. Sins can be hidden in the protective anonymity of the crowd and neither God nor parents are feared—only the policeman.

Young people who go to the city have to pay a heavy price. Two years ago I lived for several months in a village called Guapira, about a hundred miles into the interior from Salvador; it survived by growing cassava root and milling it into flour, a labor-intensive process that meant grueling work for the women and children. As *Carnaval* week approached I went to Salvador to observe what would happen to six or seven of Guapira's children who had gone to the city to work.

Carolina, then twenty-seven, was one of them. When I found her she had just been abandoned by her lover, a dockworker named Afrodizio. Stranded without any means to support herself and two illegitimate children, Carolina had moved into a girl friend's hut in the

favela of Pau Miudo, Small Stick, the meanest of the immigrant shantytowns which were spreading up Salvador's hills like fungus. Carolina
took in laundry, washed it in a canal each day and managed to earn
the equivalent of about twenty dollars a month. "We eat," she wrote to
her mother in Guapira, "but only with the help of our neighbors."
Carolina feared that unless she could find a husband, she might be
forced into prostitution to support her children.

In Carolina's home back in Guapira, there was an altar with its
plaster statue of St. George just inside the door. Her mother prayed to
the saint, asking his protection, the first thing each morning; she also
believed, as did all the Guapira women, that sinners could be turned
into werewolves and that women who slept with priests became head-
less donkeys; the unschooled villagers, living in what was barely
more than a wild frontier, also believed that plants were governed by
the moon and had human-like sensitivities, and that if a menstruating
woman set foot in a field being sown, she would curse the crop. To
Carolina, after her years in Salvador, these were just superstitions. Yet
she was aware that they gave precious comfort in a village where
drinking water was infected with schistosomiasis and other worms,
where a bite of the dreaded *barbeiro* cockroach, which came out of
cracks in the mud walls at night, could cause inescapable death in five
to fifteen years from *chagas* disease. And where, if you felt a stabbing
pain in your insides, no medical care was available; the nearest doctor
or hospital was ten miles over a rutted dirt road passable only by foot
or horseback.

Carolina's family of eight might live in a mud-and-wattle palm-
thatched hut and eat little but *feijão, arroz* and *farinha*—black beans,
rice and cassava flour—and spend most days working long, back-
breaking hours in the fields. Yet religion conferred meaning and dignity on their lives. And, like her parents, Carolina yearned for a
religion rich in miracle, mystery and myth. In Salvador her Catholicism, formed in the village's agricultural setting, with its annual rebirth of life and the mystery of growth, began to weaken; she was told
many Catholic relics were bogus and the miracles doubtful. Soon, at
night school, retaking her education from the first grade as most of
Guapira's children were forced to do in Salvador (few would credit
the years they spent in Guapira's primitive one-room schoolhouse),
Carolina learned men could walk on the moon or blow the planet up.
Salvador was full of all kinds of Protestant sects and conflicting ideologies, each attacking saints like St. George and St. Anthony as frauds

and idolatry and appealing to Scripture or scientific logic. Some said the Bible was more myth than history, to say nothing of the divine revelation Carolina's mother had taught her it was. In Salvador, Carolina discovered, holy days became holidays, the beaches were crowded, the churches half empty; in the evenings it was King Kong or Kung Fu.

Like most girls from Guapira, Carolina first found work as an *empregada*, housemaid for a rich family. After she became pregnant with Afrodizio's first child, they turned her out. The boys from Guapira had it no better; most shared a cubicle in some crime-infested *favela* or slept on the docks or at a construction site, cooking their own cheap, unnourishing meals; many went jobless.

One day Carolina learned the *favelados* planned to invade some government land and seize plots to build shacks and settle there. She joined them, the marchers grew to more than a thousand and they tore down fences and everybody rushed to grab a plot of ground. This invading squatters' army sang the Apaches' *Carnaval* song:

> My body is inviolate; it is mine; what
>   do you have?
> Come close to me, come close to me, you
>   will find out.

Within hours truckloads of policemen came. They began taking apart the shacks so frantically thrown together. A neighbor sobbed to Carolina, "What can I do? I've got eight children but only two can go to school. I've no money. They can't take away this chance to get a house for nothing!" Carolina heard screams and shouts; some of the squatters were resisting. A policeman came to tell her, "It's much better if you take your babies and leave now, *senhora*. We are going to tear down everything."

So, it's *Carnaval* again and let it all explode. Leave St. George; he's nothing but a piece of clay. Leave that phony promise of salvation. Leave those bogus myths of forgiveness, charity and love. This is the here and now, the music is all we've got. So listen to the *trio*'s drumbeats, hear those screaming guitars, see those flashing lights and shadows, c'mon, Carolina, and you and me and everybody, take it all in, the whole ear-splitting, all-obliterating din. Let it all combine to break into your mind from without, trampling down all resistance with its force—and when it passes through you the codes and culture of a lifetime will be annihilated. C'mon, join the mob. *Turn, turn, turn, turn, into a wolfman.*

A night in Casablanca. The waterfront bar was crowded with sailors, dockers and *kif* peddlers; they drank, they talked and they smoked hashish. The prefecture has since closed it down; but this was ten years ago and, quite innocently, I had wandered into the most notorious dive in the old *medina*. The big Senegalese whose front teeth had been knocked out was talking about Germany: "Yeah, plenty fucking in Hamburg." He was waiting for a false set so he could ship out again.

"You know I got land—five hectares," said the heavy-shouldered docker, Mustafa. "Only beans and wheat, but the harvest is coming. I'll go home for a week, two weeks, look at the land, see if the crop is good or not."

The big sailor laughed. "Mustafa, you are still a farmer. Why don't you go back home and stay in your village?"

"*La, la.* For a farm man, he must have money. I know how to work all right but where do I get the capital? We got only rain, no irrigation. Hell, I'd go back if I could. Look at my vest. I've had it for fifteen years now and it's a goddamn rag. I think I spend my life for nothing."

"This is the life anyway," said the small bearded black man, speaking for the first time. I noticed his Dutch sailor cap was pulled down low, but not low enough to hide the knife scars. Against my protests, he and Hamid, the Berber of the lot, bought two more bottles of wine. I was drunk now anyway; somehow every time you put down your glass it was filled up again and the next thing I knew the docker and the big sailor were gone and we were sitting on cushions in a low, dark place full of Arab junkies; pipes of hashish were going around and some fat Berber women with jangling glass bracelets on their wrists and ankles were beating tambourines and belting out pure emotion in harsh, shrill voices as if they meant to hurt. Then it got blurred again until I was aware of the reverberation of footsteps on cobblestones and, sure enough—that moment you're afraid of—there we were heading down a narrow alley of shuttered houses toward a dead end. Just as this came to me, the Berber yanked off my watch and somebody else grabbed my billfold. I ran, instinct stronger than the hash and booze—then heard footsteps running after me.

The Casablanca *medina* is a labyrinth. Even in the daytime when you're sober it's easy to get lost, and now it was a reeling nightmare. My pursuer caught up and we fought in the darkness until he got a stranglehold; for a time I was too scared to grasp what he was saying; a voice was arguing, in a heavy Moroccan accent, that now that I'd been robbed, it was too dangerous to try to get out of the *medina* alone; a foreigner found without money might be stabbed or beaten. It was the bearded black and, incredibly, he was offering to take me back to safety. He led the way to Boulevard Mohammed el Hansali, where we hailed a cab, and he dropped me at the cheap *maison de passe* in the French quarter where I'd found a room. The watchman was standing by the door, looking unreassuring in a black, hooded *jellaba*. After the taxi pulled away, he asked, "Where did you meet *him?* That's Barek. He's a big gangster in Casablanca."

I looked for him and found him in the *medina* the next day. Why? Curiosity and a superstitious disbelief in chance, I suppose. Then in the taxi he'd mentioned that he had originally come from a village. I was in Morocco to find a village. Why not his? And what made a villager, once in the city, into a criminal? If you're sympathetic, you might say a poor man, jobless, maybe with a hungry family, is desperate enough to try anything. If you're hostile/afraid, you blame criminality on childhood experience, psychic debility or even derangement. Or you blame the cultural breakdown of a society. In Barek's case, there was an element of all of these. In the months we spent together, he sometimes violently lost his temper; then he would threaten me, "Someday, *khafir,* I gwine kill you!" I think he meant that, caught up in the heat of anger, he feared he might. It was as if, like Legion, he was tormented by hidden demons. But Allah and his angels were there, too.

*

Morocco is a brown and arid land except in the spring. Then it turns a lovely green. That was one of Barek's curious English words—"lovely." The Moroccan soil, washed by heavy rains from the Atlantic, also sends up a fantastic profusion of wild flowers: white and yellow daisies, orange and red poppies, the blue of violets. In the weeks we spent in his village, up on the Romanni plateau beneath the Atlas Mountains, Barek used to pick these flowers by the armful; he would give them to old women in the village, but he picked them compulsively, without reason; he just wanted to gather the flowers up.

In his description of the village on our bus journey, Barek had pictured his *douar,* as he called it, as bright, cozy and comfortable. We had to walk a mile from the station along a high country road and when we reached the home of Hadj, a farmer and uncle whom he had not seen for fifteen years, I could see how apprehensive Barek had become. In Casablanca, we had struck a deal: he would spend some weeks with me in his village and in return I would try to help him get a passport so he could go to France. Barek admitted to having been in jail a couple of times—for fights, he said, over Zora, his girl, who worked in a bar and went with foreign sailors. I soon forgot the doorman's description of Barek as a "big gangster" and did not learn for years that by then he already had a long criminal record for robbery and for getting into street fights while drunk.

Barek was then thirty. He was a short, muscular Arab with African blood. Both of his parents had died before he was nine. He soon ran away to the city and after years as house servant, errand boy, sailor, docker, pimp and street peddler, with knife marks on his forehead and teeth marks on his knuckles, he felt himself to be very much a man of Casablanca. From his words it was evident that he loved the sun-drenched port city with its bleached white buildings, the mysterious Arab *medina,* the docks with their giant forklifts and freighters going to all the world, and the fleets of tattered fishing dhows.

Hadj's homestead, as we approached, was a single low-roofed hut of mud-plastered brick, a black cooking tent, two mean-looking sheds of straw and stone for the cattle and—nothing else. A hill descended sharply to a riverbank, where files of white geese moved among the green grass and wild flowers. Just on the opposite bank began an olive orchard, rows of long stone barns with rusted tin roofs, and a big, square, old-fashioned villa, the manor house of a Frenchman who owned most of the village land. The rest of the village huts, perhaps forty in all, clustered around a giant eucalyptus tree, with willows and mountain ash peeping out of bramble fences. The huts looked poor and mean but the village was cheerful; all day you could hear the village sounds: chickens squawking, dogs barking, birds calling, and the cries of children playing around the big tree.

"It is lovely here," Barek said. "The valley is so green."

"Too green," Hadj's wife told us, over mint tea. "We've had too much rain. Hadj says the field work is two months behind. And still it rains." The youngest of the family's five sons, little Musa, was palsied; his legs were misshapen as twisted ropes, spittle dribbled down his chin and he was unable to control his facial muscles; he had intelligent eyes. The child was so deformed it was painful to look at him but when we were at the house Barek always held him in his lap, carried Musa about on his shoulders and played with him; he was the only one who did. Soon little Musa adored him; this was not lost on the child's mother, who told Barek, "Always I think about my boy. I think when I die I'm going to leave him like this, with his sick feet, talking no good. Always I think what will happen when I'm dead."

In our days in Romanni, we worked with Hadj's oldest and only married son, Mohammed; we went at first light to the fields for a day of weeding, cultivating and mowing, cutting a cartload of fodder at sunset. These were the best of times, working in the fresh spring air and, especially, walking homeward at dusk on a high ridge road over the intensely green valley, Barek stopping to fill his arms up with flowers. He loved the wide, spacious sweep of the land, the clean air, the sun, which sometimes broke through the blue rain clouds, and the green, a vivid green I have never seen before or since, of the young wheat and pea fields. "The green of the fields," Hadj's wife would say, "is good for the eyes."

Hadj, with fifty rain-fed acres, was the only Arab landowner in the village. All the surrounding fields belonged to the Frenchman, who lived in Paris. Years before Hadj had rented him twelve acres, but the Frenchman had refused to give it back when his lease expired. The local authorities would not give him a hearing; Hadj suspected that they had been bribed. He was forced to hire an advocate and, while he got his land back, it cost him his savings.

Each morning perhaps a hundred workers, mostly old men, women and children from the *douar*—the young, able-bodied men shoveled sand from the riverbanks and stayed independent—worked in the Frenchman's fields under a Berber overseer, who carried a heavy staff and gave no one a moment's peace.

"Why don't the French all go from here?" Barek exploded one day. "So these people have land to live."

"This is the life," an old woman rebuked him. "We have nothing to make of it. We are poor laboring people. It has always been like this. The rich eat the poor. We wait for Allah to judge them."

Sometimes an American Peace Corpsman, a blond Swedish-American from Minnesota named Steve, came to try and persuade Hadj to invest more in modern methods. But it meant taking credit. Hadj would have none of it. "I pay my taxes," he said. "That's all. If you have only fifty acres and you owe the government a million francs, how do you sleep at night?" "The land is everything," Barek said. "If you have good land, it will give you good wheat."

One day he told Mohammed, "When my father died, we had a hungry time. We had about ten or eleven cows. Sometimes I go with my mother after the cows, sometimes with my little sister. I was so hungry I broke into the flour sack to eat. My mother, she catch me and she slap me. 'Black boy,' she would say, 'black boy, you are no good!' So I stay two, three years here in the village. Then I leave my home. I leave my mother also. Soon she is dead."

Barek told Mohammed about his girl, Zora, and that she supported her mother back in a village near Rabat, but not that she did so by sleeping with foreign sailors. ("Never a Moroccan," Barek later told me.) He told about street fights after drinking, but never spoke about his long record in Casablanca's Prison Civile; he liked to talk about the life along the Boulevard du Mohammed el Hansali, with its date palms and tourists buying Moroccan carpets and leather; about the Café Brasserie du Maghreb where he and his friends gathered for coffee and gossip in the mornings; and the Café Bouchaib, where jobless dockers played *tooti, runda* and other card games all day long. One day he did tell us about the last time he fought with a gendarme who abused Zora and about how Zora came to the prison, broke down, and ripped aside her veil, sobbing, "No, no, Barek! Every time, every time! Don't you drink so much in the street and fight!" Barek said, "I want to stay in Casa and look after her, but better I go to France and catch a job. What is my life here?"

"Why not find a job in Morocco?" Mohammed asked.

"Where? Where?"

One rainy day, Barek, Mohammed and I sat around the hut of Hamid, an old retired soldier who had fought in Indochina, drinking wine and smoking hashish. Hamid, a toothless, wrinkled laborer whose wife had left him, showed us a faded photograph of himself in uniform; he looked manly and strong, another person from the pathetic wreck he had become. He wanted to know about Barek's life in Casablanca.

"My life? What is there to tell?" But Barek took a few more swigs of wine and told how it was in the city, when he arrived there as a runaway boy; until then he had never worn shoes. First he worked in a cheap dockers' café, sleeping on the floor, never changing clothes, splashing cold water on his face. Then he'd found a job in the kitchen of a rich Moroccan and stayed seven years. "That man," Barek said. "Always he was good to me. He sent me to French school for five years." Barek was proud of his literacy. But his family found him and brought him home again; so he ran away for a second time.

"I loved Casa. I don't like to sit all the time in a small village like this. Why? Why? I don't know why. That's the way it was, anyway. Back in Casa, I found three French whorehouses. Many seamen went there. I'd wait by the cars in front of those private houses and when somebody came out I'd say I was the watchman. I cleaned the windows on their cars and they gave me ten, twenty francs. If I had enough for a movie, I'd go."

Barek drank some more wine; he began to speak with some kind of inner ferocity and we could see he was wound up. "You want to know about my life? I'll tell you." Once when he was a seaman, he said, he left the key to his room in Casablanca with an older brother who had come to the city, Abdesalem. When he returned from sea, a trip to Holland, he found someone else living in his room; his brother had sold all his possessions and used the money to gamble, losing everything. "Now in that room," Barek said, "I leave six or seven pairs of pants, three or four towels, some stuff to cook with, pots and things, ten shirts, three blankets, one mattress, bed, table, chairs to sit on—everything I got in the world is in that room." He found his brother and demanded, "Who give you leave to sell everything like this? Sell my clothes? Everything I got?" Barek's eyes brimmed up, remembering. "Always I respect him, look up to him. That day I punched the son of a bitch in the face. He was bleeding and I hit him again and again. I want to kill him. He's my brother. So I never see him again. I promise this is true."

"It's a hard life," Mohammed said.

"God gives everyone such a life," groaned the old soldier. "And who is there to look after you? To help you in this life?"

"Nobody!" Barek spat out the words. "I got nobody but myself!"

He went outside and we found him with his head down against the wall, tears streaming down his face. He turned away, ashamed of us seeing him and swore, "That son of a bitch! He make me cry like a woman!"

Hamid shrugged. "He'll get used to it," he said.

*

Barek's main hope in France was that an acquaintance, one Pierrot, would help him; they had played together on the same soccer team until Pierrot, a Jewish Moroccan, had migrated to France. Barek had not heard from him for several years but it was said he had done well. Getting a passport had proven to be easy; we flew to Madrid and went on to Paris by train. I had to accompany Barek that far as it was the only way to get him past the French immigration authorities. We did get stopped at the border, but only until I produced an old, fortunately undated White House press pass. I was writing a story on North African migrant workers in Europe, I explained, and Barek was my interpreter; in a sense, this was true.

In Paris, things went wrong from the start. At Gare Austerlitz, Barek asked the cab driver to take us to the Arab quarter; instead he drove to St. Germain and we got caught in a Saturday night Left Bank student *manifestation*. Traffic stalled and students swarmed around us, pounding on the hood and our hastily rolled-up windows and shouting slogans: *"Guerre au racisme! Français, immigrés tous unis!"* Many carried torches and some, seeing Barek, would shriek, *"Solidarité! Justice aux immigrés, les Arabes, les Africains!"*

We were exhausted already, and it was a nightmare for us. "Keep your window up," the driver cried. "There's trouble with the *flics* ahead. The tear gas can knock you out." "What is it?" I asked. The driver shrugged. *"La révolution."* When we tried to get out and walk, he insisted we pay a double fare. "You got me stranded here. I could be here all night. Pay me double or you don't get your luggage." You could hardly hear; horns were honking, students shouting; we paid and fled on foot, *"Guerre au racisme! Guerre au racisme!"* fading behind us. We reached the Métro but it was early morning before we found the Arab quarter, just off the intersection of Barbes-Rochechuart; unable to find a hotel, we spent the night in a *hamam* near a mosque, a Moslem refuge from the culture that has made Paris a beacon of the civilized world. Or Barek did. I was too angry. I had been in Paris once before, with my family, when I was nineteen; we had stayed at the old Continental on the Rue de Rivoli, breakfasting on a balcony overlooking the Tuileries gardens. This was the other side of Paris, one tourists don't see. I stared into the gloom of a dim, domed chamber; beads of water dripped from the ceiling and drowsy figures moved about, Arab outcasts. Men breathed heavily in deep slumber, flung about the heated tiles like dead white fish washed up by some catastrophe. But, side by side with his Arab brothers, Barek slept.

The next day we found a room in a hotel, the American, a wooden firetrap I read burned down not long ago, killing eighteen Arab guests. That second night we sat in confusion in a sidewalk café on Barbes, staring at flashing neon, revolutionary graffiti, heavy traffic grinding down the Boulevard de Rochechuart and sidewalks mobbed with people. Across Barbes were rows of shiny bars, all chrome and mirrors. The mirrors, one saw, reflected mostly black and brown faces, Algerians, Riffis, Africans standing with drinks along the bars; on the sidewalk was a French Salvation army band, behind them the white lights of porno film houses. Barek was dazed with fatigue, but was reassured by the Egyptian music coming from the jukeboxes and the signs in Arabic everywhere.

"What I want to know," he asked a youth from Senegal who had just sat down and said to call him Zeke, "is how one man from Morocco, when he wants to find work, can find a job in Paris?"

"Maybe it's dangerous to look for a job in Paris right now," the Senegalese said. "Many French boys, they don't get jobs. Maybe seven, eight hundred thousand French people, they don't find work. If you're an Arab, nobody wants you. Before it was free. Not now. Now you got to have French nationality. *Beaucoup racisme.*" Zeke, a tall, skinny, pitch-black youth in tight white pants and an electric pink shirt, told Barek there were other ways to make money in Paris. We went along with Zeke to Place Pigalle, where tourists, he explained, after days touring the Louvre, Notre Dame, Sainte-Chapelle and the Arc de Triomphe, came at night when they were ready for action.

Crowds were thronging up the hill toward Montmartre, where we could see the floodlit domes of Sacré Coeur. The Moulin Rouge flashed red lights, a marquee advertised *Oh, Calcutta!,* strip shows displayed life-size cardboard cutouts of naked girls, you could see transvestites dancing in the windows of Madame Mathur's, and Zeke

pointed out the big cinema houses of the Luxour, Trianon and La Ci-
tale, where French men could be picked up and robbed in the base-
ments. We soon had enough of Place Pigalle and Zeke came with us
back to Barbes where we saw a large crowd of men milling around
behind the Métro station. "These boys, they go all over Paris," Zeke
explained. "They pick pockets, steal watches in the Métro stations,
maybe steal somebody's clothes. So they sell it here. Anything you
need you can buy here cheap." Next came the narrow Rue de la Char-
bonniere, so dark you could hardly see your way, where Arabs and
Africans were standing in queues outside the whorehouses; one
woman cursed from behind a barred door as we went by, "*Salud, ta
guèle, fichez-moi la paix. I don't like black men!*"

We offered to buy Zeke a drink in gratitude for our tour; Barek was
relieved to find a place where the *patron* came from Casablanca. They
began to talk when a handsome young man broke away from a group
of Greeks at the other end of the crowded bar. "Excuse me," he told
Barek, speaking Arabic, "I heard you say you're from Casa. Excuse
me, but you're Moroccan and I'm Moroccan. Don't think I like these
Greek guys I'm with. They're rich and I just go with them. I used to
work at Simca but they laid me off. You understand?"

The *patron* leaned across the counter. "This is no good, the things
you do," he told the youth in an undertone. "You must drink but you
are supposed to be gentle to these people, not beat them and rob them.
You give my café a bad name."

The youth turned savagely upon him. "You shut your mouth! This
is not your business. You just sell your wine." Soon other Arabs joined
the argument and there were shouts of "*Dieu moc boue!* Your father
is a pig! Queer! *Zumle a karasa!*" The *patron* finally threw the trou-
blemakers out, furiously shouting, "Finish! You no more come to my
place!"

"I hate Paris," Barek said as we walked back to our hotel. "Better I
go to Marseilles. I got a couple of friends there."

The next day Barek phoned Pierrot, who invited us to spend the
next Sunday with him. We met in a café across the street from his em-
ployer's house, an imposing gray stone mansion on an elegant chest-
nut-shaded boulevard not far from the Arc de Triomphe; it could have
been an embassy. At a glance, I could see that Barek's friend, who was
blond and wore a well-tailored suit, had become a Frenchman; my
heart sank since Barek, with his dark skin, beard, boots and shabby

tweed jacket, was unmistakably a poor Arab. Pierrot warmly em-
braced Barek Arab fashion and seemed genuinely delighted to see
him. *"Salaam aleik!"* he exclaimed, and then said he had the whole
day free and what would we like to see of Paris? Over coffee he told
Barek how well he was doing, earning more than three hundred dollars a month. He had a motor scooter and was saving to buy a car; he
was looking for a better job so he could get married. He had taken out
citizenship papers. Indeed, to me he seemed already French.

Pierrot was friendly and enthusiastic; he wanted to know about all
their mutual acquaintances back in Casablanca. We climbed the Eiffel
Tower, watched a soccer game (Barek: "These French can't play like
Moroccans"), spent an hour in the Louvre, strolled through the Tuileries and reached the Champs Élysées just as tiny golden lights were
blinking on under the red-and-white café awnings, and the Arc de
Triomphe looked like a pale blue apparition of itself in the traffic
fumes; it was the Paris I remembered.

By now, both Barek and I realized that Pierrot was choosing to
treat Barek as if he were a visitor on a holiday; there was no offer of a
place to stay or help to find a job. Nor would Barek ask him. I
remember him saying, as we sat drinking coffee in a café on the
Champs Élysées, "Paris is lovely. I think before it is like Casablanca.
I never think it will be like this." I sensed he was self-conscious of his
beard and shabby clothes (he shaved off the beard the next day without saying anything). In that moment, Barek's fate was suspended; we
both were praying Pierrot would offer real help. But why should he
have? Why should he have endangered his own chances of becoming a
Frenchman? The moment passed. Pierrot was shaking our hands and
then moving away, fair and inconspicuous, into the well-dressed people of Paris. I wanted to call him back. Then both Barek and I hurried
to the nearest Métro entrance like fugitives, fleeing one of the most elegant streets in the world; getting back to Barbes was a relief.

Barek spent his last days in Paris grimly taking the Métro and buses
to industrial suburbs and applying for jobs. His fellow French appli-
cants did not disguise their hostility. He filled in forms and was told to
return. I knew he never would. When he grew too discouraged, I went
with him. We found the big Renault plant in Billancourt on strike and
lost our way back to the Métro station. All the streets seem to look
alike; long and deserted, with empty plant buildings on both sides. At
last we saw the main boulevard ahead, but halfway down the sidewalk

were five mean-looking French youths, tight jeans, shaggy hair and pasty faces. I told Barek we could walk around them; we kept going. Barek muttered, "Excuse me, I just want to pass." One spoke to him, ignoring me. "What do you want here, black boy?" Barek stood perfectly still. When one boy stepped toward him, he went berserk. His arms shot out and the boy went down on the pavement. The others tried to jump us, but we ran straight down the road, hearing their abuse behind us.

The next day we went to the Simca factory. No hiring. Six thousand Moroccans were already on the payroll and there were layoffs. We saw how the workers lived. New barracks had replaced the old *bidonvilles* but there were still six men to a room. The Parisian press that week had reported the death of five Africans, trying to warm themselves by a makeshift fire in a "hostel" in Aubervilliers. Earlier fifty North Africans were found to be living in a five-room house. These barracks were not much better. As we walked back toward the city we found ourselves in a treeless, garbage-strewn wasteland near the Seine. A notice pasted on a telephone pole warned that any immigrants who illegally smuggled relatives into France would be immediately deported. In the distance, behind a high steel fence, was a new apartment complex; children were playing on a green lawn. Barek said the workers' barracks were like the Prison Civile in Casablanca; he said you could see what the life of a poor Moroccan would be in Paris.

We wandered aimlessly on—both, I think, sensing that we were reaching the end of our journey. Along the riverbank derelicts were living in shacks among heaps of refuse. I thought: it will have to be Marseilles now, if Barek really does have friends there. We turned back.

There was trouble at the Clichy Métro station. The ticket puncher, an old woman in a blue uniform, was crying *"Le ticket, le ticket!"* Two Moroccans, both dead drunk, argued that they had given theirs; she insisted they had not. She began to furiously pound on her booth to summon her supervisor. They began to abuse her. "You're not true French. You're from the Maghreb, same as we are. Some old bitch from the Maghreb." The French crowd surged around them with undisguised revulsion. *"Les Arabes . . . les Arabes . . ."* we could hear, as if it were a dirty word.

Changing trains, we found the same two Moroccans just ahead of us in an underground passageway. A French family, elegantly dressed, with a little boy with a red pompom on his hat, suddenly came to a stop just in front of us. One of the Moroccans was urinating. The man, furious, lifted a rolled umbrella he was carrying and whacked it down on the Moroccan's head. "No, let him alone!" the man's wife shrieked. "He's drunk!" The other Moroccan started shoving the Frenchman and the woman screamed, "Stop! No! No! Oh, please, somebody help us!" People began pushing, some to see better, some to get away, mostly to just get past. Then three French youths, their long hair flying, came from somewhere and we saw they were punching Arabs, other Arabs on the platform ahead, and when one of them jumped one of the Moroccans from behind, yanking his head back with a violent jerk, Barek moved in, his fist smashing into the white face as if all his resentment had suddenly exploded. The train came just in time and, shoving and kicking Barek myself, I managed to force him inside.

*

"Someday, *khafir*, I gwine kill you!" Voiced, fiercely, on the way back to Barbes. But I was hot, feverish, sensed something physically was going wrong. And there was the premonition that Barek was somehow on the edge of a cliff and one had to pull him back. The next morning I took him to the American Embassy and tried to get him a visa; he didn't fit any of their bureaucratic categories and was refused. Back at our hotel, I collapsed with fever and chills; Barek was terrified, didn't know how to find a doctor, but the hotel brought one. He diagnosed bronchitis; for two days I was semi-delirious. Barek brought hot tea, changed the sweat-soaked sheets, kept watch. On the third day, when the fever subsided a bit, I calculated what money we had left after hotel and doctor were paid: two hundred and fifty dollars. We had to do something. I phoned Pierrot, who agreed to come and put Barek on the train to Marseilles; I gave him two hundred dollars, then called the airport and booked the first flight to Dulles. I never saw a grown man cry like Barek did that night. I never will again. Then it was over.

A month or so later a letter postmarked Casablanca came. Barek wrote that he had reached Marseilles and stayed nine days, had "had some trouble with some Algerian guys," who robbed his money. The Moroccan Consulate sent him home. "Don't worry I lost my passport," Barek wrote. "I still have it with me." He remembered how he "picked flowers in the fields" in Romanni.

More than a year later I learned Barek was in prison, sentenced to fifteen years for "organizing a criminal gang and robbery." Hamid and another man, caught stealing from a French tourist, implicated Barek in their confessions. The sentence was stiff; there was speculation that Casablanca was trying to rid the waterfront area of undesirables. In early 1973 I went to Casablanca and with help from his Arab underworld friends was able to visit him at Casablanca's Prison Civile. The Arab who brought me lost control and wept hysterically. But Barek, seen through the double bars of the *polwar*, was calm and smiling. I could hardly hear him above the shouts and weeping of the other prisoners and their families. "I didn't do nothing," Barek called, his voice barely audible above the noise. "Don't you worry none about me." Only the water that welled up in his eyes gave lie to the grin.

That was eight years ago; at this writing Barek has been in prison for ten. Our lawyer, Bensaid, is hopeful that with so much time served, the sentence so unduly severe, and a good behavior record, we can get him a pardon; Morocco's King Hassan gives them three times every year. In 1979 I saw Barek again, at a prison farm near Settat, a small town a two-hour drive from Casablanca. This time, except for the lawyer and two guards, Barek and I talked alone; he looked unchanged. Zora, he said, had never written nor come to the prison, but an eighteen-year-old niece, Aminah, came about once a month, the only member of his family who did. I asked Barek what he would do if we could get him a pardon. "Go back to Casa," he said.

"Why do you help him?" Bensaid asked as we drove away.

"Because he needs help. He is poor and unlucky."

Bensaid shrugged in the French manner. "Ah, but you would have to help half the world."

I don't know half the world, I thought. But if half the world gives love to crippled children and picks flowers, it can't be all bad; it only needs the right kind of help. So I didn't reply to Bensaid; it was too hard to explain. I just looked out the window, staring at the passing landscape of dull, ripe wheat, ready for harvest—but seeing a green valley.

NEETIL VILLAGE, SUDAN

Africans are forever walking, walking along in their flowing white tunics with a comfortable, easy, loping gait natural to people who, with no other way to go, are used to journeying by foot across the big, empty spaces of their continent. That's how I met Kuwa, on a dusty track near the small town of Dilling, a couple of hundred miles southwest of Khartoum where the Sahara ends and the African savannah begins. Kuwa was a giant of a man, ebony black and as tall and muscular as the Nubian slave of Western mythology. When Mohammed, my interpreter and, like Kuwa, a member of the Nuba tribe, asked where we could find a village, Kuwa at once invited us to his. It was another five hours' walk in the bush. Arriving weary and footsore, we moved in with him, his four wives and nine children that very night, sleeping in one of the many small grass huts in their thorny-bush compound. Then the real walking started: to Kuwa's sorghum fields a mile away, to the river to water his cattle, into the bush to collect firewood, into Dilling on market days and, once, through a haunted mountain gorge, to meet a dying king.

At the outset I'll confess that I find black Africa, at least way out in the bush hundreds of miles from anywhere, peculiarly intimidating. Maybe it's the oppressive heat and monotony of the savannah, the way the desert dunes, prairie acacia and grassland shrubs go on and on with little relief or variation; or the drums, somewhere way off in the distance, faint but almost never silent; or the wildlife, harmless and fascinating as it is, unless you happen to get caught in the bush unarmed and alone. Maybe it's simply the strangeness of it all, but in Africa I feel an uneasy sense of being cut off I almost never experience elsewhere—or not for long. Often when you go to new places, you feel a little uneasy at first. You don't know anybody, you're not sure of the do's and don't's. In the Nuba Mountains, it was a relief to be accompanied by Mohammed, a young journalist known in Khartoum as a champion of the Nuba people and their customs. When we set out to make the two-day journey to Dilling, flying first to the Sahara town of El-Obeid and then making a long day's journey across drifting sand in an antiquated truck which kept breaking down, there was many a time I would have turned back without him. Yet once we settled down in Kuwa's village of Neetil, surrounded on all sides by the Nuba Mountains, Mohammed turned into a jittery critic, finding fault with everything. Our long daily walks in the bush distressed him; the solitudes unnerved him; all the talk of *ju-ju* magic undid him. I felt like asking, "I thought this was your home; what is it you're so nervous about?" I didn't because I suspected his anxiety might be because he did know what we were getting into so well. As a foreign outsider, having complete trust in Kuwa, I could relax just because I was totally ignorant about Africa, like those tourists who sometimes jet into the midst of a revolution, see the sights and jet out again, oblivious to any crisis until they read about it later in the newspapers. At any rate, within a week of our arrival in Kuwa's village, Mohammed, who had promised to stay forty days, was suddenly gone, fleeing back to the city with his fancy clothes, tape recorder and camera. It is not necessarily the foreigner who suffers the worst culture shock in villages.

I was a bit angry and afraid, but nonetheless, he had gotten me there and Kuwa, at forty-eight a retired soldier, was a perfect host and guide. He had spent fifteen years in the Sudanese army and had served in Equatoria, Ethiopia and what was the Belgian Congo; his proudest memory was of shaking hands with Queen Elizabeth while a member of the Khartoum presidential palace guard. The Nubas, since conversion to Islam in the 1960s, no longer went naked except on ceremonial occasions; but they still hunted with spears and cultivated their slash-and-burn sorghum and millet patches with hoes, having never known the plow. Physically impressive, they seemed to thrive on their unvaried diet of sorghum mush, a little meat and okra, washed down with coffee, tea or home-brewed *merissa* beer (it went down like buckwheat pancake batter). To me, it grew more *unappetitlich* day by day; in five weeks I was to lose more than twenty pounds. Maybe only the fittest survive.

Kuwa himself seemed modern-minded; he spoke some English, knew about jets, penicillin, and the Apollo moon landing, and had seen many foreigners in his army days. He knew a world existed where men put their faith in technology, not in gods; he was proud of the village school's rudimentary science laboratory; his main ambition was to educate his children. So it came as a surprise when he said one day that he was soon going to be his Nimang subtribe's *kudjur* or rainmaker-faith healer; Kuwa was about to become one of the last of the witch doctors.

The landscape of the Nuba Mountains is very strange. There is the starved greenery, red soil and hot sweet smell so common in black Africa, with its hint of smoke from the grass huts and fires from the bush as ground is cleared for planting. The "mountains," small and craggy and barely worth the name, rise from flat savannah plains in reddish, boulder-strewn cones about one or two thousand feet in height. It looks like an array of miniature, extinct, pointy volcanoes. So many of the boulders are precariously poised on the slopes it looks exactly as if some giant geological explosion had flung them into the sky and they still lie about wherever they happened to land. As we were on the eastern edge of the Sahel's three-thousand-mile sweep, the Sahara's southward creep had drifted sand dunes right into the village; most days sand-dusty mists gave an impression of fog. Neetil, like all the other Nuba villages we visited, was a small settlement of conical grass huts clustering around the foot of a mountain by the same name; Kuwa said there were exactly ninety-nine mountains, each with its own subtribe. Above the village on Neetil Mountain there were acacia woods inhabited by hyenas, baboons and exotic birds; the old men remembered elephants, zebras and giraffes, but these had fled south long ago. Neetil was also situated along that great African divide between the Islamic north and the Christian-pagan south. The ruined churches and abandoned Victorian bungalows we saw in the bush testified that Islam, like the Sahara, was creeping south too.

Sudan nowadays has caught the world's attention because, as Africa's biggest country—one third the size of the United States—it has two hundred million acres of land deemed arable, less than a tenth of it ever farmed. Dreams of becoming "the breadbasket of the Arab world" have caused the Khartoum government to invest in big, subsidized mechanized farms. Only recently has Sudan begun to discover, as all governments do, that raising food production means transforming village culture. Go too fast and you turn an agricultural people into a mass of culturally uprooted and politically restive laborers. Keeping the African ancestral faith would be the surest way to keep the social peace, but this would mean little change at all. Most of the fifteen million Sudanese follow the same combination of cattle grazing and rain-fed sorghum and millet cultivation that Kuwa did; but a tribesman and his family, using hoes, can only grow eight or ten acres of sorghum a year; there is virtually no surplus, beyond what is eaten, to create cities or, as happened in Egypt to the north, a great civilization. How to wring out a food surplus?

As a start, the government has set up schools, dispensaries (simple ones, but they give out iodine, sulfa and enteroviaform) and mosques in most of the tribal villages. It has also kept the village courts set up by the British (who went home in 1956), even if they are often overwhelmed by civil suits on marital disputes, assault, petty theft and defamation, many of them brought for the sheer pleasure of litigation. The government has done less well providing pure water; Neetil's wells, when I was there, had dried up during the long years of the Sahel drought; women had to carry water in heavy tin cans on their heads almost a mile. Rabies was endemic, yet any kind of serum, even a tetanus injection, as I was to discover, meant the long day's journey back across the desert by truck or the single daily bus to El-Obeid. And the government had yet to make its peace with the *kudjur*, who, as magician, rainmaker, soothsayer, medicine man, priest and social leader, stood at the very center of Nuba tribalism; his power came from the belief that he could control supernatural spirits, who are also known as *kudjurs* (an Arabic word from which we get "conjure").

I first made an acquaintance with *ju-ju*, or magical, fetishistic objects used in Africa, in the Dilling marketplace. There, spread out upon the earth, in one stall after another, were such delights as baboon and dog heads, feet of hyenas and gazelles, dried snakes and chameleons, bristles, roots, hoofs, eyes and such putrefied bits and pieces of God knows what, I stopped asking. The gate of Kuwa's compound back in the village was also adorned with *ju-ju:* a spear, a shield, bits of bone, roots and hair and an enormous and particularly repellent dried lizard. *Ju-ju* can be used for either black or white magic but it seems a pathetic substitute for science and medicine because, like the more gruesome of the African masks, it tends to be scarier than the evil it's supposed to chase away. In the Nuba Mountains there was a lot to be afraid of: rainstorms, forest fires, earthquakes, drought and plagues of disease, aside from the everyday dust storms and sweltering heat. Neetil's new school, dispensary and mosque were new in the past decade; one could understand why the Nuba religion chose to make ordinary men like Kuwa intermediaries with God, whom they called *aro* or *kuni* or (my favorite) He Who Lives in the Sky.

Trio Eléctrico, Salvador, Brazil.

Carnival reveler in Brazil.

Carolina.

Barek, a Moroccan immigrant to France—now in prison.

Moroccan peasant.

Old Nuba tribesman in Neetil village, Sudan, sings of his people's miraculous origin and history.

Kuwa, a Nuba tribesman.

Nuba tribesmen.

Sultan Ahmed in Neetil village.

The author and Tashi Sherpa, his guide-interpreter, on the Tibetan border above Nepal's Langtang valley, 1961.

Sherpa woman and grandchild.

Ngodup's father, Khampas.

Tibetan children.

Tibetan refugee.

Tibetan refugees.

Ngodup.

Friend of Tonio in Tulungatung,
Philippines.

Catalino, Tonio's father.

Carabao pulls cart in Tulungatung village, the Philippines.

A man did not choose to be a *kudjur;* the spirit chose him. With Kuwa it happened fourteen years before my visit; he was home on leave from the army and was encountered, usually in the dead of night, out walking in the bush alone, speaking, as the villagers described it, "in a low thrilling voice" that was not his own. When he also began to display amazing gifts of healing and prophecy, Kuwa was taken to the Nimangs' old, disenthroned king, Sultan Ahmed, who declared him to be a *kudjur.* Soon the spirit, speaking through Kuwa's voice, revealed his name was Neetil and that he was the common ancestor of all the Nimang people; he said that henceforward death, illness, harvests and the subtribe's welfare and happiness would be Kuwa's concern. Kuwa wore this mantle lightly. When I was with him, he usually downed a peg of liquor first thing in the morning and he cultivated his fields, grazed his cattle and goats, collected berries and roots and helped his neighbors to build and repair their grass huts just like anybody else. But his willingness to become a *kudjur* earned him a sharp rebuke from the village schoolmaster, an Arab from Dilling.

"How can you, Kuwa," the schoolmaster protested, "provide the young people with the education and jobs that matter to them? You cannot. The *kudjur* only exploits fear and ignorance. We must abolish these superstitions." But I noted that the schoolmaster, as a good Moslem, believed in *djinn.* The village *maulana* was more sophisticated. A Moslem missionary trained at Cairo's great Al Azhar University, he warned Kuwa, "The *kudjur* is a *setan,* an agent of the Devil. It is written in the Koran that a *setan* just plays tricks with the people; in the end he will abandon them to burn in the fires of hell. A *kudjur* claims he is possessed by a benevolent spirit from God to take care of rain, war and disease. Sometimes *kudjurs* do seem to have supernatural powers. Rain can come. The sick may be cured. But this is mere coincidence. Allah alone created the world and He is responsible for everything. You must pray directly to God, Kuwa. No human being can come between a man and Allah."

*

Day began, in the five weeks I stayed with Kuwa and his tribe, with the crowing of a rooster, who nestled with some hens and chickens under Kuwa's cot at night. Each of Kuwa's four wives slept in her own grass hut, with her children. Kuwa, his oldest son, Ali, home from a factory job in Khartoum, and I slept in the men's hut, which was just

big enough for three cots; the door was so low, about three feet, you
had to virtually crawl in. When I complained I was getting bitten by
tiny spiders which dropped from the grass roof or came out of my
bed's wooden frame at night, Kuwa laughed and said, "Never mind,
once they fill their bellies they'll let you sleep." The hell with that, I
thought, and borrowed a steel cot from the village dispensary. Mornings were cool; Sindia, Kuwa's favorite and youngest wife, brought
morning tea. Kuwa would pull a grimy white Arab gown over the old
army pants he slept in, splash some water on his face and wind a white
turban around a bright orange skull cap. By sunrise we would be on
our way, walking, walking, walking.

*

A few of the Nubas still go naked, mostly older people we met far
out in the bush. Their nakedness was adorned, you even might say
covered, by all manner of necklaces, earrings, bracelets, feathers, tat-
tooings and lacerations; some, especially on ceremonial occasions or
just to keep the flies away, smeared their faces and bodies with white
dung ash (I was tempted to try it against the flies but in that crowd a
white face looked ghostly enough). Clothing, only universally worn in
the past twenty years, imposes an economic hardship on the poorest
Nubas, as does anything they cannot grow or make themselves in their
almost money-free economy. They complained about it to me.

*

The sound of drums is distinctive to Africa; they almost never
cease. On nights of the full moon in Neetil, all the young people would
gather near a huge old *tebeldi* tree to dance; Kuwa, too old to join in,
and I would go to watch. Girls formed a circle first while the boys, as
hangdog as Iowa farmers at the start of a country dance, stayed back
in the tree's shadows. The main beat was played by an old man who
banged his hands against the ends of a cylindrical drum which he
carried hung about his neck; two younger men with their drums
placed upright on the ground struck the surface with the palms of their
hands. Soon the drums imposed their own monotonous deep beat over
the confused hum of the crowd and the girls in the circle quieted
down, swaying with the beat, their eyes wide open and expectant. Suddenly, as if he could control himself no longer, one young man would
leap into the circle and start to dance. His expression and whole manner of being seemed to say he was not doing this of his own free will

but because the growing power of the drums forced him into it. Soon the youth fell back into the circle, other young men slipped into it and the dance really began.

One, two or three men would advance toward some favored girl, nod, mutter an invitation, and move back again. Then as the drum-beats quickened, each man, his body held loose, chest thrust out and shoulders back, would start plunging his right leg up and down, knee bent, in a pounding, throbbing movement which carried his entire body forward in the same rhythm. Girls also began to dance, facing some boy and doing the same movements, but shyly and less vigor-ously. The dance was explicitly sexual and yet chaste; you could not help but admire the grace, composure and splendid sense of rhythm of these young African dancers and their youthful endurance as they moved their bodies for hours in time to the monotonous, obsessive beat. It was as if, just as in the Brazilian *Carnaval,* they were caught and held by the power of the drums, not just that they wished to dance but that they *had* to dance, their faces shining and streaming with sweat and even, as the night wore on, wearing expressions of strain and fatigue. But they kept going. And, as Kuwa explained, it was all see and no touch. Promiscuity was very rare; if a couple slipped off into the bush and a girl became pregnant, the boy faced a two-year jail sentence. Or the girl's father might punish her by arranging her mar-riage to an ugly or older man; the Nubas had their own strict sense of decorum and morality. Kuwa himself felt the pull of the drumbeats and complained, "They're all babies." I too felt the power of the con-tagious rhythm, something, one felt, that came straight from the heart of man's innermost depth; probably this rhythm is one of the most val-uable legacies Africa has given the rest of us.

*

I grew to fear the baboons. Almost every day they'd swoop down from the cliffs above Neetil and snatch somebody's goat or hen. "They move about in a big family," Ali explained. "You can see them beck-oning with their fingers to call their children. Oh, very clever, these baboons; if you sit on a rock and one sees you, he'll try to sneak up behind you and take your stick or rifle and run away. Curse their fa-thers!" Ali claimed that baboons raped girls if they caught one in the bush alone and that they had been known to kill a man. "The baboon is an old, old, old man," Kuwa said. "Like we were before."

*

Rape was the most common crime among the Nubas, usually committed with the girl's tacit consent as a way of persuading her father and family to agree to a cheap bride price, for the going rate of a hundred Sudanese pounds, two bulls to sacrifice at the betrothal and marriage ceremonies, plus clothes for the bride and some goats for her father was more than most young men could afford; many were forced to postpone marriage.

While I was in Neetil, a violent rapist also appeared in a stretch of acacia forest toward the next village of Salara. "Nobody lives around there," Kuwa explained. "It may be one man or a gang of men. No one knows. Two women were walking to Salara and suddenly a man came out of the trees, his head covered with a black cloth. He had a heavy stick and nearly killed them. When the women were found, their clothes were ripped off and one did not recover consciousness until we carried her home. One blow broke her jaw. Both were spitting blood and lost some teeth. It has happened twice since. One of the girls was famous for her beauty."

*

Some of the mountains were haunted; the worst was Karjung, which we often passed. "It is a bad place," Kuwa said. "Lately those who pass by say they hear noises, but can't see anything. Devils with bat-like wings live there in caves. They come out at night." Karjung to me looked like Walt Disney's Bald Mountain in *Fantasia;* sheer gray cliffs rose to peaks streaked with white, the offal of vultures; trees clinging to the lower slopes had gnarled, claw-like branches with bony-white bark. Enormous crows were always flying about and harshly cawed when we passed; Kuwa said the winged devils who lived on Karjung sometimes swept down and carried off men and women who were never seen again. He said you could see fires burning on the highest peaks at midnight and that to gather firewood or cut down a tree from the slopes of Karjung was to invite certain death. Here, as throughout the Nuba Mountains, Kuwa never let me go outside the village unless he came along, which suited me just fine.

There were many such haunted places around Neetil village, most of them forested peaks or bottoms of dry riverbeds. Kuwa was forever telling about eerie lights in the forest, stars moving strangely across the sky (satellites?), certain hideous *bhati* phantoms with long hair and bent legs and bodies whose presence was announced by a sudden chill and evil smell. Perhaps it was all Kuwa's talk of ghosts and magic that got to poor Mohammed. Born in Kadugli, another Nuba town not far away, he seemed to have a special aversion to Kuwa's supernatural beliefs; maybe they awoke in the citified journalist deeply buried feelings he preferred to keep that way. What Mohammed liked was the modern world of press conferences, taxis, telephones and tape recorders, its lack of mystery; he still writes every so often, but never mentions the Nuba Mountains. Once, when I wrote an article about Kuwa for the Los Angeles *Times*, the story was hotly denounced by several Africa scholars as presenting "a Hollywood stereotype." This suggests there is something psychologically fragile and guilt-ridden about our picture of Africa; like Mohammed, we too may prefer a reassuring facade. But behind it lies a reality that will remain until we can reach deeply into Africa with our science and technology: the disease, superstition and fear that still grips its villages. Kuwa himself more than agrees.

*

Then there was the episode of Kuku, the cattle thief who could turn himself into a hyena. One day in the bush a crowd of men approached, at first looking menacing, as they all carried rifles, spears, axes or heavy sticks. Then we saw that they were driving ahead of them a powerfully built man whose clothes were ripped and torn. This was Kuku, who, the men claimed, had been caught red-handed trying to steal a herd of cows. "A gun cannot kill him," Kuwa told me as these vigilantes passed. "He is from the Kolak tribe. They are all dangerous. Kuku wants to be a big hero. He never minds anybody. If he wants, he can escape from jail by making himself invisible. Or he can turn into a hyena. He has the magic to do that for him."

Kuku's trial, at the police station in Dilling, was an event and we all attended. Kuku seemed to enjoy his starring role and declared in a deep bass voice, to the crowd's laughter and enjoyment, "Judge, I confess I am a big thief." He appealed to the old tribal laws. "I never stole a cow in Dilling or from any member of your Dilling tribe, Judge. I must ask this court to set me free."

The judge, Magistrate Ahmed Ibrahim, a Nuba himself, though the first I saw with suit, tie and spectacles, held up a tattered old copy of the British colonial penal code and waved it at the accused. "Kuku," he said in a stern, cultured voice, "you have committed an offense in the eyes of this law. A crime is a crime wherever it is committed." He sentenced Kuku to two years in jail and warned him that if he ever took as much as a fountain pen that did not belong to him, he would get ten years next time.

Afterward, over tea, the magistrate explained that until very modern times the Nubas had lived outside the law or government; they were still a proud, warlike people. Kuwa's own Nimang subtribe had not been conquered until 1917 when the British quelled its last revolt by cutting off the Nimangs' food and water supply and hanging their chief, the present old Sultan's father. With so much land, Ibrahim explained, anyone could plant a patch of sorghum or millet wherever he wanted. So land had no special value and instead, traditionally, a man's wealth had been measured by the number of his wives and cattle. This had led to endless tribal wars; neighboring subtribes were raided for cattle and women, who were carried off as slaves; the periodic fighting also tested the courage of the young men. Bravery like Kuku's was still much admired.

Ibrahim, a law graduate from Khartoum University, also said some slavery was still going on; children were being carried off by Arab camel caravans. The Nuba Mountains, just on the edge of the Sahara, had long been a center of the African slave trade. Once, the magistrate said, he had arrested thirty-one vagrant children in Dilling. "They were all hanging around the cinema and sleeping there at night. Nobody asked for any one of them. These children could be carried off by the camel Arabs without anybody knowing about it. They sever their tendons to keep them from running away. I'm convinced it still goes on." Another survival from slavery days, he continued, was the still common practice among the poorest Nubas of indenturing small sons to semi-nomadic *baggara* or cattle-raising Arabs. The children became cowherds and the father in return got a cow each year in payment, the boys themselves nothing.

I was shocked and with Ibrahim's help spent a week with some of these indentured herdsmen out in the bush. We slept at night inside a bramble enclosure around a big tree, spears at the ready in case of hyenas. Meals were twice a day, cold sorghum mush, okra and cows' milk, at dawn and sunset. One of the herdsmen, known simply as "the Wali," after his subtribe, had been "sold" by his father when he was six years old. He guessed he was now about twenty. "We have only to go with the cows, to graze them and water them, that's all," he told me. "If your father doesn't tell you how old you are, you would hardly know." He agreed his life was hard. "Maybe someday I'll go north. I came here long ago and never went back to my family. My master would not let me go." Six years before, the Wali's father, who perhaps had died, had stopped coming and he had kept the annual cow payment himself. "Perhaps," he said, "when I have ten or twelve cows I will go back to my tribe and marry, and cultivate some fields and die there." Despite his bleak circumstances, the Wali seemed to be an exceptionally happy person; he took pleasure in small things and I frankly enjoyed the days accompanying him. He had never seen a white man before and thought I looked gruesome. "Your hair," he said one day, "is like dead grass blowing in the wind."

*

My stay in the Nuba Mountains ended suddenly; one morning in the bush I was attacked by a rabid dog. It sank its fangs deep into my right ankle and it took Kuwa and me two days to reach the nearest hospital, at El-Obeid, across a stretch of the Sahara; thank God, there was a plane going to Khartoum and I could get a seat on it. It was the longest three days of my life, since I did not learn until I reached a British-run clinic in Khartoum that one has fourteen days in which to start the anti-rabies injections (I had half expected to begin frothing momentarily). Kuwa was splendid, refused to leave my side until he got me on the plane and, though I tried to give him money to pay for my stay in Neetil, flatly refused to take a penny; it was, significantly, the only time this happened in a village; even in the Punjab, where there was a strong tradition of hospitality without cost, you could recompense the village family with gifts. Not so among the Nuba, which says something about so-called civilization.

*

A week before I left Neetil, Kuwa and I went to see the old Sultan, who, long stripped of his political power in the tribe, lived in seclusion at the end of a rocky gorge. As we walked through it, myself growing nervous at the steep cliffs on both sides, white-streaked with offal from the many vultures winging about, and noisy from the hordes of baboons, shrieking their usual hysterical threats, Kuwa, who took such things for granted, pointed out the peak where Sultan Ahmed came to make rain. If there was a drought, all the people in Neetil came in solemn procession to sacrifice a bull. Then the old man climbed the cliffs to the highest peak and there plunged his spear into "solid rock." In Kuwa's words, "The blade enters the rock and stands quivering. After that the power possesses the Sultan and he asks the blessings of God so rain will come. If all is well, and God agrees to give rain, Sultan Ahmed withdraws his spear and comes down to the people." Everyone then celebrated with *merissa* beer, drums and dancing. I didn't need to ask but did anyway; yes, Kuwa said, rain always came.

As we neared a cul-de-sac at the end of the gorge we could see a compound of grass huts enclosed by the usual thorny bush. Several of the huts were larger and grander than those in the village, but the roofs were rotting and everything had a tumbledown look; there was a general air of decay. At the time of our visit Sultan Ahmed was said to be nearing the age of one hundred; we had to wait for him to appear for some time but when he did he was physically impressive, looking about thirty years younger. He was a tall, very straight old man with piercing if yellowish and rheumy eyes; his face seemed permanently etched in lines of pain. His tunic and turban were streaked and grimy, but his arms were adorned with silver and copper bracelets, he wore a necklace of ostrich eggs, several valuable-looking rings pierced the lobes of one ear and a red ruby hung from a golden cord around his neck; Kuwa said the ruby was to protect him from the ghosts of all the men he had slain in battle; the Sultan had been a famous warrior in his youth.

He seemed very frail and feeble now and from time to time during our visit closed his eyes and seemed about to nod off into sleep. But I think he was just straining to remember things long in the past.

"Whenever the people come to see the Sultan and ask for help," Kuwa said by way of introduction, "he will ask God to bless them." From the looks of things, few came anymore.

As if reading my thoughts, the Sultan spoke. "Whenever a man comes to visit me, I will allow him to come, if he comes with good in his heart." He shut his eyes for what seemed a long time; when he opened them again he stared fixedly into Kuwa's face.

"I am dreaming again of famine and disease, Kuwa," he said. "I have had such dreams for seven years now. What does it mean? Through my dreams at night the prophecies have always come to me, whether there was to be an illness or famine or evil in the land, all these things. Seven years ago we used to go down to the river places at night. There we made our sacrifices. The *aro* spoke to us and we followed its ways. In the past times, the people used to come to me and we would go down to the river at night and follow the *aro*. Whether they were ill, or going to die, or some evil was going to come to them. And I cured those men there. Now the harvests are poor and the land is not fertile and the rains are few these seven years. Why? The people have become Moslems. They are leaving their faith. They do not follow the *aro*."

Kuwa spoke gently. "There is a change in the ways of living, Sultan."

"Because of these schools and modernization," the old man said with deep bitterness, as if these very words were curses. "The people become Moslem. I myself call myself a Moslem. But the true way of God comes from our ancestors. The power chose to work through my grandfathers, my father and myself. Now the power chooses to work through you, Kuwa. You cannot say yes. You cannot say no. You cannot refuse the power or it will do you any evil. As long as we live, we must follow the way of the *aro*. And in my dreams, it speaks of drought, famine and death. The people will be punished."

As we walked home, Kuwa was lost in thought. At last, groping for words, he broke the silence. "The people have always seen the Sultan as the instrument of God," he said. It is better to let a religion, especially a tribal one which is both a faith and a way of life, die out slowly from feebleness and old age, than to try to destroy it all at once. In the old man, but in Kuwa too, you could see the grief and pain a man feels when everything he believes in starts to crumble into nothing.

As a small boy, growing up in a nomadic herdsman's family on Tibet's great Chang Tang Plateau, Ngodup spent his days running up and down the frozen dunes with his father's yak and sheep. In Zhungru, the western Tibetan area where he lived, temperatures rose to 70 degrees by day but fell below freezing at night. Such extremes of heat and cold, the rarefied air of the high altitudes, giant hawks and roaming packs of wolves were not the only dangers. Khampa bandits on horseback sometimes rode up to demand food, money, clothes, rifles and knives. This was tolerable as the fast-moving Khampas had no interest in the family's real wealth, its livestock; Ngodup's father had about two hundred yak, seven hundred *lepcha* sheep and twenty-five horses; this was average for a nomad family in Zhungru.

Zhungru was such a small province it was not subject to the Tibetan government, but was directly ruled by the Dalai Lama's household in Lhasa, which regularly sent officials to collect cattle, butter and cheese. Zhungru also had one lamasery, Dsalung, and a borax mine. Sometimes Ngodup's family roamed as far as Bangba Chugdso, a place of grass and snow-covered mountains, where his father sometimes snared musk deer with loops. Once they visited Ngodup's grandmother's native region of Yangbachen, where there were vast juniper forests; his father purchased dry wood to sell in Lhasa.

One morning, when Ngodup was seven years old, the Khampas came riding up. This time they came not to plunder but to warn the nomads that there had been an uprising in Lhasa. The Dalai Lama had fled over the Himalayas to India and Chinese soldiers were coming from Bangba Chugdso. "You must run as fast as you can," the Khampa leader told Ngodup's father. "The big people, the rich people, and the lamas are being robbed and killed. You must run." That day many of Ngodup's neighbors fled toward the Tsangpo River and Nepal. His father and an older brother went also. But Ngodup's grandmother was too old and frail to travel and the rest of the family stayed behind with her, tending the herds. One day Chinese soldiers came to their camp. They asked for Ngodup's father. They warned his mother not to join him and said, "There is no reason to go. We have come to bring you a new life. So why should you want to run away?"

In the days that followed the family heard reports of lamas being sent into forced labor, of public executions and whole families being marched off to China. When Ngodup's father secretly returned for them one night, they were ready to go. They fled with just a single horse for the grandmother; one of Ngodup's two brothers and a sister were to follow with the rest of the horses, sheep and yak. They never came. Many years went by before the family learned they had been caught by the Chinese and forced to return to Zhungru. Today both are married, with children, and follow the old nomadic life.

The family managed to reach the Nepalese border town, Dolpo. Without money, they sold the horse for two hundred rupees, a fraction of its worth, yet considered themselves lucky—some were selling horses for bread. Ngodup's brother went off to join the Indian army and for the next three years Ngodup, his parents and his grandmother became beggars, wandering up and down the Himalayan frontier towns. *"Biccha magne! Biccha magne!"* they would cry, in the age-old beggars' lament of Tibet. They went from one house to another, their sheepskin covered with patches, filthy, their hair long and unkempt as was expected of beggars. Finally they reached a Tibetan refugee camp at Dorpatan, a week's journey from Dolpo. They were turned away but were given enough food to reach the western Nepalese town of Pokhara.

Here a United Nations relief official settled them in Tashi Palkhiel, then a settlement of grass huts in the hills just outside Pokhara. Soon permanent stone houses were constructed and, at age eleven, Ngodup entered school. "I couldn't understand the teacher because she spoke Tibetan," Ngodup told me years later. "I knew only the Zhungru nomad dialect. After six months or so, I could understand and I learned to read and write." After five years Ngodup was sent to Katmandu for three years' paramedical training so he could come home and set up a village dispensary. His final examination was to treat ninety-seven patients in a single day. Ngodup wanted to continue his studies and become a doctor, but he had no money. Today he runs the village dispensary and weaves rugs in the Tashi Palkhiel cooperative, where average monthly earnings are forty dollars. In most families several members work, including all of the village's women.

I first spent some weeks in Tashi Palkhiel in 1973 and Ngodup has since come with me on several treks in the Himalayan border region. Like most Tibetans, he has an unusually happy, easygoing disposition, taking each day as it comes. But like most, he would like to go back to Tibet and take up the old nomadic herdsman's life. By air, Zhungru lies only 170 miles north of Tashi Palkhiel; to go on foot, which means a circuitous mountain trek through Dolpo on the border, takes at least four weeks. Today the nomads from Zhungru trade at Dolpo twice a year and Ngodup's brother and sister send messages down with the Tibetan mule trains. As Ngodup explains it, "What can I say? Once we have freedom we won't stay in Nepal, even though we have good houses and a pleasant life. We will follow His Holiness Dalai Lama and go where he goes. Tibet is our motherland, where we were born." He gropes for words. "The life of a nomad is free," he says.

*

Someday he may. The news that comes out of Tibet with the bell-tinkling mule caravans over the high Himalayan passes into Nepal suggests that much of Tibet's traditional nomad life goes on little changed under Chinese rule. Local border trade has picked up in recent years and many of the eighty thousand Tibetan refugees who have settled for the past twenty years in Sikkim, Bhutan, Nepal and India, like Ngodup, manage to keep in touch with relatives back home. Tibet, it seems, is still mostly a land of shifting encampments of yak-hair tents whose people are forever searching for pasture for their herds of yak, sheep, goats and horses. In such a harsh environment, this is not surprising. The nomads mostly occupy a high plateau, extending six hundred by eight hundred miles, between the Himalayas and the Kunlun Mountains, at altitudes of twelve thousand feet and more. They graze their herds on barren, treeless, windswept wastes broken by thousands of saline lakes and many rivers. Tibet is the source of all the great rivers of Asia: the Sutlej and Indus, the Ganges and Brahmaputra, the Salween, Mekong and Yangtze. Snow-covered mountain ranges soar above twenty thousand feet and there are great jutting rocks of shale, schist and limestone; according to Ngodup's father, violent gales, dust storms and icy winds blow almost every day.

Until the Chinese occupation, the wheel, considered sacred, was never used: horses, camels, yaks, sheep and men were the only transport over rugged tracks and precarious bridges spanning deep, narrow gorges. Even the way of death was harsh, bodies being cut up and fed to buzzards, a custom still practiced in Tashi Palkhiel.

One man in four was a Buddhist lama. Some of the monasteries were vast; the Dalai Lama's Potala Palace in Lhasa is said by Tibetans to number ten thousand rooms. While the ecclesiastical dignitaries were mostly high-born nobles, the Dalai Lama himself was usually a poor herdsman's child, chosen through oracular revelation, born at the moment of his predecessor's death and believed to be his reincarnation. In 1973 the present Dalai Lama shocked everyone by saying, "I might be the last Dalai Lama." Yet, south of the Tibetan border, even lamaism shows vigorous signs of life—at the Dalai Lama's court in Dharmasala in India, among the four million people of Tibetan origin in the border regions, and in the many successfully rehabilitated refugee villages like Tashi Palkhiel in Nepal and India, where the old ways and views of life have been recreated and passed onto a younger generation. Tibetan schools are filled, ancient lamaseries have been refounded and such traditional handicrafts as rug-weaving have replaced herding as the culture's economic base.

The four noble truths live on, enough at least so that the pragmatic Chinese are starting once more to see the Tibetans as a minority whose separate race, culture, language and identity will not go away. They have tried to make a more convincing case to Tibetans, at home and in exile, that conditions are improving. The exiled Dalai Lama retorts: "If things are so good, why not let the exiles visit their families?" As China woos exiles like Ngodup, many of the Tibetans' host governments are growing less hospitable. Bhutan has demanded that all its Tibetans become Bhutanese citizens and stop being loyal to the Dalai Lama. India's quarrel with China ensures a welcome there for now; even so, the Dalai Lama has felt compelled to say he has lived there so long he feels like an Indian. Americans, anxious to woo the Chinese, now require Tibetans with American citizenship who want a passport to list China as their place of birth. By orders from Katmandu, Tibetans have been banned from going anywhere near Nepal's western Mustang region, a ten-day trek from Tashi Palkhiel, ever since Nepalese King Birendra's Gurkha troops forced thousands of Tibetan Khampas to evacuate the region in 1974. Eight Khampa leaders were still imprisoned in Katmandu in 1979, supposedly awaiting trial for "illegal possession of arms." What everybody knows but nobody will officially admit is that these arms were supplied by the C.I.A. (parachuted down in boxes from American Air Force cargo planes over Mustang in 1960–61).

If governments turn their backs, a large number of culturally disaffected Western youths trek to remote Tibetan refugee settlements, such as Tashi Palkhiel, to study lamaism. Buddhism spread to Tibet, in a decadent form, only in the seventh century, twelve hundred years after Gautama's death. Tibetan lamaism is influenced by Tantric rituals, the demonolatry of Bon, the ancient Tibetan religion and, finally, Mongol shamanism, with its "possessed" oracles, amulets, magic charms, beliefs in ghosts and monsters, and mechanistic prayers (all those prayer flags and prayer wheels forever fluttering and spinning).

Yet in few other forms of Buddhism have Gautama's lofty ethics or his "four noble truths" (existence involves suffering caused by desire; escape from perpetual rebirth comes only by ridding oneself of desire) survived quite so triumphantly in the daily lives of ordinary people. In the end the real contest in Tibet seems likely to be between Maoist materialism and its work ethic and lamaism's world-rejection, which, both among the Tibetan refugees and the disillusioned Protestant youth of the West, has real appeal. This is what makes the Tibetans so exceptional. At a time when, as we have seen in Brazil, Morocco and Africa, traditional cultures are breaking down, the Tibetans seem to be, in the face of tremendous odds, keeping their culture alive.

*

In the months we have spent together, in Tashi Palkhiel, but mostly out trekking through the Himalayan passes, to Jomoson, Langtang Valley and Helambu, Ngodup and I have talked much about his religion. To Ngodup the world as we know it is an endless repetition; unless you renounce desire—for pleasure, success, or life itself—your destiny, working itself out through your Karma, will be reborn again and again until the breaking up of the universe. Ngodup accepts Buddha as the originator of the Wheel of Life, a diagram we studied as portrayed on the walls of the portico in Tashi Palkhiel's lamasery. The wheel is clenched tightly in the claws of a monstrous animal which Ngodup says symbolizes the hideousness of clinging to life. Between each of the wheel's six spokes are painted the realms of possible reincarnations: the Lha (gods) country, where gods and goddesses dwell in gardens and palaces and pluck the fruit of wish-granting trees; the Lhamayin (titans) country, where one finds the roots and the trunk of a tree about which envious, warlike men fight in vain against the Lha; man's country, with all its woes of birth, struggle, and death; the animals' country, where beasts prey on each other and are hunted by men and forced to bear their burdens; the Yidag (ghosts) country, haunted by the spirits of the miserly and gluttonous, with huge swollen stomachs and spindly legs and necks; and Nyalwa (purgatory), where savages with animal heads inflict torture on those condemned by an inexorable judge, the King of Death. Even the lotus-born Lha gods, though they may live for thousands of years, at last die miserably to be born again, even as animals.

Ngodup also explained his belief in the "four noble truths" and the "noble eightfold path." And every morning when he awakes and just before going to sleep at night, with the help of his rosary, he recites *Om mani padme hum* one hundred and eight times. Ngodup said he does this as a way of praying that all creatures, human and animals, will be allowed to go to heaven, or Dewajen. The utterance of *om* is to free the Lha, *ma* the Lhamayin, *ni* man, *pad* animals, *me* those in purgatory, and *hum,* those in hell. When I told him about my childhood prayer ("Now I lay me down to sleep . . .") he found it very strange; Tibetans, when they pray, do not pray for themselves, but for all living things.

Aside from Buddhism, Ngodup had all sorts of older Tibetan folk beliefs. He believed all Tibetans are descended from a demoness, Daksin-mo (hence their fondness for raw meat) and a monkey (hence man's wisdom). Not only, in this way, did Ngodup believe man was descended from the ape, but he had a Flood legend, when all Tibet's highest mountains were covered by water. His creation story was of a God-like spirit, Adi-Buddha, creating fire, water, wind and earth, then shaping them into four worlds—white, blue, red and green—each separated by seven seas and seven mountain ranges, in the center of which was a gigantic mountain, Rijel Lhunbo. Time in the Tibetan cosmos accelerates; as men grow more sinful, lives become shorter. "Someday," Ngodup said, "old age will come at ten and marriage at five."

In Ngodup's stone house, one small room was kept as a chapel; inside were three altars, adorned with offerings of butter and tsamba (ground barley, the Tibetans' staple diet), lamps, silver goblets, bowls, flowers and incense sticks; idols and sacred texts were placed behind. Each evening lamas came to recite Buddhist scriptures, beat drums and clash cymbals, noise meant to remind the spirits of the family's needs.

Unlike most peasants, Tibetans are sexually tolerant; a girl who has a child before marriage is not condemned nor is the child taunted as a bastard. Both polygamy with sisters and polyandry with brothers occurs; Ngodup's soldier brother, away serving in the Indian army most of the time, had proposed that Ngodup take a wife for both of them; then she would always have a man in the house.

Tashi Palkhiel had a sorcerer, or Mo-ba, who treated illness, and all sorts of *dres,* or ghosts of men who had died with unexpected violence, who haunted the place of their death for what would have been their natural lifetime. (I was said to have seen one, which I will describe in the chapter on the supernatural.) Certain lamas, called Podebs, performed the funeral rites of the dead, while others, Jobas, after praying, beating a drum and blowing a trumpet, cut the corpse up and fed it to vultures. Ngodup said the corpse is usually laid face down for this. But once in Tashi Palkhiel a dead man was lying face up when the Joba made the first incision in the chest. The man's arm flew up in some muscular reflex and hit him. Ngodup, who has a good deal of humor, thought this very funny. There are also zombie-like *rolangs,* humans not given proper funeral rites, who prey on the living and can only be killed by a lama, wolf or *dremo,* the Tibetan name for *yeti.*

Belief in the *yeti,* our old friend, the Abominable Snowman, is universal among Tibetans, who take it for granted that a six-foot-tall apeman, with black-brown hair, a monkey face, a robust jaw, no fangs, no tail, and arms that reach down to its knees, is a natural part of the local fauna. In Tashi Palkhiel I found no less than eight villagers, all of them elderly, who claimed to have seen the monster. Ngodup's father, who was in his seventies, told me that in his yak-herding days, *yetis* would often try to attack the herd, seizing the yak by their horns, twisting them and breaking their necks. "They ate the yak meat and left the skin on the rocks," he said. "If we found a yak's skin, we'd know a *dremo* had gotten it." Ngodup told me, "If you want to trek with me to Dolpo near the border, you can see a *dremo* for sure."

I made a cowardly mental note to stay away from Dolpo. Belief in the *yeti* depends on where you are. Usually, trekking in the Himalayas, there are lots of people about: bronzed Tamangs and Gurungs, trident-carrying, ash-smeared *sadhus* on their way to some remote shrine, tousle-haired Tibetans moving in mule caravans with bales of wool. Or Pan-like cowherds piping flutes, bare-legged porters with muscles like rope, old women bent double under bundles of grass, herds of goats, laughing children. Most of the time Ngodup and I were

climbing up and down sun-drenched ridges over vast misty valleys ter-
raced with wheat, rice and vegetables. There are many villages, changing from lowland thatched brick houses to the drafty stone Sherpa or
Tibetan stone chalets as you go higher.

Only the highest Himalayas are really deserted, the land of what Sir
Edmund Hillary called "the perpetual challenge of icy spire and rock
tower, high in the thin, cold air." It can be wonderful in solitude to
watch a sunset reflected against the ramparts of the Annapurna range
or fishtail-shaped Machhapuchhare; then the sky grows dim and they
are swallowed up in mist and darkness. No worry, I used to feel, if
Ngodup was wrong and, as Hillary wrote, it is all "a fascinating fairy
tale, born of the rare and frightening view of strange animals,
moulded by superstition, and enthusiastically nurtured by western expeditions." But were you really in solitude? Maybe there was *something* watching you from the forest that loomed so darkly between you
and the safety of the nearest village—a man-monster, a *dremo-yeti*,
Gigantopithecus still at large. Frantically scrambling down the track
in sudden panic, almost falling, I would be the last one to dispute the
yeti's existence right then.

There is something very satisfying about the mystery and wonder of
it, as Ngodup knows from the steadily arriving Western youth, who
ask him, "Are you Hinayana or Mahayana?" and say, "That's far out,
man. You're into it." He told me, "Most of these European people,
call them half-and-half hippies, want to know how life was in Tibet.
Some are interested in monasteries, all are interested in the mountains.
They ask about the *yeti*, they're afraid of leeches, they want to know if
there are Khampa bandits in the Himalayas. I say, 'Who can tell?
These things happen.'"

A few he criticizes. "A real hippie is a man whose character is
different from other men. The way he dresses, the way he talks. We
Tibetans, we're not rich in culture or education. But I think these hippies are worse. They say, 'My fucking government, I don't like it.'
They criticize their parents, they smoke hashish all the time, they don't
want to work. Among Tibetans, nobody smokes hashish, ever." (This
appears to be true. Among the Nepalese villagers themselves, however, moderate smoking of hashish is an old, established custom; some
of the Peace Corps volunteers assigned to remote mountain villages
got the habit.) Ngodup goes on, "And Tibetans are honest up to now.
Maybe we are proud." Or maybe they are not trying to escape a con-

sumer culture which, to some estranged youngsters, seems to have lost its meaning.

This was brought home to me one night at a wayside inn in the high Himalayas. The young trekkers around the fireside ranged from fresh-faced sportsmen to wan and sick-looking youths, ravaged beyond their years by drugs. Ngodup spoke of Tibet. "Many lakes and hills of sand. Mountains higher than the Himalayas. I can't explain it. It's an unbelievable thing." "Tell us about the Potala," said one of the young women. "It is a place where gods and goddesses live, oh, many. And thousands of rooms. I can't tell but my father says there are too many. By the grace of his Holiness Dalai Lama we may some day see it for ourselves."

Anywhere else, the youths might have listened cynically, waiting for the rip-off. That night their faces glowed in the firelight like children hearing a fairy tale.

TULUNGATUNG VILLAGE, PHILIPPINES

"This has always been a peaceful place," old Catalino would often say, as if the words themselves could protect the village. Sturdy, good humored, patient, he was like his son Tonio; it seemed nothing much could change them. Very likely their *barrio* of Tulungatung, with its *nipa* stilt houses ablaze with bougainvillea and dangling pots of flowers had looked much the same ever since the first Malays came up from Borneo and settled, chasing the black Aete aboriginals into the jungle.

Ferdinand Magellan's three ships, the first to sail around the earth, landed three centuries later. The Spaniards founded Zamboanga City as a seat of Castilian culture and called the peninsula around it the "land of the flowers." But they failed to convert to Catholicism all the Moslem Malays, whom they called Moros; many retreated with their sultans to strongholds on other parts of Mindanao, others went to Brunei and the islands of the Sulu Sea, where they turned to piracy. In one form or another, this Christian-Moslem struggle has gone on ever since. Black Jack Pershing's doughboys failed to subdue the Moros in the nineteenth century; so have the armies of every successive Philippine government since independence and World War II.

I first spent several months in Tulungatung in 1972, picking the village because one of Zamboanga's former mayors, Caesar Climaco, offered to let me stay in a treehouse he had built there, high in the branches of an enormous Spanish acacia tree. The treehouse, constructed of mahogany, had thick walls like a watchtower, comforting on a coast where Moro pirates still plundered fishing boats at night, tossing their victims to the sharks. Other Moslems waged a seemingly endless terrorist war against armed bands of Christian settlers, who were encroaching on Moslem land as immigrants from the over-populated Visayan islands and Luzon. The fighting came and went but, as I found in visits in 1972, 1974, 1978 and 1980, Tulungatung itself, a Christian village with a Moslem chief, somehow always managed to escape the violence, except for the odd cattle rustling or coconut theft.

People sometimes ask about the Moro pirates. Once, in 1974, I interviewed some at a notorious penal colony, San Ramon, an hour's bicycle ride from Tulungatung. Armed Filipino guards stayed outside, but locked my interpreter and me inside the main prison yard. With the help of some of the convicts, we located several pirates, moustached and swarthy Moros who, evidently because they were dangerous, were in leg-irons right out of the Middle Ages. They were amiable, proudly boasting about their murderous way of life at sea, saying it was handed down from their fathers. Each claimed to have killed fifty or sixty men. They were also curiously emphatic in reporting that, back home in their Sulu Island villages, they were model law-abiding citizens. One got an impression of unromantic and schizophrenic psychopaths, who savagely slit throats without remorse as part of a day's work and then went dutifully home to their wives and children.

During these years the fallout of modernity has pretty much settled on Tulungatung's enduring fabric; now Isuzu buses ply the coastal highway into Zamboanga City, with American pop and rock music loudly playing on their drivers' Sony cassettes. The latest American-bred dwarf rice is grown in Tulungatung's fields. Young men, if they have the pesos, go into town Saturday night to a dance, a porno *bomba* film, or a Kung Fu or Clint Eastwood shoot-'em-up. Comic books are the *barrio*'s standard reading fare. What makes the Philippine village unique in Asia are the legacies of its three hundred years of Spanish rule and, equally important, forty-two years of American colonialism. The main American impact came in the spread of popular, English-language education, both in village primary schools and city universities; it contributed to the Philippines' land ownership pattern, with the small-town middle class owning much of the countryside, and left the Philippine people extremely receptive to American pop culture, which, together with the Latin culture and Catholicism of the Spanish, has all but obliterated the ancient Malay customs.

Especially in Manila, so much pop music is played so much of the time, it becomes the electricity of the air. It sometimes seemed as if Ferdinand Marcos and his ex-beauty queen wife, Imelda, were part of an opera with Beatles themes and Amazing Spider Man lyrics. Some of Marcos' speeches had such a cartoon stridency we might have been seeing them above his head in comic strip balloons. Even in Tulungatung, you get pure she-loves-me-yeh-yeh-yeh pop and you get it all the time. Coke, Action Comics and Clint Eastwood go right along with the transistors that endlessly spill out pop and rock. As Pauline Kael, the wittiest observer of American pop culture, has written of the West Indies, pop and tropical islands seem to just naturally go together, "part of the crime, corruption and tourism." And among young Filipinos like Tonio in Tulungatung, a good many of their ideas seem shaped by movies and comic books. In no other village have I found anything like the deep influence of pop culture you get in the Philippines; maybe it's just another way of saying it's more Americanized.

Yet, even in Tulungatung, as in most Filipino *barrios*, it's the timelessness of the place that really tells: the hush at dusk when trade winds stir the coconut palms; the hands of an old man, brown and fragile as last year's leaves, raised in prayer in the *barrio* chapel, a heavy-aired, medievally Castilian refuge with its incense, candles and fat old Spanish priest. Like all *barrios*, Tulungatung has its burnt little plaza; a pool hall and tavern where you can get pleasurably groggy on *tuba*, the sour-tasting homemade coconut wine; the *barrio* school where children go about their vegetable garden with sprinkling cans; the cockfighting pit where *machismo* is ritualized and a lucky bet is the best hope of paying one's debts, the Catholic chapel, Chinese rice mill, and, down by the sea, the cemetery of whitewashed tombs and angels with moss-covered wings.

No electricity or paving; during the rains Tulungatung slips into mud; in dry weather the ground is as hard to the bare feet as stone. The *barrio* is steamy and sleepy by day. At night it wakes into sound: snickering cicadas, croaking frogs, screaming jungle birds, yelping pye-dogs, crying babies, crowing roosters. Inland rise the hills, where there are logging camps. These hills used to be covered with mahogany forest. Now there are signs of slash-and-burn cultivation everywhere—stumps of trees and ashes of fires where ground has been cleared for corn, cassava and coconuts by the *kainjinero*, poor men with no land on the coastal plain. A flat, open expanse of rice paddy extends to the sea, divided into small holdings of two to fifteen acres. Almost all of it is tilled by leaseholding tenants or sharecroppers. The rice fields are mostly owned by small absentee landlords—merchants, teachers or civil servants. In the Philippines, the impoverished countryside is owned by the prosperous little towns. My guess about what happened is that after near serfdom under the Spaniards and forty-two years of village primary education under the Americans, two or three generations of peasants got educated, moved into middle-class occupations in the nearest town, and started getting rent from the less enterprising left behind. These tenants really live in their fields; once out of the cramped villages hidden in the treelines and away from the mountains, there is that same sense of air and release you get on the sea. The whole Philippine archipelago is like that: river and swamp, mountain and forest and then you come out of the trees into the big open rice lands where the people are. Their dilemma is, with a third or fourth of each crop going to a town landlord, there is no surplus left, after they feed their families, to modernize agriculture.

*

Tonio has kept trying. When he began farming at the age of twenty-eight in 1967, he rented two and a half acres from a schoolteacher in Ayala; the new "miracle rice" had just come to the village and he harvested almost six tons in his first crop. But double-cropping meant he could no longer burn off his fields and leave them fallow once each year; unchecked, the local insect population just kept growing. When I arrived in 1972, Tulungatung had been plagued for three years by an infestation of army worms, green leaf hoppers, and stem borers such as never seen before; half the village's harvest was destroyed and Tonio harvested only three and a half tons. His father, Catalino, told me, "The rice crop was doubled but we grew deeper and deeper in debt buying chemicals to fight the insects. And what good does it do? We tried to follow all the modern methods but the insects got worse. It's no good. We are tortured. Why doesn't the government give us free or subsidized insecticides and show us how and when to apply them?"

Beset by insects, the unwillingness of Tulungatung's small absentee landlords to invest, and the rising costs of insecticide and fertilizer, agriculture was actually sliding backward in Tulungatung. A few of Tonio's neighbors talked of giving up the new seeds and modern methods altogether.

Then, during my second visit, in 1974, I found that everything was going right. In a new government program, which Marcos called Masagana, or "abundance," for the first time bankers came right to Tulungatung to extend credit per crop season at 12 percent interest. Agricultural technicians, the first seen in the *barrio* for years, also came to see that the money borrowed went for land preparation, new seeds, insecticide and fertilizer, and that it was correctly used. Tonio took a loan of $172, invested in inputs and once more harvested six tons. Soaring commodity prices enabled him to sell rice to the Chinese miller in Ayala for $6.50 a forty-four-kilo sack, 50 percent more than the price two years before. Prices Tonio obtained for maize doubled and for coconuts quadrupled. He was able to pay off his crop loan, hire a mechanical thresher for the first time, buy three pigs and get married. Cattle and coconut theft had faded away.

Going back in 1978, I found that it had all come unstuck again. The price of rice was up to $7.50 a sack, but the cost of fertilizer and insecticide had risen even more. Not using enough, Tonio had harvested only three-and-a-half tons of rice again. Like his neighbors, he had gone back to threshing with his feet. Although his wife, Maria Elena, earned a wage teaching at the village school, she and Tonio now had three small children to feed—a baby had been born each of the three years of their marriage—and after eating and paying rent, the crop was gone. Tonio told me, "Almost everybody in Tulungatung has left Masagana. That's why we don't have a good harvest this year. Nobody has the money to buy fertilizer and insecticide. Most of us are not able to pay the bank what we owe and I'm one of them. What am I going to do?"

Land reform is the answer in the Philippines; without it, it's probably the last nation in Asia where the communist-appropriated slogan of "Land to the tillers" still has real zing. Marcos, who is smart and well read, knows this: he made land reform the justification for imposing martial law in 1972. In a 1974 interview, he was still plainly wrestling with the need to do the sensible thing, but his old Filipino "guns, goons and gold" political instincts seemed to be getting the better of him. He still talked a good game of populism but by then it already seemed to be just stardust he was throwing in his own eyes so he wouldn't have to see what a dangerous corner he'd gotten himself into. (He invited me to spend a day with him as he reviewed troops, cut ribbons and ate a late lunch in his Malacañang Palace office; I was too busy taking notes to eat much so he insisted I take a sandwich along when I left. I went by a surprised British trade delegation and the lurking security hardboys, munching my ham and cheese on rye with satisfaction.)

It was fully evident on a 1980 visit to Manila that Marcos didn't move far enough fast enough when he still had the power. As a senior scientist at the International Rice Research Institute at Los Baños put it, "Unless small absentee landlordism is eliminated, the Philippine farmers won't be able to afford the inputs to modernize. If Marcos moved in with enough irrigation, fertilizer, credit and technology, the farmers might prosper enough to buy their land if the townspeople found it profitable enough to sell it. But it's a very long shot." More than ever Manila fit Jean-Luc Godard's remark that life is getting to be like "living inside an enormous comic strip." Manilans were playing a new game, "His and Hers," a bit like Monopoly (he has Boardwalk, she has Park Place); players had to guess which hotels, newspapers, members of parliament and so on belonged to Marcos and which to Imelda. Whatever oomph Marcos' promised "New Society" ever had, it was gone.

*

Most villagers really demand only three things of government: some rise in living standards, the delivery of a few basic services without too much inefficiency and corruption and freedom from lawlessness. For Tulungatung, the problem of how to modernize its rice production is still unsolved. Local crime and the danger of getting sucked into the Christian-Moslem terrorist fighting has worsened. During my last visit you could hear firing most nights; Tonio said it was mostly government soldiers, kids getting drunk and firing at nothing. Christian-Moslem tensions in Tulungatung began in 1972, my first time there, after a brawl at a Saturday night dance. Two truckloads of Moslem toughs showed up in Tulungatung but got stopped by the constabulary. The Moslem chief of a neighboring village got a note signed by the "Ilagas" or Christian terrorists, threatening a massacre. Moslem fishermen started arming themselves and so did the Christian loggers up in the hills; for a while it got pretty dicey.

Even this land war, like Filipino crime, has a bastard pop quality to it, the rhetoric on both sides as bloody and slam-bang as the Kung Fu, Italian spaghetti Westerns and Hollywood gangster films that partly inspires it. It makes you wonder; in almost every Saturday night movie we saw in Zamboanga City, you got smacked in the face by so many falling, drowning, burning, shot-up, hacked-up bodies—and the worse the atrocity the more the audiences laughed and seemed to enjoy it—it seemed like the film producers were consciously out to instill a taste for savage cruelty. The impact of violence in TV, movies and horror comics upon American social behavior is much debated. What about its impact on the rest of the world? The same police sirens, screams, high explosives and pistol, rifle and machine-gun fire are coming out of their screens too.

Like most of Tulungatung's older men, whose memories of the atrocities and deprivation under the Japanese occupation were still fresh, old Catalino was bitterly critical of both the Christian and Moslem terrorists for keeping the pot boiling. "When the Ilagas kill a Moslem," he told Tonio in disgust, "they cut off an ear and take it home. They even kill women and children. The government must stop it."

"They never will," said Tonio. Like some small-town media freak in our own country, Tonio had made heroes of the Christian terrorist killers. He told me the Christian commander, a woman, was said to have risen from the dead to give her men supernatural protection against bullets and knives. "Even if they are hit in the chest," Tonio claimed with admiration, "the bullets just fly away. The Ilagas use only bolo knives, while the Moslems have Armalites and Garands."

Such talk alarmed Catalino. "Our Moslems here are educated," he reminded his son. "They know what is good. But those Sulu islanders are illiterate. They have always fought the government. If these outlaws ever come ashore and seize the village, Tonio, we must obey them."

Even the rise of Marcos had reflected pop fantasy; he was the Philippines' Audie Murphy, its most decorated soldier of World War II. Like the hero of an action movie of thirty years ago, Marcos embodied strength and how to fight and win. Some of his follow-me-men aura still survived when he imposed martial law in 1972 on the grounds   I-am-the-one-lone-leader-in-a-country-crawling-with-Commies. Sometimes in Tulungatung we tried to catch Marcos' radio speeches but the transmission was so poor all we could catch were a few phrases: ". . . land to the tiller . . . equal justice for all . . . dignity for the working man." Tonio explained the crackling static: "It's because they're all clapping. Imelda is clapping beside Marcos."

Tensions eased after martial law when government troops came to seize everyone's weapons. Catalino was doubtful this would stop the terrorist fighting. "The Moros will never give up their firearms," he said, "even if Marcos sends all his soldiers and planes." Tonio agreed. "These Moslems like guns so much they'll sell their land for a weapon, they'll even give their wife."

Catalino was hopeful. "Maybe Marcos just wants to be a dictator.

Maybe he wants to do good things. I don't know. I just watch and wait."

There was a Spanish streak to Tulungatung's undertone of violence as well. You could see it Sunday afternoons when everybody went to the cockpit down by the sea; by midafternoon the bleachers would be packed with hundreds of village men, intense concentration on their work-hardened faces. It was an uproar; everyone kept shouting his bets; the bookies, called *kristos,* yelled the loudest. You kept hearing, *"Sombrero, sombrero!"* to back a favorite whose owner wore a straw hat. You had to watch the *kristos* very closely because as they shouted one thing, they placed their own true bets with gamblers across the pit, moving their hands and fingers in quick, sudden gestures. When a fight began there was a dead hush. Two roosters were released to shuffle and peck at each other. Then suddenly the moment of attack came and like unfettered prisoners, like the birds they really were, the cocks shot into the air in a fury of gleaming spurs and scattered feathers. Blood would spurt, one drop to earth and the cock would shudder in its death spasms. Pitiless, the other would usually jump astride, pecking away while all the *aficionados,* Tonio as kill-crazy as any of them, shouted, *"Ito na! Ito na!* It is! It is!" The cockfight was a mysterious *macho* ritual—you never saw a woman among all those passionate, hard-bitten faces.

Tonio told me how he had once owned an imported Texas rooster. It won eight times in Ayala. He trained it and fondled it, as the villagers were forever doing with their fighting birds, and thought of little else day and night for months. He treated it with the utmost tenderness until the Sunday afternoon he put it into the Ayala cockpit and saw it die. "I bet everything on that cock, borrowed from Catalino and my uncles, even sold my shirt to raise some pesos," Tonio recalled. "When it won, it was glorious." When it got its throat cut, Tonio took the loss philosophically. But after that he talked only of its victories, how much money he made and how the fighting cock had won him much honor. "It was brave and not afraid to die," he said.

*

Tulungatung's people also had an abiding faith in God. Tonio said the Lord's Prayer each morning when he awoke. Most *barrio* families knelt together after the evening meal. Yet few villagers went to Sunday mass and the older men like Catalino often complained about the venality of the Spanish priest, Father Perez. "The shepherd doesn't attend his flock," Catalino said. "Priests are supposed to save souls, not make business." Whenever the bells tolled for a funeral and we would hear them in the fields, Tonio would joke, "Another eighty pesos for Father Perez." There was much humor about the old priest, who would give fifteen pesos during sowing in return for thirty pesos' worth of rice at harvest. Other jokes were about themselves. Tonio told about a villager who, in the Ayala church, knelt before the statue of Jesus being crucified; the man frantically prayed for a better life. "Here was Jesus in agony and suffering on the cross and this foolish Pedro throws himself down and cries, 'Oh, Lord, give me money, give me clothes, give me food, give me everything!' At last Jesus looks down and says, 'If my feet weren't nailed down, Pedro, I'd kick you!'" Tulungatung also had older, pagan Malay beliefs; dwarves were said to live in certain old trees, sometimes invisibly, sometimes taking the form of ghosts who tried to carry you away. Tonio told about how he was once bewitched by a dwarf in the shape of a beautiful woman. "She was incomparable," he said. "Like a saint, a virgin. She is more beautiful than anyone." After running amok and becoming delirious with fever, Tonio had had to be tied down and cured by an old village woman with herbs and the smoke of a magic fire. "Before that I didn't believe in dwarves," Tonio told me. "But after it actually happened to me, it must be true."

*

Mrs. Bernardo, Tulungatung's volunteer family planning worker, often grew discouraged. She went about the village most days, a stout woman with a yellow parasol who had given birth to seven children of her own before her conversion to contraceptives. Often, she complained to me, women would hide from her. "Many are afraid their health will be affected or they say, 'It's against God.' So many men take many children as proof of their sexual powers and *machismo* or tell me they're God's blessing. One needs patience in this work. Like I meet Father Perez. He'll call, 'Hey, Mrs. Bernardo, where are you going?' I say I am going out to motivate. He says the Pope is against contraceptives, only the rhythm method. I tell him, 'Father, supposing the lady is irregular? Some are twenty-eight days, some thirty days. There are so many failures in rhythm.' All he does is quote me the Bible, 'Be fruitful and multiply.'"

"Maybe Father Perez is like that because the number of baptisms would go down," Tonio joked. "And many people are getting stabbed these days. If it got peaceful, the church bells would never toll." He told Mrs. Bernardo he'd heard the Pill made women fat.

She snorted. "So much false gossip going around. That even if you have an IUD you can get pregnant." Tonio laughed. "Some sperms are very tricky," he said. "Maybe they can jump around the IUD." Mrs. Bernardo was used to such banter. She unrolled a condom and waved it at Tonio. "When erect already, that is the best time to put on this stocking. If you want to make it slippery, use oil. The Moslems in Recodo village use pomade but it doesn't work very well. Best is brilliantine." Mrs. Bernardo knew her stuff and how to hold the men's attention. "They're very fond of stabbing in Tulungatung. Sometimes they stab their best friend, sometimes their worst friend. They drink and forget. Tulungatung is almost all condom too. All condom. Mr. Mulorino, Mr. Enriquez, Mr. Araneta. In Recodo it's IUD and pills. In Ayala, pills, condoms and Emco vaginal foam. How about you, Tonio?"

"Ha!" he grinned. "If you really want to practice family planning, you'd better cut off your organ."

*

The reckoning in Tulungatung came at the end of the harvest. For days it was pounded and crushed by bare feet or a carabao's hooves and winnowed from high bamboo platforms to catch the sea breeze. Finally, it was measured out in baskets. For Tonio, after paying his rent, there was just enough to feed his growing family. He was forced to borrow once more from Father Perez—the old, profitless cycle. "All that plowing, planting, weeding and harvesting," he told me. "All gone with the wind."

A neighbor was more worried about crime. "These thieves," he said, "they're not afraid of martial law any more. Last week somebody entered my house and took my brother's pants. Right while he was sleeping. These goddamn stealers. I'd put them in the electric chair, before a firing squad. It's no good if a Filipino steals right in his own *barrio*."

"They're hungry, that's why," said Tonio.

Old Catalino sighed heavily. "This was always such a peaceful place. You could go anywhere, come home at any time of night, and nobody would ever bother you. Not like this time now. People are afraid."

Tonio's good spirits deserted him. "Everything is getting worse again in the *barrio*. I don't know what you have to do to have a good life here." He glared up at the sky. "What is God doing up there?"

Step down the sun-dappled path, past the once gracious French architecture shaded by the old tamarind trees; the patients stroll about, looking, in their flappy blue pajamas, like little boys. Large windows are open in all the wards; you can walk along the wide, hushed verandas and see all the wounded lying in their beds. The patients are separated by injury. In the first ward, all the men have one or two eyes bandaged. Then come the lung patients, some of them looking healthy and crouched on the floor, playing cards. A bit further on are abdominal wounds and burn cases awaiting plastic surgery. Inside, the pale yellow walls smell of antiseptic, urine and pain. There are too many wounded; they lie in the halls, on the veranda floor, waiting to be tended, some moaning, one man vomiting down his chest.

But the grounds are superbly tended. The gardener has cunningly clipped the hedges into a green menagerie of leafy elephants and pelicans, kangaroos and rabbits, as humorously comforting as wallpaper in a children's nursery. Dusty, antiquated ambulances rattle by, engines wheezing and flags flying, rather comically, like inadequate stage props in an amateur production of *What Price Glory?* Planes drone lazily overhead; the sleepy gardens, young green after the just-ended monsoon, are fragrant with newly cut grass.

It's funny—after all these years I can still smell that grass, as if it and not the horror were what mattered. It was early 1965. The South Vietnamese Army was being defeated, losing a division almost every week, and this was Cong Hoa, the country's biggest military hospital, where they brought the dead and wounded of this, the losing side. In the emergency room, combat casualties lay on stretchers waiting for a doctor. An ambulance driver patted the shoulder of what seemed a mere boy, saying good-bye with a forced grin. They had just driven fifty miles from the Delta, he told me, barely escaping a Viet Cong roadblock. Helicopters were available only at night, when the highway was deemed even more dangerous.

The wounded youth was handsome, with delicate features; one eye was bandaged. His name was Nguyen, he told my interpreter; he was twenty-two and from a small village, Long Phu, on the central coast, where his widowed mother owned orchards and twenty acres of rice land. She lived alone. His two brothers had been killed in the winter's fighting at Quang Ngai. Nguyen was then a student; he had been drafted and after three months' training sent south to serve as a rifleman in the Mekong Delta.

The doctor came at last, a frail Vietnamese of middle age with a sparse moustache. He said he had studied medicine in Toulouse; when he came home he was conscripted. That had been eight years ago. He hoped to return to civilian practice—"Our country has less than two hundred civilian doctors now, you know"—but he smiled hopelessly. Every day there were at least a hundred new casualties; some days two or three hundred. The doctor said the wounded did not talk about the war. "They are just soldiers and go on fighting. They do not talk about politics because they do not wish to interfere."

After he read the student's chart, the doctor's manner softened. He patted the boy gently on the shoulder and lifted up the cotton sheet from the foot of the stretcher.

"Foot blown off with a mine," he told me in English. He spoke to the boy again in their own language, then turned back. "After treatment here, the boy will go back to his unit in My Tho to wait for the local military council to meet. The council will decide whether he can go home or not, of whether he must stay in the army to do some light job. He wants to go home. He should go home. When the wound has healed, we will send him to the rehabilitation department for an artificial limb. He says his wife came south with him. She rents a house outside the camp. They have a two-month-old son. It must be a very small house." He said that as a private with one son, the boy got the equivalent of eighteen dollars a month; totally disabled, he would get thirty-five dollars a year. The doctor thought there were at least fifty thousand partially disabled veterans in the country already; perhaps it was a blessing he did not know the war would last another ten years.

The doctor spoke to the boy again. "He says he is an infantry rifleman and that he has never killed anybody." A wounded sergeant in a nearby stretcher muttered, "Who knows where the bullets go?" The doctor lifted up the bandages from the boy's forehead; the right eye was shut and swollen. Unclipping an X ray from the foot of the stretcher and holding it up to the light, the doctor motioned me over. The black film showed the boy's skull; in the black socket of his right eye was a jagged rectangular shape a quarter inch long. "Steel fragment. That eye will have to come out." An orderly called the doctor and he went away.

I saw that the boy was moving; painfully, and with great effort, he reached down, groped for the X ray on his legs where the doctor had left it, clutched it and held it up to the light. We didn't dare stop him. There was no outcry, just thought—the deep private thought of someone faced with the final, tragic collapse of so much of his life. After a moment he lowered the X ray carefully back to where it had been, put his head down and stared upward.

I told my interpreter to ask if there was anything we could do. At first the boy did not seem to hear. We waited. Then he spoke and said, yes, he wanted to send telegrams to his wife and his mother, who did not know what had happened to him nor where he was. The words started pouring out then; my interpreter could only catch part of it. "The war must end . . . so there is no more killing . . . so I can go home. . . . I want to go home . . . I want . . . my brothers . . ." He was crying hard now and the tears streamed down from his good eye. In shame he tried to dab at them with his pajama sleeve. I thrust some piastre notes into my interpreter's hand to give to the boy and went outside to stare hard at the hedges shaped like rabbits and elephants.

After some time the interpreter brought out two telegrams for us to send. The first was addressed to Mrs. Ho Thi Loi, Long Phu Village, Bai Dinh District, Binh Thuan Province.

I was transferred to Cong Hoa Hospital this morning, the nineteenth of April, and am being treated at the eye section. My wife and baby are still in Go Cong Province; they do not know where I am. I will send them a telegram through a foreigner who came to visit the hospital. I was wounded in the left foot and it was amputated. My right eye is also wounded and might be operated on in the coming days. Come and see me if you have the time and means.

Your son

To his wife:

I was transferred to Cong Hoa Hospital in Saigon this morning and am being treated at the eye section. Come and see me if you have the money.

Dearly yours,
Nguyen Van Quy

*

The war is over now, has been over many years. The boat people have put the lie to the once widespread notion in our country that ordinary Vietnamese like this boy ever wanted the communists to win. For years this mistaken belief seemed to me one of the worst injustices we inflicted on the Vietnamese. It happened because surfaces were almost never reality in Vietnam. It took me a long time to discover this. The first year I covered the war for the Washington *Star,* 1964, I engaged almost entirely in straight reporting of the military war. The second year was devoted to pacification, the third to internal Vietnamese politics and Hanoi's political strategy, and the last, 1967, to the breakdown of the ordinary South Vietnamese's traditional Confucian culture, which was (and probably still is) the main obstacle to a successful communist Indochina. What began as the reporting of events (conventional journalism) ended in the study of the culture of ordinary people (amateur anthropology). It was that kind of war; by 1967 the restoration of traditional Vietnamese values was the only chance left of saving the country.

For the Vietnam conflict was never a Chinese-style "people's war," but only a revolutionary type of warfare designed to enable a minority to gain control over the people. The men who ran it in Hanoi were a very small group of highly intelligent, absolutely ruthless, absolutely determined men who were out to build a power structure and intended to let nothing and no one stand in their way. The key phrase upon which Hanoi based its strategy in the South was "exploiting internal contradictions in the enemy camp." The Viet Cong's strength did not feed primarily on ideas or peasant grievances but relied upon terror, intimidation and exploiting personal ambition.

Unlike the sophisticated Saigonese, the Vietnamese villager, like villagers everywhere, was plain, straight and conservative, with traditional and material drives. He wanted to own a few acres of rice land near his ancestral burial ground, build his house and raise his family. Once he experienced communist rule, he knew what it meant to these wants and to himself as an individual. Hanoi's "two main slogans" in the South, both based on deception, were "National Independence," effective propaganda against the French and American soldiers, and "Land to the Tillers," effective propaganda among the landless. But even these were not enough to win sufficient popular support. The real basis of the Viet Cong's hold on the villagers was terror.

It went on all the time. By subverting the government's police force with its own agents and infiltrating its terrorists, Hanoi prevented the establishment of permanent security in the towns and villages. Without this security, there was no law and order. Without law and order, the government administration could not function. Without functioning administration, it was impossible to create a genuine non-communist political base. And without such a base, the struggle was doomed.

An example: in early 1966 I stayed overnight in the town of Tan An, just south of Saigon, well protected by an American infantry brigade. Searchlights beamed across the surrounding countryside, American howitzers pounded the rice fields with harassment and interdiction fire and one felt just about as safe as you ever could in Vietnam. About midnight four terrorists murdered a policeman and his family in their home a block from the house where I was sleeping. They wore South Vietnamese army fatigues, two carried Thompson submachine guns and they came upriver by sampan and walked through the streets unheeded, people assuming they were just another government patrol. They left behind propaganda sheets declaring, "This execution is to avenge crimes against the people by dirty landlords, the puppet government and the American imperialists." I retraced the assassination squad's steps the next day. Everyone was unusually silent, looking once and averting their eyes. Those we could get to talk said, "We know nothing," "Nobody saw the killers," "The policeman was too openly loyal to the government side," "We are poor men and just go about our business and feed our families." They were all desperately afraid.

Most villagers just want to be left alone. Again, I remember a fisherman interviewed during South Vietnam's 1966 elections. He was mending a net on the odd heap of bamboo poles, split bamboo matting and planks on stilts that he called home; it was on the banks of the Bassac River near Can Tho. The fisherman kept mending his net as we talked, his calloused fingers grasping a primitive wooden needle to stitch and replace the rotted braid. Both he and the art seemed as old and enduring as the sluggish Bassac. "I have no mind about Saigon," he said, his sun-bronzed face wrinkling about the eyes. "If the government wants me to go voting, okay, I will do my duty. But after voting I will live here, go on fishing and my life will be the same." While it was impossible to read the heart of a Vietnamese fisherman mending a fishnet, I got an impression of neither hostility nor interest. Just natural indifference over something he felt was unlikely to make any real difference in his life. The inner walls of his hut were plastered over with whatever scraps of paper had come his way: lottery tickets, yellowed Bombay film ads, illustrations from a cheap biography of Buddha, and a glossy poster of Lyndon Johnson. You could make out the words: "We are in Vietnam because the American people have promised to help the people of South Vietnam preserve their independence and build their nation." The fisherman said the paper was stiff and helped keep out the cold night breeze from the river.

*

The villagers were the key. But how to get to know them well enough to help them against the terrorism which was destroying their confidence and their culture. Of all the Americans involved, the Marines tried hardest, moving squads of men into villages to live for long periods. One of these villages, Kim Lien, just north of Danang, will always be for me a metaphor for the entire Vietnam war.

A Marine squad, which fluctuated in size from eight to fourteen young Americans, first moved in to live in Kim Lien in early 1966. Its people had then been subject to communist terrorism and indoctrination for twenty years. Even so, things went well at first. The Marines trained seventy village-recruited youths as a militia; a color guard raised and lowered the red-and-yellow South Vietnamese flag each day. The Marines put money into Kim Lien; they hired ten men as grass cutters and another seven as construction workers; they raised $700 to make a sandy beach on a nearby riverbank, where they took the village children swimming each day. They bought candles, mirrors, mattresses, cigarettes, films and whatever else they needed in the village itself.

Volleyball games were played every evening on a new playground; two navy medical corpsmen opened a village clinic; a Marine band and drum-and-bugle corps came to give concerts. If a villager died, the Marines bought a traditional funeral banner; they went to weddings, took meals in the villagers' homes. Their sergeant visited each of three hundred or so houses to personally explain why the Marines were in Kim Lien. Soon the village had its first latrines, a barbed wire perimeter fence, a fancy new entrance gate, new wells, a new portable sawmill, a new irrigation system fed by a mountain stream. Soon the young Americans were enormously popular.

Was it enough? Ten items of the Marines' Daily Log for August 12, 1966, the day I happened to visit, tell the whole story:

1. Made roving sick call.
2. Two Marines ate chow in woodcutter's house.
3. Two more ate *boi beo* (noodle soup) in a fisherman's home.
4. Held English language class.
5. One Marine bought haircuts for two boys.
6. Completed two more new wells.
7. Organized volleyball.
8. Swim call for boys.
9. Distributed modeling clay to children.
10. Found anti-VC posters torn down in the center of the village.

A Marine sergeant told me, "This ville is full of VC. Anything we put up, they rip down at night. We keep putting stuff up and they keep tearing it down. An old man told me today, 'We don't want you to help us build a well because we don't understand what you're saying and you don't understand what we're saying. Besides my brother-in-law might kill us. He's up in the hills with the VC.'"

One of the Marines, Corporal Lyttleton T. Ward, Jr., a twenty-one-year-old Virginian whom the villagers called Tom, was one of the few Americans I met in Vietnam who had spent a long time in a village and knew the Vietnamese language fluently. Tom told me, "I don't think the VC have ever left this village. We're all just sort of living here together. Oh, we like to think if we got clobbered one night, somebody would come and warn us. We've been probed a few times. Whenever that happens old Mr. Thi moves his cows over to the other side of the railroad tracks the afternoon before. We could tell battalion intelligence, but they wouldn't believe us. But the morning after some action, sure enough, that's where Mr. Thi's cows are. He's a very old man and has his finger in every pie. He stays away from us and we stay away from him. But he's not a VC; he's just trying to save his cows."

Tom went on, "It's like when we play volleyball every night. A former VC officer is captain of the villagers' team, probably still is a VC. But he's a real go-getter. Gives us a heck of a lot of help when it comes to putting in wells, even if he probably is still a Charlie. They probably come over to play volleyball to see where our grenades are. Some guy accidentally hits the ball under the grenade bunker and goes crawling in after it. Oh, the VC propaganda team comes in and stays a month or so, trying to throw some little wrench into our gears. The days they put out their biggest load of pamphlets, people will bring them in and show them to us. All about the American Nazi Party and the Ku Klux Klan.

"Our biggest problem is the village chief. Oh, he smiles a lot, a real yes man, but he's never given us cooperation. The most helpful man in the ville, like I told you, is the VC officer. He gets everything organized."

While Tom took me around Kim Lien, I had my Vietnamese interpreter talk alone with the village chief. According to him, the chief said, "I know who the VC in Kim Lien are, but I can't arrest them. If I did, I'd be killed or kidnapped and tortured. Kim Lien supplies food for a hardcore VC company living in the hills. They're all from the village. The commander is Vi, Nguyen is his deputy and Thanh is the chief political officer. I know them. Sometimes I've even seen them here in the village. But what can I do? When the GIs first came, I thought of killing myself."

My interpreter also talked to the Marine squad's Vietnamese interpreter, who, aside from Tom, was the only way to communicate. A former clerk from the Ministry of Health in Saigon, bitter to be drafted, he complained, "The GIs should not treat Vietnamese as inferiors. Without me, how can they work in this village? Even if they speak Vietnamese fluently, like Tom, they don't see how terrified these people are. People here in Kim Lien are quiet with the Marines, okay on the surface, but in their hearts they're afraid to have Americans in their village."

And it wasn't only Kim Lien: the whole country was that way—a Trojan horse of Hanoi's agents, informers and terrorists virtually riddled Saigon too. As I wrote in *The Long Charade,* published in 1968:

A charade, like any theatrical performance, never looks quite the same to anyone once he has watched it backstage. The players posture and grimace as before, fighting their mock battles before the footlights. But the illusion of reality is gone. Looking back on those years in Vietnam is, I find, like remembering it all as seen from the wings, where everything is quieter and darker. The performance out front goes on as before—the horror shows of fiery suicides and flaming villages, the stage-managed riots and rebellions, even the last bloody battles of the cities—but now I can see Le Duan in the shadows above, jerking the strings.

Le Duan, who was shortly to succeed Ho Chi Minh as the leader of the Vietnamese communists, was the master strategist of the whole terrorism-based performance, just as Tom's VC officer possibly was in Kim Lien.

Kim Lien's reckoning came September 10, less than a month after my visit. I didn't hear about it until the following spring when I drove out to the village with two Marine sergeants from the Danang press camp and found that the Marine squad was gone. One of the schoolteachers told us about it:

"The VC came from the sea one night and overran the Marine outpost down by the river behind the schoolhouse. Three Marines and one VC were killed and the Marines lost a machine gun. It all happened in about fifteen minutes. They pulled the Marines out of Kim Lien after that. Tom was all right. I hear he's back in America."

The teacher, a frail man who was visibly frightened himself, said he no longer slept in Kim Lien at night, nor did the village chief. "He only comes in the daytime to sign papers," he said. He said the chief had also withdrawn the Marine-recruited militiamen who had been guarding a bridge called Nam O down the highway. And that a platoon of Viet Cong were openly living in houses just across the road. "What does it mean?" he wanted to know. "Are the Americans going away?" He asked if we had any news of Tom. "People here liked him. He always made jokes and helped everybody. Tom used to say, politically speaking, that the villagers who cut wood and lived inland were pro-VC and the fishermen along the beach were pro-government. That was wrong. The Marines lived on the fishermen's side; they were safe at night. Now everyone is afraid. We miss Tom and the Marines and wish they were back living here. Now the VC go everywhere." The teacher, probably feeling he had said too much, went away then and the two sergeants and I walked around Kim Lien.

It was evident right away everything was wrong. The Marines' clinic had been torn down, the volleyball court was overgrown with grass and—always the surest sign the Viet Cong were around—there were no children in sight. Aside from the teacher, the only sign of life was three women dressed in black, sawing logs; as soon as they saw us, they looked away. A few military vehicles went by on the road to Hue, the notorious Street Without Joy. Otherwise Kim Lien looked deserted. "Let's get the hell out of here," one of the sergeants said. I felt like gunsights were trained at our backs, a not uncommon sensation in Vietnamese villages, no matter how careful you were. Bob Hope had a gag for it: "They tell me the enemy is very close; imagine me not knowing which way to run."

A couple of nights later the Viet Cong blew up Nam O Bridge, cutting off ground transport of military supplies from Danang to the DMZ for days. The Marine command said it had taken a lot of preparation and that the Viet Cong demolitions men must have been living in Kim Lien for some time. Our defeat in Vietnam was not a failure of power but a failure of knowledge.

JOYPUR VILLAGE, BANGLADESH

It is a land of golden dreams and dreadful night, fiercely naked in the size of its population and the depth of its poverty. It is the great delta of the Himalayan-watered Ganges and Brahmaputra rivers, wet, flat, silt-rich and so amazingly fertile that despite frequent cyclones, floods and drought, it has managed to precariously support ninety million Bengalis. If the United States were so densely populated, it would have six billion people. It was created after a brutal civil war in 1971 that saw the most heinous atrocities in a quarter century. As its first prime minister, the since-murdered Sheikh Mujibur Rahman once told me, it is "poor, poor, poorest of all the world." It is what Henry Kissinger called "the international basket case," the tag end, down as far as you can go, the rock bottom: Bangladesh.

Land holdings are fragmented and small, few more than one or two acres; most are subdivided further still into tiny, disconnected plots. Rice and a few vegetables are the subsistence diet; nutritionists say that the meager daily average intake of food is scarcely above the starvation level. Along with malnutrition, cholera is endemic and malaria is coming back. Some 94 percent of Bangladesh's people live in sixty-five thousand villages, making it the most rural of any major country in the world. Agricultural productivity is too low to keep pace with population growth, yet the country endures. Most experts agree that if the Bengali peasant is given the opportunity and training and enough money is put into agriculture, Bangladesh can quite easily double present rice production and have more than enough to feed projected future populations. Unlike some of the more arid parts of the planet, where population seems to have outstripped resources, and no corrective technology exists, Bangladesh has reasons for hope.

*

In the monsoon, out in the countryside, Bangladesh is an unexpectedly beautiful land, with a soft languor and gentle rhythm of its own. Great whirls of white, thick cumulus clouds, towering thirty to forty thousand feet, drift over its wet, pale-green surfaces. Mist hangs over the endless sea of rice paddies like steam over a vat. By day, when I visited it some years ago, the village of Joypur was deceptively peaceful. With just over fifteen hundred people in a hundred and forty families, it lay steamy and somnolent in the sun—its busy activity off in the fields, or hidden from view in the women's courtyards. Chickens scratched for grain, naked children played in the dust, there was the soothing creak of bullock carts; a tailor sat crosslegged before an ancient sewing machine. There was the drone of the pump engine at the village tube well, which watered sixty of its two hundred and fifty cultivated acres. The lack of more wells was a bone of contention; water meant the difference between one and three crops a year and two more deep wells had been promised.

At dusk the village came to life. As crows left the village in screaming flocks for their night roosts in the fields, the men came to settle in groups before one of the open pavilions and talk—rich, warm Bengali talk, argumentative and humorous, fervent and excited in gossip, protest and indignation. The men were barefoot and clad only in *sarong*-like *lungis*—from habit and the high price of cloth. A few still had rags tied about their coarse black hair against the day's fierce sun or sudden monsoon rains. They were, for the most part, cheerful, with shy manners that abruptly exploded into excited chatter, their heads bobbing from one side to the other. Most were undernourished, though a few robust figures stood out—like muscular Rashid, respected as the best farmer in Joypur, or silver-haired Abdur, the head of the cooperative society—as if, as E. M. Forster wrote, "nature remembers the physical perfection that she accomplished elsewhere, and throws out a god—not many, but one here and there, to prove to society how little its categories impress her."

Against the murmur of their voices, fireflies darted over the ponds and the winding path to the outside world; slowly the flickering lamps in the enclosed women's quarters were extinguished and cicadas snickered from the fields. It should have been calm and idyllic, like the Bengali villages in Satyajit Ray's films. It was not; as night fell, fear seeped into Joypur. The talk, as it often did in those days, centered on growing lawlessness and the gangs of *dacoits*, or bandits, who attacked villages at night.

"We are always afraid," fretted Ram Lal, the coppersmith and one of Joypur's few Hindus. "The government cannot cope with all this lawlessness. The prime minister, no doubt, is a good man, but those about him are corrupt and dishonest."

Sitting crosslegged beside the coppersmith, an old whitebeard cackled, then collapsed into a coughing fit. "Hee," he exclaimed, when he recovered, "when an elephant tries to catch a frog, the frog will jump quickly. But once the frog is under the elephant's heel, he lies there pretending he is dead. That's how it is for us."

"The situation deteriorates day by day," said the bespectacled schoolteacher, feeling called upon by his position in the village to say something. The fall of darkness made everything outside the halo of an oil lamp look black and impenetrable. Across the courtyard Rashid's wife, shrouded and bent over a cooking pot, waited for water to boil. Everyone rested from the day's labor, speculating what the *dacoits* would do next. They had come once, just after eleven o'clock, fifteen or twenty young men armed with Sten guns and rifles who landed in small boats from the river. Some wore masks; others had smeared war paint on their faces just like Indian braves in some Hollywood film. The villagers suspected it was an inside job. The raiders attacked two houses whose owners had just sold their rice harvest; one man refused to open his door; they fired through it, wounding him. Some of the villagers felt they were not true *dacoits* at all, but younger, better educated men, probably students, perhaps from the university. Some thought they were liberation war fighters, now better armed than the police and embittered against the government, who saw no other way to get money. Others speculated the night-comers were communist Naxalites or Moslem Leaguers or Bihari militiamen or Awami League bully boys. Or maybe just bandits after all. Who could tell these days? Elsewhere, they heard, it was worse—daylight bank robberies, hijackings, murders, rapes.

Worst of all, in the Joypur villagers' minds, was a seizure and looting of their local *thana,* or district police station. From Moghul times, the police *thana* always had been a Bengali village's main link to the government. What were they to think at the spectacle of thirty anxious policemen, armed with old Lee-Enfield rifles and cowering behind their rusted barbed wire at night lest the *dacoits* strike again?

Who would protect Joypur? No one but themselves. They formed voluntary night patrols, men who went about each night, ready to sound a general alarm if any suspicious outsider was seen. Ram Lal, as a Hindu, was the most fearful of all. He had heard that in some raids the *dacoits* told the people that what the Pakistanis had not destroyed in Bangladesh, the Indians plotted to steal, and that the government favored Hindus and did not stand by the tenets of true Islam. Ram Lal knew all too well the age-old phenomenon of Bengali Moslems reacting to pressure in unpleasant anti-Hindu ways. He and his wife were among the ten million refugees who fled to India during the civil war; as he told her, "We are a minority and we must always worry about how we will be treated by the Moslems." He knew the government was not antagonistic to non-Moslems; but if times were bad, Hindus were made the popular scapegoats and must flee.

Now, as the men sat in silence somewhere out of the darkness came a bird's mournful cry, "Trrrr, trrrr . . ." Ram Lal shuddered.

"Did I feel a raindrop?" asked young Rashid.

"Hah," snorted the old man. "We are not salt that will melt away." After a pause, he went on, "Even the educated people are *dacoits* these days. But they do it sitting in a chair in Dacca. Only the foolish *dacoits* come to your door."

"They do, they do," affirmed Ram Lal, drawing nearer his Moslem neighbors, just as if he had grown apprehensive.

Ahmed, a rugged-faced, sinewy man who was one of several itinerant landless laborers in Joypur, made fun of the paunchy Hindu. "*Dacoits* don't bother poor men," he scoffed. "All we possess is our bedding. Who will slit our throats for that?"

"Whatever comes, it is Allah's will," muttered another laborer. Ahmed and his fellow workers had journeyed two days by riverboat from their distant village—part of an army surging across the Bengali countryside looking for field work, in return for rice and a few rupees a day. Rashid let them sleep in a lean-to on his threshing ground.

Rashid himself was troubled. "We got independence but not peace," he complained. "We have to fear these *dacoits* will plunder us at night. Who dares to sleep in his own house? Without security, what good is freedom?" In the yellow glow cast by the oil lamp, his face had a spectral look.

Silver-haired Abdur agreed. "Before we listened to the government's words. Now who can believe the rascals?"

"The *dacoits* are not the worst of it," Rashid continued. "Look at me. My whole life is growing rice. But these days I cannot grow a good crop for want of fertilizer, insecticides and fuel to keep the irrigation pump going. If we had a sure supply of these things, I for one would like the government to stop its subsidy. Let us pay cash. Now it's impossible. Those foxes in the government are selling our fertilizer out the back door at black market prices."

"Some high hands are involved in it."

Rashid was stirred up. "For the last two years we are learning from the radio that corruption will end and the government wants us to grow more food. But there is no change at all. During liberation even a dying man wanted to hear the politicians' words. Now no more."

"Ah, brothers," sighed the old man. "I hoped things would get better so I could take my rest. Now I must go on working."

"Those who can afford to stop at sixty," said Ahmed, the laborer. "Those who can't go on until they drop in the fields." Ahmed felt justly aggrieved. His wife had to have an operation at the hospital in Dacca that cost him the equivalent of seventy dollars in rupees. Already in debt, he had to mortgage the quarter acre of land he inherited from his father. For the first time he joined the hungry, roaming men looking for field work in strange villages. "First my wife got ill, then came a plague of insects, then a flood, and finally rising prices. This is the worst year of my life, worse than ever before." By harvesting in the day and threshing at night for a month, he had managed to send home a five-dollar postal money order. "I may have to go home empty-handed now," he told the men, since there was no more field work available in Joypur. "It is peaceful here, but all I do is sit around and think how I can take money home to feed my four children."

Rashid sympathized with him. *"Khub bhalo katse,"* he said. "I eat good. I have my independence and dignity. I can employ men. If you lose the land, you are a slave to others."

"Work can keep your health," retorted the old grandfather with spirit. "An idle man gets lead in his bones. Well, Bangladesh will always live in want." He thought of the many such conversations he had heard over the years. It was different in his youth, he told the men, when Joypur had only half the people. "Ponds full of fish, fields full of grain . . ." He chuckled at the memory. Ahmed was not amused. "You speak like Sheikh Mujib," he said, "and his dream of a golden Bengal."

Rashid, a fervent Moslem, did not curse or complain out loud, remembering Allah's will. But he was determined to improve his lot. Although he had completed only five years of school, he kept careful records of his earnings and expenses. With two acres, he owned two bullocks and supported a family of wife, two children, and a widowed mother (typically, he married when his wife was thirteen, he twenty-two). A student also lived with the family, tutoring Rashid's children in return for rice and a place to sleep. He taught them Bengali, English, mathematics and the Koran; it was a not uncommon arrangement in Bengali villages, where learning is held in the highest esteem. That year he had raised seven tons of IR20 and IR5 dwarf rice, plus some traditional varieties, by triple cropping half his land. The total worth of the harvest gave him, after food for the family and expenses, nearly a five-hundred-dollar profit, allowing him to build a new house.

Future hope in Bangladesh rests with Rashid and millions like him; in the eight years since then, as law and order improved and they got the needed supplies, Bangladesh was to see yearly rises in food production of 4 percent and 5 percent. But even today too many Ahmeds still exist, men for whom, in the words of Rabindranath Tagore, "the horizon is fiercely naked." The great Bengali poet was comparing pent-up human wrath with the ominous silence, heat, and despair of a drought, when "lashes of lightning startle the sky from end to end."

Memories are a form of metaphor. When we liken one thing to another we are remembering. When I remember Bangladesh now I think of a rainy night in Dacca in 1973; I was returning home from an interview with the prime minister when my car fell behind a crowded bus. Sheikh Mujib had spoken with genuine feeling of his love for his people, but he had already shown himself to be a manifestly incompetent administrator. "If I have to buy so much food from outside to feed my cities," he had told me, "how can I find money to invest in agriculture? It is my most terrible problem." The bloody upheaval that would end his government and his life within the year had, when it came, a tragic inevitability about it. But when you lead a nation of ninety million, almost all of them very poor peasant villagers, you sure as hell better give agriculture your top priority. Soldiers with machine guns broke into his home and massacred the whole family.

In the wet, heavy traffic and darkness that night, my driver was afraid to pass the bus. Emaciated, near-naked mobs of Bengalis pressed in on us from all sides. *They* didn't know we were coming from their prime minister; some of them looked baleful enough to set upon the car. It was one of those ghastly nights in Bangladesh when your nerves are just about to give out: heat, dripping monsoon rain, smells of tropical rot and stale urine, headlights flashing on scabrous walls plastered with hate-America graffiti, that panicky get-me-out-of-here feeling. Some corpses, hideously decapitated, had been found just a few days before right out on the same street where I was staying. My Bengali interpreter, cultivated, conscientious and self-conscious, stared fixedly at the snarled traffic, taking in all the squalor. "My father loved Macaulay," he blurted out in near hysteria, "and he wore a suit, tie and vest every day of his life."

The bus was one of Dacca's old double-deckers. Despite the drizzle and darkness, men were riding on the roof, clinging to the sides, the doors; the rear bumper seemed to drag on the pavement. The bus creaked forward, not fast, but fast enough so that men who could not find a grip or had lost theirs ran behind, apparently thinking it would stop farther on. But the bus did not stop. It just disappeared into the dense Bengali night. And so did the men, running soundlessly, hopelessly, after it.

Mexico, both modern and primitive, is a society with a dual reality. Pre-Columbian civilization, with its Aztec domination, ritualism and human sacrifice, subtly thrusts itself, when you least expect it, into the present. Tepoztlán is the most American-studied village in Mexico, or anywhere in the world when it comes to that. It has long been the focus of anthropological debate as to whether village life is happy and satisfying or filled with fear, envy and mistrust. When I first went to Mexico, flying up from Rio de Janeiro in the spring of 1977, I naturally sought out Tepoztlán, only to find it was a village no more. But it does say something about contemporary Mexico and where it is going.

Today Tepoztlán has handsome villas everywhere; in the lovely valley below, the old bean and maize fields have become the walled estates of millionaires, with a trailer camp and YMCA recreation park thrown in here and there. *Time* and a daily English-language newspaper are sold in Tepoztlán's plaza, TV antennae sprout from every rooftop, a new chromium-and-glass cinema shows bloody and macabre Mexican shoot-'em-ups, and express buses leave every hour on the hour for downtown Mexico City, seventy-seven kilometers or seventy minutes away by four-lane superhighway. Some three thousand bus fares are sold daily to the city of Cuernavaca, fifteen miles below on the plains, home of many a retired American. Many Tepoztecans daily commute to jobs there. Kellogg's Corn Flakes, Nescafé and ice cold beer are standard fare in the village grocery shops. Among the new residents, the German colony is the biggest, but there are plenty of rich Mexicans, Americans, Italians and French, and an artists' colony of painters and film actors. Even Hollywood invades every once in a while to shoot a movie, such as *Butch Cassidy and the Sundance Kid*.

On weekdays the plaza and market look as desolate and dingy as in any village, but on weekends thousands of tourists pour in from Mexico City, filling five hotels and a dozen restaurants. Real estate values have skyrocketed. Tepoztlán's land sells for two hundred and fifty pesos, or about ten dollars, a square yard. If one counts seven small outlying hamlets, the Tepotzlán *municipio* now has almost twenty thousand people; it is a fair-sized town, no longer a village. A good many Tepoztecans remain part-time cultivators, growing corn, beans, and alfalfa on two thousand one hundred hectares of land four miles down the valley, a *hacienda* confiscated and turned over to the people during the 1910–1917 Mexican Revolution. But many villagers have joined the middle class. Most menial work in Tepoztlán, for example, is done by immigrants from neighboring Guerrero state. Another measure of prosperity—one important to us—is the fall in the number of men who temporarily migrate to the United States as agricultural workers. In 1948, there were thirty; by 1957, more than six hundred; in 1980 there were only nine, which suggests that Mexicans will stay home if they can afford to. This prosperity has been largely fueled by land sales, mostly since Tepoztlán became fashionable among the rich after the superhighway was built and Mexico City itself became one of the worst-polluted cities anywhere. (The combination of a high altitude and fifteen million people in a single mountain-enclosed valley is deadly.) The movement out of the peasantry into the middle class also reflects remarkable advances in the Mexican economy and in education during the past twenty years.

Evidence of the older civilization is still there, as almost everywhere in Mexico. You can ascend the cliffs that surround Tepoztlán on three sides to an Aztec stone temple where children were sacrificed to the rain god, Tlaloc, in 1580, by having their hearts cut out and the blood given in offering. There is still a record of how Tepoztlán, along with other villages in pre-Hispanic Huaztepec province, gave tribute of warriors' armor with shields to Montezuma's Aztec court. One can see fragments of a thick wall said to be part of the house of Martin Cortés, the Spanish conqueror's son. And the old men can still relate almost bullet-by-bullet accounts of the fighting that waged back and forth through Tepoztlán between the Zapatista guerrillas and the federal troops during the revolution, just a little over sixty years ago.

As in many Mexican small towns, the dense foliage of trees conceals the houses until Tepoztlán is actually entered. An old Spanish church on the plaza is by far the largest building; its great walls, crenellated to serve as battlements, and its two tall bell towers, rise above the treetops and are just about all one sees when approaching from down in the valley. An American visitor wrote of Tepoztlán's streets in 1930 that they were "very still; in them no wheel ever passes." And in his book, *Five Families*, Oscar Lewis described it in 1959:

> The ancient highland village of Azteca [Lewis gave Tepoztlán a fictional name] lay quiet and serene on the mountain slope in the early morning darkness. . . . Spreading from the top of the slope to the broad valley below, eight barrios, each with its chapel and patron saint, formed little communities within the larger village. A paved road connecting Azteca with the main highway cut across the village and ended abruptly at the plaza. Here were the municipal building, the central church, the mill, a few small shops, and a bare park. Extending up and down the slope the old terraced streets, laboriously constructed of blue-gray volcanic rock, were lined by small, one-story adobe houses with their patios of semitropical plants and trees set behind stone walls.

Today most of these old houses have been rehabilitated or torn down and one would no longer say, as Lewis did in the 1940s, that the streets are "uniformly quiet and rustic and stamp Tepoztlán as a village." There are still steep cobbled lanes but cars move up and down them; on weekends there can be traffic jams. At the same time a good many Tepoztecans still ride horseback.

None of the many books Americans have written about Tepoztlán quite prepare you for the spectacular beauty of its setting. Nestling into a sloping alluvial valley, the community is surrounded by very sheer cliffs and fantastic and massive rock outcroppings. These are partly forested with pine, fir, oak and madrona, and offer breathtaking vistas of stone cliffs. With mist and a mossy green color in every direction, the views resemble those in the Bavarian or Tyrolese Alps, which may explain Tepoztlán's popularity with rich Germans.

One evening I was talking to a woman, who as Macrina appeared as a character in *Pedro Martinez,* one of the Lewis books, when her husband, drunk on tequila, arrived home from the fields on horseback. He at once declared, "Americanos can never understand the life of Mexico." But they keep trying. At different times in the plaza, I ran into two anthropologists still studying Tepoztlán, Claudio Zomnitz, a young Chilean, and Philip Bock from the University of New Mexico. This persistent effort to unravel the mysteries of this single village baffles me. On a visit in 1980, Tepoztlán's old men, still dressed in

Vietnamese refugees, 1966, in the Mekong Delta.

Planting rice in Bangladesh.

Threshing wheat in Huecorio, Mexico.

Aurelio.

Aurelio's grandmother and niece.

Prem (Mauritius).

Octave, the author and Karl, 1969.

Octave and Karl, Creole fishermen on the southern Indian Ocean island of Mauritius, prepare in 1970 to dive in their lagoon for fish and octopus while Prem, the author's interpreter, takes down their dialogue.

Old man in the excavated palace of Darius the Great near the village of Shush-Daniel, Iran, site of the Biblical city of Susa. The granite horses' heads were supported by colossal pillars.

Sherif and Karim (facing camera).

Yahkoub.

their loose, white *calzones,* tattered *sombreros* and *huaraches,* and still carrying water to their homes from the nearest public fountain, like the old women queuing up to have their corn ground, seemed to be just about the only relics left of a true village past which was likely to die with them. Then the closeness of its soaring cliffs and forests, the dense foliage all about, give Tepoztlán its own special, haunted, slightly claustrophobic ambience. It is a place of incredible beauty, perhaps the most beautiful setting in all Mexico, but I doubt that truly representative village life was ever found there.

*

Mexican village life matters to us because it is thrusting itself upon the American consciousness in a way no other peasant society can. This is not only because of Mexico's newly rediscovered oil riches, with proven reserves a third as big as Saudi Arabia's, but because Mexico's population has quadrupled in just four decades, the fastest growth of any major country on earth. Mexico had only 18 million people in 1940. If one counts 6 to 12 million *"illegales"* in the United States, it has 76 to 82 million now and it is projected to have 130 million in just twenty more years. This will be half as many people as the United States is expected to have.

Until very recently many Americans thought about Mexico, if they thought about it at all, as a particularly friendly, reliable "good neighbor," drowsing peacefully under its sombrero in the shadow of a cactus and a Spanish colonial church. In the fifty or so years that Americans have gone to Mexican villages to study the peasantry, 20 percent of these peasants have become industrial workers, another 16 percent of them service workers. The country has sustained yearly economic growth rates in real terms of at least 6 percent, one of the best development records anywhere; Mexico's soldiers have stayed out of politics and its civilian presidents have peacefully handed over power every six years for half a century. There are around 8 million Mexican-Americans, or Chicanos; some thirty-five thousand retired Americans live in Mexico and, in good years, about 3 million Americans visit Mexico each year to view its scenic beauty, pre-Hispanic ruins, colonial architecture, the art of Orozco and Rivera, and beaches, like those at Acapulco.

Yet most gains have been eaten up by runaway population growth, which peaked at 3.7 percent in the mid-1970s and now is claimed to be down to 2.9 percent, still very high in a population where 46 percent are under age 15; this growth is partly caused by fervent, conservative Roman Catholicism, partly by the *macho* (ostentatiously virile) pride in being father of a large family and partly by a more generalized *macho* feeling that to restrict population would be to fall in with a *gringo* plot to curtail Mexico's destiny. Figures in Mexico need to be treated with caution. In 1980, the average Mexican had a yearly per capita GNP of $1,290, less than one-seventh of the $9,700 of an American across the border. Mexico is one of the most unequal countries in the world in terms of national income, though: 30–40 percent of the population cannot afford an adequate diet and, in 1969, the top 20 percent of families received 64 percent of all family income.

A peasant villager consumes an average of 2,604 calories per day, just what a Ugandan does. Agriculture in the most backward villages hasn't changed much since the Spanish conquest of 1519. Add low standards of housing, education and health, the extreme gap between rich and poor, and an almost total lack of popular political participation and you find the true Mexican village as poor and traditional as any village anywhere. Indeed, I find a Mexican village to be much more "foreign" than, say, one in Brazil or even northern India. The reason may be the country's two-thousand-year history of violent ups and downs: the rise and fall of the great Mayan and Aztec civilizations; conquest and colonization by the Spaniards; the struggle for independence from Spain; an imported Austrian emperor; dictatorship; revolution. The whole Mexican political system seems designed to stave off another revolution; every six years you get a new president, with new faces, new hopes.

What makes the Mexican villages different from all the others in the Third World is that they lie just across our common border. Short of building a 1,950-mile fence and constructing a symbolic iron curtain with Latin America, it is impossible to isolate ourselves from the problems of the Mexican village—not enough land and water to go around and not enough jobs. When it comes to bridging the gap between rich and poor, village Mexicans do it with their feet. How many "illegal aliens," "undocumented migrants," or "wetbacks" (so called because of their swim across the Rio Grande) cross the border each year is unknown, but the Immigration and Naturalization Service (known as *migra* to the migrants) catches and sends back more than 1 million each year. "STATE IS THREATENED BY ILLEGAL HORDES" screamed the Los Angeles *Herald-Examiner* in August 1977.

Possibly the very best thing we could do to solve the "problem" of the illegal aliens is to legalize them; a leading expert, Wayne Cornelius of M.I.T., has proposed issuing 750,000 temporary work permits a year. Jorge Bustamente, a Mexican authority on emigration, thinks legalization might let his government off the hook of trying to find the solution to unemployment and poverty within Mexico. The roots of this poverty lie in the land. What happens in the Mexican villages, especially if the present flow of illegal migrants turns into a flood, if not an inundation, is going to bring home to Americans the harsh realities of the human condition when population growth at last outruns economic resources. Let us take the example of a village where I lived for six months in 1977 and which I revisited in 1980, Huecorio.

Calm and peaceful, this small mountain village spreads from the marshy shores of Lake Pátzcuaro, famous for the butterfly nets of its fishermen, up the rocky and eroded slopes of an extinct volcano. The air, at six thousand feet, is bracing. The view is spacious and scenic. Forests of pine and fir cover the misty peaks around the thirty miles of shoreline; the lake itself is strewn with islands. The lower slopes are a patchwork of tiny fields enclosed by rock walls. In spring these fields are golden with the wheat harvest. By the time I left in 1977, they were green with corn and beans.

Like most Mexican villages, Huecorio is picturesque. Its small plaza and cobbled streets are lined with walled-in adobe houses, half hidden, like those in Tepoztlán, behind foliage and flowering bougainvillea. Traffic rumbles through on a new paved road. Television antennae bring in "Charlie's Angels" and "Hawaii Five-O." Instant coffee and breakfast cereal are standard fare in four or five small shops.

Yet, even much more than in Tepoztlán, you can feel the years under you. Gone is the great Tarascan Indian empire that ruled this lake region until the Spanish conquest. Gone the god of fire, Curicaveri; gone the nobility, the commoners and slaves, the priests and human sacrifices. The stone temples are in ruins and the few pure Tarascans who survive have retreated to the islands of the lake, human relics who fish from ancient canoes.

Huecorio's people are the mestizos of modern Mexico; the mating of Spaniard and Indian took place about eighteen generations ago, and only the rich black hair and the lustrous skin of the pure Tarascan remain. Yet scratch the surface and you'll find many ancient Indian beliefs persist—fears of eclipses, sorcery, evil winds and spirits, a faith in healing herbs; even the practice of *el robo,* bride theft, still goes on. Beans and tortillas have always been Mexico's staff of life, in the pre-Columbian empires as today. Wheat has replaced maize as the main cash crop and plows substitute for the old hoe cultivation, but few other modern agricultural techniques are practiced. We still cut wheat with sickles just as they do in India and threshed the grain by driving horses to stamp upon it, as the *carabao* or human dancers do in the Philippines.

There was also a deeper, more intangible legacy of the Indian past, the brooding introspection Mexican intellectuals such as Octavio Paz have described as reserve, insecurity, solitude. On the surface, Huecorio's people were merry, their courtesy affable and sincere, their fiestas noisy and exuberant, their family attachments warm and evident; of all the villagers I have seen, Mexicans show the greatest affection for their children. But daily behavior tends to be stolid, a bit surly, except for the effusive, almost overbearing friendliness of the men when drunk, as the Huecorians often were. As we walked to the fields in early morning, it was not uncommon to find someone we knew, lying in a rumpled heap in the ditch, dead drunk. These part-Indian mestizos, still strongly influenced by pre-Columbian civilization and in an incompletely developed relationship with the Spanish culture of the Mexican cities, seemed unhappily caught in a cultural no-man's-land; this leads to some very contradictory character traits: warmth but suspicion, passivity but violence, vision and cynicism, idealism and gross corruption. Almost all the men had worked in cities at some time, but the familiar universe of the village eventually drew them back. Put plainly, though I worked in the fields with a family only in the mornings and escaped to library research in the afternoons, I found the Mexican villagers, in six months with them, unusually heavy going. What their dual culture lacks is a unifying harmony; instead there is a fatalistic acceptance of society being divided into the strong and the weak.

In Huecorio this psychological tug-of-war was especially evident because the main source of cash income was the United States. The men of Huecorio began migrating to California in 1943 during the *bracero* program initiated after farm labor shortages in World War II and continued until the mid-1960s. Then Congress, under pressure from organized labor, put an end to it. When I was in Huecorio about half its labor force of 250 men still went, but illegally.

Aurelio, whose grandparents I helped in the fields and who served as my interpreter, had been to Los Angeles many times; nearly a full-blooded Tarascan, with long, coarse black hair, he looked like Geronimo and had worked in a car wash. To go, he said, meant a three-day bus journey to Tijuana, a $250 bribe to a *coyote* or fellow Mexican waiting across the border with a car, and a scramble over, under, or through a barbed wire fence while trying to hide from the patrol cars of the American immigration agents. Once safely in Los Angeles, Fresno or Bakersfield, most Huecorio men worked as harvest hands, though some, like Aurelio, took menial jobs in the cities. He had even attended high school in Los Angeles, working nights. Wages ranged from $7.50 an hour at a General Motors plant, the best job held by a Huecorio man, to $40 a week washing dishes. In Huecorio itself, a field laborer with no land of his own could not make more than $750 to $800 a year. In the San Fernando Valley, he could make that much in a month. By sharing a one-bedroom, $250- to $400-a-month apartment with four to nine other men, he was able to save $3,000 to $5,000 in a single year to bring back home.

"In L.A. I had a nice car for nine hundred forty dollars," Aurelio told me. "Here having any car is impossible. I have to go anywhere by bus or walk. There I had heat and air-conditioning and a telephone. Huecorio has one phone, in the schoolhouse, but it's been out of order for three or four years." Calls had to be made at the villa of a Mexican general's widow, who lived in a Spanish-style hilltop mansion about a quarter mile from the village; with perseverance her servants could usually find whoever was being phoned, at least to tell them to call back. With their savings, Huecorio's illegal immigrants had bought land, bulls, dairy cows, and horses. One man had purchased an irrigation pump and tripled the productivity of his truck garden. Another bought a house for $2,500, which he rented for $20 a month. One man bought a sewing machine, gave up farm labor, and became a tailor. Others opened *tiendas,* or small shops. Two got taxis. In effect, Huecorio's illegal migration proved to be a remarkably efficient form of foreign aid, and helped, by providing us with cheap labor, to fight inflation.

Everybody, it seemed, sooner or later came home again. When I asked Aurelio why, he said, "I mean people aren't laughing all the time, but they're happier here. Because they don't have to worry like people in L.A. do. Like, if I lose my job, how am I going to pay the rent?" We talked a lot about it over tequila in one of the village *tiendas* in the evening; the consensus among men who had worked in *el norte* seemed to be that Huecorio was the place where they were born, where they had their homes, land, animals, and permanent livelihood, and where there was safety for them and tranquillity. As long as they could survive in the village, they would stay. In Huecorio, they had dignity.

A few were bitter about abuses they had suffered as illegal immigrants—the bribes they had to pay corrupt Tijuana policemen, or the occasions they got caught and slapped around by American immigration agents or were jailed or just trucked back across the border. A few were chauvinistic, saying, "I am a Mexican, and I would not change my country for anything." There were *macho* sentiments—"An American woman rules the house, but here a man is boss"—or objections to all the regulations and taxes of American life—"I felt like a slave." What surprised me was how many had enjoyed life in California or Texas and would hear no criticism of it. One of these was Fidel, a father of nine children with whom I threshed wheat for some days. Fidel, a plump middle-aged man and one of Huecorio's more solid citizens, was a veteran of six trips, some of them as far north as Illinois, Wisconsin and Montana. "I liked everything about *el norte,*" he said. "Nobody treated me badly and I said good-bye to ignorance. Best of all, there was sufficient work for decent pay." In 1980 he went back for a seventh stay.

Huecorio had avoided a major crisis, but there were indications that one might be ahead. There was an acute land shortage—only 915 acres of arable soil, or less than one acre per person. This land, moreover, ranged from irrigated, alluvial soil along the lake shore, where an acre was worth something, up to wind-and-water-eroded plots on the volcano slopes, extremely poor land that produced little. After the Revolution, three acres of land apiece from a confiscated *hacienda* were allocated to 134 Huecorio families (I stayed for a time in a motel run by the son of the dispossessed *haciendero*). The average holding today is just thirteen often badly eroded acres per family, three fewer than Mexico's national average. Even then, the land is fragmented, with each family's holding consisting of five or six widely scattered plots. The wheat field of Aurelio's grandparents, for instance, was way up on the volcano's slopes; we had to begin each day with a steep one-hour climb. (I kept hoping the volcano really *was* extinct.)

Anthropological studies going back fifty years have found that Mexico's village women have long wanted fewer children. They held back from using contraceptives because of the opposition of the Roman Catholic church, but more important, its reflection in community pressure. In Huecorio, as in all villages, I found fear of the neighbors' censure or "What will people say?" is a far more potent force than government fiat or fear of God. It is this kind of *social* pressure, which village priests exercise against contraception, that is the main obstacle in Latin America (and in outlying Catholic societies such as the Philippines).

Huecorio by the late 1970s had 134 full-time farmers, exactly what it had in 1922. But now there were 38 part-time cultivators and just over 60 field laborers, a sharp rise. It was evident that agriculture had become increasingly labor-intensive to absorb more hands. The population had grown from 421 in 1922 to 1,100. With little drop in the extremely high birth rate or family size, the only alternatives for Huecorio's people were to search for nonfarming jobs, educate their children better or migrate either to Mexico City and other towns or, seasonally, to the United States. Huecorio had done all three. In 1962 there were only three college graduates; two decades later the village had produced a doctor, two lawyers and half a dozen engineers. Another 85 men and 14 women worked in Mexico City or other urban centers, often leaving their families behind.

Mexico City remains one alternative, but its population is said to be 15 million or more (estimates go from 12 million to 17 million) and, at current rates of growth, is doubling every six years. It will soon be the earth's largest city. Already air pollution from industry and more than a million and a half cars at an altitude of eight thousand feet gives Mexico City the worst eye-burning, throat-searing smog I've seen anywhere in the world. The thinner oxygen at the high altitude makes people more susceptible to upper respiratory disorders; some days when you stepped out of the Hotel Geneve in the city's fashionable Zona Rosa, the sky looked yellow and smog misted over buildings a block away.

Another grim adjustment to overpopulation has come in diet. Meals in Huecorio seem ample compared to villages in other countries—Mexicans are always eating—but nutritionists say this apparent abundance is illusory and about 4 percent of the village people suffer from malnutrition. Alarmingly, Huecorio consumes only 15 percent of the food it grows. An average Mexican eats just under a quarter of a pound of maize each day; Huecorio can grow only enough for 150 days a year. The rest, like Mexico itself, it has to buy outside. This means selling much of its fruit, vegetables, eggs, milk, pigs, cattle and fish to pay for enough maize. More and more, Mexico depends on the United States for food, a record 9.5 million tons of it in 1980; Americans also took 70 percent of Mexico's exports, supplied 60 percent of its imports and accounted for almost 70 percent of Mexico's $6.8 billion in investment from abroad. Such are the geopolitical facts of life ever since we finished taking half of Mexico's territory 128 years ago. (Texas won its independence in 1836, the Oregon Territory went in 1846, California and the Southwest changed hands in the Guadalupe-Hidalgo Treaty of 1848 and the Gadsden Purchase of 1853.) We tend to forget this expansionism; Mexicans talk as if it were only yesterday. Someday, if immigration gets really out of hand, they may win it back simply by outvoting the Anglos.

Poor Mexico, as the old saying goes—so far from God and so close to the United States. Huecorio's fate and our own would be bound together even without the 600,000 barrels a day of Mexican oil we were getting in 1980. If Pope John Paul II had a change of heart about contraception, if scientists could come up with technology to grow more on small, dry-land holdings with scanty rain, if Mexico used its oil money to invest in agriculture and reconstituted its worn-out soils, then things might get better in Huecorio so its men could stay at home. Decentralized industry could be the answer. In the meantime, before oil can enrich the impoverished countryside, many of the too-many Mexicans will suffer. Instead of anti-wetback outcries, we need to help Mexico in the task of education, organization and management so that enough of the oil money eventually finds its way into the pockets of the poor. Otherwise we'll all be in real trouble.

Always, when the day begins, the men of Grand Gaube, a fishing village founded by freed African slaves a century ago, set forth into their island's lagoon in small wooden pirogues. Most sail just as dawn is breaking. Like Karl, who dives for octopus, they make their way, half asleep, from their thatched huts through the whispering casuarina trees to the cove where the boats are anchored. On one shoulder, Karl carries mast, furled sail and diving gear. I follow with snorkeling mask and fins.

It scarcely seems possible that twelve years have gone by. Then, in the last months of 1969, Octave, Prem, George, Karl and I set forth in this same way every morning; our last expedition, when a storm came up at sea on New Year's Eve, I had put into a book. Now Octave of the high spirits and splendid physique was a land-bound mason, married, with several children, grown placid and remarkably fat. Prem, the Hindu among us, was in London studying law. George fished alone with a line. Only Karl, a surly, untalkative youth of twenty then, was still at it. From the day I returned, taking a beach hut near the water, Karl came to get me every morning, taciturn but welcoming. Although Karl made his living at it, there was a hint of the mutually understood ritual about our daily fishing trips this time, as if, while we knew we could not recover the past, we could at least try to repeat it.

So that each day, as before in semidarkness, we would hear the dip and push of oars and the gruff, familiar greetings from one boat to another in the local Creole *patois*. The older men still fished with lines or cages, though nets were now forbidden many months each year. Much larger numbers of younger men than before now dove underwater to spear octopus or harpoon fish, a measure of how badly the lagoon had been depleted. They did not go far out. Beyond the reef, a half mile from shore, the coral fell precipitously into the abyss. Mauritius, almost entirely ringed with coral reefs enclosing shallow lagoons of clear blue-green water, is the exposed tip of a volcanic colossus jutting up from an ocean floor two thousand fathoms below.

To Karl, who has been diving almost daily for fifteen years, the underwater topography of the lagoon is as familiar as the island's craggy peaks, vast sugar plantations, forests and scattered towns. Each pass through the reef has its own character. Barracuda Pass used to deserve its name; Karl says fewer of the *lichen tazar,* dog barracuda, which used to send us scrambling back into the boat, are to be seen now. Kalodin, where I saw a six-foot shark just a few yards away in 1969, is light and shallow. Ramzan is all caves and tunnels, where nasty lamprey eels may dwell. Basmaurice is a sunken isle. Troualbert, named after London's Albert Hall, is the most beautiful, a deep break in the coral, shaped like a giant green underwater amphitheater, misty and silent.

Once the mast is stepped and the boom rigged, Karl's old patched sail draws the trade wind and the pirogue skims over the water, waves slapping the bow. More often than not this time we go with Karl's friend, Fleriot, who owns a new Johnson motor. No one but me misses the sail. At thirty, Karl's chocolate-brown face scarcely looks older than it did when he was twenty; his eyes are still a startling blue. Thick black curly hair frames a face that is both Gallic and African and neither—the humorous, hot-blooded, sad, patient face of the Indian Ocean Creole. Karl has changed: he no longer is forever getting into drunken fights and spending a night in jail as before; nor does he joke as he did ten years ago, teasing George about masturbation and shocking the prim Prem with stories of his sexual exploits.

Once the sun appears, blindingly over the horizon as we near the crashing reef, we sometimes stop to watch a small fleet of net fishermen moving into the tossing waves. Net fishing is only done for a few months each year now, to spare the depleted fish. These men splash their long wooden gaffs on the water's surface, hiss and beat *batage* sticks against the wooden seats like jazz drummers, to frighten the fish into their nets. Tossed into the foaming spray, these nets flash with beaded light; everything glitters in the wet sunshine.

After watching them haul in a netful of fish, we sail on to a shallower place where the floor of the lagoon is brilliant with open stretches of white sand and yellow seaweed, like a desert landscape. The water is pale green, only six or seven feet deep, and Karl is soon paddling back and forth steadily, his spear in his left hand as he swims with his right arm, his blue fins leaving luminescent bubbles in their wake. He searches the coral formations for a glimpse of octopus eyes. I follow him, preferring several hours' swimming in the salty sea to staying in the boat, which will soon be crawling with a dozen half-dead octopi. A small octopus under a flat rock, feeling Karl's shock waves, turns from dark brown into a pale gray and squeezes itself softly into the dark crevice of the rocks that are its home. But too late. Karl's barbed *larfine* cuts through the water and pins the octopus to the coral. Karl plunges the point in and out as a cloud of brown ink spreads across the water. Still the creature lives on, its three-foot tentacles clutching at Karl's arm as he rips it off the *larfine* and, holding it away from himself as best he can, carries it back to the boat with one hand. There he has to rip away the tentacles again. If Fleriot is along he beats the squirming head with a tiller stick, rips the octopus inside out and tosses it to the bottom of the hull, where the tentacles keep clutching, not relaxing until the octopus is dead.

These days, often by himself, Karl hunts just three or four hours until he has a dozen or so octopi for a combined weight of six or seven kilograms. The catch will go to Bennie, the Hindu fishmonger, back at the cove. By noon, satisfied he has enough, Karl sails back to Grand Gaube, content now that the day's work is over. Karl sings a *sega*, the Creoles' own fast, calypso-like music: "The Heavens have chosen my island to make Paradise . . ."

Mauritius comes close. A fisherman once told Mark Twain, when he came on a visit, "Mauritius was made first and then Heaven; and Heaven was copied after it." Tiny (thirty-eight miles long, twenty-nine miles wide) and remote (twelve hundred miles out in the Indian Ocean from the eastern coast of southern Africa), it is one of a scattered group of islands known as the Mascarenes. Justly famous for its many waterfalls, shooting stars, and frequent rainbows (these have something to do with the mist; we saw splendid ones almost every day), it has an eerie sense of spacelessness and timelessness, with its fog and mists swirling slowly about the green volcanic mountains. Charles Darwin noted in his H.M.S. *Beagle* diary that "masses of white clouds were collected around these pinnacles, as if merely for the sake of pleasing a stranger's eye."

Seen from a jet, the island looks so small and isolated, it seems like a sea bird resting on the waves. This and its people—by an accident of history the 900,000 inhabitants of Mauritius include Chinese, Indians, Arabs, Africans, and Europeans—give the island its special fascination: it is uncannily like the world in microcosm. Indeed, that is why I went there twelve years ago, to study the population crisis. The World

Bank's then new population division had suggested I go, saying that Mauritius was "perhaps experiencing the first true Malthusian breakdown." I went and it was. Its future prospects looked hopeless. Flying in from Bombay in 1979, after an absence of ten years, as our jet approached to land, I was reminded once again of how the Earth must look to astronauts: small, finite, fragile, its air and clouds, oceans and rivers, the great swirls of white against bright blue surfaces bringing home the planet's inescapable unity. I always thought poet Archibald MacLeish got it right. Inspired by televised shots of man's first view of earth from the moon on Christmas Eve, 1968, MacLeish wrote: "Riders on the earth together, brothers in that bright loveliness in the eternal cold . . ."

Mauritius has the same gaps of money, race, power and ideology that divide the planet, and its hopes of survival are rooted in the same need to curb births, reshape the economic processes and remedy the grosser inequities. Astonishingly, on such a small island, the rich, who are almost all white, have their golf, theater, cars, upland chateaus and coastal beachhouses, read *The Economist* and *Le Monde*, buy their clothes, books and art in London and Paris, and are conversant with the latest Ingmar Bergman film or Saul Bellow novel. The poor—black, brown, and yellow—often exist on bare subsistence, and some, in their small stone or wooden huts, have hungry children. Yet all the island's people share the same TV, the same network of modern roads and buses, the same schools, the same jet airport, and the economic interdependence that has made the earth itself so intimate and vulnerable a place to live.

How did this happen, so far away from anywhere? Until the Age of Discovery, Mauritius was unpeopled. It was so cut off that its ecosystem developed separately, and unique species of birds, insects and reptiles lived here, including the now-extinct dodo. That plump bird with the twisted beak danced the quadrille with Alice. It was not until the development of lucrative sugar plantations in the Caribbean that Europeans settled Mauritius. The Dutch came first, but were driven away by rats from their ships which, unchecked by natural enemies, multiplied. Then came the French, who brought mongooses; after many nobles fled to the island during the revolution of 1789, it was declared an independent colony with ten thousand Frenchmen and thirty thousand African slaves. The British seized it as a crown colony in the early nineteenth century, but aside from ruling Mauritius and demanding a share of the sugar profits, they made no attempt to settle. They left it to the French and their black slaves to transform its rocky, inhospitable soil into great plantations. Then, under pressure from liberal London, slavery was abolished. The freed slaves, now mostly Creoles of mixed French and African blood, deserted the plantations forever, moving into fishing villages along the coast, like Grand Gaube, or working as artisans or dockers. The French were forced, as they were in the Caribbean, and as the British were there and in the Fijis, to bring indentured Hindu and Moslem caneworkers from India; by 1860 the population reached 160,000 and Chinese and Arab traders came to cater to its needs.

After World War I, sugar prices soared, and the French plantation owners grew very rich, building themselves fabulous estates in the misty upper reaches of the island. The British built roads, schools, hospitals, water and sanitation systems, and, with DDT, eradicated malaria. The mortality rate plummeted. Demographers, noting the population passed 420,000 by 1944 and was pushing 800,000 by 1969, projected it would reach a "catastrophic" 2 million by 1982. Britain hastily granted Mauritius independence, setting off riots because few wanted it. A Hindu doctor who had lived fourteen years in London and had attacked "British imperialism," Seewoosagur Ramgoolam, was knighted by Queen Elizabeth and was elected the island's first Prime Minister. The Indian caneworkers now had a slight majority of the votes, a strange denouement in a society where the French had brought their language, culture, and miscegenation, and the British their ideas of human rights and liberal government, racial prejudice, and the color bar.

Mauritius became the United Nations' fifth smallest member. Soon an unending stream of experts were arriving from UNDP, UNESCO, UNICEF, EPTA, ILO, FAO, IBRD, IDA and WHO (in 1980 they were still coming). Russian and American naval ships began to call. Even the Chinese, Libyans and Egyptians opened embassies, making the people of Port Louis, the harbor and only town of any size, seem like a cast of characters in search of a Graham Greene novel. When I first came in 1969—a year after independence—Mauritius numbered 420,000 Hindus—who ran the government; 10,000 whites—who ran everything else; just under 140,000 Moslems; 25,000 Chinese and 230,000 African-descended Creoles. Aside from 70,000 caneworkers and 4,000 fishermen, there was little employment. Almost 35,000 were on the government payroll; another 15,000 were on public relief.

In Grand Gaube, where I spent five months, the old fishermen spoke of the coming Apocalypse and the young of impending revolution. A new Mouvement Militant Mauricien, known as the MMM, called for violence "to sweep all the capitalists aside." It was led by a young white of French descent who had taken part in the May 1968 Paris riots. Many of the rich were fleeing to South Africa. A fisherman told me, "There is talk of rising up and killing all the whites." If Mauritius was a preview of what to expect in an overpopulated future, we were in trouble.

*

Now, twelve years later, Mauritius is still, in its fashion, a microcosm of the world. It is doing unexpectedly well. The birthrate has plummeted from 48 to 23 per 1,000; it looks like population will stabilize at about a million. Contraception has won the same acceptance it is starting to win everywhere in the world. The island has been made another tax-free Hong Kong, luring foreign capital with its concessions; imported wool has made tropical Mauritius the world's eighth largest maker of sweaters. Tourism has grown so fast—luxury hotels have sprung up along the beaches—that it is hard to get air bookings in and out. A sugar boom in 1973–74, when record crops happily coincided with record world prices, fueled the entire island economy: new houses are everywhere, there is heavy traffic of mostly new cars and trucks on the roads, and most people voice a generally-held feeling of well-being. Politically, the MMM has transformed itself from a group of hotheaded young revolutionaries into a labor party that stands for elections; its unions now control the ports and buses. In the last general election the MMM got more votes than any other single party and there are some expectations it could win complete control of the government in the early 1980s. What would happen to the Hindu-white arrangement that has always kept the island going then? If it fell, would Mauritius, like Madagascar or Tanzania, have a socialist regime? To the whites, who keep bank accounts and apartments in London and Paris, this question is everything. In Grand Gaube, where the fishermen will sail their boats into the lagoon each day no matter who runs the island, it counts for little. If the MMM came in, the fishermen might at last get help in buying bigger boats, better nets and motors.

For a fishing village, like all villages, has its own rhythms, as I suspect it always will. Life is hard; some days Karl catches almost nothing; mishaps at sea can result in drownings. And the poorest people on the island can be the most extravagant, going barefoot but paying ten dollars to dance all night at a village *bal*. Karl and his friends may get into drunken brawls and knife fights Saturday nights, but they always meekly follow their wives to six A.M. mass Sunday mornings. Rare among the world's villagers, men like Karl place little value on money; no fisherman, however poor, will ever accept payment for sailing with him. A former American diplomat in Mauritius, who has settled since his retirement in a villa near Grand Gaube, agreed with me that these poor Creoles, of all Mauritians, lead the most satisfying lives.

Life is a succession of todays: the pines, coves, silence, sea; the pleasure of sailing across the dazzling blue-green water of the lagoon; the thrill of maneuvering the boats to catch the shoals of fish and tossing the nets into the crashing surf; the adventure of diving in the milky-green silent underwater world along the reef, where cliffs of pink, yellow and lavender coral glow in prisms of sunlight, and the rampart falls to the blue-dark depths of the ocean beyond; the sudden, spontaneous bursts of joy, jokes and singing coming home with a good catch.

Mauritius is beautiful, especially sailing in the lagoon. There is no other adjective: it is not just scenic, picturesque or charming. Almost every day as you sail back to the cove at midday, after a morning's adventure in the strange, silent, underwater world, amidst the fishermen's *sega* songs and humorous spirits, you get an almost painful feeling that every second left is precious and you want to stay there in the boat, sailing across the water in the bright sunshine with these friends, just as you are, forever. The fishermen feel it too; much of their singing is of the island's beauty. There is a simple truth about it, far removed from our own over-complex twentieth-century ways. Riders together.

The Shah of Iran, in his thirty-seven years of rule—secret police and torture aside—did just about all the things any developing country might expect of its leader: he carried out sweeping land reform to end a feudal Islamic system of near serfdom, sent huge numbers of students to learn the West's technology, did much to liberate his country's women and created a modern urban middle class. He presided over an Iran where real income had been rising at over 15 percent a year.

Yet his people wanted to kill him. The Shah's fall questions the twentieth-century assumption that a people who are growing richer will support their leader. In Asia this assumption still seems valid; a steady rise in GNP is the best prop for semi-dictators. Even in Iran we don't yet fully know how false it proved to be; it will be a long time before the peasants and the middle class get to tell their story. Ayatollah Khomeini and his *mullahs* took over mostly with the support of city slum dwellers. But it does raise the question whether growth that is fast enough to hold back communist revolution is so fast that it causes unbearable strains on Islam, especially out in the villages.

Until, like chain lightning, street mobs in one Moslem country after another took to sporadic rioting, rulers of these countries would seldom admit to the existence of an Islamic revival. The stock answer, including the Shah's, was that since they and their countrymen were devout Moslems already, there was nothing to be revived. And, indeed, compared to present-day Christianity, Islam is woven deep into the fabric of a Moslem state. The rituals—the profession of faith, fasting, pilgrimage, alms-giving—are widely observed; most people would declare themselves believers. Yet the new vitality and political clout of fundamentalist Moslem groups in countries stretching from Mauritania to Malaysia by way of Egypt, Turkey, Iran and Pakistan can no longer be written off as coincidental. Some observers of Islam, such as *The Economist*'s Levant correspondent, Godfrey Jansen, say what is happening is that the assertion of Islam's relevance to politics and to law is breaking through the weakening structures of several Moslem states at the same moment, most spectacularly in Iran. Khomeini himself seemed likely to be one of those media creations that come and go with such speed, especially since the Shah's death in 1980 deprived him of his main issue. However, the Islamic challenge he represents is likely to be with us from now on. Since about one-fifth of the world's people are Moslem (there are about 750 million Moslems living in seventy countries), this resurgence of Islam commands our attention.

The visions of crazed, hysterical mobs, of bearded men in robes and turbans, of stoned adulteresses, flogged criminals, blood dripping from a convicted thief's amputated hands, are barbarous and atavistic. What matters most about the new militancy is that it is a form of reaction, of disillusionment with the process of modernization, industrialization, urbanization, Westernization—call it what you will—and the fear that older values are about to be irrevocably lost in the stampede toward a consumer society. Further, this disillusionment can be linked, as Khomeini tried to do, with racial feeling. The reaction was so violent in Iran because the Shah and his men tried to yank the country into the modern world ahead of the crowd. What the Shah tried to do, I feel, did not so much bring about his downfall as the speed and manner of the yanking; ordinary people will sacrifice a lot if they feel they are being deprived of their dignity. As the Shah revealingly told Barbara Walters in an off-camera remark not long after his fall, "If only I had had three more years. Then they would have known what it was I wanted to do." A year later he said in a David Frost interview, "It was not so much a question of thinking it was time to go, rather I was thinking it was like an end to something; of me, an era, of something." He hadn't grasped his people's need for dignity and the confidence they badly required to be carried along with him.

Let us take one specific episode: the attempted agricultural transformation of Khuzestan, the southwesternmost desert province of Iran, where all the oil and Arabs are. During the past year Khuzestan has become familiar the world over as the battleground of the Iran-Iraq war. In the winter of 1970–71, I lived for some months there in a village called Shush-Daniel; I went back again in 1974. Since it is less than half an hour's drive from Dezful, the village almost certainly was overrun by Iraqi troops, though I've been unable to confirm this. It was, of course, a peaceful backwater a decade ago; yet on both visits you could already see that Iran was trying to do too much too fast, was stumbling and could lose its footing altogether.

Khuzestan wasn't always a desert. First settled around 8000 B.C., it was transformed into a green and fruitful plain by the Elamite peoples who, about 4000 B.C., invented the decimal system and probably invented irrigation. Together with the Sumerians less than one hundred miles to the west, the Elamites founded civilization. Shush-Daniel, now just a small village, was the great Biblical city of Susa, which survived as a populous urban center for five thousand years, longer than any other city has ever managed to survive. The Assyrians destroyed it in 640 B.C., killing or carrying off all its people. But in 521 B.C., Darius the Great rebuilt it and established his Achaemenian court there; the agriculturally revived region became the breadbasket of the Persian Empire. Incredibly, the Sushiana plain—you can drive all around it in a day—has been either ruled or plundered by the Elamites, Sumerians, Babylonians, Assyrians, Medes, Persians, Parthians, Greeks, Sassanians, Romans, Arabs, Mongols and Tamerlane. And now the Iraqis.

Susa's great palaces mysteriously crumbled to dust, its fertile land faded into desert and its population vanished in the fourteenth century. Nobody knows why. What is known is that a long agricultural decline began with the Arab conquest of Persia and its conversion to Islam in the seventh century. The peasants were too heavily taxed, the Caliphate in Baghdad grew too corrupt and inefficient, salinity ruined the land and imported slave labor proved no salvation. Then as now, Islamic fundamentalism and technology proved incompatible.

Why all this history matters is that it formed the mind of Mohammed Reza Shah Pahlavi. Even as a young man he spoke of Khuzestan as Iran's "future salvation." A sickly boy who read a lot, he vowed to someday recapture the "great civilizations" of the Elamites and Achaemenians. When this son of a onetime army sergeant chose to be known as His Imperial Majesty, King of Kings, Light of the Aryans, he did so self-consciously; these were the titles of Darius the Great. The same was true of the fantastically extravagant 1971 celebration at Persepolis of the anniversary of the founding of the Persian Empire 2,500 years before. The Shah had a dream: to create another Persia.

To understand this dream, forget tacky Tehran (which looks like the seedier side of Chicago in 1932) and go to the ruins of Susa, a huge, mile-long plateau composed entirely of rubble, potsherds and human bones. Or enter the throne room of Darius, excavated in 1970, so well described in the Book of Esther:

> There were white cotton curtains and blue hangings caught up with cords of fine linen and purple to silver rings and marble pillars, and also couches of gold and silver on a mosaic pavement of porphyry, marble, mother-of-pearl and precious stones. Drinks were served in golden goblets. . . .

From this vast room, in those days set in palm and cypress gardens, but with the same view you get today of the snow-peaked Zagros Mountains and with some of those same marble pillars you can still see lying around, Cyrus freed the Jews from Babylon, the Prophet Daniel advised the court (his tomb is in the village), and Esther, hailed by Jews at Purim, ruled as the queen to Darius' son, Xerxes (Ahasuerus in the Bible), the same Xerxes whose sack of Athens galvanized the Greeks into the Age of Pericles; it was in this same room, on one spectacular day in 325 B.C., that Alexander the Great and ten thousand of his Greek soldiers took Persian brides to fuse the European and Asian races. (Alexander lingered on for two more years, setting fire to Persepolis, probably when drunk, before setting out for Carthage, but dying on the way in Babylon, at the age of thirty-two.)

But for Susa all this was practically modern history; it had been a city for well over three thousand years by then, a contemporary to Ur of the Chaldeans. Its great temple, Dur Untashi, not fully unearthed until 1962, is the biggest and best preserved of some twenty *ziggurats*, or pyramid-like earthen temples, found on the Mesopotamian plain. Predating even Egypt's pyramids, these man-made mountains, our first attempt at monumental architecture, inspired the Tower of Babel legend. (The uppermost tier, towering 165 feet in the sky, was painted blue, so it did indeed seem to be "a tower with its top in the heavens.")

What is today Khuzestan's lifeless desert—grassless, empty and sandy if unirrigated—was a watered green plain as far back as the later chapters in the Book of Genesis; it remained cultivated land for almost ten thousand years, a staggeringly long period of time. A few canals, weirs and underground tunnels, part of a huge irrigation system built by seventy thousand captured Roman legionnaires under the Sassanians, are still in use near the town of Dezful. Who can blame the Shah for wanting to make such a desert bloom again?

*

In Khuzestan—and the Shah spent a lot of time at his winter palace there, sometimes taking long walks through the ruins of Susa (watched by the shades of Cambyses' royal bodyguard, the famed "Ten Thousand Immortals"?)—you can set foot into the ancient past in an eerily unattended, on-your-own fashion as you rarely can do elsewhere, even in Egypt's most labyrinthine and spooky pharaonic tombs, where there are usually lots of tourists and guides about. Once, while I was spending some weeks with a family of Arab Bedouin shepherds, we grazed our flock near Dur Untashi, which the Bedouins simply called Chogha Zanbil, "overturned basket of earth." What looked like sand dunes as we approached turned out to be heaps of debris; shards of glazed blue and green pottery, pieces of bone that crumbled between your fingers, bits of black obsidian. The shepherds looked for copper coins; these could be sold in the Shush market. At last, when we got close enough and climbed to the top of a dune, there it was: the temple in the desert, rising singular and splendid from perfectly flat ground, ringed with crumbling walls and ceremonial staircases, fully sixteen or seventeen stories high. When I first caught sight of it, the best I could do, after a childhood of old Claudette Colbert and Elissa Landi movies, was cry out, "My God, it looks like a Cecil B. De Mille set!" Or even more, like D. W. Griffith's huge Babylonian set in *Intolerance*—so big, as Pauline Kael put it, neither the camera nor Mae Marsh and the other players seemed "to know what to do with it." Everybody was reduced, just as we were now, to the size of ants.

We decided to explore the royal Elamite catacombs beneath the temple. One of the shepherds explained, "This place is very old. Before the Prophet Daniel." Nobody else seemed to be about for miles around and I was afraid we might run into hyenas; but curiosity overcame fear and we descended tremendously long steep stairwells, lighting our way with torches of sagebrush. The torches kept sputtering out, but in repeated scary sorties, we discovered three gigantic halls deep underground, each connected to the others by low, narrow tunnels. The air was rotten and pestilential; the catacombs were at least three thousand years old, yet if you touched a wall the white gypsum came off on your fingers, it was so perfectly preserved. There were pits of ashes and great sinister-looking slabs of marble.

Assurbanipal, the Assyrian ruler, when he destroyed Elam in 640 B.C., ransacked these catacombs to unearth the bones of what were then ancient Elamite heroes; he took them back to Nineveh, where libations were offered to awaken the souls of the dead, so they could taste the bitterness of defeat. Assurbanipal boasted to posterity, in words carved in stone:

> The dust of the cities of Elam, I have taken it all away to the country of Assur . . . I deprived the country of the presence of cattle and of sheep and of the sound of joyous music. I have allowed wild beasts, serpents, the animals of the desert and gazelles to occupy it.

He'd done that all right. There we were, in 1971, precisely 2,611 years later and, except for the temple in the desert, there wasn't a sign of life anywhere save for a few wandering Bedouin nomads, hyenas, jackals—and me. I sang a few bars of "Strike Up the Band!" and shouted into the void, "Take that, Assurbanipal, wherever you are!"

The life of these Bedouins was Biblical and harsh. We slept in the black tents of three brothers, Yahkoub, Husein and Kazim, whose cousin, Sherif, was my interpreter-guide (and protector; among the Bedouins you needed a formal introduction or you were robbed and had your throat slit). The brothers' herd of four hundred sheep provided meat to eat, wool for clothing and cash for wheat, sugar and tea. Yahkoub, the youngest and our favorite (we secretly tried to teach him to read), told me, "If a man has enough sheep, he is in need of nothing more. Some Bedouins say we have too many sheep and every year, if the rains are few and the government takes more land to irrigate and farm, there is less and less grass. But I say to them, 'Who gives the grass, you or Allah?'"

We slept on rugs and carpets right on the desert sand; it was freezing in the early morning as the icy cold came up from the ground; I soon suffered lumbago, shuffling around in the mornings half bent over like an old man (who thought the Sheik of Araby romantic?); it still bothers me a bit on rainy days. After splashing some cold water on one's face and a hurried breakfast of sweetened tea and unleavened bread, we spent the whole day walking with the sheep, hoping Yahkoub and Husein would leadeth us on to green pastures. Yahkoub ran endlessly back and forth with his rod and staff, his long woolen robes flapping, trying to close up the herd and shoo ahead laggards and strays. Amazingly, he could talk to the sheep; a certain high-pitched squeal and they would all stop and graze; another weird cry and they were all up on their feet and moving out. Often Yahkoub

played upon a reed flute he had made himself; the melody was simple
and strange, like the first music known to man. Once a sudden thun-
derstorm came up and, without shelter in the perfectly flat plain, we
had to run and dive into a shallow ditch. Just as the lightning was
crackling all around, a ewe gave birth. Yahkoub ran to help, gently
drawing a fleecy black lamb from the womb. I watched, astonished, as
the lamb at once shivered, wagged its tail and looked around at the
universe with seeming enthusiasm—or maybe dismay. Once the ewe
had licked it clean, Yahkoub wrapped the lamb inside the folds of his
cloak, where he carried it to keep it warm until we got back to the
tents that night.

This is a book about villages and nomadic Bedouins do not really
qualify; their way of life is older and more brutal. Husein, as the eldest
brother, had the authority for all daily decisions as to where to seek
pasture or pitch tents. He also meted out cruel justice, beating his wife
if she forgot to tether a donkey or leaving his near-blind old mother,
too frail to walk any more, in a corner all day like a heap of filthy
rags, unhelped and unattended. After one of the dogs attacked and
killed a sheep, Husein put the animal in a deep pit with his victim's
carcass; the dog ate until the bones were picked clean and then he was
left to starve; every night we could hear him howling and whimpering.
Sherif, whose family had left the nomadic life to live in Shush, admired the Bedouins' predatory ways. "In the old days," he said, "all
the Bedouins were hunters, warriors and bandits, all crafty, brave
men. No digging in the ground, no planting, no herding sheep, just
riding up and taking what they wanted." The occasional Bedouin
horsemen's band still came in and raided Shush, shooting up the streets
and robbing a few houses on the outskirts. To the Arab shepherds,
Iran meant the local Persian soldiers, whom they feared and hated. If
sheep strayed into any settled farmer's field, these soldiers would beat
the Bedouins and try to steal a sheep or two. The Shah was a very distant figure; none of the dialogue I took down among the herdsmen
mentioned him.

*

In his dream to make the desert bloom again, the Shah turned to
David E. Lilienthal, former chairman of the Tennessee Valley Authority. In 1959 Lilienthal came up with an ambitious plan to reir-
rigate northern Khuzestan with dams and canals. Work on these went
ahead, but initial attempts to quickly modernize the indigenous vil-

lagers failed. Impatient, the Shah brought in privately financed American and British companies which were given the task of creating big agribusinesses of the kind that had transformed the desert valleys of California. The existing villagers were told to hand over their small land holdings for wages and dividends; some got jobs with the big new mechanized company farms, many ultimately moved to Tehran and other cities (where, if jobless, they may have joined in the anti-Shah riots).

The three showpiece projects, just below Khuzestan's big new Dez Dam, part of the overall plan, were agribusiness outfits run by Shell Mitchell Cotts (British), Iran California (American) and Hashem Naraghi, an agile Iranian entrepreneur who had gone to the United States penniless after World War II and made a fortune out of almond growing. All were mammoth units of up to twenty thousand hectares each, all of it scientifically leveled by giant scrapers. George Wilson, then the seventy-eight-year-old retired president of the California Farm Bureau, told me why he had come to Khuzestan with Iran California: "Gol darn, I was helped as a boy without anything and I'd like to help others before I die. And I want to prove a point: that American technology is not enough if you want to get real production. The only way you'll really get it is to get American farmers in here with the equipment, financing, chemical fertilizer and know-how."

Even then, in 1971 when the agribusinesses were just getting started, Wilson had misgivings about how Iran was going about it. To make room for the three big British and American farms, Wilson had discovered, fifty-eight villages had been arbitrarily uprooted. The peasants were simply told they had to sell their land; few wanted to. They protested, but nobody aside from Wilson seemed to have paid any attention.

"I don't like it," Wilson confided to me. "We've got to help these farmers get back their own land. We've taken it away, now it's up to us to get it back to them. In our outfit, Iran California, we've got our sights set whereby in three years we can say to our best men, 'You take fifty acres. If in five years you can prove you're a good farmer, we'll lease it to you cheap.' There's been no trouble so far, but there will be if we don't establish a record of turning land back to these local villagers. Otherwise someday there'll be a revolution. We'll do it quietly and if it works, we'll do a little more. And when our time is up, we'll present everybody with a *fait accompli*. With all the new dams, land leveling, canals, access roads and modern farming methods, we can bring this desert back to life and eliminate the dangers of flood and drought for the first time ever. And with cold storage, packing and better seed selection, we can eliminate a 30 percent loss of production. We want to do better by these people than what's been done by 'em before."

Development, like hell, is approached along a road paved with good intentions. Why did the Shah turn to big foreign-run farms in the first place? Another side of the problem he faced was that his major land reform of the mid-1960s had given most of Iran's village families their own land. No doubt about it; it was one of the best land reforms of modern times. Before it, Khomeini-type ayatollahs had owned much of the land, accumulated by the mosques since early Moslem times, and the Iranian peasantry were little more than serfs; many were ill-treated. After his land reform—the Shah called it his White Revolution—Iran was mainly left with family-size farms which had to support six persons on five to seven acres. Irrigated land, which could be modernized quickly on small holdings, is scarce on the Iranian plateau. Then village Iran has an extremely diverse population. In Shush, for example, I stayed with a Kurd family, had an Arab interpreter and worked with farmers from the Lur and Bakhtiari tribes; there were also Turks and Baluchis. Each ethnic group had its own way of farming, all of them very backward.

The Shah was also trying to modernize his cities, to catch up with European industry, very fast. In the early 1970s, when he was making his crucial decisions about Khuzestan, the income of Iran's city people was going up five to ten times faster than village incomes. Rapid industrialization, with oil and gas paying the bills, was creating an intense demand for better food—meat, eggs, milk, fruit and vegetables—things denied to poor Iranians for centuries. The World Bank's agricultural economists kept warning that Iran should not try to meet this demand domestically. They argued that the Shah should concern himself instead with the impact upon the villagers of the cities' new wealth; they proposed providing more cash, credit and technical aid directly to the peasants who made up, and still do, six out of ten Iranians.

The Shah, eager to realize his lifelong dream of restoring Khuzestan, did not listen. To modernize the peasantry, he felt, would take at least a generation. Iran could not wait. A shortcut to self-sufficiency in food was heavy investment in modern agribusiness companies and big mechanized farm corporations. It is a mistake political leaders—in Russia, China, Egypt, Sudan, so many countries—keep making; it has never worked.

*

In the souls of the people the grapes of wrath are filling and growing heavy, growing heavy for the vintage.

—John Steinbeck

Damn Steinbeck. The Okies were dirty and ignorant; why some of those people lived just like animals. Sure, we turned 'em away. But only because we already had twenty more families living in the barn. I'll bet you almost every one of the children of those Okies went to college and got good jobs today.

—George Wilson, 1971

During the months I spent in Shush-Daniel that winter I took down many conversations among the villagers about the new agribusinesses. Here is an excerpt from one; the speakers include Karim, a short, stocky Kurd farmer, forty-six, with whom I was staying, who acted as interpreter; Murad, fifty, his neighbor, a Lur farmer; and Yusef, a younger man. All their faces were seamed and weathered by the desert sun and wind; all wore white cloths loosely wrapped about their heads.

"The Company, he lie," Murad said. "He tell the Shah he give good house, good money to these people if he take their house, their land. What he give? Nothing!" Murad had been farming all his life. His father was the first man to cultivate a wheat and vegetable patch at Shush; before that the village had been completely surrounded by sand. Yusef was working for Iran California as a driver, earning the equivalent in Persian riyals of four dollars a day.

"So what's better, your job or farming?" Karim asked.

"Farming is better."

"Damn you and your farming," Murad joked.

"No, *baba*," Yusef said earnestly. "I had twenty hectares of land in Safiabad. The Company took it. The government took my land and didn't pay. Just told me, 'You go and maybe afterward I'll give you some money.' Now at Iran California when the men cut fodder, I fill up the wagon and pull it back to the storehouse on the tractor. Drop off a load and go back."

"So what's good? Before or now?"

Yusef shrugged. "I don't know. Maybe before is better. Now I gotta buy clothes, milk, everything. I have money and after a couple of weeks I got nothing. I work eight hours, six days a week. Six in the morning the bus comes to take all the people. Come back at four."

"Who's making the money?" asked Karim.

"I dunno," said Yusef. "The Bank Melli pays you. Everybody has a card. You stand around the window until a man calls out your number —number two, number forty, number sixteen—like that, every fifteen days. Five o'clock get up, the bus comes at six. Go to sleep at nine, work every day but Friday. Before, back in my village, if a man wasn't busy, he could go to bed and get up when he felt like it."

Murad: "Those people who go to work with you on the bus in the morning, you know them?"

"The guys on my shift, I know."

Murad shook his head. "I work for myself. You work for the Company."

"What's better?" Karim asked. "To be with Iran California or Naraghi?"

"Iran California is better. Naraghi is hard-working. He drives his men hard. We work eight hours; with Naraghi it's ten hours a day."

"When they bulldozed your village at Safiabad," Murad asked, "what happened to the people?"

"I dunno. I went down to Abadan to look for a job. I went over to Kuwait for a year."

Karim: "I heard from some men at Safiabad that when Naraghi takes the land, the young men get jobs and the old men stay at home."

"Yah," Murad agreed. "If he takes the land, he takes a check from the bank, gives money. If a man has sons, working men, he gives them jobs."

"No, baba!" Yusef interrupted. "Naraghi he first gives a man money, a check, and after that he sells that man some house. They make every family a new house. My brother got one. He had to pay for it. He got paid for his land but he had to buy the new house to get a job. He's working for Naraghi as an irrigator. I myself was farming government land. I had no paper so I got nothing."

"No, baba!" Murad exclaimed angrily. "Your land in Safiabad, it's the same as our land here in Shush. Nobody here's got a paper. This land was not the government's before. It was desert, sand, nobody's land. This was for the people to water and plant. So they gotta pay you. You've got one God and one Shah. No more. They gotta pay you."

Such talk made Karim, who feared the ears of Savak, the Shah's secret police, uncomfortable. "Murad's an old man," he said. "Maybe Murad says . . . well, he's busy all the time cutting grass, cutting wheat. Murad doesn't know what he says."

Yusef changed the subject. "Some foreign people work at Iran California. American people. They eat different. I never tried that American food."

Murad laughed. "American people don't like a lazy man like you sitting around on the ground, Yusef. If not working, they want you to stand on your feet, not sit."

Yusef agreed. "If you sit and rest, the Americans look at their watches. They ask, 'Are you sick? Are you tired?'"

While I was still in Shush, word came down that the government would take the village's land to expand Iran California's huge farm, probably in one more year. It was all Karim could talk about; one thing he said stuck in my mind. "I don't know what's better," he began one day. "Before my father and Murad's father, they had land, they had cows, they had sheep. They don't work for no Company. They don't work for no other man. Now clothes are dear, food is dear. My boys, they gotta go work for the Company. It's good pay. But, you know, a man wants more, he gets more, then he's gotta pay more and it seems maybe he's back where he started." Karim spoke in the English he had picked up while working in the oil fields near Abadan.

"I think maybe it was always this way. Take before in the old times, before Darius and Alexander, maybe those old Elamite people, maybe they have trouble with the land like we do now. Maybe their king was like a big Company. He brings five thousand, ten thousand men and that king he don't put those men in the jailhouse, but the same like a jailhouse. Every morning that king gives those men a place to wash and a place to shave and he puts them on the road to work, puts them in the field to work and they go home at night, the same like a jail. That king don't need to pay his men much, only food to eat. These men they're cutting, digging, maybe make cement, make a roof, maybe they watch horses, watch sheep. After six o'clock, the king brings them back to the mess hall and back to jail. All those men, all they think about is, 'How much you gonna pay me?' And maybe after a while the king gives them a little money so they can send it home to their wives and children.

"I think Iran California is like that king. Iran California, he pays laborers maybe two hundred fifty riyals one day. Maybe that man is working all the time cutting sugar. If he cuts his foot, he gets paid. If he loses a leg, okay, Iran California pays for that. Maybe somebody's working in the sugar, he's dead in the sugar. The Company's gonna pay his family. So maybe that man who works for Iran California is like that man in the king's jailhouse in old, old times. He's in the jailhouse but life is easy, easy. I think it was always like that, always the same. A man wants to know, 'How much you gonna pay me?' And he gives that money to his wife and children and he knows that money is coming in.

"You take Murad. Murad is free. He don't work for nobody, no Company and no king. I work for him and I cut my foot and who's gonna pay me? Murad works for himself. Murad drops dead in his field, who's gonna pay his wife and children? Nobody.

"Now the big Company it's gonna come to Shush, take our land. It's no good for Murad and me. But maybe it's better for our boys. They get jobs. They get electricity, good water, they get schools. Maybe it's like the old king's jailhouse but they don't worry about Bedouins coming in and burning their house down. But they have to buy everything in the shop. Bread, tea, rice, everything. And if they want to get their money, they got to stand by a window like Yusef and some man calls out a number. That's no good. Before a free man don't have to do like that. So what is good?"

*

By 1976 all three of the big agribusinesses, including Iran California, had failed; the American and British farming experts went back home. Blame was put on the inevitable difficulties of managing such large-scale undertakings, misunderstandings over what the government promised and the owners expected, delays in the delivery of equipment and in canal building, and the salinity of the soil. A small experimental farm was carved from the land. The Shah's dream was dead.

I planned to return to Shush in January 1979. I was too late; the Shah fell that month. Sherif, who had written often, sent one last letter; all the foreigners, he said, even the French archeologists, were gone. No word about Karim, Murad, Yusef or Yahkoub, even before the war. At this writing, I do not know what has happened to them. Sand must be drifting over the great plateau of Susa, that fabulous rubbish heap of potsherds, broken bricks, fragments of marble pillars, shards of sickles and spears, human teeth and bones. One can only imagine the wind howling over the dunes, whirling up sand and dust; perhaps now and then an eagle circles or a murderous old hyena crawls out of its lair and trots across the wasteland. But mostly there must be a stillness settling like dust over the Mesopotamian plain, as if nothing had ever disturbed it.

"What are you doing?"

"Buldev's got a thorn in his foot. I'm trying to take it out."

Surjit looked at her husband with exasperation; he was squatting over the foot of their nephew, Buldev, probing for the thorn with a needle. "Now what?" Surjit asked herself. She was perched on her low footstool before the open fire, shucking peas and boiling potatoes for the evening curry. "Hurry up," Surjit called. "I want Buldev to carry fresh dirt to the cow shed. And I want to wash those clothes you're wearing. They're filthy."

"Shan't I even finish my work?" Saroop complained in his defeated way.

"Ouch, it hurts!" Buldev protested. He was a sturdy, muscular eighteen-year-old, whose father, an opium addict, had died of a police beating in jail, leaving Buldev landless and penniless; now he worked as Surjit's hired laborer. She was more dependent upon his strong back than she would admit.

"Hurry, hurry, get the dirt. Buldev, you still have to go and help Pala cut fodder before it gets dark." Satisfied to see Buldev rise and limp off, Surjit stirred the curry. Without her seeing to every little thing, she felt, the family would starve. Surjit was a handsome woman of forty with black hair and the high color of outdoor living and robust health. Beside her, Saroop looked much older; his once handsome face was worn and sunken from years of eating opium, his body wasted. Unlike her husband in his soiled clothes, Surjit, in a yellow *salwar-kameez* and fleecy white shawl, did not fit her surroundings: the mean little mud hut with its log beams aslant and its sagging thatched roof seemed about to collapse at any time. The farmstead was set in recently cleared jungle, far from the nearest neighbors. Everything about it looked makeshift. Behind the hut corrugated tin sheets propped up by stripped branches passed for a cattle shed. Here Surjit's two bullocks, a buffalo and a calf were tethered. *Charpoys,* string cots on which the family slept, were scattered about every which way in the yard, piled with touseled, dusty quilts and pillows. Surjit's hearth was black with soot and swarming with flies. Everything seemed harsh, blighted.

Saroop stood in the hut's doorway, stripping off his dirty shirt and unwinding his turban. Surjit watched her husband as he rolled up a tiny black pellet of opium and gulped it down with a glass of water; how emaciated he was becoming, she thought, cursing opium as she had done a thousand times. When her family visited, she would conceal all affection for Saroop, telling her father his opium cost only two rupees a day. "So it is all right," she would reason. "If you keep a daily laborer these days, it's five rupees in Bhadson. Whereas my husband is quite a good worker." Once it had been different; they were wed in 1947 just before India had been partitioned; Saroop had been a good catch, a rich landlord's son. When they suddenly had to flee from what was now Moslem Pakistan one day, leaving land, home, possessions, everything behind, Saroop had proved too soft to start in again; as a refugee his self-esteem had crumbled and he became addicted to opium. Surjit had gone the other way; she had hardened and now was fiercely determined to make something of herself and her family. She was prepared to be ruthless but it was not easy. "It's lonely here," she would often complain. "The children's grandma never visits us. She says she's got no company here and no new faces to see. And she's getting so fat, Saroop. Fat as a pig!"

What kept Surjit going were her two oldest sons, Pala and Kaka; they would soon be young men. A third boy, little Bara, had been born crippled, with a twisted leg. Surjit's oldest daughter was already married and lived in her husband's village; Guri, the younger girl, would someday do the same. As a refugee, Saroop had been given fifteen acres of land but even before the last two children were born he had mortgaged it heavily to buy opium. Surjit wrote in desperation to her father, Sadhu Singh, who came at once to find his daughter and her infant children close to starvation, without grain, cooking utensils or fodder. The father swept up the family, including Saroop, took them back to his own village, Ghungrali, and gave his son-in-law all the opium he wanted, telling him, "You enjoy yourself to the full; you be happy." In this state Saroop agreed to sign a *mukhiarmanan* or legal transfer of financial responsibility to Surjit. She promptly sold the mortgaged land and bought twenty acres in the jungle, where it was going cheap, having just been confiscated by the government from the estate of a bankrupt prince. Sadhu Singh and Surjit's brother,

Charan, bought bullocks, farm implements and cooking utensils and helped to clear the land. In the winter of 1969–70, Surjit was able to plant her first wheat crop on seventeen acres.

At that time I and my interpreter, Krishanjit Singh, were staying in Ghungrali, twenty-five miles away, doing the story on the Green Revolution which appears in the next chapter. A village, as I have said, is a man's world. It is even more so in the Punjab, where women are so sequestered one can by custom only speak to those older than oneself. Even Charan's wife, though she cooked and served our meals, kept her face covered when we were about. When Surjit invited us to come to Bhadson, I jumped at the chance. Without prying neighbors, Surjit felt largely free of village social pressures. She allowed us to smoke around her homestead—"We couldn't care less; as you see it's a lonely place"—and talked with us by the hour over endless cups of tea on the open veranda that served her as a kitchen. At the same time life in Bhadson was much harsher than in an established village; some nights jackals would come sniffing right up to the cots where we slept in the open. Surjit said her family rarely visited, explaining, "I don't know what will happen to the family. Father and Charan between them must spend twenty rupees by evening. They are racing to see who can ruin the family first. Ah, well, everybody has to hang himself. You know the saying, those who have twenty rupees in their pockets, they are kings in the Punjab and can stand around and order others."

Surjit told us of the long struggle to clear the land of trees and stumps; that year the boys had sown her first crop of new high-yield dwarf wheat from Mexico. The family's whole future depended on a good harvest as she had borrowed heavily to buy the new seeds and fertilizer. It was also evident, though Surjit did not speak about it, that much depended on the strength of Buldev. Surjit drove him fiercely though his foot became infected from the thorn.

She was soon relating her future dreams. "Now, as you see, brothers, I feel a little relieved. I had to really go through hell for years together. All the time I was praying to God, *Hey, Sadhe Padshah,* Oh, Holy King, shall I ever be able to see good days again? Now he has heard my appeal and after the harvest I'll be better off. I am only waiting for my children to grow up. Within a few years I shall be quite free of my burdens. I shall bring brides for Pala and Kaka and marry off this little girl. I'll just be sitting on a bed in the kitchen in a few more years. I'll just be sitting and sleeping in the same bed. I'll get up and start churning milk early in the morning so the children can have a nice long sleep. I won't give my daughters-in-law any trouble. Now listen, brother, God has heard my appeal and He'll hear this also."

She planned, she said, to add four rooms, two on each side of the present hut, so each of her sons would have a place to raise his family. "I have faith in the Maharaj," she went on. "He Himself will do everything for us. Oh, I have a heart as big as a lioness. A hundred people can come and stay with me and you won't even see the slightest wrinkle on my forehead. Everybody brings his own food stamped by God. We are nobody in between. I have seen really bad days. Now they are just about over."

Much of the time in Bhadson, when we were not sitting and talking with Surjit, Krishanjit and I followed our usual technique of following everybody about and stenographically noting down all they said and did. What follows is a typical evening. Surjit was preparing the evening meal, Saroop and the two oldest boys were carrying sugar cane in from the fields and Buldev was working at the water pump, recently electrified. "The more you take out of your body the better it becomes," Pala, the eighteen-year-old, was saying. He was a scrawny, humorless youth who seemed to think of nothing but work; Kaka, a year or two younger, was easier-going and better looking. "Now, father," Pala went on in a grim attempt at joking, "you should work hard and get thin so we can save money and spend less wood when we take you to the cremation ground."

Saroop chuckled. "Son, you need not build a wooden pyre. Just throw me into a canal. My tiny body will be washed away."

"No, no, Father," interrupted Kaka in a shocked tone, "we'll bring heavy loads of sandalwood."

Surjit called everyone to come to supper, but Pala protested they wanted to finish the work first. "Pala's such a cruel man," Surjit told us with pride. "He won't even let the others stop the work for eating." The family soon gathered, taking seats on the edges of two string cots placed on either side of a crude wooden table. Buldev, though a nephew, was given a low stool to indicate his inferior, landless status: had he been an untouchable laborer he would have had to sit on the ground. Since the mud hut was so small, we always ate outdoors; Buldev, Krishanjit and I slept on cots in the cow shed. In the middle of the meal the electricity stopped and so did the water pump.

"That black electricity has run away again!" Buldev exclaimed. Pala ran to start the diesel engine; he was trying to lift water from the tubewell to irrigate the ripening wheat. "Now Pala wants to fix the engine, too," Surjit said worriedly. "Maybe he'll break something."

"Nothing goes wrong," Saroop reassured her in his habitually weary way. "Don't worry." But Surjit sent Kaka on his bicycle to try and fetch an electrician. Buldev was still eating but she ordered him, "Go, run, help Pala. Eat, eat, hurry." The meal finished, Surjit took Saroop's dirty clothes to the pump to wash.

"Give my turban a little starch," her husband called after her.

"Oh, you just wrap it around any which way," Surjit snapped back.

"I'd like starch. I must feel young sometimes." His sagging, tired face said it was too late.

"Bah! You don't care how your turban looks." Surjit noticed Buldev was idle. "Buldev! Did you give food to the pig?"

"I thought Kaka had given. My foot is hurting. When I stepped on that thorn. I want to go to a doctor."

Surjit threw up her hands in annoyance. "It's like a marriage of barbers around here. Everyone's a gentleman and nobody will wash up the pots and pans." She gave Saroop's clothes a vigorous scrubbing. Pala ordered Buldev to feed the pig, water the cattle and then cut more oats. Then Buldev noticed Pala was carrying some oats in his *chadra,* a sarong-like cloth many Punjabi peasants wear instead of pants. Buldev yanked it away from him, shouting, "My *chadra* is not for that!"

"Oh, the fine prince!" Pala exploded sarcastically. "He will first get himself beautifully dressed. He has been uprooted of his style of dress on our poor farm."

"You tell me I'm uprooted? You who wear pants like a gentleman just to work in the fields. You expect me to go in rags?"

Pala, seeing Buldev was really angry, backed down. "I don't say anything. Do whatsoever you want. I am only suggesting you can wrap the oats in that dirty cloth you always wear." In defiance, Buldev limped angrily over to the pump, stripped down to his shorts and squatted under the cold stream of pump water, splashing it over his head. When he finished he shook out his hair to dry in what was left of the setting sun. Surjit, now really becoming alarmed, called to Buldev, "Now be a tiger! You have taken a bath. You look fine. Now go and water the cows."

Buldev scowled at her. "I've just taken a bath. Why don't you send one of your sons? You always treat me like somebody else's child."

"What have I done to you?" she cried. "Have I fired a bullet at you? I'm just asking you to do a little job so I can milk the cow."

"I won't do it. I'm tired."

"What have you been doing all day? Now Pala must fix the engine and cut the oats too." Surjit turned to Saroop. "What has come over your nephew? He goes ten days without washing and now he spends the whole evening taking a bath!"

"Let him be. His foot is hurting him. Everything will be all right." Saroop always tried to keep the peace. "Come and take tea, Buldev."

"I don't want any."

Surjit lost her temper. "I know you don't want any! I know that very well. The neighbors have been whispering in your ear. You are listening to malicious gossip that we won't feed our nephew if he doesn't work. Well, just sit all day long and we'll give you food. But you can't expect us to touch your feet and beg you to take a cup of tea." Surjit banged down the kettle, her voice getting shrill. "I can't stand this sort of attitude. Your head has been turned by some village gossips, Buldev." She taunted her husband. *"Your* nephew won't take tea."

Pala chimed in, "All Buldev wants is a good beating." Buldev limped off to the field.

Surjit turned her anger on Pala. "And if Buldev goes away, what then? Where will we get the money to hire somebody in his place? And with the wheat harvest coming?" Soon it was quiet again as Pala followed Buldev to the oat field. But not for long. We heard shouts and ran to see Pala and Buldev rolling over on the ground, fists flailing at each other. Pala broke away, howling and clutching his jaw; his lip was bleeding. Buldev, who seemed to have gotten the best of it, was sobbing. "Pala ordered me to carry oats. Here I am dying with pain and not one of you bothers. I'm wise enough not to have a contract with you, Surjit. Otherwise you'd treat me worse than a slave."

"It's his foot," I told Surjit.

"No, that's not the trouble," she replied emphatically. "Today some neighbors came and filled his ears. They told him, 'You'll get your leg amputated if you keep working for them like a donkey. Why do you put up with it?' I heard those jealous gossips. They'll take every chance they can get to hurt us. Someday I'll show them."

That night as we lay on our cots in the cow shed we could hear the family arguing. "How can you depend on such people?" we heard Surjit ask. "They have no house anywhere in the world." Pala growled, "We'll tie him with ropes and teach him a lesson." "No, no," Surjit's voice again. "He'd run away. What then? Do you think you and Kaka and your father could harvest the wheat without him?" Then Saroop, weary and conciliatory, "Go to sleep now. It doesn't matter. Everything will be all right." (Krishanjit was noting it all down as I held the flashlight and ordered, Surjit fashion, "Don't miss anything.")

The next morning I hired a horse-drawn *tonga* and Krishanjit and I took Buldev into the nearest town to see a doctor; he gave Buldev a penicillin injection for his infected foot and told him to stay off it a couple of days. On the way Buldev related his life story in the grimmest fashion: his father, an opium addict, a beggar, a thief, sold all his land and died in jail; his mother, also addicted, sold Buldev into bondage to a brutal master for a little opium money; this farmer, when drunk, used to harness him to a plow and drive him across a field with a whip. In a lurid narration, he told of wandering from farm to farm, working as a cowherd or laborer, of shoot-outs and bare escapes from the law, how he once escaped to a Sikh temple and served the monks for a year as a water carrier. And the women, "all blood and bone and promises until your money is gone and they kick you out." He called himself a "vagabond," said he could always find work as a field laborer and that he had always spent whatever money came his way, saying, "You don't know my life."

When we got home I could see Surjit's distress. "What did the doctor say?" she asked at once, evidently prepared to be sympathetic. But Buldev was no help. "Can't you see the bandage?" he growled at her. "It hurts."

At once forgetting a vow she had made to hold her tongue, Surjit snapped, "Have you got a bullet in it? It's just a scratch from a thorn. You make herds out of the hair of a sheep!" But she kept out of his way the rest of the day, which Buldev spent lying on his cot. That evening Surjit's daughter, her son-in-law, their baby and several other relatives came to visit unexpectedly. All was forgotten as Surjit, a generous hostess and good cook, prepared fresh chapattis and a delicious curry while Saroop broke out several bottles of home-brewed liquor. Soon the men were gulping down whole glassfuls in the Punjabi style, followed by gasps, purplish-red faces and hasty drinks of water.

The daughter told how her husband had been sick for three days. "There he was," she said, "lying deaf and dumb, looking always in the air. He was completely useless."

"Those black-faced bastards," Surjit called from the fire. "They must have put pills in his liquor."

"No, no," protested the son-in-law. "It was not liquor that put me in a daze for three days. It was my old auntie. She bewitched me and put her ghost inside me. She is dying and has some land."

"How much?" Surjit asked.

"Twelve acres and no sons. My relations took me to a sorcerer who said not to drink milk or liquor or eat eggs or meat. He said my auntie will die soon and I will inherit some of the land. I recovered. My relations told the old lady. Maybe she will change her will."

By the fire Surjit muttered under her breath, "Pills in the liquor."

Back in the cow shed, we found Buldev was cursing Saroop. "He was a party when my father sold our land," he told us, evidently after some brooding. "It was his fault. He made my father an addict. Send him to me. Tell him I want some chewing tobacco." We went back to the family and told Saroop, who went to talk to Buldev for some time and then returned. Saroop told Surjit, "Buldev wants to go back to Ludhiana to his mother's house."

"When?" It was what she had feared.

"Tomorrow."

Pala went to talk to Buldev, telling him, "If you go to town like this, with your foot in bandages, how will we show our faces to your family? You just want to pour insults on us!"

Saroop tried persuasion. "Don't you think we provide you with enough food and care? What will people say, that we work your hide off when you are healthy and throw you out when you are sick? Go with pleasure, my son, but when you are well."

Then Buldev was forgotten as the meal was served and Saroop kept filling up the men's glasses. Soon everyone was talking at once; only at intervals could one hear Saroop's drunken voice above the rest shouting, "Who knows about tomorrow? We may die tonight! Here, Pala, son, catch another glass!" Saroop started singing, about Bhandi, beautiful Bhandi, who was lost at the fair. Then he would shout again, "There's still a little, little bit more in this bottle!" "We don't want to dirty any more glasses," the son-in-law cried. "Why don't you take it?"

When Buldev appeared, standing sullenly some distance away, Surjit called to him to come and eat. He joined them but instead of taking his usual footstool, sat on the ground. "Why are you sitting like that?" Surjit demanded.

"I would do so," he said.

"Why do you not greet my son-in-law?"

"Because you never introduced me."

"But you know him?"

"And he knows me. Why does he not greet me?" Surjit braced herself as Buldev went on. "From tomorrow," he said, "you must pay me five rupees a day like any other worker. Or I'll go. Otherwise you'll show me no respect. And to hell with your wheat crop. It can rot in the fields. And why is nobody watering it tonight? The wheat is starved for water."

"Yes, yes," mumbled Saroop, who by now could barely sit up. "We must water the wheat." He tried to rouse Pala, who had fallen against the pillows in a senseless stupor. Kaka and the other men were just as drunk.

Buldev addressed Surjit. "If you wish they can sleep in their beds tonight. I'll stand alone the whole night, watering the fields. If any of you thinks he is more sturdy than I, let him come also. But don't you be barking at me tomorrow. I may do anything. Sleep all day in my bed. Whatever I like. After all, we are of the same blood."

Buldev headed toward the fields. Saroop somehow managed to get to his feet and staggered after him, crying, "Now, my son, you are a tiger! You are a real tiger and will water our fields. Pala and his mother are cut from one piece of cloth. But you and I are cut from another." Saroop did not get far, but soon stumbled and fell into a stack of cane. At once Surjit ran to him, helped him to his feet and brushed chaff from his shoulders. She supported him and, with him leaning on her, the two of them made it to his cot. Surjit settled him down, gently, as if he were a sick child, and drew his quilt over him. I remembered Buldev telling us on the trip to town, "Oh, they have fights but in the end she always gives in to him." Surjit withdrew something from Saroop's shirt pocket; it was a packet of chewing tobacco and she ran after Buldev and handed it to him, without a word.

Buldev grinned. "Now I'm well armed," he said. "Watering, I need not stand on my foot much. If it doesn't rain I won't be bothered at all tonight." As he headed into the darkness he shouted at the sky, "Come, Old Grandfather, be good to us!"

Soon Surjit, rejoining the women, was telling them where she would someday build her kitchen; she would put her bed there, she said, where, if God willed, she'd just be sitting and sleeping, quite free of all her burdens.

*

That first wheat crop was harvested. With what she made and against much advice, Surjit invested everything in seeds, fertilizer and hired machinery and planted all her land in cotton. The next year, buying five more acres, she began double-cropping wheat and rice. When I went back to Bhadson to see her in 1980, she owned one of the richest farms around; a high red-brick wall enclosed a modern homestead consisting of an eight-room brick house, a large cattle barn and other outbuildings, a bio-gas plant to provide both cooking fuel and fertilizer, the latest undergound irrigation system, two large new tractors and a combine. The whole yard covered one full acre. Her youngest, crippled son had been successfully operated upon; he now played football for the state agricultural university, where he was studying engineering. Three attempts to arrange a marriage for Pala had failed, but Surjit had found a wife for Kaka whose uncle was a powerful member of parliament, and also headed the committee that ran all the Sikh temples in Punjab; Surjit has become very pious. No one is quite sure just what happened to Buldev. There have been reports he joined the army in Delhi or was seen driving a truck in Rajasthan; others claim to have seen him in this village or that, working on somebody's farm, which seems more likely.

Saroop, who looks dignified since his beard turned a snowy white, is formally the master, but everyone knows it is all in the hands of Surjit. Nothing is done without her consent. She never rests, driving them all as hard as ever, bullying and cajoling, generous and anxious, as if her fear that Buldev might run off before the harvest had never quite left her. She sees to everything, is said to be getting a name in state political circles and is proud and fiercely ambitious, that bed in the kitchen long forgotten.

GHUNGRALI VILLAGE, INDIA

"Dhakel has molested a little girl!" The cry broke the quiet at Charan's well, where his harvesters drowsed under the shade trees after the noonday meal. I remember sitting up, half asleep, and seeing two men run toward Dhakel's well, their sickles raised like weapons. Dhakel was there, stumbling around under the trees, probably in an opium stupor. In a minute we were all on our feet and running too to try and stop a killing. As it turned out, the girl was not so little and Dhakel had come across her cutting wheat by herself and merely tried to kiss her. In the Punjab, because she was an untouchable Harijan and he a landowning high-caste Jat, this was cause enough for murder.

Revolutions claim victims and I suppose you could say the Green Revolution claimed Dhakel. Charan saw this right away. "This would never have happened if Dhakel had been cutting his own wheat," he said. Nobody, not even the Harijans themselves, went as far as I did, blaming the rich, progressive farmers like Basant Singh, forever thinking of economy of operations and returns, never weighing the human cost. Somebody had to pay. I was sorry it was Dhakel, still young, with a wife and small children, going his own way, a minor figure in the village scheme of things. Later on, when ordinary life went on as before, except that Dhakel was no longer respected, the episode seemed to symbolize how the caste system and India's unstoppable agricultural revolution are locked into a collision course.

In the late 1960s the Green Revolution was going to solve all the problems of India's agriculture. In the mid-1970s, the fashionable view was that it had failed, leaving the rich richer and the poor poorer. Both judgments were wrong. What actually happened was steady progress, the more striking because it contrasted with a century of stagnation, when India's food production stayed almost static as population rose. Now, in the past fourteen or fifteen years, production has doubled, despite setbacks in 1965–67, again in 1972–74 and the poorest monsoon in a century in 1979 (weathered without famine because of huge grain stocks at hand). India, at last, is likely to surprise everybody and, like most of South Asia, grow plenty of food in a few more years.

Can the Hindu caste system, which has always held India's 576,000 villages together, survive the coming of modern farming? Evidently not, if one looks to the prospering Punjab, where the familiar trinity of tractors, combines and electric power is rapidly displacing human labor. Strip away the age-old economic basis for caste—the exchange of labor and services in return for grain and fodder—and the old sahib-serf relationship shatters like overripe wheat. At least it does for the untouchables, whom Mahatma Gandhi called Harijans, the children of God, and long the true tillers of the soil in the Punjab, doing much of the actual field work under landowning Jat overlords. The Jats still don't know what hit them, many evidently confusing the old subservience with some notion of their own inherent superiority; since they are generally, but not always, taller and fairer, there is a racial element too. The old interdependence is gone and with it the old sense of community.

Instead a new Harijan credo of "now we are free" and "my sons will never work for Jats" has swept village Punjab, where India's old "Upstairs, Downstairs," sahib-and-slavey days seem gone for good. Atrocities against Harijans by higher castes, who do not seem to want to grasp the economic reasons for what is happening, get reported in the Indian press almost every day. The incompatibility of castes and modern farming will determine the shape of village India for a long time to come.

This has all happened very quickly. Even in 1970, when I first went to Ghungrali, much of the old, traditional village way of life remained. Then, two years after planting its first crop of high-yield, Mexican-bred dwarf wheat, Ghungrali had just begun its transformation from age-old subsistence agriculture to modern commercial farming. The village still resembled the usual Indian huddle of walled brick and earthen houses, with the usual temple, school, stagnant pond and giant banyan tree. No one in Ghungrali, unlike Surjit's family in their jungle clearing, built houses in their fields, as they are starting to do now, and every morning we rumbled out of the village in a creaking bullock cart.

The roads were dirt and rutted in those days and as you rode along the cart's wooden wheels would groan and creak at the slightest movement; we carried copper drinking vessels along, for water, and these, hanging from poles fixed to the cart's side, would chime in, like bells. Charan, briefly introduced in the last chapter as Surjit's brother and the Jat farmer-landlord with whom I stayed, would crouch on his haunches on the cart's wide tongue, holding the reins and coaxing the bullocks forward with a falsetto mixture of praise and curses, *"Tat-tat-tat-tat-tat-tat! Ta-hah, ta-hah!"* Not that he needed to show the bullocks where to go; they had been following the same ruts to the fields for many years; it was as much their daily lot as the cool shade at Charan's well, almost a mile from Ghungrali, where they munched grass all day, or slept, rolling over on their sides.

Charan's hired laborer, Mukhtar, a Harijan, was usually along, as was my interpreter, Krishanjit. Unlike in the relatively free atmosphere of Surjit's homestead, Krishanjit had to observe village custom in Ghungrali and could only smoke in the fields or in Charan's cattle barn. A sophisticated Sikh who had cut his hair and wore no turban after many years in Delhi, Krishanjit had been raised in a village not far from Ghungrali; but he had quarreled with his father, a rich, high-caste Jat landowner, and never went home. In 1981 he lived in Canada.

One morning Mukhtar told us his wife had awakened him during the night to see a giant star with a long fiery tail. He said old men among the Harijans were saying it was an evil omen. Such a comet had been seen in the sky over Ghungrali just once before in memory—in 1947 just after India's partition. Some 15,000 to 20,000 people—the village's Moslem inhabitants, plus Moslem refugees who had fled to Ghungrali for safety and had not yet gone to newly-created Pakistan— were massacred in a single afternoon by Hindu soldiers and Sikh mobs from the cities; their bones were still entombed in sealed wells throughout the village.

"Yes," Charan agreed, "they say that when such a star appears, the village will suffer a disaster." Charan was then thirty-nine, the same age I was. He was a giant of a man, with a bushy black beard; he towered over most of the other villagers and when he laughed, as he often did, he had a look of great vitality and physical strength. This was deceptive; he suffered badly from asthma and even then depended upon Mukhtar to do most of the heavy work on his farm. Like all of Ghungrali's 65 Jat families, Charan and his family, including the newly married Surjit and Saroop, fled their old homes in Pakistan without advance warning in August of 1947, making the journey to the new Indian frontier in a caravan of 22,000 bullock carts. As a boy of sixteen, he had known near-starvation, helped fight off Baluchi attackers, seen friends butchered by Moslem soldiers and just escaped a flash flood in which many drowned. Cholera claimed his only brother and, once in India, Charan's fat, lazy father, Sadhu Singh, who had spent his life as a wealthy gentleman farmer, told Charan, "I have never taken my hands out of my pockets and I never will." The old man stuck to his word. Aside from Surjit, married to opium-addicted Saroop, Charan was left with three more younger sisters and his parents to look after and became his family's sole provider. For years he worked with the Harijans as a daily-wage laborer, farming his own rented land at night. "But you know," Charan once told me, "those hardest years were my happiest. Maybe work is good for a man."

When Charan's father and his uncle, Sarban, whose only son, Dhakel, was then still a small child, were each allotted fifteen acres under a refugee resettlement program, the family moved to Ghungrali, which was not far from Sadhu Singh's old ancestral village. The brothers took a government loan for a tubewell, for water was everything in the arid Punjab; with it you could turn a desert into a garden. That was in 1953; within four years Ghungrali had forty-six tubewells; in 1981 there are more than a hundred, all powered by electricity.

The new Mexican-bred wheat was first planted on a small seed plot in Ghungrali in 1965 by another Jat refugee from Pakistan, Basant Singh. The most enterprising man in the village, Basant Singh had arrived penniless; he was allotted only two acres. He soon married an heiress with thirty acres, finagled the only license to sell liquor in Ghungrali and assiduously cultivated the agricultural officers who, with a bottle here and a bottle there, kept him informed of the latest technology. Always out in front, Basant Singh was the first farmer in Ghungrali to use chemical fertilizer, in 1960; two years later he bought its first tractor and in 1970 its first combine. He sold his first few seed crops of the Mexican wheat at enormous prices. By the winter of 1967–68, the dwarf wheat was grown on all fourteen hundred acres of Ghungrali's wheatland.

The Punjab Plain is perfectly flat. Since most of the farms are a uniform fifteen acres, the landscape tends to look the same everywhere, the only variation clumps of trees around the wells and pumphouses. When I first saw it in the winter of 1969–70, it was almost entirely planted in wheat, much of it still green, but a field here and there, sown early, had already started to ripen. But what wheat. It was so short and stunted it barely came up to your waist (by 1980, the latest varieties, fully grown, just reached your knees). The wheat was a thick tangle of plump grain heads on short, stiff stems, so luxuriant it looked almost artificial. In those days the varieties were given names like Khalyan Sona, PV 18, 227, RR21, Triple Dwarf. When we passed a field, Charan, a good farmer, would often comment, "This PV 18 is sick. It has a disease." "Not enough fertilizer on this field. Nirmal is a poor farmer." "Now, look at this good crop of Triple Dwarf. Yes, that's right."

Charan's uncle, Sarban, with his son, Dhakel, farmed the land just to the south; north of Charan's fields was the farm of old Pritam Singh, a hardy, saintly old man of whom I grew very fond over the years. Tall, broad-shouldered, unstooped, Pritam was seventy-two when I first met him; he wore a clean, faded blue cloth wrapped around his head and usually carried a walking staff—very much an Old Testament figure. Pritam was one of the few Jats who, despite his age, still did daily physical labor side by side with his Harijan field-hands. Like Charan himself, Pritam seemed to be one of the vanishing giants of the earth. *"Sat Sri Akal!"* he would call in the traditional Sikh greeting whenever we passed in the bullock cart; he always had a comment on the weather. "God is after our wheat, Charan. With these thundershowers it goes down and becomes shaky at the root." Pritam felt Ghungrali had a bright future. "If people go on minding their own business, there's no doubt about it. With this new wheat, we're getting richer day by day."

At that time Charan was a heavy drinker. I can't say I blamed him. He had worked for twenty-five years to build up his farm, suffered asthma, endured daily petty quarrels with his meddlesome father and been guilty of so many follies and injustices he said it was painful to remember them. He was aware that he neglected his gentle and kindly wife and that he was partly to blame that his half-educated sons looked down on him and were disappointing to him. Charan seemed to realize that he was a mediocrity, a bit of a drunkard, short-tempered and a companion to some of the worst wastrels in the village. Yet he seemed resigned to it and always looked forward to laughter over a bottle with some friends of an evening. Charan had discovered what we all eventually do: that every man must be satisfied with what he is.

One morning, I remember, when we arrived at his well, Charan was furious to find someone had poured out a drum of residue from some crushed sugar cane; he had hidden it in his toolshed and planned to distill some illicit liquor. One of his laborers, an old graybeard of the lowest Mazhbi barn-cleaning caste, a humorous man whose name was Krishan, but whom everybody called Poondi, "little bug," clearly enjoyed telling Charan what had happened. "It was your father." Poondi chuckled; he had a deep bass voice. "He came last night after you went home and made us pour it out. He said, 'It does not behoove us to make drink. It is beneath our dignity.'" Poondi gave a hoot of laughter.

Charan cursed, "I'll rape his mother! It would have made at least thirty bottles!"

*

If you go to Ghungrali today, sooner or later you will hear about the "boycott" in the winter of 1969–70; everyone uses the English word. The village has never been the same since. The boycott ended, quite suddenly and, as it turned out, permanently, the traditional interdependence of Ghungrali's 65 Jat families and 160 Harijan families. That Ghungrali had a caste system at all may come as a surprise because all its people, Jats and Harijans alike, are Sikhs; it did to me. The Sikh religion, a fairly modern attempt to combine the best of Islam and Hinduism, is based upon human equality. The Sikhs' sacred scripture, the Guru Granth Sahib, an anthology of its religious teaching, is specific about this:

The Hindus say there are four castes
But they are all of one seed.
'Tis like the clay in which pots are made
In diverse shapes and forms—
Yet the clay is the same.
So are the bodies of men made of the same five elements.
How can one amongst them be high
And another low?

Yet caste was rigidly followed in Ghungrali, as throughout Sikh Punjab. There were three castes in the village: the Jats or farmer-landlords, such as Charan, Basant Singh, old Pritam, or Charan's cousin, Dhakel; and two kinds of Harijan untouchables: the Chamars or traditional leather workers, who then included almost all the field laborers like Mukhtar; and the barn-cleaning Mazhbis, such as Poondi. All of them prayed together in Ghungrali's *gurdwara,* or Sikh temple, which stood on a hill with its white onion towers and loud public address system. Outside the temple, the Harijans, whether Chamar or Mazhbi, suffered constant discrimination. Intermarriage was unthinkable. Harijans could eat in a Jat home only if they crouched on the earth and used no plate or utensils, just taking food in their outstretched hands. Jats never ate or drank in a Harijan house. When Krishanjit, as a high-caste Jat, and I took meals with Mukhtar or Poondi, the whole village was scandalized.

Race came into it. The Punjabi Jats are relative latecomers to India. They may have been originally descended from the Scythians, the nomadic people who displaced less warlike rivals on the Eurasian steppes, seizing their pastures and establishing themselves as overlords of settled agricultural populations, much as they had done in Punjab. Even today the Jats retain the old warrior spirit, glorying unabashedly in the strength of arms, the destruction of foes and the number of their cattle; they form the main ranks of India's army. The Jats—now divided into Hindus, Sikhs and Pakistani Moslem Punjabis—did not enter India until the time of Caesar and did not fully occupy the Punjab Plain down as far as Delhi until the collapse of the Mughal Empire in the late nineteenth century. They thus escaped the influence of the holy men of the Gangetic Plain who succeeded elsewhere in India in setting its spiritual, world-rejecting tone. The most European of Indians, the Punjabi Jats pursue the good life and leave metaphysics to the *bhaiyas,* or brothers, as they somewhat contemptuously refer to other Indians. Many Indian film stars are Punjabi Jats. In contrast, the Mazhbis—short, squat, muscular and chocolate-colored—are descended from India's aboriginal Dravidian race. The Chamars are of mixed blood; a few in Ghungrali were as fair and tall as Jats but possessed no land to give them status. Caste weighed heaviest on the Chamars, who bitterly resented it, while the Mazhbis, though lowliest of all, were Ghungrali's most cheerful and humorous lot.

Caste in Ghungrali also had an economic basis: the age-old *jajmani* system, a traditional exchange of labor and services for grain and fodder. Under long-established custom, a landless Harijan harvester received a fixed part of every wheat crop he helped to mow and thresh—traditionally one bale of every twenty—which was enough to feed his family for a year, or until the next wheat harvest. He also received the right to cut grass for his cow or buffalo on the Jats' land undisturbed. This left the Harijans in poverty, but insured that each family would get enough wheat and milk, the Punjab's two staples.

Ghungrali's wheat harvest always begins on April 13, Baisaki, or the Sikh New Year. In 1970, a few days before Baisaki, Ghungrali's richest Jats, led by Basant Singh, decided they were losing too much wheat under the old *jajmani* system. With the new high-yield wheat, they argued, it was enough to give a harvester one bale in thirty, not twenty as before. They persuaded all the village Jats to go along with this, in the interests of "unity."

The Harijans were dismayed. They angrily rejected Basant Singh's offer, saying they would accept either the old twentieth bale or fifty to eighty kilos of threshed grain per acre, depending upon the crop. "Grains we won't give," Basant Singh replied. He called a meeting of the Jats. Afterward a Jat spokesman announced over the temple loud-speaker, "No Harijan can enter the Jats' fields. No Harijan can take grass from our land to feed his cattle." The Harijans decided to retaliate by not harvesting the Jats' wheat at all; instead they would go and cut and thresh the wheat in the surrounding villages. Thus the "boy-cott" began.

Few of the villagers at first took this mutual refusal to engage in traditional relationships seriously. No one, not even Basant Singh, I think, realized it would permanently divide the village. Charan first thought it was so much foolishness. "It's impossible," he said. "This village can't survive without a settlement." So did his old father, Sadhu Singh, who harumphed, "It's all a fuss over nothing. You'll see. Once the wheat gets ripe and starts to shatter, how the Jats and Harijans will go running to each other!"

Pritam had misgivings from the start. He warned, "What we have sown, we shall reap also." Basant Singh scoffed at such fears. He declared, "Either we shift to machinery or get labor from outside. It's the only solution. Pritam says this boycott is harmful to Ghungrali. But the poor are making more money than ever and spending it on hashish, tobacco and liquor. Their real enemies are their bad habits."

The Harijans were anxious but stuck together. Mukhtar, though he had worked for Charan for twelve years, told him, "If the Jats boycott us, we must boycott them. It means I cannot work for you anymore, Charan *sahib*." The government tried to head the trouble off, sending a police inspector to Ghungrali. He told the Jats, "Don't strangle these poor people. Don't kill them this way. I don't say the Jats should be giving with four hands, but don't make the Harijans starve either. I want this trouble to end with a little adjustment on both sides." He was no match for Basant Singh, who said it was too late as Jats had already left Ghungrali to fetch outside harvesters. "We no longer need our village Harijans," he told the policeman.

The Harijans themselves did make an attempt to reach a compromise. They said they would accept a separate rate for each farm, depending upon how abundant a farmer's crop was. When Basant Singh and his men argued that this would be "too much trouble," a Harijan protested, "It can't be any more trouble than the village is facing now. We can't go to your fields. We can't cut grass for our cattle."

Basant Singh cut him off. "If you won't accept our terms, there is no reason to talk further. It is all over. Finished. Now you are free to do what you will and we are free to do what we will. *Sat Sri Akal!*" A few days later Ghungrali learned that Basant Singh had bought the village's first combine; he would not even need harvesters himself. Charan cursed him and said, "There are real hypocrites in this village."

The day before Baisaki and the wheat harvest began, Ghungrali always held a bullock cart race, inviting all the men, Jat and Harijan alike, from the surrounding villages. The race had always symbolized their mutual dependence; though caste might separate them the rest of the year, in the wheat harvest Jat and Harijan would cut side by side, joking and often competing to see who worked the faster. The annual race heightened this sense of community, everybody cheering for Ghungrali's carts as they competed with those from other villages.

It was a splendid day; hundreds of men and boys lined the eleven-acre-long course in the fields just west of the village; since it passed Basant Singh's farm, he stood by his well with a rifle to make sure none of the crowd trampled his wheat. In the dusty luminescent light, everything was a dreamlike pastel color: the wheat, the sky, the trees, men in clean white shirts and yellow, pink, pale green, red and orange turbans. The sense of sinking caste differences was very strong. It was to be the last bullock cart race Ghungrali would have.

Charan and his cousin, Dhakel, then a handsome, beardless young man in his twenties, had goaded a third cousin, Sindar, who worked with Dhakel, into entering the race. Sindar, a cheerful braggart, was forever going on about his exploits. Just before the race we all went for a drink at Dhakel's well and sat swigging down the fiery home-made liquor as Sindar fussed over the bullocks. "Oh, today you shall run like the wind," he told them. "Today I shall crush someone under the hooves of my bullocks. I don't know about the others. But no one in this village can beat me." When Dhakel suggested he should sit down and rest, Sindar was indignant. "Oh, why should I do that? Should I grab someone's penis? No, we'll go straight to the race." We could see others heading that way.

"Clear the way! The first cart is coming now!" one of the villagers was shouting over a loudspeaker rigged up on a truck near the finish line. We arrived just in time. "Oh, come with pomp and show!" the announcer went on. "Come with courage. Oh, Bhajan Singh of Mal Majra village, come!" Charan soon went off with his cronies to drink. He was red-faced and staggering by the time it came Sindar's turn to race. Hearing that Sindar was to come next, Charan pushed back the nearest bystanders, bottle in hand, calling out, "For God's sake, please clear the way, brethren. You are masters of your wills. It is your village. But clear the way."

"Bring that red flag up, just watch the red flag," the announcer called. "Run! Go! Oh, green and red turbans, please clear the track. *Shabash, sha-b-a-a-ash!* Here comes Sindar Singh of Ghungrali. Look how the bullocks come! Like air! Look with your full eyes wide open but clear the way, my friends . . . Sindar, Ghungraliwallah, is com-ing. He's running like a railway train. See how he flies. . . . Ooop! What's happened?" Something had gone wrong. Men pushed into the road to see. "Friends, clear the way. Stop running this way and that. What? Ah-h-h-h, the bullocks are running into the wheat field! Clear the way! We can't see. Oh, Sindar's cart has left the road! His bullocks are heading across the wheat field. Oh, look! Now he's turned them around again. Oh, he's bringing them back. They're back on the road. Clear the way, clear the way! The bullocks are coming with great dig-nity. Don't worry, friends, they'll get here some day. *Shabash, sha-b-a-a-ash!* Sindar Singh, *Ghungraliwallah!"*

Sindar's cart finally rumbled across the finish line to shouts and jeering, by far the slowest time of the race. Sindar, humiliated, disap-peared at once. Charan shouted, "Seeing Sindar race, I get drunk without liquor!"

At Charan's well that evening, after another bottle or two, Sindar was back in form. "Our game was wrong," he insisted. "The people frightened my bullocks, the bastards. They kept pushing into the road. I rape their mothers." Old Poondi, who had been cutting grass on Charan's land, laughed. "Sindar has been having diarrhea ever since he lost."

"Why should I have diarrhea?" Sindar squawked indignantly. "Even if my bullock cart falls in a well, I won't have diarrhea." The talk shifted to the boycott. "Maybe the Harijans will move away, get jobs in the city," said Sindar, relieved to change the subject.

"Never mind," said Poondi. "City life is good. A law is going to be enforced where poor people will only work eight hours a day. Then we'll apply to the government for a paved road and we'll buy bicycles and go to town every evening."

"Take your children in big baskets if you go there," joked Sindar. "When they go hungry you can always throw them on the railway tracks."

Dhakel, a quiet youth who seldom spoke much, was worried about the harvest. "If we could get Harijans from Ghungrali," he said, "I'd gladly give one bale in twenty. We don't want those Hindus from outside. You can't depend on them." Soon everyone fell to cursing Basant Singh and his men for stirring up the trouble. "I think he drinks in secret and is also an opium addict," said Charan, who thought nothing of the kind. "In the morning he takes opium and in the evening he takes liquor," Sindar joined in. A fresh bottle was passed around.

"Basant Singh abuses Harijans."

"He is his own air."

"That bastard is arrogant and proud."

"Fuck Basant Singh," said Sindar. "Let's go to America."

Dhakel, quickly sober and serious, objected. "Our America is here in Ghungrali."

Charan laughed. "It is all the fault of that star with a tail. It wanted to show its power and made Ghungrali its victim."

*

In the days to come, as Basant Singh harvested his wheat with his new combine, most Jats hired migrant workers from Uttar Pradesh or Bihar. Such able-bodied young men as Dhakel and Sindar cut it all themselves, but Charan, with the help of Poondi, was able to hire a dozen Mazhbis. This was lucky for me. In Charan's fields the harvest was done in the traditional fashion. We cut the wheat as Punjabis always had, the men crouched low on their haunches in a wide, spread-out line, slashing sickles at the dry stems, grasping a handful at a time, advancing slowly, rocking from side to side, moving steady and rhythmically down the field. At first I found this murder; I didn't have the right leg muscles and had to keep standing up to stretch; it took some days to get used to it and I was always stiff and sore, with legs like noodles, by night. All day for ten days our sickles flashed in the hot sun, making the same sound: *grrch, grrch, grrch.* As their muscles grew more tired, the younger Mazhbis cursed and told jokes more, while the older men became quieter. Gathering the sheaves into bales, we sometimes divided into two teams, the young racing the old to see who was fastest. *"Shabash,* boys, we have to show our strength to these old men," one of Poondi's sons would shout. "We'll make them spit like stallions! Work with energy!" Poor old Poondi could be heard, breathlessly shouting back, "Show your strength, men! Make the parrots fly!"

Charan's asthma kept him from mowing in the dry, dusty wheat himself. Instead he kept busy all day, running back and forth from the well, carrying tea and meals. Water we simply drank from pails with a dipper. I sweated so much in the scorching, dry heat, I must have drunk gallons every day, but it was pure water from Charan's well. Charan himself was tirelessly good-humored, forever making jokes and cheering everyone up as if his geniality alone sustained the brutal labor. On the last night of the harvest he had a pig butchered and roasted at the well yard and when we gathered at sunset to wash at his pump, Charan produced a dozen bottles of newly brewed liquor. After bathing, the exhausted, hungry Mazhbis fell to eating and drinking like birds of prey, leering at the plates of roasted pork and stuffing as much down as they could; few had meat more than two or three times a year. When the pig was gone, Bawa, one of Poondi's sons, held up the platter and drank down all the gravy; he must have had a cast-iron gut. The Mazhbis kept drunkenly praising Charan, exclaiming, "The way Charan treats us we could sacrifice our lives for him. He is a prince among men." Poondi, drunk as a lord, shouted, "Where men work, there is God!" Charan kept producing more bottles from somewhere, laughing and bellowing in his hoarse, deep voice, "Have you ever seen so many bottles? These are the young ones of the last. Drink up!" Once he cried, "Enjoy, for we only live once! I'm not happy, I'm super-happy. I'm so happy I could jump up to the sky!" We had a marvelous time of it.

When we finished Charan's harvest, we went to help Dhakel, or I did, while Krishanjit, who felt above physical labor, took down the dialogue in his notebook. This encouraged Sindar, who kept up an endless running commentary: "God has made our bones of steel! Whatever happens, we will keep cutting wheat. Oh, I rape their sisters! After this we must get drunk for four days. Oh, I remember one time in Isaru. We were threshing. A real good girl came along to beg some grain and she brought two more girls back the next day. We had three trips each. How they were jumping like springs underneath! All were happy and all were the gainers. Oh, I should have been a woman. I could sit inside the house all day. But you know at midnight you get a foot-long penis inside you. Then you'll say, it would be better if I was a man. So what God has made, that is right. One time in Mal Majra village . . ." The sickles kept flashing, cutting the wheat stalk by stalk, row by row, field by field, and acre by acre, to the accompaniment of Sindar's cheerful nasal voice. By the time we had finished Dhakel's ten acres, Ghungrali was surrounded by bare stubble fields and threshing grounds.

One evening, just at the end of my stay, I was riding back to Ghungrali on Pritam's bullock cart. We passed Mukhtar and his wife, who were carrying bales of green fodder home from the next village. Pritam had just remarked, "Who would leave this lush grass by the roadside if the Harijans were allowed to cut fodder for their cattle?" Seeing Mukhtar, the old man told him, "It is not good, the way we are treating each other, but I think it will all be settled very soon." For some time we went without speaking, the bullock cart creaking gently, Mukhtar and his family a huddle of dark, barefooted figures, walking silently beside us. When Mukhtar did not reply, Pritam went on, "Now you go to other villages. We mind it very much. Look, we Jats have to feed your children. Your daughters are my daughters and your sons, my sons. We must see that they are fed. That is the way it has always been in Ghungrali."

Mukhtar had told me he vowed his son would never work for the Jats. Now, at last, he spoke to Pritam. "Yes, you are right, *Sardarji*. But it is written that we should cut the wheat of another village."

"Yes, it is written." Pritam sighed. "But it will be all right in a few more days, my son."

*

Poor Pritam. In the years to come Ghungrali was never to be "all right," in his old traditionalist sense, again. A way of life had gone and nothing would bring it back. Before returning to Ghungrali to see the changes the next decade would bring, let us look for a moment at India itself.

Soothsaying is India's specialty. Anyone trying to tell its fortune for the next twenty years is likely to come up with one of two scenarios. The first is more of the same: an India with more industry, more people (just over a billion) and more food (around 185 million tons), but essentially the same old antheap of hungry people and hungrier cows. The second forecast postulates something like 900 million Indians but has them eating more while exporting surplus grain from an annual production of over 250 million tons. This India would have doubled its cropland under irrigation, enabling it to triple-crop with rotations of high-yield, fast-maturing wheat, rice, other crops and nitrogen-fixing pulses, reducing the need for fertilizer; a farm family of six persons could feed themselves and earn $500 cash a year, cultivating just two or three acres.

This second India would meet its energy requirements partly through bio-gas, trees and solar power. There would also be a multi-billion-dollar hydroelectric dam-reservoir-canal complex to channel the melting Himalayan snow of Nepal down to the parched, flood-prone Gangetic Plain; a system of underground caverns, aquifers and tubewells would store the monsoon rainfall instead of having 80 percent of the waters of the Ganges and Brahmaputra flow unused, as they did in 1980, into the Bay of Bengal. Two of India's poorest states, Uttar Pradesh and Bihar, would be transformed into a granary that alone could feed the entire country.

This scenario may sound a bit like science fiction, but in New Delhi I find that its main prophets are India's most respected agricultural scientists and economic planners. In an interview in 1978 when he was still prime minister, Morarji Desai, then eighty-three, told me, "We know now, with the farm science we already possess, that we can produce twice as much food in the next twenty years, maybe three times as much." Another convert to optimism was Norman Borlaug, the Iowa plant breeder who won the Nobel Peace Prize in 1970 for developing dwarf high-yield wheat in Mexico and getting India and Pakistan to grow it. (His story of how the Green Revolution got started and how scientific agriculture is changing China follows in Chapter 22.) As Borlaug put it during several days of talks I had with him in Mexico in the fall of 1980, "Hell, yes, India has the potential."

Today India has more untapped agricultural potential (land, water, sun, energy) than any other big country, including Brazil or Sudan. It has almost as much cropped land as the United States (350 million acres to 380 million) and a lot more than China, which has just under 250 million acres (yet China produces a lot more grain, 241 million tons to India's 128 million in the 1975–77 average year). India can double the amount of land that can be brought under irrigation, from a current 128 million acres to 277 million, or almost two-thirds of its cropped land (China has 116 million irrigated acres, just about half its total). Then India applies only 6.5 million tons of fertilizer annually, in comparison with the 5 million tons Egypt applies, though India has fifty-eight times more cropped land. The result is extremely low yields—a fourth of Japan's in rice, half of Holland's in wheat.

It has always been evident that once India had the technology and got its priorities right, its agriculture would start to really move. From independence in 1947 until the mid-1960s, Jawaharlal Nehru followed the Russian example of investing heavily in industry without first putting agriculture on a sound basis. Only in the 1970s did it become fully evident that Indian industry couldn't expand much more and was hamstrung until more purchasing power got into the hands of its villagers, who still make up 80 percent of India's people. The wisdom of giving agriculture top priority, as was done from the start in Maoist China, was slow in coming. Raj Krishna, one of India's leading economic planners, has summed up the problem:

> The overall prospects for India's economic development remain unknown. The resources and the knowledge to eradicate deprivation exist. The failure to use them is purely managerial. The Indian political system has simply not produced a leadership that is knowledgeable and sincere enough to break the syndrome of slow growth and growing poverty.

Krishna, whom I interviewed in New Delhi in 1978, felt India could advance quickly if there were "shifts in leadership." Dr. Borlaug, who has exchanged letters regularly with Prime Minister Indira Gandhi, felt she was on the right track investing heavily in irrigation (in 1978 India began irrigating 7 million new acres every year, more land than there is under irrigation in all Egypt); he has urged her to expand grain production, storage and fertilizer output and even mobilize the Indian army to plant trees in the Himalayan foothills. In reply, over the years, Mrs. Gandhi has emphasized the need for better technology for rain-fed, dry-land areas, especially for higher yielding sorghum, oilseeds and pulses.

Morarji Desai, who served both Nehru and Mrs. Gandhi as finance minister, told me way back in the 1960s that he felt India should reduce the maximum acreage per household, spend much more on irrigation, encourage multiple cropping and protect village industries. These were all sensible policies which he started to carry out as prime minister. (While in Indonesia in 1979 I wrote Desai that he should take a look at Java's successful way to get more income to the poorest villagers through WPA-type road-building projects; he was interested and the AID mission in Jakarta provided him with their studies.)

When he finally came to power, Desai was too old and too politically shaky to do much more than establish a new direction in which India, especially in the priorities given irrigation and the power and pumps to run it, now seems fated to go. Politically, because the minority "haves" in each village naturally benefit faster from agricultural advance than the majority "have-nots," and any New Delhi government must push food production to feed what were over 690 million Indians in 1981, the opposition—any opposition—seems likely to quickly grow more popular with the poorest peasantry than whoever is in power. I think this explained Mrs. Gandhi's remarkable comeback, though she faced, once in power, a Sisyphean struggle to try to balance growth and equity. The fatal plane crash of her son, Sanjay, in 1980, one of those accidents that change history, established one thing: It is time, at last, for India and its politicians to show political maturity by starting to build up constructive alternatives to India's post-independence leadership.

In a sense, as we go into the Eighties, the Indians are holding their breaths; an agricultural revolution on the scale of America's, or even China's, seems too good to be true. The scientists fear extension may be too slow. (India is now trying to field one agricultural graduate for every 800 farmers.) Planners like Krishna fear the bureaucracy will be too cumbersome and corrupt (though Mrs. Gandhi put the fear of God into a lot of civil servants). But a huge new scientific agricultural establishment has grown up since the early 1960s, with twenty-one agricultural universities and thirty research institutions. And no Indian with any technical knowledge doubts that a historic transformation is underway. It's not just that food production and food stockpiling averted famine and set new records in the 1970s. Confidence really stems from what Indian science has come up with and what India ought now to be able to do with its land, water, sun and energy resources. A new India, likely to take us all by surprise, is coming.

In Ghungrali, this new India is already here. All of its 107 tubewells are electrified; after dark you'd think you were in suburban Chicago. The village now has 40 tractors and 2 small combines; huge German combines come under contract to do some of the harvesting. Fertilizer consumption has risen from nothing to 800 tons a year. Sophisticated piped irrigation, to prevent evaporation, is coming in. So are bio-gas plants to supply both fuel and fertilizer. Rice, sown for the first time in Ghungrali in 1977, has replaced wheat—still grown in winter—as the village's biggest cash crop. In 1978–79, Ghungrali started to triple-crop for the first time, a wheat-pulse-rice rotation made possible by a new quick-maturing, sixty-day pulse, *mung,* which fixes nitrogen from the air into soil, sharply reducing the need for chemical fertilizer.

All Ghungrali's old dirt roads have been paved; the bullock carts these days have rubber tires and no longer make that satisfying creak. New express buses go right from the village banyan tree to the Punjabi cities of Chandigarh and Ludhiana. Two doctors come daily on motorcycles to hold office hours; a new resident nurse, partial to Vitamin B-complex injections, gives competent initial treatment. Almost all of the Jat families and two of the Harijan families have children in universities; a big new worry is where to find jobs for so many graduates. One possibility is emigration, and remittances from educated sons and daughters abroad now arrive in Ghungrali postmarked Dubai, Munich, Toronto, St. Paul and Yuba City. Now Jats include television sets in their daughters' dowries. In 1978, Basant Singh bought Ghungrali's first privately owned car.

Charan has changed even more than the village; his beard is now gray, he hasn't touched a drink for several years, he dresses carefully; indeed, he's become something of a patriarch. In 1978 he arranged marriages for his two oldest sons, Sukhdev, now a member of the Punjab police, and Kuldeep, twenty, who has taken over most of the farming. A third son went to college, as did Charan's only daughter, Rani, and the youngest boy is still in high school. In 1979, Kuldeep rebelled and ran away to try to join the army; a compromise was reached after Charan agreed to buy a big new tractor and wagon and let Kuldeep operate them on hire for others. Charan also rented out half his fifteen acres, sparing Kuldeep some drudgery. The two daughters-in-law are part of Charan's household; in 1979, he became a grandfather. Old Sadhu, his own father, has become a tottery, frail old man who no longer interferes but drowses all day, fretting about this and that, on a *charpoy* under some trees near the cattle yard.

I was astonished by the change in Charan; it seemed more like a whole generation, not just ten years, had passed. One day, like Sadhu before him, Charan discovered a drum of crushed sugar residue hidden in the well house; Kuldeep was planning to make liquor. As indignant as if he himself had been a lifelong teetotaler, Charan poured it out, to the amusement of Poondi and me. Charan complained, "I will never allow a son of mine to make this stuff at home. There are so many better things than this country liquor, I don't understand why they want to make it!"

Yet hardly changed at all was old Pritam, now in his eighties, but still going to his fields each day. Pritam had grown rich, bought a tractor and had a grandson—a college graduate educated in Bombay—to help him. But he still labored side by side with his workers.

When I asked Kuldeep if he remembered the boycott—he was only ten years old at the time—he said, "Yes. The Harijans never came back to work for us after that. These days most of them are taking jobs in the towns, working in the oil and rice mills or loading wheat at the freight yard. Some do this lifting and loading work. It's hard but high paying. They get ten, twenty rupees a day. They have become too greedy." But Ghungrali's Jats were still paying five or six rupees a day for field work, not much more than they paid in 1970. For a time the Jats had plugged the labor gap with seasonal migrants from the poorest areas of Uttar Pradesh and Bihar. These Hindus from the Ganges basin were an alien, pathetic lot, with a different religion, culture and language. As agricultural modernization spread toward Calcutta, even this source of labor was drying up. Charan told me that the number of Jats going bankrupt was growing; so was the number of alcoholics and opium-eaters increasing. A few of the richer farmers like Basant Singh were evading the legal eighteen-acre-per-family ceiling to amass more land. Almost all of the Jats were in debt—on the average, $5,000–$10,000, up from the $1,000–$2,000 of 1970. Yet with a medium-size holding of fifteen acres like Charan's—land, house, machinery and all—a Jat's assets easily came to $50,000–$60,000 at 1979 Indian prices. The cost of inputs was rising and the Jats talked much about demanding "parity"; but the price they were getting for wheat was already higher than what an American farmer gets. In 1979 five Jats with small holdings were forced to sell out and move to the city and more feared bankruptcy when their mortgages fell due. Charan said that whereas in 1970, a man with ten acres could do well and manage to have a tractor, a tubewell, a threshing machine and livestock and to hire two daily laborers, this was now only possible with fifteen acres. Surjit, with twenty-five, is prospering.

Richer Jats seized on this as evidence that Ghungrali could no longer support small farms. Their typical argument: "Fifty to a hundred acres are needed to economically operate a tractor. For the past ten years we have all gone deeper and deeper into debt and can never repay. Any farmer with less than ten acres must sell his land." Basant Singh himself, who in 1978 bought twenty acres more to farm fifty-two, told me, "Even a hundred acres is too small. To really mechanize in the Punjab, you should go to a thousand acres. And we've got to mechanize. It's the only solution to the labor problem."

Ghungrali's Harijans, as I had feared, had been reduced to a rural proletariat. Perhaps the biggest surprise I had in Ghungrali was to hear that they liked it. Mukhtar, who worked at a rice mill in town, had bought a small piece of land and built himself a new brick house; he owned two bicycles, a milk buffalo and a large Japanese-made transistor radio as well. "It's better now," he told me. "We get more money in town. We only work eight hours. And we are free. These Jats can no longer rule over us. They can no longer treat us like animals. Now I can go out and do a day's work and talk to people freely." Mukhtar had cut his hair and in his town clothes there was no way to tell if he were Jat or Harijan. "One thing is certain," he said. "I'm doing my best to give my son a good education. If he fails, then he may be a factory worker or a mechanic. But he'll never work for the Jats."

Mukhtar said about eight out of ten of Ghungrali's Harijans commuted to town jobs, either bicycling five to ten miles each way or taking the new bus. No Harijan family had moved out of the village.

A few of the Harijans voiced regrets—very few. Banta, one of

Charan's Mazhbi harvesters ten years before and a graying man of middle age, said, "If the Jats had paid more generously, we would not have gone outside to work. Had I not been tilling their fields for thirty years? One time the university gave Basant Singh ten shirts as prizes for a wheat crop I helped him to grow. I asked him for one shirt, but he refused. He is that greedy." Like most of Ghungrali's people, Jat and Harijan alike, Banta was worried about a decline in morality. "These days," he said, "some Jats, those who have become drunkards or eat opium, may even refuse to pay their workers. That never happened in the old days. It costs too much money to complain to the police. We poor people cannot afford it or the time." He said that also, for the first time ever, the Harijans had to watch over their daughters. "Some of the Jats' sons try to molest them when they go to cut grass. So we leave it to God and go our own way, keeping to ourselves. God will punish the Jats, not us."

With the collapse of the old sense of community and the moral code that went with it, I found a new resentment being voiced by the Harijans. Even humorous old Poondi spoke with frank rebelliousness. "Oh, Dick *sahib,* we used to be dying the death of dogs," he said, "slaving in the fields while these Jats sat and enjoyed themselves." Poondi admitted he did not object to the hard physical labor itself. "Life comes with work," he said. "If you work hard, you live much." He said it was more a question of dignity, explaining, "Once I cut wheat for a Jat and he served the other Jats meat. For me only potatoes and vegetables. I asked him, 'Why? Did I cut less wheat?'" Poondi made a gesture of resignation. "But don't speak. Fear God. The British ruled India for a hundred years. Why did they not give the Harijans one or two acres each? What did we do wrong to them?"

This new aggrieved spirit extended to other Jat abuses. Many Harijans told me the Jats had prevented them from receiving their share of government emergency relief after a hailstorm destroyed half the wheat crop in 1976. Then the Jats had repeatedly frustrated a government plan to redistribute eighteen acres of village land historically set aside for the Harijans, so each family could have its own small plot to grow fodder. When I last visited, several Jat families were farming this land.

Even in everyday field work, the Jat-Harijan estrangement seemed complete. Kuldeep and the new young generation of Jat farmers, unlike Charan and his contemporaries, no longer greeted, talked or joked with Harijans, even those of their own age. They scarcely knew their names. Even the migrant workers felt uncomfortable. Typically, one of them told me, "Once we go home to our villages again, we'll never come back. We don't feel at home here. These Punjabi landlords never speak to us except to give us orders. They expect us to work ten or twelve hours a day without stopping."

The wheat harvest, when it came, was a great disappointment. Not enough immigrant harvesters could be found and the big combine operators refused to cut any wheat less than a hundred acres. As a last resort, Ghungrali's Jats turned to the village Harijans, contracting each field for seventy to a hundred kilos of grain per acre, a payment much more favorable to the Harijans than ever before. The Harijans, by taking leave from their town jobs and putting their wives and children to work mowing with sickles, once more were able to earn enough wheat to feed their families for a year.

So the Harijans came back into the Jats' fields, but not in the old, traditional way. The Jats were no longer obligated to serve their harvesters food, tea or even water. Nor were the Harijans obliged to carry bales to the threshing ground as before. The Harijan-Jat estrangement in the village now spread to the fields: the Harijans cut the wheat, the Jats stayed at the wells or in the village. Each group kept to themselves. Among the Jats I knew, only old Pritam continued to serve his harvesters tea and water. When I asked him why, Pritam said, "Because they are poor." But when the old man asked a Harijan laborer to help him lift a bale and the man refused, Pritam was enraged. We found him trembling with anger. "That man used to be like a son to me," he said.

In contrast to the old harvest spectacle of large groups of men, Jat and Harijan mixed together, mowing in good-natured, bantering company as we had done with Charan and the Mazhbis ten years before, now there were only small groups of Harijans—a man and woman and their children—working in silence. It was grueling work for the women, who traditionally had never cut wheat.

Charan and I attempted to contrive an old-fashioned harvest, hiring Poondi's three strapping sons and Mukhtar. Poondi's daughters came too, working apart and modestly covering their faces when I brought them water or tea. Neither Kuldeep nor any of the younger Jats joined in; Kuldeep told me that since the wheat was to be cut by contract, he saw no reason to get involved. I and my interpreter bought liquor in town and invited both Jats and Harijans for a drink after work in the evenings. Old Poondi and Pritam, who came over from his well, enjoyed it, if only for old times' sake, but among the younger men the old spirit of sharing a common community task was dead.

Aside from Pritam, only Dhakel seemed to miss the old harvests. Sindar had left years before, selling his land to buy a truck. Working alone at his well except for his elderly father, who was frail and badly addicted to opium, Dhakel had become something of a drunkard. He complained he had no one to talk to because his two hired laborers, immigrants from Bihar, did not speak Punjabi. When the harvest began, Dhakel came often to cut wheat with Poondi's sons, Mukhtar and myself, clearly enjoying himself. He told me one day, "Before the harvest was the best time of the year. Everybody worked together like a family and we cut jokes and raced to see who was the strongest and could cut the fastest. Now I've hired these Biharis. They don't even speak our language. How can I work with them?" Dhakel was drinking more and more and some days, when he did not show up in our fields, we would hear he was lying in a stupor at his well. When his Bihari laborers quit, he was forced to contract the harvest of the rest of his fields to a Chamar Harijan family from Ghungrali, headed by Munshi, a white-bearded old man I had not known before.

Then it happened. It was almost the last day of the harvest; about noon we heard the cry, "Dhakel has molested a little girl!" We saw Munshi and one of his sons, both carrying their sickles, running toward Dhakel's well. They were shouting, "Have you no daughter in your house?" When Munshi saw us coming too, he called back, "My daughter was cutting wheat alone. Dhakel went there and seized her! He has done this to us!"

Dhakel was staggering about, drunk. When Munshi's son reached him, he seized Dhakel's shoulder and shrieked, "I'll not leave you alive! I'll pull your sister from your house and rape her!" Just as we got there, the youth raised his sickle as if to rake it across Dhakel's face. Munshi swung his sickle at Dhakel's chest. Dhakel threw up his hands and thrust the two sickles away; at once his hands started to bleed. It was a terrible scene. Mukhtar and Poondi managed to drag Munshi and his son back. Then Dhakel's elderly father, who apparently had been asleep in the well house, came out and shouted, incredibly, "Leave this! Leave this! Get back and start cutting my fields!" This enraged Munshi all the more. "I'll not cut your fields!" he roared. "Send your son to the village! Who will save him? We will have our revenge!"

Old Poondi looked beaten when we returned to Charan's fields. "We live together," he said. "We work together. If such things happen, who will work for these Jats? But Munshi should keep quiet now. He should not do anything in the village. Terrible things are happening these days."

"If this had happened to us," one of Poondi's sons said, "we would not have left Dhakel alive. We would have cut off his head then and there." He turned on his father. "Why did you go there? Let this happen. Let them kill him."

"No, no, my son," Poondi protested. "There must be a compromise. We have to live with the Jats."

Charan, who was in town that day, came straight to his fields when he heard the news, but Dhakel had already fled to another village. "This is shameful," Charan said. "If I had been here, I would have beaten him myself. I could have given him two or three blows and that would have ended it. He must have been very drunk. The girl was only thirteen. Dhakel has three children himself and a fourth on the way. He's not a young boy."

For days Dhakel stayed out of sight. Ghungrali talked of little else. I went with Poondi and some of the Harijans when they went to see Munshi and his family. The men were prepared to compromise and settle for an apology. Not Munshi's wife—a wrinkled, shrill-voiced woman, prematurely aged by long years of heavy work. Her hatred of the Jats was chilling.

"We will take our revenge!" she vowed. "If Charan gets involved, we will not spare his family also. I have resigned myself that my sons are as good as dead. Whatever the sacrifice, we'll not leave Dhakel alive!"

Poondi could not believe that Dhakel's father, Sarban, had not come to beg the family's forgiveness. "Not a word!" Munshi's wife shrieked. "Not a word!"

From the village temple that evening came the familiar Sikh prayer:

We reap according to our measure—
Some for ourselves to keep, some to others give.
O, Lord, this is the way to truly live.

BERAT AND SIRS EL LAYYAN VILLAGES, EGYPT   13

Those who say technology causes as many problems as it cures can find plenty of evidence in Upper Egypt. Here, along the 650-mile valley from Cairo to Aswan, a huge change took place sixteen years ago. In 1964 the Aswan Dam began storing water, forever ending the Nile's annual August flood; two-thirds of the valley's 2.5 million acres were shifted from using that floodwater to perennial irrigation. The abrupt result was a change from one to three crops a year, from mineral-rich silt deposits to artificially manufactured fertilizer and from pharaonic water lifts to $400 Russian-made diesel pumps—all among Egypt's most tradition-bound people.

The Upper Egyptians, or Saidis, still veil their women, practice vendetta law and prize family honor. Women who sin against sexual conventions are killed by their fathers and brothers. Still in use are the hoes, forks and threshing sledges depicted in ancient tomb paintings. Women blacken their eyes and henna their hair, just as Nefertiti did. Most cropping patterns, water control and village disputes might come straight from the annals of Meches, who recorded day-to-day life in his village in 120–111 B.C.

In his eighteen years in power, President Gamal Abdel Nasser, a Saidi himself, installed a primary school, a doctor and an agricultural cooperative in each of Egypt's four thousand villages. Yet today only about half of Upper Egypt's children go to school; education for the many is merely memorizing the Koran from an old village sheikh, whose notion of geography is likely to be that the earth is flat and surrounded by sea and the mountains of Kaf, where the *djinn* live.

In just a decade and a half the agricultural props for this enduring Arabian Nights mentality have been knocked away. Yields per acre have dropped as year-round irrigation causes salinity and chemical fertilizer fails to provide a substitute for the Nile's lost silt. The feudal aristocracy has been largely destroyed by land reforms. But in Upper Egypt a new *kulak* class of *fellaheen*-entrepreneurs has emerged, lacking the old paternalism. They monopolize diesel pumps, sell water to poor neighbors and sometimes start blood feuds. In an upsurge of retaliatory crime, masked bandits burgle the houses of the newly rich.

The widespread introduction of sugar cane has tripled many family incomes. But expectations have risen faster, as income meant for reinvestment in the land is too often squandered on feasts, weddings, death rites, drinks and hashish—or, among the pious, all-night prayer performances and pilgrimages to Mecca. Most *fellaheen* are in debt.

Is it true, then, to say that modernization in traditional society inescapably leads to such social and psychological turbulence? No. For if change has produced a raucously explosive Upper Egyptian grasshopper, it has also produced a passive, polite Lower Egyptian ant.

North of Cairo, in the triangular 100-mile-long Delta, where six out of ten of Egypt's 22 million *fellaheen* are crowded 2,300 to the square mile, you find another lifestyle altogether; a strong work ethic, thrift, rigid Allah-fearing religious restrictions and extreme courtesy mixed with reserve. Staid, orderly and crime-free, Delta society puts its faith in technological progress. Upper Egyptian weddings are uproarious with dancing, bands of musicians, pistol firing and drunken brawls; a Delta wedding, with its cassette player and men sitting about on mats and smoking endless cigarettes, is decorous and deadly dull.

Why the difference? A milder climate in the Delta, generally richer soil and much more historical contact with Europe and other Middle Eastern countries play some part. More important, the conversion of the Delta's 3.5 million cultivated acres from flood irrigation to perennial irrigation took place after the construction of dams, barrages and canals by Egypt's Turkish ruler Mohammed Ali and his successors from 1805 to 1882. Delta village society has had a century longer than Upper Egypt to culturally adapt.

Delta *fellaheen* have partly licked the salinity problem and, using only a quarter as much chemical fertilizer as Upper Egyptians—applying cattle dung instead of burning it for fuel—get steadily rising wheat and maize yields. Women work beside the men in the fields. Students seem to be everywhere, tattered textbooks in hand, memorizing their lessons. Primary education is universal in the Delta and even the poorest *fellaheen* scrape together enough to send at least one son or daughter to university or technical school. And, because they are better educated, a disproportionate number of village Deltans made good in the Cairo government; Anwar Sadat was one.

*

In the summer of 1976, after two years of familiarity with Berat, a village on the Upper Nile near Luxor, I spent three months in a second village, Sirs el Layyan, forty miles north of Cairo in the heart of the Nile Delta. Everyone argued you couldn't claim to know village Egypt without spending some time in the Delta; they were right; it was another country altogether. I was the first foreigner to be given permission to study a Delta village after the 1967 war with Israel (being a member of the press did the trick) and the *fellaheen* of Sirs el Layyan, unaccustomed to seeing an American walking around their fields, were at first reserved and secretive. (I slept at UNESCO's center for literacy training in the Arab world, a big, walled compound just outside the village. There were about twenty teachers and civil servants from each Arab country, including Libyans, Algerians, Iraqis and South Yemenis, to whom an American was something of an oddity too.)

Right from the start I missed the open, free and talkative Saidis. Somehow the Upper Egyptian grasshopper—explosive, fiery-tempered, full of jokes—has an extraordinary zest; Berat village seemed to be continually exploding with emotion, everywhere a fierce flaring of laughter, anger, fear. So alive with humor, intelligence and intensity were its people that the docile, hardworking, ever-aspiring Delta ant seemed in comparison admirable but not much fun. One finds regional differences in all countries, but in Egypt they were more striking and unexpected. One kept looking for reasons why.

The Delta's climate, for one thing, is much milder. Except in August, which was very hot, it was remarkably cool in the morning and evening; I wore a sweater. There was even a little rain, whereas Upper Egypt has almost perfectly blue, cloudless skies every day of the year. In the Delta, the Nile itself is also missing; its two branches to Rosetta and Damietta on the Mediterranean coast are much narrower and less impressive than the undivided river which begins just north of Cairo; sometimes they are indistinguishable from the canals. Also, in the Delta there is an abundance of tall, quick-growing trees—eucalyptus, casuarina and sycamore; you can rarely see very far into the distance. I got a feeling of Java or Bangladesh.

Upper Egypt, in contrast, possesses a stark grandeur with the broad Nile and the very narrow green valley on its banks, seldom more than five or ten miles wide; pink cliffs rise like mountains on either side, for the Nile Valley is really a trough, cut deep into the desert floor thousands of years ago. The trees of Upper Egypt, mostly date palms and acacias, are smaller and sparser, almost transparent; the sky seems larger, the landscapes more spacious; there is a sense of fantastic remoteness.

Above all there is the Nile itself. To fully experience this wonderful river, it is best to sail down it by *felluca,* skimming over the water, waves slapping the bow, as your tattered, patched gray sail catches the desert breezes. The banks are surprisingly green, a patchwork of wheat fields and sugar cane, with the huddled masses of earthen houses and the smoke from cooking fires and the cries of a *muezzin* wailing from a mosque, "Come to security, come to God!" There is always movement somewhere, but it is the gentle rhythm of a loping procession of camels, the trotting of a donkey, other *fellucas* gliding by. You can idly observe the flight of egrets, white wings fluttering low over the water, and kites, crows and hoopoes along the banks. Men fish for spiny-backed *bulti* and Nile perch, women wash clothes and children swim. And nothing can be more satisfying than the sight of a ruined pharaonic temple rising from the desert's edge, the pink Sahara cliffs behind.

Upper Egyptians call the Nile *el Bahr,* the sea, the giver of life. With the valley so narrow and few bridges spanning the river, the *fellaheen* must cross the Nile frequently in small ferry boats; especially in the early morning or at dusk, when traffic is heaviest, these brief journeys invariably seem like a rite of passage. The heavy, clumsy ferry leaves the bank and heaves through the water so slowly that it is only by watching the bank recede that you can tell the ferry is moving. Men hang over the sides, watching the river, shrouded in their scarves and tunics, hunched over, chatting quietly, greeting friends or lost in contemplation. It is not hard to imagine you are all sitting on some strange aquatic animal, swimming out to an unknown land. Then the ferry swings into midstream and all too soon is bumping heavily against the landing stage. There is always a mad scramble to get off, yet the *fellaheen,* though they must cross the river thousands of times in a lifetime, never seem to get their fill of the river, murmuring and lapping against its banks from the heart of Africa to the Mediterranean.

In midday there is another Nile as the sun shines blindingly on the water and seems reflected in the air itself, which is pure on the river as it never is in the sand-dusty villages. Its water is then of a color impossible to name: it is at once a soft combination of dark blue, silver and green; in parts the water shines copper-like and in parts liquid sunshine goes from shore to shore. No other river seems to exhale such a life-giving warmth; as Herodotus said, "Egypt is an acquired country, the gift of the river." The Egyptians say that once you have drunk the water of the Nile (and in Egypt there is no other source of water), you will always return to the river. I believe it.

The Delta, lacking the Nile proper, also feels semi-urban; you are never far from Egypt's two great cities of Cairo and Alexandria. Cairo, with its Cheops Pyramid and the Sphinx, Saladin's wall against the Crusaders, Mohammed Ali's Citadel, the Mamelukes' city of the dead and medieval Cairo with its thousand minarets, retains much of the character of Upper Egypt. It is modern Cairo along the Nile, with its skyscraper hotels, like Alexandria with its beaches and open-air restaurants, that somehow seems to belong more to the Delta and the Mediterranean than to the old, enduring Egypt. In the Delta, where half of the population lives in small towns and a few scattered cities, it is impossible to say where town ends and countryside begins; its population density of 2,300 per square mile is one of the highest on earth. In Upper Egypt, where there are no cities of any size—Luxor and even Aswan are fairly small towns—three-fourths of the people are deemed villagers; with the empty desert all around there is no sense of crowding.

Yet none of this explains the differences in the cultures and characters of the Upper and Lower Egyptians as much as the century's time gap in agricultural development, the century between the end of the Nile's annual August flood in the Delta and the Upper Nile.

*

Mohammed Ali and his successors, by constructing the series of dams, canals, barrages, drains and water pumps beginning just north of Cairo, made possible year-round irrigation and multiple cropping, so that two to three crops, not just one as before, could be grown each year. The kind of village society that has since gradually evolved in the Delta suggests that technological change, providing a culture has enough time for its adaptive mechanisms to go to work, need not automatically have a disruptive impact on social values. In Upper Egypt, as I tried to illustrate in my book, *Shahhat*, the sudden shift in irrigation and farming methods since the Aswan Dam ended the annual flood in the 1960s has created a good deal of social turbulence. We do not find such turbulence in the Delta, where, since the big change came a century ago, a society has come about that restrains individuals in favor of the collective good.

Does what happened in the Delta have broader application? Can we expect other extremely crowded rural societies to go the same way? Its religion—the core of its culture, Islam—is just as strong a faith as in Upper Egypt, though many of the old supernatural supports are gone. There is a strong work ethic, value is placed on industry and thrift, courtesy is mixed with reserve and there is a firm commitment to technological progress. That village life in the Delta is remarkably orderly, crime-free and stable suggests that groups of people living together in extremely crowded rural countrysides do tend to adjust by sacrificing some of the more psychologically satisfying kinds of behavior and a good deal of individual freedom. The cost paid—aside from the year-round hard physical labor that intensive, nonmechanized agriculture requires—seems to be a fairly rigid rule by conventions, religious restrictions and obedience to authority. One finds similar patterns in equally crowded Java and Bangladesh.

*

Egyptians ask you if you don't find their rural landscapes monotonous. I never did along the Upper Nile. In the Delta the network of Nile-fed canals, the huddled mud-brick houses and the occasional minaret, the bright green of Egyptian clover and young wheat against the darker green of the many trees—well, it does sometimes seem to go on forever. The mild climate, abundant sun and water make the Delta a virtual greenhouse, producing some of the earth's highest yields in rice, beans, cotton, sugar, onions, wheat and maize. There is little mechanization and one sees few tractors.

Four things in the Delta struck me right away. First, the fierce work ethic; men may spend sixteen or so hours in the fields, and instead of the Saidis' jokes, gossip and sexual banter, one hears shouts of "Work! Don't speak so much!" "Leave that stubble clean, *nahdoof!*" and "You work like a boy, not a man!" I also missed the sorrowful songs, more like weeping, which can give a solemn dignity to field labor in Upper Egypt, as well as the sudden volcanic eruptions of tempers and the mock-furious shouting matches. The Delta *fellaheen* worked much harder, often staying in the fields all day except for an hour's siesta after the noon meal. As I have seen nowhere else, they sometimes harvested wheat by sickle by night as well as day. Most of the time, their long tunics or *galabias* tucked up at the waist, they labored with hoes. Unlike the Upper Egyptians, who never enter a field without removing their shoes, few worked barefoot. Then, mowing clover, or harvesting grain with a sickle, they bent from the waist, rarely squatting down on their haunches as Punjabis and Saidis do.

Second, there were round, cement cisterns in many fields, scattered in long lines a hundred meters apart. These were part of a tile drainage system which is starting to successfully combat the problem of salinity from such constant irrigation; tile drainage, though badly needed, is still little used in Upper Egypt.

Third, in the Delta one sees a constant procession from fields to the villages and back of men leading camels, donkeys and buffaloes laden with manure or fresh dirt. Great heaps of manure and dirt sit about the edges of the fields; nearly half of the Delta's labor force is engaged in the unceasing task of refertilizing the land with animal manure to replace the minerals and nutrients lost when the Nile stopped flooding the Delta a century ago. In Upper Egypt dung is still mostly used as a cooking fuel.

Fourth, Delta women commonly work in the fields, the older ones in the same long black dresses all women in Upper Egypt wear, but in the Delta the younger appear in brightly colored gowns, their heads wrapped in kerchiefs. Upper Egyptian women, once they reach puberty, rarely do field work; they go about freely in public, doing marketing and attending weddings, funerals and other social occasions, but always in long black wool cloaks; these cloaks, flowing behind and almost touching the ground as they ride their donkeys, give them a peculiar medieval look, like noble ladies in Cervantes' Spain.

The last conspicuous difference is the large number of students one sees in the Delta. Egypt supplies one-third of the Middle East's Arab migrant labor; without these Delta youth the Arab world would find it impossible to fill the void in teachers and technicians. In Upper Egypt only a handful of village children reach college.

*

The cultural differences between Upper and Lower Egypt are even more striking if we compare individual people. Let us take Shahhat, the Egyptian I know best, and a Delta *fellah,* Fatih, who is the same age, twenty-nine in 1981, cultivates the same size holding, two and a half acres (a bit above the all-Egyptian average of two acres), also became head of his family when his father died in the mid-1970s, and is married with small children (Shahhat has just one, Fatih, who married earlier, four).

Shahhat's village of Berat, four hundred and fifty river miles south of Cairo, has about 7,000 people who cultivate 1,300 acres; Berat is divided into eleven distinct hamlets, each close to its ancestral fields and possessing a separate identity. Shahhat's family was deeded two of its acres from Sombat, a former feudal estate, in 1965. The village has its own agricultural office, government primary school and dispensary, staffed by a doctor. Berat's real center is El Kom, its largest hamlet, with its biggest mosques, graveyard, office of the *'omda* or headman, several *kuttabs,* or traditional Moslem schools, Berat's sole opium and gambling den and its leading shopkeepers, sheikhs and sorcerers.

Sirs el Layyan is much bigger and much less traditional. Its 46,000 people cultivate 3,600 acres; the average holding among 8,000 families is one and a half acres. No longer worried, as the Saidis still are, about banditry, most Sirs el Layyan families have built small second houses out in their fields. The village is no longer completely dependent upon agriculture; there is a glass factory, two wheat mills and nearly 3,000 villagers work in Cairo, about two hours away. Statistics are all but nonexistent in village Egypt, but my guess is that about 5,000 men and 2,000 women work full-time in agriculture. Remarkably, the village has more than 7,000 students enrolled in five schools; the fact that nearly 900 schoolteachers living in Sirs el Layyan, I think, explains much that is urban middle class about its culture. Government services are much more sophisticated than in Berat; the Sirs el Layyan hospital has four doctors, and there is a veterinary clinic, experimental farm, day care and family planning centers and a welfare office.

The family income of both Shahhat and Fatih in the year I took for comparison—1976—came to just about the Egyptian equivalent of $1,200. Shahhat headed a family of seven, including his widowed mother, but also fed a steady stream of visiting friends and relatives, including half a dozen small nephews and nieces, on a fairly permanent basis. Shahhat owned a buffalo, a donkey and eight sheep. Fatih's family of ten included younger brothers, his widowed mother and his wife and children, but he fed no one outside the family during the time I knew him. He owned a buffalo, a camel and four sheep.

Shahhat's biggest cash crop of sugar cane brought in a net profit of about $600 a year; he also grew maize, beans, lentils, sesame, wheat and Egyptian clover. From time to time, Shahhat earned extra money selling wine, candy or vegetables or cooking *kunafeh,* a kind of vermicelli, during the annual month-long Moslem fast of Ramadan. Fatih's main cash crop was seed potatoes; he also grew wheat, maize and clover. His mother churned butter, which she marketed in the village for a profit of about $250 a year.

Earnings were similar; cash spending was not. Fatih's family, in an average month, spent $30–$35 (in terms of 1976–77 buying power): $8 for meat (a kilo every Thursday night is an Egyptian Moslem custom), $10 for cloth, $6 for tobacco, 20 cents for matches, $3 for sugar, $3 for tea, $1 for kerosene and $1.30 for soap. The poorest family I could find spent about $25 a month, nobody less. Shahhat's family, with much the same land, livestock and cash income, spent $50–$60 a month, the difference coming in cigarettes (Fatih rolled his own, Shahhat bought Egypt's most popular brand, Cleopatra), meat, sugar and tea (which Shahhat's mother, Ommohamed, was forever serving visitors in traditional hospitality).

But above household expenses, Fatih also spent $20–$25 a month to send three younger brothers to school, one of them to a commercial college to study accounting; Fatih calculated the older boy would be able to get a government job paying $40 a month; this would finance the college educations of the two younger boys. Neither Shahhat nor any of his five surviving brothers and sisters had attended any school but the village *kuttab* to memorize the Koran, which cost very little—perhaps $3–$4 monthly.

When Shahhat's father had died in 1974, Ommohamed had borrowed $600 from the government, using future sugar harvests as collateral, to pay for *zikrs,* or all-night prayer performances, on the seventh, fortieth and hundredth days after his death to speed the father's spirit on its journey to Paradise. Fatih, much less traditional, had held no *zikrs* for his father. He had no debts; if he borrowed money to buy seed and fertilizer, he always repaid it at harvest time.

As was characteristically Upper Egyptian, both Shahhat and Ommohamed could be wildly extravagant. Ommohamed, especially, loved the grand gesture. If there was a guest to feed—and she was justly famed as the best cook in the village—Ommohamed would prepare several meat dishes such as roast beef, chicken, rabbit or pigeon, grape leaves stuffed with rice, a casserole of eggs, tomatoes and potatoes, a spicy salad, lentil soup, fresh bread, white goat's cheese and both sugared tea and coffee. Often it meant that for a week afterward the family would have nothing to eat but bread and beans. Ommohamed was eager to outshine all her neighbors in hospitality; her door was always open and she might serve twenty to thirty glasses of tea in a day. Shahhat would grow angry at such extravagance. "Are you a *princessa?*" he would shout. "No, you are poor and without clothes!" Ommohamed would flare up just as hotly to defend herself. "You have no manners! How dare you shout at me in my house? If one is generous to others, Allah will provide!"

The *fellaheen* in Sirs el Layyan were also hospitable, once you got to know them, but the fare they offered was extremely modest, usually just their own daily diet of wheat or maize bread, cheese, a vegetable or two, raw onions, beans and sweetened tea. Most were very frugal, just as most Saidis were both avaricious and generous, forever scheming how to get money out of you, totally lacking in scruples when it came to asking for *baksheesh,* and yet prepared to spend their last (or your last) piastre to entertain you lavishly, even if it meant, as it almost always did, going into debt. Feasts, musicians, dancing, hashish, beer, liquor, magic charms, even all-night prayer performances, were to spontaneously enjoy in the present moment without much regard for the consequences; very few Upper Egyptians showed much ability to defer gratification.

In 1979, soon after his book was published, I gave Shahhat $500 to get married. I missed the wedding celebration but Shahhat described it in a letter, written in English for him by some passing American tourist. At first, Shahhat said, he was critical of Ommohamed for buying an "expensive" robe for the most revered Moslem sheikh who was to attend because "until now I have had little faith in sheikhs and their powers." At the wedding feast, Shahhat ceremonially sacrificed a large ram. "And what do you think we found inside the ram?" he wrote. "You will not believe it but it happened. The great sheikh demonstrated his power. Inside the male ram we found a small lamb!"

Sensation followed. The astonished wedding guests fell to their knees to pray. And Shahhat? "I felt terror and that the sheikh might take revenge on me." So he rushed to Luxor and hired a band to celebrate. That night all the villagers gathered to perform a *zikr,* chanting from the Koran to praise Allah and Shahhat's miraculous marriage feast. The letter ended, "Mother Ommohamed, the woman—my wife—and the rest of the family send their best wishes. Ommohamed always prays to Allah to save you and bless you." And hurry back, I thought, as the debts are mounting. Ommohamed, in the time I lived with the family, was quite capable of throwing up her hands and beseeching Allah, "How can I feed my children? How?" and an hour later rushing out to borrow from the neighbors to prepare a banquet for some guests. Of all the villagers I've known, the Upper Egyptians were by far the most hopelessly improvident.

They also had the most humor. Not so Fatih. The proverbs he quoted would have gone down well in the Bible Belt. "Work and let the day pass," "The lazy man is always depressed," "Don't sleep with your wife on the days of harvesting," and "Time is like a sword; if you cannot cut it, it will cut you." In contrast, there was always an element of amused self-parody about Shahhat. If somebody greeted him, "Good morning," he would pretend to scowl and would retort, "Black morning," a Moslem curse. Or if a passerby on the road asked where he was going, as like as not he'd reply, "Going to hell." In the fields he was forever singing or shouting in a half-comic, half-religious style, such as, "Oh, my God, Allah, help the poor people! Send us a breeze and an army of workers from the sky! Oh, holy Prophet, help us, we are Molems!" Once, when somebody cursed him as a Jew, Shahhat laughed and said, "Jew, am I? Well, Allah must love the Jews for he has given them everything."

Both Fatih and Shahhat sang popular Arab tunes, improvising their own words. Fatih's was characteristically grim:

> Poverty came one day in a *felluca*
> And I asked Poverty:
> What do you want with me?
> And Poverty said:
> To live with you always,
> Never let you be happy.
> Oh, Poverty has a stick
> And beats me on the head.
> If I see Poverty again
> I will kill him.

> Oh, hire yourself to others
> They will kill you with work.
> But he who fears rats
> Cannot breed chickens.

One of Shahhat's:

> Why, why, why, why, why, why?
> If you have money your wife respects you
> And says, "You are the beat of my heart,
> The light of my eyes.
> The days without you, I go out of my mind."
> But if your pocket is empty,
> The smell of your sweat burns her eyes.
> Why, why, why, why, why, why?
> Oh, I'll take hashish and opium
> And be strong as a bull.
> If a woman is satisfied,
> Her words are sweet as honey.
> If she is not, she can roast you like an oven.
> Oh, I'll take hashish and opium
> And be as strong as a bull.
> At noonday prayers how I'll soar!
> But when they pray at Mahgreb
> And the sun goes down,
> I'll flutter like a wounded bird.
> Why, why, why, why, why, why?

Sirs el Layyan, in its Moslem fashion, was very puritanical. There were only three cafés, all out on the main highway; the clientele ran to bus and taxi drivers and even they just took tea. Beer was sold, but customers were expected to take it home or out of sight to drink. Hashish was smoked, but only in the dead of night, when, I'm told, the village policeman took his turn on the *hubbly bubbly* or water pipe. In Berat, a favorite gathering place for younger men at night was Abdullahi's, a low, dark hovel in El Kom hamlet where everyone sat about on straw mats, drinking, smoking hashish or, crowded around a low circular table, gambling at cards. The main drink was *zabeeb*, a concoction from dates so potent that Shahhat liked to drop matches into the empty bottles to see the fumes explode. When we went to Abdullahi's, it was never long before everybody was intoxicated, so that we sat about grinning with bleary eyes, stupefied by the bad liquor and noisy uproar. In the dim lamplight, even the most innocent face took on an evil look; sin hung over Abdullahi's like a fog. But liquor, whatever you say, and as Charan, now a teetotaler, remembered a bit sadly last year, "brings people together." Even as innocuous as Sirs el Layyan's cafés were, the *fellaheen* rarely went in them, Fatih never. I think they missed something.

In both Berat and Sirs el Layyan villages there was a strong belief (among the men) in male superiority; in both, women fought back as best they could. Shahhat's favorite song, for instance, was "Shefiqa and Motwali," a kind of Egyptian "Frankie and Johnny," which has been popular for years all over the country. The theme is male chauvinist in the extreme. Motwali, a young soldier, discovers that his sister, Shefiqa, has been seduced into prostitution. He disguises himself, pretends to be a customer, confronts her and kills her, cutting off her head. Then, accompanied by a band of musicians, he carries her body through the streets and drops it at the feet of his parents, sobbing, "Here is your daughter!" A judge acquits Motwali for saving his family's honor. Shahhat found it deeply moving and was forever playing it on somebody's tape recorder. After a few drinks, it even brought tears to his eyes.

It is the sort of thing that still can happen among the *fellaheen*, especially in Upper Egypt. In Berat, while I lived there, an unmarried girl who became pregnant was murdered by her father to preserve the family honor; he waited until she was bent over a well washing clothes and held her head under the water until she drowned. So when I was in Sirs el Layyan and the unmarried sister of one of Fatih's neighbors, Helmi, became pregnant, I feared the worst; Fatih himself said Helmi "should do like Motwali."

When the police sent for the girl and questioned her, she named seven village men. One, a schoolteacher, was temporarily arrested, but hysterically protested his innocence. Several of the other men named went to Helmi's house and stood outside in the street, shouting denials and abusing the family. The baby was born, but soon fell ill with fever. Helmi's sister took it to the Sirs el Layyan hospital but they refused to treat it on the grounds that it had no father; the baby died. To worsen the girl's ordeal, a doctor, called to provide a death certificate, claimed to find evidence of strangulation. Helmi's poor sister, by now nearly out of her wits, was briefly arrested. Remarkably, Helmi steadfastedly resisted pressure from the village men to kill his sister; he accepted the dishonor.

Often the women themselves fight back. In Berat, Shahhat's cousin, Batah, a pretty sixteen-year-old, broke with Saidi tradition by refusing to marry another cousin, Ali, whose father was a notorious drunkard. Batah was secretly in love with a member of the lowly Jamasah clan, outcastes in Upper Egypt because their ancestors were once cursed by the Prophet Mohammed. One night while Shahhat, Nubi, my interpreter, and I were eating at the house of Batah's grandmother, Hasan, Ali's father, broke into the house and tried to carry Batah away. Batah resisted and began screaming; we were upstairs and witnessed what was a terrible scene from the staircase. Hasan was shouting at the girl. "Be silent! You are to marry my son. I shall take you to my house. By God, if you do not come I shall slit your throat and cut you into small pieces. Not even maggots shall find your body. We do not allow women to say yes or no." Actually, as I learned later, the Koran does require that a girl give her consent in marriage; when it came to the cult of male superiority, I found the Saidis all too ready to ignore Koranic strictures.

Batah's grandmother, a frail old lady, almost blind, rushed to the girl's defense. Batah's father was also there, but he merely said, "Yes, you speak the truth, my brother. We cannot leave things for the women to decide. You can take her. Be still, my mother-in-law. Do not speak. We want to close this subject."

But the courageous old woman ignored him, seized a butcher knife and shrieked, "I am an old woman and blind. But if you do not leave my house this instant, Hasan, I shall kill you and stay screaming all the night. There will be no marriage with your son. You and your family go far from us. If anyone tries to take Batah against her will, I shall fight you until I die. Men like you are not real men. Women are better than you!"

A man with Hasan cursed her, "Your father is a dog, old woman! Why has Allah not taken you? The good ones die and the bad stay alive." By now Shahhat had seized a glass pitcher and was about to enter the fight on the old lady's side, but Hasan left the house. For days he went around the village cursing Batah and vowing, "By the Great God, that girl should be driven from the village!" He told everyone his family had been dishonored; the son, Ali, was away in the Egyptian army but everyone feared a blood feud, with killings on both sides, especially when it came out that Batah planned to marry a Jamasah instead and with her grandmother's blessing. A day or two before the wedding was to take place, Batah went about the village, going from house to house as was the custom, inviting the women. Then, about three o'clock in the afternoon, we suddenly heard her screams. They came from one edge of the village; by the time we got there a crowd had gathered in the road. Up ahead Batah lay moaning; her clothes were ripped open. Her cousin, Ali, still in his soldier's uniform, was crouched over her; he held a revolver and shouted he would shoot anyone who came closer. As he turned and ran off into the desert, we saw he had blood on his hands.

Shahhat explained what had happened. In Saidi custom, a bridegroom ends his wife's virginity by breaking her hymen with his fingers; the girl's mother is present to hold and comfort her. The mother then displays a bloody cloth to the village women as proof of the bride's virginity. What the cousin had done was to symbolically violate Batah to display contempt for the Jamasahs and uphold his family honor. What astonished me was that village sympathy tended to be with the soldier, not Batah. In their eyes breaking with village tradition was the greater guilt.

Even Ommohamed, forty-nine at this writing and still handsome and as strong-willed a woman as you can imagine, was subject to notions of male superiority. She had married at the age of thirteen, given birth to twenty children, but lost fourteen of them in infancy or childhood. Intelligent but ignorant and superstitious, with a mind formed, like Shahhat's, by medieval Islam, Ommohamed was convinced that her many children had died because Satan and his demons had strangled them. When they fell ill she did not go to the doctor but bought amulets and charms from the village sorceress. In fear of attracting the Evil Eye of envious neighbors, Ommohamed had left her children unwashed and shabbily clad; as is common in village Egypt, infants in Berat were habitually left extremely filthy; you'd see dozens of flies buzzing around their eyes, unheeded and unmolested. This was not because the women did not cherish their children, but because they did. They had such a dread of trachoma and other endemic diseases, they were afraid to wash the children and do the things that, had they but known, would prevent them. There is also the woman's fear that her husband will divorce her or take another wife—in Islamic law he is allowed four if he can support them—if she cannot give him sons. Whatever power a woman wields, and in Ommohamed's case it is considerable, it is as the mother of adult sons.

Explosive arguments and violent threats, though rarely violence itself, were part of daily life in Berat; you never went anywhere at night without carrying a heavy stave, mostly against ferocious dogs, but for possible protection against humans, too. Some men carried knives; a few, pistols. Jail sentences for murder in a genuine feud or if unpremeditated in a heated quarrel tended to be light. In Sirs el Layyan, nobody carried weapons of any kind, not even staves, after dark. Quarrels were very rare; what few I saw, unlike the melodramatic shouting matches in Upper Egypt, were serious and more vicious. In Berat, where cattle rustling was endemic, livestock were brought into a stable, part of the house, at night. In Sirs el Layyan, buffaloes and cows were often left untended in barns out in the fields far from any house; livestock theft seemed unknown.

The sense of removal in Upper Egypt was great. Only in the past year or two has Shahhat begun to watch television—several cafés down by the Nile ferry landing have sets. He was the first to tell me about the Jonestown mass suicide-murder, for instance. Few of Berat's people take much interest in outside events, however; only a handful listened to President Sadat's radio speeches. In contrast, one day we were coming from the fields in Sirs el Layyan just as Sadat was speaking; we could hear Sadat's voice coming from virtually every house we passed. With so many radio and TV sets, Cairo so near and so many teachers reading newspapers, political awareness in Sirs el Layyan seemed high.

Not so in Berat, where if a son were drafted into the army, many families practically went into mourning. Shahhat and I, in a scene described in his book, once met a family taking their son, who had just been inducted, to Luxor to put him on the train. They were all weeping as though a funeral were in progress. The father called out in terror to Shahhat, "What is happening with the army now? Is there war? What is the news from Cairo?" In her review of *Shahhat* in the New York *Times,* Vivian Gornick wrote, "The scene tells all. It frames a life where, after twenty-five years of socialism on the radio, the world beyond the village still drops off into darkness and, alone under an empty sky, men and women struggle daily, in the crudest of terms, to experience themselves."

Shahhat was aware of birth control. He once observed, "Women take tablets today not to get so many babies; people are getting intelligent about life." In Berat pronatalist attitudes persisted because more sons meant relief from field labor, old-age security and protection in feuds; there was also a high rate of infant mortality. In Sirs el Layyan the incentives were the other way: modern medicine was available at a new drugstore, there was a family planning clinic and even the poorest families tried to get at least one child into college. In Egypt, as elsewhere, the key to fertility declines seems to be more rights and education for women. President Sadat's wife, Jihan, has even advocated sterilization and legislated two-child families. Sadat himself is much more conservative. In an interview at his seaside summer home near Alexandria in 1976, he told me, "Change in village Egypt only comes through education, only. I accuse my wife of being a philosopher. I tell her, let us look to our culture and our people."

Sadat's native village of Miet Abu el Koum was less than twenty miles from Sirs el Layyan; he described how, as a boy, he cut clover, harvested wheat, plowed and tended cattle. (When I told him I grew up in North Dakota, Sadat exclaimed, "Marvelous! You didn't tell me. You're pulling my leg. Do you know the whole state has only seven hundred thousand people but they produce eight million tons of wheat? You should have stayed home and been a farmer.")

*

In Egypt, then, the end of the Nile's old annual flood, a century ago in the Delta and just sixteen years ago in Upper Egypt, has produced two distinct village types. What I have called the Upper Egyptian grasshopper is superstitious, spontaneous, extravagant, temperamental and fatalistic. The Delta ant is gentler, practicing thrift, industry, piety, courtesy and trust in technological progress. The ant saves his money, accepts military service, likes to travel, respects the police, will visit a doctor and tries to emulate urban middle-class values. Humble, conformist and responsive to group pressure, he is, I felt, more likely to suffer from psychological repression. Gossip seemed a bit more malicious, less funny in the Delta; there was a tendency to brood and harbor grudges. In contrast, the grasshopper spends everything he can get his hands on, is forever in debt, fears military service, hates to leave home, hates the police, goes to doctors only after magic and sorcery fail, rejects city values and has a good deal more pride, personal courage and individualism. Upper Egyptians may suffer feelings of helplessness, but they try to disguise it with a *macho* front. The improvident Saidi grasshopper is less anxious and less driven than the ever-aspiring Delta ant.

Islam is a total and living faith for both. In Sirs el Layyan ritual and Moslem social restrictions were much more binding; there was more outward piety. But I felt Islam in the Delta lacked that powerful inner force a religion gains from its supernatural supports: the Saidi's is reinforced by beliefs in magic, sorcerers, demons, djinns and the power of Satan for evil and Allah for good. Berat's *zikrs,* prayer performances, were much more somber and frenzied; the Saidis were so at one with Islam they could joke about Allah, something the less confident Delta villagers, trying for a more modern and hence inescapably more secular way of life, never did. In Upper Egypt, everything is humorous, even the ways of God.

Both ant and grasshopper are caught in a never-ending race against time, weather and government incompetence to get the crops in and get paid; this cycle, for both Fatih and Shahhat, was tantamount to natural law. Inside this law both looked out at the world through holes, as it were, in the mud-brick walls of their villages. To Shahhat this world was more blurred and frightening, demon-filled and Allah-awesome. Naturally, he turned back to the tiny fortress-like world of the village, built with mud-brick houses linked end to end, no house free-standing. In Sirs el Layyan, almost symbolically, they were starting to build individual homesteads out in the fields.

In Berat two emotions—fear and desire—had much more power than in Sirs el Layyan. Among the women like Ommohamed, proud, hungry for life, desperately ignorant, there was a great deal of feverish praying and running to the sorceress. Among young men like Shahhat there was a lot of wild breaking out. Yet—what was so remarkable—just when things seemed completely out of hand, you'd go to bed, wake up the next morning and start out afresh, as if nothing at all had happened. Ms. Gornick caught this very well in her remarkably perceptive review. She observed, "Family grievances, sexual passions, quarrels over money or honor—all have the effect of chain lightning: strike a single bolt and within minutes a dozen lives are in ruins (except that twenty-four hours later the dead are laughing and talking, yesterday's despair somehow overcome)."

In Sirs el Layyan, you had neither the drama, the sense of emotional release nor the humorous aftermath and postmortems that went with them. In Berat, if I got mad at somebody, we'd threaten each other with murder and mayhem, maybe even throw chairs or knock each other down and the next day kiss and make up (literally kiss; every time I came or went from the village, I had by custom to embrace and kiss a good many of the men and a few of the women too, though only those so ugly, halt or decrepit nobody could possibly construe a sexual interest). In the polite, ever-cool Delta if you felt angry, there was no such way to vent your frustrations and resentments.

In time, as modernization moves along and traditions weaken, Upper Egypt seems likely to go the way of the Delta. This will be a long and leisurely process. At the end of my stay in Sirs el Layyan, Shahhat came down on the train, expecting to stay a week. Everyone was friendly and hospitable. Shahhat admired Fatih's industry and his willingness to sacrifice to educate his younger brothers. He was fascinated by the Delta's different way of farming. Then, at the end of the third day, he was ready to go, restless, anxious, complaining he felt suffocated. "It's like a prison here," he said.

When I think of Jakarta as it used to be, I think of it at twilight, just after a late afternoon monsoon rain. The street-stall lamps along Jalan Thamrin have misty halos and there is the occasional splash of a passing car; there was not much traffic then. Water glistens on the pavement, on the soaked canvas hoods of the line of three-wheeled pedicabs, or *betjaks,* all lined up in front of the Hotel Indonesia, which was truly luxurious in those days. Even the lean, hard-muscled shoulders of the *betjak* drivers are wet; Welcome Circle is washed by rain. Gone, at least in my memory, is the oppressive equatorial heat; the air smells of freshness, salt spray from the Java Sea, frangipani and jasmine, and the sweet, peculiarly East Indian odor of clove-spiced *kretek* cigarettes.

That's how it was that evening in December 1967, when I stepped out of the hotel wondering what I would do for the rest of the day, and the rest of my life, now that I had one. I had just ended three years and eight months as a war correspondent in Vietnam and not even a month lying on the beach in Bali had fully convinced me that the nightmare was over and I had survived.

"Hello, mister! Where are you going?"

The voice came from one of the *betjak* men; I glimpsed flashing white teeth in a bronzed, beaming face and a floppy hat and shirt soaked with rain. Where was I going? I had no idea and told him I just wanted to see the sights.

Once you got used to the *betjak* man's labored breathing and overcame the feeling of being a sitting target for every approaching car, a *betjak* ride was agreeable. You were carried along just fast enough for the air to seem cool; it was possible to lean comfortably back and look at the stars without being bitten by insects.

The driver first pedaled to Merdeka Square, where we saw Sukarno's gigantic National Monument, a pillar of Italian marble with a floodlit flame. Husen, as the driver said he was named, said there were forty kilos of gold up there costing a third of a million dollars. Then we pedaled past the glittering white presidential palace to the vast, shadowy steel skeleton of what Husen said would be the "biggest mosque in the world" someday, on to the West Irian Monument topped by a bronze giant breaking his colonial chains and back to the bright Christmas-tree lights of Jalan Thamrin. Sukarno's legacy to Jakarta might have been bankruptcy and a useless pile of hollow and half-finished monuments, but they made a perfect setting for a guided tour in a *betjak*. Then we visited a Chinese crocodile-breeding farm, took in part of a soccer game at the national stadium and, caught in a monsoon downpour on our way back to the hotel, took refuge in a roadside teahouse. There was a soldier there and after I asked him about the price of rice, how much he made and such, he became very agitated and I abruptly found myself back in the *betjak* as Husen pedaled into a drenching rain. "Hey, what is this?" I shouted. "I'm getting all wet! Why did we leave the teahouse in such a hurry?" Husen laughed and laughed. "Better we go, uncle," he finally explained. "The soldier say you ask too many questions and must be zero-zero-seven or *kommunis*. But I say, no, you are people from another people's country and so must ask many questions."

"How can I see a village?" I asked on impulse, feeling like a drowned rat as we neared the hotel. Since Husen spoke a little English he was a great guide. "Would you like to go to my village, *tuan?*" Husen asked in his ever-ingenuous way, characteristically not mentioning until we were on the bus the next afternoon that his village was 210 kilometers from Jakarta, halfway across Java.

Thus began what has become a rather long journey with Husen and what was to stretch into years of living in villages in many parts of the world. I have since stayed in Husen's village for six months in 1970, with revisits in 1973, 1978, 1979 and 1980. As with Charan in India and a few of the others, I feel Husen and I have gone from the last of youth into middle age together. (A sad and somehow unexpected aspect of my work is that everybody keeps getting older. Perhaps it's more noticeable when you only see them once every three, four or five years, though villagers do seem to age more rapidly than we do.) In 1970, when I lived with Husen the whole time, we spent about half our days in the village. Whenever his money gave out, he had to return to pedaling his *betjak* in Jakarta, in the slum of Simprug where he and his young wife, Karniti, stayed. (In those days I was practically as poor as they were.)

If there is enough food, life in a Javanese village can be idyllic;

against a backdrop of misty volcanoes, placid rivers, bright green rice paddies and clumps of bamboo, mangos and bananas, steamy equatorial days drift into balmy nights. After dark, as oil lamps twinkle on and the haunting *ning-nong* sound of bamboo *gamelan* orchestras floats over from the treelines, the countryside becomes alive with shadow plays, folk dramas, classical dance and acrobatic performances. Together with the Balinese, the Javanese are possibly the most cultured, artistic and mystical villagers anywhere. Although they are nominally Moslem, their beliefs are deeply influenced by medieval Hinduism and pagan animism; they love theater, especially the shadow play, or *wayang kulit,* the most pervasive cultural influence. It sets their standard of ethics, a strong belief in authority, the idea that good and evil spirits must be placated and general ideas about life.

One of Husen's most vivid childhood memories of his village, a beautiful place set on the banks of the wide Cimanuk River with its distant cloud-wreathed volcano and the pale green of the rice paddies against the deeper green of the fruit tree groves, was the *gamelan*'s *ning-nong* sound just as darkness fell. As a small boy, hearing it, Husen would slip away from his parents' bamboo hut, hurrying through the evening with some friend like Raskim or Djuned, with mounting anticipation as the music grew closer and louder. In the paved courtyard of some prosperous peasant, the boys would dart past the glowing orange lights of tea-stall lamps, throwing their long black shadows behind them as they converged on the large coconut oil lamp of the village *dalang,* or shadow play puppeteer. Sometimes they would pause behind the big white cotton sheet and watch entranced as the *dalang* unpacked his flat, gaily painted leather puppets, some grotesque, some regal, others comic; all seemingly came to life when their shadows were viewed from the other side of the lamplit screen.

Like water seeking its own level, the boys would scramble to the front of the men, falling upon each other like pups in a heap until the play began. For a time they would watch the puppet gods and nobles in their interminable court debates and philosophical discussions which begin the plays—but often the children fell asleep until it was time for the battles and the clowns to come on. Sometimes they sat up and watched everything and gradually, as the years wore on, the *wayang kulit* came to seem to Husen, as it does to most Javanese, a truly sacred drama. A Hindu king wrestled with demons, a holy man combatted evil spirits. The bodies of the leather puppets, hidden as they were on the other side of the screen, came to seem like an illusion, and their shadows, which trembled and breathed with life in the *dalang*'s skilled hands, the reflection of that illusion. And somehow, unconsciously, as Husen grew into manhood, he absorbed the Hindu belief that soul, shadow, spirit and ghost are one; although he is nominally Moslem, his deepest beliefs thus were formed.

Most of the shadow plays depicted stories from the Hindu epic, the Mahabharata, a great war between kinsmen, the five Pendawa kings and the one hundred Korawas—portrayed as an endless struggle, not so much between good and evil, as between base animal passions and detached, effortless self-control. Since this struggle never ended, the final battle was never shown. One Pendawa king, Judistira, symbolized the inability to act if drained too much by kindness and compassion; another, his brother, Bima, human vitality and the dangers of passionate commitment; a third, Ardjuna, cool capability and merciless justice.

But the play's real heroes were their clown-servants—above all, the fat, physically repulsive Semar, with a black, ugly-looking face, who was full of crude talk and action, such as breaking wind to chase away his comic children or throwing feces at an opponent. But to Husen and all Javanese villagers, Semar was the father of all men and, rather like Jesus in Christianity, was actually a god come to life, but in all-too-human form; he was regarded as the kind, all-knowing guardian spirit of all Javanese from their first appearance to the end of time. The shadow play was very complex, a dream world peopled with gods, kings, priests, princesses, warriors, giants, buffoons and fantastic animals; but its values were deeply ingrained in the Javanese mentality and were the measurement by which they judged their own behavior. Javanese society is highly structured and just as everyone in the shadow play had his place, so did ordinary people in Husen's mind. In the early 1970s, as Jakarta's Governor Ali Sadikin began banning *betjaks* from the center of the city, he might have seemed as merciless as Ardjuna. But to have opposed him, in Husen's view, was as unthinkable as for clown-servants to rebel against one of the gods.

Husen for years has worried that so many young people are turning away from these values. Better the dreams of the shadow play, he feels, than nothing at all. Once, after his story was published and he enjoyed a brief fame in Jakarta, even becoming the subject of a television documentary, he was asked about Jakarta's ban against *betjaks*.

Husen told the interviewer, "It is a good thing. Now the governor will help us to find a better way of earning a living." Partly he was simply playing safe, but I think Husen genuinely expected more to be done for the poor.

Husen was unusual for a *betjak* man in that he had been educated to be a primary school teacher. He ran away to Jakarta in 1955, as a sixteen-year-old, just a year before completing his training. He told his dismayed father, "I want to go everywhere, to see many places, to make many friends in my life. I do not want to be just a teacher in the village, always books and papers, quickly become old." Husen was to spend twenty years as a seasonal migrant to Jakarta; he did not return to Pilangsari to farm for good until 1976, too old—in 1981 he was forty-three—to pedal a *betjak* any longer. His life in Jakarta's squalid, crime-ridden slums was not without adventure and, before General Sadikin's ban, he truly loved showing tourists the sights. At the same time, he never lost his longing to return to the tasks and values of the village. "I am a villager," Husen once told me, "and wherever I go, I must follow the ways of my village." Today he has been married and divorced four times, with one surviving child, a boy of fourteen, who lives with a grandmother. Husen left his first wife, the boy's mother, after she abandoned him for dead when he was stricken with yaws and lay delirious for seven days on the floor of a bamboo hut in one of Jakarta's worst slums before he was found.

His second wife, Karniti, was the only one I knew well. In 1970, after four years of marriage, with her flowered sarong and long black hair falling over her shoulders, she looked the fifteen years she had been on her wedding day—despite the death of a one-year-old son from fever and two miscarriages. During the six months I stayed with them, Karniti was tortured by fears that Husen would leave her if she proved barren. This fear was justified when, after I had left Indonesia, Husen's ever-critical parents demanded he either divorce Karniti or no longer be their son. Since parental wishes are traditionally binding and the land is the only physical or psychological underpinning a poor Javanese has, Husen divorced his young wife; his parents quickly arranged a third marriage to a plump, healthy girl whom he left in three months. In the final scene of Husen's published story, written much later than the rest, he encounters Karniti one evening a year after their divorce in Jakarta's main market, Pasar Senen.

She was selling rice at an all-night stall. He scarcely recognized her. She was heavily made up, her cheeks rouged to the eyes, her eyebrows and eyelashes thick with mascara, and her mouth scarlet with lipstick. He told her to go back to the village, and tried to give her train fare. She refused. He told her he loved her and would go on loving her until the day he died, and then he went away and did not see her again.

In 1973, after a long search, Husen and I found Karniti in Jakarta's waterfront area of Tandjung Priok. She had remarried, to another seasonal *betjak* man and part-time village cultivator, but she was still heavily made up. It was a terrible slum; both Husen and I were afraid trying to find our way out after dark. But Karniti's story ends more happily. During my most recent visit Husen said that she was visiting her family across the river; Karniti looked as she had in the old days, seemed terribly pleased to see us and, bringing the youngest of her two children for me to greet, pointed to his little tassel; she had finally had a surviving son. Today Husen realizes he still loves Karniti; he cannot forgive his parents for forcing him into such a tragic mistake. He is middle-aged now and begins to look it. "When I was young, I felt life was going up, up," he told me in 1980. "Now mine has gone way down."

Over his years in Jakarta, whenever the rain fell at planting time or the rice was ready for harvest, Husen always went back home to the village, often in those days riding in the rooftop baggage rack of a dilapidated old bus, or on a grain truck; today there are modern buses that take half the time and everybody rides inside. Once outside Jakarta, Java is lushly green but so densely populated there is hardly a break in the small, white-painted bamboo huts with their gardens, plots of paddy and picket fences; town and countryside fade into one another just as they do in the Nile Delta.

In 1973, at Husen's urging, his father, then a highly traditional man in his sixties, reluctantly planted one crop of the new Philippine-bread high-yield dwarf rice, then called C-4, investing in nitrogen fertilizer and chemical insecticide for the first time. Earlier the father had flatly refused to try modern ways at all. He tripled his normal yield, harvesting six tons on his two and a half acres of rice land. But as soon as we left, Husen to Jakarta and myself to another country, the father returned to traditional methods, scattering only leaves from the *jowar* tree on the green shoots of his next crop and relying on Moslem prayers and fasting to keep insects away. The harvest once again fell to two tons.

Although as early as 1970 an agricultural extension agent told Husen his father's land could feed and support sixteen people instead of five, enabling Husen and several brothers to permanently return home, the father feared and resisted change. A proud, conservative old man, a rigid Moslem, and deeply superstitious, the father had always worked hard, tilling his paddies and mango orchards with a hand hoe, a backbreaking task in the sticky volcanic soil (as I found out in 1970 when I almost cut my left big toe off and was forced to spend a month in bed in Jakarta). As an ambitious young, completely landless peasant, Husen's father had struggled for years, doing coolie labor, to save up enough to buy his land and educate Husen. Husen, the only one of his children he could afford to send to high school, had proved the father's greatest disappointment in life. Although an increasing number of families in Pilangsari were doing well with the new rice and the government encouraged them to grow it, the father adamantly stuck to the old ways.

He still borrowed and gave loans without interest; he shared one-sixth of his rice crop with even poorer neighbors, mostly elderly women, who planted it and harvested it. He would rather have died than mortgage his land for credit at a bank in order to buy insecticides and fertilizer. Mutual aid had always had a healthy leveling effect and the father did not like the way some villagers grew richer and others poorer with the new rice. Husen's old mother was equally opposed to contraception. To the elderly couple, value had always been attached to large numbers of children, all-night shadow play performances, and religious ceremonies and feasts, which impoverished them but gave life its meaning.

Husen's parents did not seem to perceive the dangers of overpopulation but instead suspected, probably rightly, that if they gave in at all to innovations, there was no telling where it would stop. Husen himself did grasp that Java had so many people it was just as futile to resist modern agricultural technology and birth control as it was to try and stop villagers from going to Jakarta. But, instilled with shadow play values, he could rebel against neither his parents nor authority. I remember one day how ashamed he was when we heard General Sadikin reply, when asked what would happen to the *betjak* men if they were banned from Jakarta, "Let them go back to their place of origin." And do what, I thought angrily, starve?

It was easy to grow angry in Jakarta in 1973; in 1967 and 1970 Husen, like the other *betjak* men, had taken pride in his independence and being a vital part of the Jakarta scene. To be told he was no longer wanted not only robbed him of his sense of dignity and participation, but badly hurt his feelings. When Husen and I returned to Jakarta to spend some weeks, I felt a vague, troubled sense that here in the great city—with its too little industry, its stagnant surrounding villages, a heedless pursuit of the consumer society by the rich and a release from the old cultural restraints by the poor, with steadily more and more people and fewer and fewer jobs. It was here in Jakarta where everything someday would meet, clash and finally explode.

At that time, when Husen pedaled his *betjak,* he was staying in a shed with about forty other *betjak* drivers, most of them from Pilangsari or neighboring villages. Most of the men slept on an open platform on stilts, sarong-wrapped and so closely packed the air was thick and suffocatingly hot. I always felt grimy and bug-bitten in the morning and could hardly wait to pour cold water over myself in an improvised shower. Below the platform a dank, narrow corridor opened out on the banks of one of Jakarta's brown, rubbish-strewn canals, where an open privy had been erected out over the water on stilts. The bamboo walls were mildewed, ragged laundry was always dripping overhead and the bare earth underfoot was wet and slimy. Some of the *betjak* men's wives and children lived in dim, foul cubicles on the lower level.

During the day most of the men slept because under Jakarta's new laws the only time they could ply their *betjaks* on the city's main boulevards was after ten at night. Aside from Husen, the ones I knew best were Tjasidi, tall and easygoing and a little better off because he had married a village merchant's daughter and purchased three *betjaks* of his own to rent to others; Tjasta, a moustached ex-convict who seemed alienated from village and city alike; and big, tough, muscular Raskim, whose handsome face was clouded with slowly growing anger.

One day, unable to sleep and seeking to escape the groans and teeth-gnashing of the fitful slumberers upstairs, Raskim and I sat down in the corridor, trying to get a breath of fresh air. Bibi, one of the wives, joined us, chatting while she systematically removed lice from the hair of one of her small children. Raskim stared grimly across the fetid canal; above the roofs of squatters' shacks we could see the sun glittering off the windows of the Hotel Indonesia and Jakarta's other many new glass-and-concrete skyscrapers; with a small modernizing Indonesian elite determined to achieve North American lifestyles, luxury hotels and office buildings were starting to jostle for space along Jalan Thamrin, the streets were filled with new Fiats and Datsuns and new shops flooded with television sets, air-conditioners and other such consumer amenities. The whole center of Jakarta had become a kind of Potemkin inner city, one of Asia's new ghettos of affluence. But the rest of Jakarta was little changed from 1967, less an ordinary city than a vast conglomeration of *atap*-roofed, bamboo *kampongs,* held together by a network of dirt roads and lacking pure water, electricity, sanitation or schools.

"Do you think the time of being free on the roads will ever come again?" Raskim asked. Bibi said her husband claimed it was getting too dangerous to pedal a *betjak* anymore with so many new cars about. "No," Raskim disagreed, but he added, "One has to be more careful." Raskim said he still earned well, but only because he had taken to bullying his late-night customers and taking drunks to some of the city's toughest vice centers. "The police are very strict," he said. "If they catch you at anything, they stomp you." Everyone was afraid of the police. Quiet Djuned, Husen's friend since childhood, had been arrested in the confusion of a riot he stopped to watch; he was jailed for two months, spent all his savings feeding his family back in Pilang-sari and now seemed broken and subdued, keeping mostly to himself. As we talked, Husen and Tjasidi came to bathe in the dirty canal; there was no place else (some neighboring students let me use their shower, but only because I was a foreign *tuan*).

"I'm just waiting until harvest time," Raskim said. "There's too much trouble in Jakarta now. They move us poor people here and there. Once the governor makes a place nice and comfortable, the prices go up, somebody buys it and we have to get out so that richer people can build houses on it."

"We'll have to leave here too if they pave the road," Bibi said. "People are unhappy. But what can we do? We are only poor people."

Tjasidi shrugged. "It is the will of God," he muttered, as if half of Jakarta were divinely meant to live in utter squalor, day to stinking day, hand to mouth.

The *betjak* men lived in fear in those days. Where would *betjaks* be banned next? What if the police came at night and demolished the shed? Resentment was growing. I was told that during a rice crisis the previous year, when prices soared, stocks disappeared from the markets and many went hungry. The high life of Jakarta's rich went right on as always. There had been a power crisis, when the shed had gone without electricity for weeks on end, but the rich all seemed to have had their own generators and from the shed at night you could see a powerful searchlight beaming up from the Taman Ria Amusement Park. All of us had seen truckloads of homeless people being rounded up by the police at night to be dumped far from the city.

The worst came every night at ten, when Husen, Raskim, Tjasidi, Djuned and perhaps forty or fifty more *betjak* men would wheel their pedicabs to one end of Blora Bridge, which linked the road from their squatters' settlement to elegant six-lane Jalan Thamrin, the boulevard where this account began, but now with all the night-time fizz and glitter of flashing neon signs, luxury hotels, restaurants and bars and flood-lit monuments and fountains. Back in the shadows of the bridge, impatient to enter this forbidden area and hustle what few late-night fares they could for tomorrow's food, the *betjak* men confronted a line of policemen.

It was almost always a tense, ugly scene: the *betjak* men, pushed from behind as their numbers grew, slowly edged forward. The police cursed them, raised their truncheons and threatened to hit those in front. Sometimes the confrontation would go on some minutes past ten o'clock until all at once the *betjaks* would surge forward together, swarming like a locust army into Jalan Thamrin. The policemen could not stop them and did not try. During those weeks in Jakarta, this small, nightly repeated drama came to symbolize to me what was going wrong. Husen had then spent eighteen years coming to Jakarta, but he had managed to cling to his traditional village values. In the others the old ties were starting to snap: Djuned seemed to have a nagging wonder what he was really living for; Raskim grew steadily angrier and was slipping toward violence and crime; those like Bibi were totally defeated. Day after day I watched them pedal their *betjaks,* strain their legs and backs until the muscles stood out like ropes, eat hungrily of their unnourishing food, and voice a vague, baffled sense of being taken. I left Jakarta fearing what would happen if they could not feed their hunger. I was glad to go, expecting violence.

*

Five years went by before I returned to Asia, years mostly spent in Egypt, sub-Sahara Africa, Mexico and Brazil. During these five years the Tanaka riots and most press reports from Indonesia suggested that things were growing steadily worse. In mid-1978, in Manila and prepared to revisit Jakarta, I seriously considered whether I should really go. Then came a letter from Husen; he was back in Pilangsari for good, the rice crops were better than ever before, and there were more shadow plays than he could remember; everybody was doing fine. That same week I read a report on Indonesia in the Washington *Post* headlined "Big Failures, Small Successes"; it generally portrayed the same desperate situation in Jakarta I remembered. It all didn't hang together.

So in August 1978 I went back to Pilangsari. I was to find that there had been a miracle in Java. Fertility had declined, how much was hard to tell, but it seemed Java's 1970–78 officially announced drop in annual population growth from 2.5 percent to 1.4 percent applied; few young couples wanted more than one or two children; almost all of the wives were taking the Pill.

Use of fertilized high-yield dwarf rice was universal; nobody, including Husen's father, would admit to ever opposing it. Average yields on two and a half acres were up to six tons; a few enterprising villagers were getting as much as ten. Pilangsari's old Dutch canal, Husen explained, had, at last, been repaired in 1974, ensuring a year-round water supply; there were double or triple rice crops for everybody.

Pilangsari had a new school. Hondas were replacing bicycles. New Japanese buses and trucks rushed people along freshly paved roads to market towns at frightening speeds. (They left such carnage in their way that I felt somebody had better start enforcing speed limits fast; during my first week there, two big trucks crashed into the ditch just in front of Husen's house.)

Husen had gone back to farming and so had the rest of his family. Only one of the father's nine surviving children remained in Jakarta, the youngest son, who drove a mini-bus. Husen was reaping windfall profits planting a new labor-intensive banana variety; he irrigated and fertilized his banana trees for the first time. The headman said the percentage of brick houses replacing the old bamboo huts had risen from about 30 percent to 85 percent, most of the money coming from rice. Husen's father was building a substantial new seven-room brick house.

"It's his monument," Husen grinned. As far as I could calculate, since 1967 the cost of living in Pilangsari had tripled or quadrupled. But there had been about a 500 percent rise in the price of rice and a 120 percent rise in overall production, which means people were really better off. Even the landless were more prosperous. So many new brick houses were going up, anybody could earn eighty cents a day shoveling sand from the river's banks; in Pilangsari that was enough to feed a family.

Most remarkably to me, the old traditions seemed to be flourishing too. There was still the welfare system of giving one-sixth of each rice crop to the mostly old women who planted and harvested it. Nor had there been any decline in the number of shadow plays and other village theatrical performances; rather, it seemed to have increased.

"We have come onwards," Husen told me, speaking English (incredibly he retains it from one visit to the next, though he almost never uses it in between; villagers have marvelous retention). In Jakarta I found that all of the *betjak* men we knew, except Tjasidi, had returned back to their villages for good; Raskim and Djuned were again farming (though Djuned was killed shortly thereafter in a bus crash). In talks with Husen, Raskim and others, the push seemed to be that it was harder to find work in what was rapidly becoming a modern city; I had noted in Jakarta that the old Potemkin city had almost become the big, real city at last. Jakarta's streets had so much traffic, it was wildly unsafe to ride in a *betjak,* even had they been allowed (they still could be seen in 1980 in outlying neighborhood districts, but never any more in the city center). The pull was that the villages, by multiple-cropping perpetually irrigated rice land, could now feed and employ everybody again. And in artistic, cultured Java, the real bright lights are back in the village. Nobody had made a statistical study, but my guess was that Jakarta was probably the first great Asian city to experience reverse migration, with more peasants going out than coming in.

Husen put the exodus from Jakarta into a charming folktale: a Jakarta king once invited all Pilangsari's people to a feast, then grew angry when all they brought him as a gift was a bunch of bananas. He threw away the bananas without unpeeling them; had he done so he would have found each was solid gold. Or as Raskim put the moral: "Better to come home and live in dignity than stay in Jakarta and be treated like garbage. Now if a man works hard, there is enough in the village to eat." This was statistically confirmed; Javanese villagers, on the average, are eating an additional kilo of rice each year.

I went back to Jakarta astonished, to stay with an old acquaintance, Tom Niblock, the Agency for International Development's mission director in Indonesia. I told Tom that, in one Javanese village at least, development worked. He was fascinated by my account, especially since a number of American and Indonesian economists—most notably Dr. William Collier of the Agricultural Development Council, who worked out of a nearby hill town, Bogor—were arguing the reverse: that everything in village Java was getting worse. The truth, as they told it, was that the landless and nearly landless 40 percent to 70 percent of Java's villagers were getting nothing but poorer, even poorer than they were five or ten years ago. The new high-yield rice was to blame; it had driven down wages, put field hands out of work, shattered village welfare institutions and led to land concentration.

"I can't believe it's true," I told Niblock, whom I had known for many years, first in Vietnam, then in the Philippines. Okay, poor people, when they get a bit less poor, are likely to buy motorcycles or television sets, or to eat more or build new houses. Investment in business, farming, education or health can wait a bit—zooming down a highway with a transistor blaring feels like progress. But when this happens in thirty-five thousand villages at once on the world's most crowded island (Java has nearly 90 million of the 145 million Indonesians) and there are plenty of new roads, schools, irrigation canals and multi-cropped paddies of high-yield dwarf rice to go with it, it plainly *is* progress. And I had seen it, going and coming to and from Pilangsari, right across west-central Java.

Niblock asked me if I would be interested in coming back to Java for four or five months to visit as many villages and talk with as many villagers as I could to see whether my very optimistic impression from Pilangsari stood up. He would put me on the payroll as an AID consultant, provide a car, driver and interpreter, and I would later be able to use my findings in this book, as well as provide him with a report. (As it turned out, I provided him with seventeen, running to 510 single-spaced pages, possibly more on village Java than anyone is prepared to read.)

Since I had commitments in Africa I could not return until just before Christmas; I stayed until mid-May 1979. I was to find that the task of an AID consultant was no picnic; I think I worked harder, rushing from one village to another and writing it all up, than I ever have in my life.

It soon became evident that some of the Americans involved in development in Indonesia represented the kind of anti-growth, anti-technology lobby I had encountered elsewhere. I felt that they were unduly influenced by such works as E. F. Schumacher's *Small Is Beautiful* and the Club of Rome's *The Limits to Growth*. Both works, read carefully, make a lot of sense; the problem was that their recommendations had been misunderstood and often had become mere slogans. Schumacher, for instance, attacked past aid programs for helping to create dual economies, causing rural disintegration and mass urban migration and unemployment. His answer was to channel future aid directly to villages, thereby creating a new agro-industrial culture based upon "intermediate technology." This he defined simply as "technology with a human face." Get the credit, fertilizer bags and mini-tractors down to the small farmer and you keep their kids on the farms.

This is good common sense—but when it came to putting Schumacher's ideas into practice, they did not work so well. Existing aid institutions, organized to provide conventional technical assistance—unlike, say, Jesuit priests or Peace Corps volunteers, who live with the people they are trying to help—lack sufficient firsthand knowledge and empathy. A human approach to technology does seem to require a human relationship between helper and helped. Small is beautiful, but it is still small.

Smart is better. Schumacher wrote, "The best aid to give is intellectual aid, the gift of useful knowledge." What's most useful in villages is modern scientific agricultural knowledge: agronomy, plant breeding, entomology, animal husbandry, irrigation engineering and, for women, up-to-date skills in handicrafts, marketing and ways to earn cash. Schumacher's ideas are perfectly sound; what went haywire is that too many academics, misconstruing them, said that what the villagers really needed was a lot of simple little easy-to-run Tinker Toy gadgets, not our higher, grown-up kind of technology. Others transformed the message of *Small Is Beautiful* into a stale, precooked campus populism; aid was bad because it led to intervention—more Vietnams—and anyway helped the rich and not the poor.

The Limits to Growth was similarly misinterpreted. When it came out in 1972, it served to dramatize the finiteness of the world's resources with its message that the planet, at then-current population growth rates, would reach "overshoot and collapse" by the middle of the next century. This book was ballyhooed like a three-ring circus. Anthony Lewis and Claire Sterling sent advance blurbs from London and Paris. The earnest young MIT computer team led by Dennis and Donella Meadows was presented to a super-elite gathering at the Smithsonian; since they had used some of my village findings I got invited and found myself seated between Katharine Graham and a white-thatched senator. Everything sounded terribly weighty and earthshaking and big-time.

In 1980 I met Dennis Meadows, who is now at Dartmouth, and asked him if his computer models were still predicting mass starvation and political chaos. "Nothing has happened in the last eight years to change our basic forecast," he said. What about the very rapid advances in food production in countries like China and India and the marked decline in population growth rates almost everywhere, I asked. Meadows replied, "Our conclusions hold for the East as well as the West. We'll see overshoot and collapse within the next thirty years."

Environmentalists, over the past decade, have also taken up the cry, warning that the earth's oil, mineral reserves and fresh water will only go so far (especially since the United States, with less than 6 percent of the earth's people, consumes about a third of its annual resources to support luxurious lifestyles unseen since imperial, plutocratic Rome). Indeed, by now there has been so much doomsaying one gets to feel like a jaded connoisseur of disaster prophecies. Still, it was a bit much to read *The Global 2000 Report to the President* in 1980 and find that even the U.S. government, or at least the Carter administration, for the first time, had added its voice to such tired, ritualized gloom. This report, prepared by the State Department and the President's Council on Environmental Quality, blitzes you with one future catastrophe after another: Mexico City, Calcutta, Bombay, Jakarta, Cairo and Seoul swelling to zillions (when actually at least three of them are losing population), 500,000 to 2 million species of plants and animals perishing in the next twenty years, acid rain falling, CO_2 rising, predictions that "people will get poorer," and of "increasing illness and misery." But its statistics, consistently underestimates, need to be treated with caution. They've got the average Chinese eating 217.6 kilograms of staple food in 1973–75 and going up to a scanty 259 kilograms in the year 2000, whereas in Peking, when I was there in mid-1980, the most reliable estimates of *current* per capita consumption ranged from 286 to 307 kilograms a year.

What makes matters worse is that while all this money was being spent on studies to predict mass hunger, the modest $145 million budget of thirteen mostly new international agricultural research centers, which play the most vital role in helping the world grow more food, was being cut. To give one example, the International Maize and Wheat Improvement Center in Mexico, the first to be created, is where Iowa plant breeder Norman E. Borlaug developed the dwarf, high-yield wheat that rescued South Asia from famine in the 1960s and won him the 1970 Nobel Peace Prize. It exchanges germ plasm and trains agricultural scientists from all over the world in two of man's three basic grain crops. In 1981 it got only $20.8 million, almost $1 million less than it wanted, meaning it had to curtail some of its training programs.

This doesn't make sense. Hyped-up doomsday forecasts, even if they didn't cost money better spent on spreading agricultural knowledge, are fundamentally insensitive; they blunt our ability to perceive the world as it really is. *Small Is Beautiful* and *The Limits to Growth* performed valuable roles when they originally came out, but the half-baked sloganism that has since been made of them has been mindless. Ideas date just like anything else.

It's as if Americans were being told to stop aiding and stop growing because it's hopeless anyway, and to stay home where we belong, looking after endangered species like the bald eagle, having fun, getting rich and pursuing a state of permanent carefree orgy. This is nonsense for a nation that most of mankind still expects to lead it. What might remain academic issues to be chewed over at endless university seminars become serious questions of practical policy when Congress starts believing the slogans and laying down mandates based upon them. This has resulted in a lot of "help the poorest of the poor" nonsense (they're all poor).

What is worrisome about the drearily familiar disbelief in economic growth is not just that it still goes over big with the Harvard professors who theorize that the rice and wheat revolution has run out of steam. In Indonesia in 1979, I found that such trendy pessimism had even seeped into the thinking of the generals and technocrats who ran the country (but rarely set foot in a village themselves). It was small wonder that foreign observers were still making the usual noises about impending social unrest.

Well, they're wrong. In four months of visiting thirty-five villages scattered the length (620 miles) and breadth (never more than 125) of Java, I found pessimism about the island's future wildly unjustified. There were a few pockets of deep, grinding poverty—wherever there was too much water (flood plains) or too little (dry upland plateaus or brackish coastal flats). With these few exceptions, Java had prospered dramatically between 1974 and 1979. When asked, "Are you richer or poorer than you were ten years ago?" every *single* one of a couple of hundred villagers replied that he was better off; some laughed even to be asked. I was not the only one who asked the question; I dragooned Husen and my driver, Djuhayet, both of them villagers, as polltakers among the very poorest people.

True, those with land had prospered more (they always do in times of rapid technological change—them that has gits) but it was Pilangsari all over again. The landless poor had not been left out; daily field wages had gone up, on the average and in terms of the food they could buy, by a quarter to a half kilo of rice per day since 1970—not much, but something. And family earnings had risen much more because of the much bigger demand for field labor. With irrigation spreading as new systems were built and old ones repaired, the introduction of multiple cropping of high-yield rice meant a lot more work and income for everybody, owners and field laborers alike.

Now, what do we mean by "poor"? It's a relative term if there ever was one, because one man's comforts are another man's necessaries. In Java I would define poor as someone who lived like Husen did when I first knew him in 1967. His family lacked the means to procure anything but a windowless bamboo hut with an earthen floor, lit by oil lamps, took its water from the river or a spring and possessed neither bicycle nor radio. A "rich" villager lives as Husen comes close to doing today; he has a brick house with a tile roof, polished tile floors and glass-paned windows; he no longer sleeps on a straw floor mat, but instead has an iron bed with a mattress and mosquito net; he lights his house with a petrol lamp or electricity (sixteen of the thirty-five villages we surveyed had rigged up their own homemade electricity with diesel-run generators), draws water from his own well, has an attached private privy, and probably owns a motorcycle or a television set. When I talk about Javanese villagers prospering, I am talking about moving from the first standard toward the second.

Notions of "rich" and "poor" are scaled to fit a certain environment. Java's is unique in three main ways. First, the island has fifty of the earth's five hundred known active volcanoes; eighteen on Java have a history of recent eruption. Gunung Merapi, Mount Fire, erupts at least once every five years (its crater glowed at night the last time I was there, and if we had to go near Merapi I'd always tell my driver to step on it). Mount Sinila, dormant for twenty years, suddenly went off in March 1979, and wiped out six villages. Bali's Mount Agung, just to the east, claimed fifteen hundred lives in 1963 during a once-every-five-hundred-years ceremony at Besaki temple on its upper slopes. (Lava flowed all around it, but the temple and its Hindu priests were miraculously spared. That's Bali, life imitating an old Dorothy Lamour-Jon Hall movie.) And Krakatoa, just west of Java (Hollywood got its directions mixed) when it erupted in 1883, killed thirty-six thousand, set off tidal waves all over Southeast Asia and encircled the entire planet with clouds of ash. Its volcanoes save Java; they enrich its soil with lava and explain why two-thirds of the Indonesians are jammed onto just one of nearly 14,000 islands in a 3,000-mile-long archipelago, most of them still uninhabited and fully half of them not yet even named. Indonesia's perpetual 70°–90° temperatures and torrential rainfalls of 60 to 120 inches a year make for badly washed-out and weak soils. If the lush-looking rain forests on many of the outer islands are stripped away the biocycle is wrecked and what remains is a wasteland. Fly over Java and you'll see that the densest clumps of palm-shaded villages and the richest irrigated paddy land are around the cloud-wreathed (and sometimes smoke-wreathed) live volcanoes, particularly old faithfuls like Merapi and East Java's Kelud (which has a lake inside and squirts out boiling hot water).

In pagan days the Javanese quite sensibly worshiped their volcanoes as abodes of destructive and fertility-bestowing deities (the Balinese still do). But today the Javanese are nominally 90% Moslem. Java's syncretic religion is its second unique quality. Islam, brought by Arab traders in 1400–1600, is superimposed upon layers of paganism, mysticism, Hinduism and Buddhism, all kept very much alive in almost constant village music, dance and theatrical performances. (There's always something going on in the villages; only westernized Jakarta is Dullsville.) Amazingly, we found in our thirty-five villages a sharp rise

in the number of shadow plays, folk dramas, classical dance performances and *gamelan* orchestras, despite rising costs and the spread of
television, cassette players and radio; traditional culture was more
than holding its own.

This mysticism and artistry may work against Java now that science
and technology are the keys of the kingdom. In 1949, the year of final
independence from the Dutch, all Indonesia had only one Ph.D.
(who, like Pooh-Bah, promptly became finance minister and just
about everything else) and no university (one was opened right away
and there are forty more now). Although there are close to three hundred Ph.D.'s today and five hundred more candidates, Indonesia is still
entering the scientific era almost from scratch.

The third thing that makes Java unique is that its population crisis
really got going about a hundred and sixty-five years ago. Since 1815
yearly growth has rarely been under 1 percent or over 2 percent, apparently because of what anthropologists like to call "agricultural
involution." (Clifford Geertz coined the phrase; it means the more
hands you put to work in growing wet rice, the more rice you get.) So
everybody got fed, but today you've got something like ninety million
people crammed onto a rather small 50,000-square-mile island, 1,725
to the square mile. (This is not up to the Nile Delta's average of
2,300, but is still plenty, and in parts of north-central Java density
reaches 5,000 per square mile, the world record.) Some 30 percent to
50 percent of the Javanese own no land except their own house and
yard and another 10 percent to 20 percent own just a tiny plot. Those
who do own land have average holdings of less than an acre; I found
farms of a quarter-acre to half an acre not uncommon. Almost everybody has to earn money some additional way; only about a fourth of a
villager's time is spent growing rice. This makes Javanese villages
hives of activity, though almost everybody is pathetically unskilled.

We found that the most visible burst of prosperity was among what
I defined as the "rich," usually land-owning group (in the thirty-five
villages we counted forty family-owned mini-buses, twenty-one trucks
and twelve cars, something unheard of in village Java in 1967). But
the "poor" were also taking part, buying bicycles, transistor radios,
lamps and flashlights. They also rode motorcycles that doubled as
taxis, and traveled to jobs and markets along new roads on new mini-
buses. The home-building boom had meant jobs in construction, digging sand for cement and quarrying stone.

I remember one pathetic bamboo hut in a remote little village called Bojong, near west-central Java's southern coast. The owner, a muscular, landless worker of forty named Sahib, invited us inside but served no tea (a sure sign of poverty; Javanese invariably offer you tea as a gesture of hospitality, or coffee and cakes if they can afford it). Sahib's wife, a worn-looking woman who labored in the fields for daily wages like her husband (she told him to put on a shirt as we sat down), said a Petromax lamp, a flashlight and a bicycle were all they had been able to buy in recent years. Their windowless, earthen-floored hut was such a wretched hovel that I thought, at last we've found an example of "the poor getting poorer." Not so, Sahib's wife protested. "Our house is bigger. We saved enough from our wages to pay for it. Oh, you may not think it looks like much now, but it's five times better than it was three years ago. And now I've got four chickens." Sahib agreed. "There's a lot more jobs since we got a new irrigation canal. The landowners produce more and they need more help." He was able to work 250 days a year and his wife about 180, he said, much more than before. What did he need? "Technical training," Sahib replied right away. "So we could learn how to do something we could do at home; then my wife wouldn't have to work in the fields so much."

It was the same way over much of Java; we'd drive along some remote back road, pick the poorest men and women we could find at random, swoop down on them and do an interview; they all felt they were better off. Back in Jakarta the anti-technology economists, even if just in town for a few weeks from some American university, would tell me all those new motorcycles (averaging forty-six per village in the ones we visited, and the trucks, mini-buses and cars too), plus the ten to twelve television sets per village and all the new brick houses replacing bamboo huts, didn't mean anything because they belonged to the naughty, selfish, landowning minority. Official statistics were cited as proof (although in Indonesia, as in Egypt, most statistics are wrong, fiddled or nonexistent). All I could say was, go out to the villages and see for yourselves.

Java matters because two-thirds of the people of the earth's fifth most populous nation live on this one little island. If the Javanese can make it, everybody can. The main cause of Java's rising prosperity is the rice revolution. As in the shadow play, it's a battle you never win, but you must keep fighting. Java gets a record rice crop one year, a plague of brown plant hoppers the next; a new hopper-resistant strain is brought in and production shoots up until the insects adapt; then the villagers start in all over again. As Husen says, it's as if the evil giants and ogres keep arising, just like human passions and lust, and you have to keep struggling with them, just as the Pendawa kings and Semar and his comic children do. Indonesia still has to import rice to feed its cities, but everyone agreed there was more rice in the villages than ever before and people were eating more. No government in the Third World really knows how much grain gets harvested or eaten in its villages. Because Indonesia follows the common Third World pattern of rigging food prices against farmers, they eat more and don't deliver when the price falls too low, so the cities suffer chronic food shortages and the government has to import wheat and rice.

These truths were happily brought home to the Indonesian government by a threatened rice glut in 1980. After orders were placed to import 2.6 million tons from overseas, the villagers surprised everybody and grew close to a record 20 million tons of rice, 10 percent more than the bureaucrats had predicted. Experts ascribed the bountiful harvest to below-normal flood damage, more fertilizer use and wider planting of high-yield rice.

Like almost every country in Asia, Indonesia could rather easily solve its food problem for a generation. The facts: it has just over seven million hectares of rice land, 60 percent of it on Java, which produces 95 percent of the country's rice. The World Bank officially deems six million hectares of this land fully irrigated. The World Bank is wrong. Go to any village and you'll find that almost nowhere does enough water get down to the families with fields farthest from the main canal, because of an antiquated system of moving water from paddy to paddy through bamboo tubes. The irrigation system may look good on paper and you get adequate water if your fields are near the canal, but those on the outer fringes go without too much of the time. With modern irrigation techniques such as those found in Holland, Java could produce three or even four rice crops a year on the same piece of land, instead of one or two as now.

The villagers know this. In the thirty-five villages, I put the same question to a couple of hundred of them: "What do you need?" The answer, almost every time, was, "Improved irrigation." (Followed by roads, schools, credit, electrification, non-rice crop technology, pure drinking water and more technical training, in that order.) And if I asked, "What's the main reason for there being new jobs and more income in this village?" I'd get the same answer: "Improved irrigation." (I had no idea how a village irrigation system worked when I started out and had to get an American engineer to come around the rice paddies with me one day to explain the damn thing.) The villagers usually had a good grasp of what water was available to them and many proposed specific ways to irrigate 10 percent to 30 percent more of their village land. One trouble, some said, was that nobody had ever come and asked them about it. (This didn't surprise me. Tran Van Huong, when prime minister of Vietnam in the 1960s, once told me no American had ever asked him, "What do you need and how can we help you?") Yet if only one-half of those six million irrigated hectares in Indonesia were double-cropped and produced four tons per hectare (and Java's average is over three tons now), Indonesia would have rice coming out of its ears. Village by village, the story of irrigation on Java is far from over.

Other signs of village prosperity we found:

· Infant mortality rates were going down, along with dramatic fertility declines.

· Rural industries and handicrafts, except possibly for handloom weaving and *batik*-making (machine-made *sarongs* are sturdier), doubled or tripled production, earnings and employment between 1970 and 1979.

· Migration from the thirty-five villages to Jakarta and other cities was down, just as in Pilangsari, to about one third of what it had been ten years earlier.

· Village primary school attendance had shot up, from 10%–15% to over 50%, mostly in 1973–79 when President Suharto, with World Bank help and oil revenues, built 31,000 new village schools, hired 200,000 new teachers and handed out 200 million new textbooks, an impressive feat anywhere. Primary education is hoped to be universal and compulsory in the Javanese villages by the mid-1980s.

Our other big finding, after the need for more irrigation and the importance villagers put on it, was the changing social role of Java's women. In Java, women are bigger breadwinners than men; they number 60 percent to 70 percent of all home industry workers, do 80 percent to 90 percent of all rural marketing and retail trade, do most rice transplanting, weeding and harvesting (men do the backbreaking land preparation, working the sticky volcanic soil with hoes) and actually work an average of eleven to twelve hours a day (five on household chores, six earning cash outside) compared to a village male's seven- to eight-hour day.

Now these long-invisible women are getting easier to see. It started when a network of forty thousand "mothers clubs" was set up to promote birth control. But everything leads to everything and before long these clubs were demanding to know more about nutrition and child care (they now get training in weighing babies and treating ane- mia, diarrhea, worms and tuberculosis). Then came demands to help them earn more income (by increasing the productivity of their fruit trees and vegetable gardens, and learning how to raise fish, eels, sheep and chickens or make earthenware or weave cloth and mats). It makes sense; the more money you make, the better your food, the better the doctor you can afford, the more your babies survive and the fewer you'll have. Everywhere we went in Java, we found women stirring: I'd go into a house to interview *him*, but before long I'd be inter- viewing *her*. Ask a woman what her village needs and she won't men- tion something general like irrigation. Instead you get a shopping list: "Two sewing machines, ten bottles of Vitamin A, a scale to weigh ba- bies . . ." It was also likely to include drums, gongs, sitars and xylo- phones; a spontaneous village movement to create all-girl *gamelan* or- chestras has sprung up all over Java (except in Yogyakarta, the *gamelan* has always been the domain of men).

There's a lot to be done. Java needs help for the landless, fertilizer subsidies, land trusts, reforestation, more roads, rat control (to stop them from eating 10%–20% of every rice crop), land reform to stop Chinese merchants or army officers from buying village land, credit and so on and on. Sharecroppers need to be guaranteed at least 50% of their harvest. Up on the nonirrigated mountainsides, new cash crops need to be introduced to encourage the Javanese to terrace and plant grass and trees and do what must be done to stop Java's critical problem of soil erosion. (It can be done; one enterprising young agronomist from Colorado, Enrique Barrau, showed a handful of mountain villagers how to increase their cash crop incomes thirty-five- fold by planting special terrace grass and trees while triple- and inter- cropping new high-altitude strains of rice, maize, peanuts, cassava and sorghum—an amazing display of what modern agricultural science can do.)

It's mostly just learning how. People like Husen's parents have made, in just five or six years, what for them was a very tough adjustment to a new, scientific way of doing things. Husen's father would never tell me now, as he did in 1970, scornfully rejecting the new rice, "If Allah blesses us, we won't starve." (I was amused to find that in 1980 the old man couldn't or wouldn't remember ever opposing the high-yield rice varieties.) Because this adjustment was made, the Husens and Raskims and Karnitis and Bibis *can* go home again—to stay. And their children can look forward to much more rewarding lives. Dwarf rice, the Pill and the whole lot of new techniques did not reach Java until 1966–67, when President Suharto's "New Order" regime and the technology that could really bring about a new order more or less arrived on the scene together. I'm glad I happened along then too, in time to see the desperate "before" that gives today's hopeful "after" its meaning. The villagers of Java are still very poor; what matters is that they are much less poor than they used to be. Now they're naturally eager for all the new technology they can get. They badly need more, of almost every kind. As I found on a visit in December 1980, now that agriculture and birth control are going so well, Java badly needs thousands of small-scale factories to give all the landless jobs. This means more highways, credit and rural electrification, probably with financial, managerial and technical know-how gotten from the Japanese, whose private and government aid to Indonesia is now five to ten times our own. Indeed, one came away from Java feeling the Americans, like the Cheshire Cat, are fading away; it may be that soon all that will be left is our benevolent smile. This, of course, could change under Reagan's administration. I know how Husen himself would answer. "Onwards," he would say.

II. IDEAS

LOOK TO SUFFERING, LOOK TO JOY **15**

Columbus discovered America in 1492; America, you might say, discovered the villages in 1926. That year, a twenty-nine-year-old student from the University of Chicago, Robert Redfield, went to live in a village fifty miles south of Mexico City. His book, *Tepoztlán—a Mexican Village,* published in 1930, was the first village study written by an American; a warm and sympathetic interpretation, it became a classic and standard reference.

Seventeen years later, in 1943, another twenty-nine-year-old, Oscar Lewis, a New Yorker, went to live in the same village. His book, *Tepoztlán Restudied,* which came out in 1951, strongly attacked Redfield's work. Lewis charged that Redfield falsely gave village life "a Rousseauan quality which glosses lightly over evidence of violence, disruption, cruelty, poverty, disease, suffering and maladjustment." Redfield found Tepoztlán idyllic; Lewis found it awful, full of "fear, envy and mistrust."

Redfield fired back, saying that Lewis lacked "humanity" and had "taken his own values" to the village. In Sweden in 1953 Redfield said that anyone who studies village life is bound to be influenced by his own "personal interests and cultural values."

"There are hidden questions behind the two books that have been written about Tepoztlán," Redfield said. "The hidden question behind my book is, 'What do these people enjoy?' The hidden question behind Dr. Lewis's book is, 'What do these people suffer from?'"

Thus began a debate about the character of village life which outlived both men and still goes on in a lively fashion today. Redfield went on to study the Mayan Indians of Yucatan; as a philosopher and humanist, with many original ideas on peasant society and culture, he became one of America's most eminent social anthropologists. Lewis turned to studying urban slum dwellers, first in Mexico, then in Puerto Rico and Cuba; he formulated a controversial theory that all the world's poorest people, in village and urban slum alike, suffered from a common "culture of poverty," identifiable by seventy specific traits. His later tape-recorded autobiographies enjoyed great critical and commercial success. Lewis won fame, but it is Redfield who is most often quoted by serious scholars.

Remarkably, right on through the rest of what were very illustrious careers, Redfield kept emphasizing *enjoyment* and Lewis *suffering*. While the work of Redfield can mostly be found in libraries, along with that of George M. Foster, the third pioneer in village studies in Mexico, the Lewis books are widely available. This distorts our perception of the Mexican poor and, to some degree, all poor people. Until 1977 and my first visit to Mexico, where I discovered the books of Redfield and Foster, I felt I owed a great debt to Oscar Lewis. I had modeled my own village work after the early Lewis technique of portraying the daily life of poor people by drawing upon observation, interviews and stenographically recorded conversation. I tried Lewis's later method of long tape-recorded autobiographical interviews, but soon abandoned it; I found that simply noting down conversation as it naturally happened got you a lot closer to truth.

As I hope to get across, a journalist is not an anthropologist, just as a story is not a study. A journalist sees the way culture is changing in the world's villages as a significant current event to be reported in the press. A social scientist sees such change as an episode in man's cultural development to be investigated and conceptualized for the benefit of scholarship. Putting it another way, a reporter writes his impressions. The distinction gets blurred because anthropologists may slip over into journalism, as Margaret Mead sometimes did, or journalists into scholarship.

Not all anthropologists would agree. Dr. Foster, in a foreword to a book of mine, wrote, "Certainly to live for a year in a small village, in intimate association with a single family, and its friends and enemies, is anthropology and not journalism." Margaret Mead wrote in 1978, "In the past our method of making an anthropologist was to take someone by the scruff of the neck and leave him (or her) alone in a community in a strange culture. If he (or she) survived the experience of culture shock once, twice, three times, then he (or she) was an anthropologist. We did not know of any other way to make an anthropologist. We still do not."

Why does this if-you-go-to-a-village-you-must-be-an-anthropologist notion matter? Because it creates practical problems for both reporters and anthropologists. Editors are more likely to print stories on poor people if they happen to live in cities. Anthropologists have lots of relevant things to say but, if their work is about villages, they seldom get the general attention they deserve. The aims, methods and results are not the same. Just about all the two have in common is a similar beginning.

To understand people well enough to write about them, you need to live with them, share some of the struggle and the idleness, the losses and the gains, and in time come to identify with them. In anthropology you also have this "participant-observer" method. From the beginning, I saw the value of doing the same daily work as the people I wanted to write about; hard physical labor was the central fact of their lives. This meant herding sheep and cattle, diving for fish and octopus, cutting cane, threshing sorghum, digging up cassava root and, mostly, sowing, weeding, harvesting and threshing wheat and rice. Housing might be a black-tent Bedouin encampment, Charan's cattle barn, Husen's bamboo cottage or Kuwa's grass hut, sleeping on string cots, carpets, straw mats, the occasional bed, or in Brazil, a hammock. We ate mostly bread or rice and a few vegetables, washing it down with tea, coffee, beer, rum or homemade liquor (ten years of village living can turn you into either a vegetarian or an alcoholic). Common work, common food, common discomforts soon break down any barrier of reserve; I suppose it's a kind of mutual commitment. Always, in a few weeks, whoever was being written about would come to take our mutual enterprise very seriously.

For my interpreter and myself, it got to be a routine; usually he (rarely she, except in cities) noted down as much dialogue as he could during the working day, while I pitched in as a fairly mute co-worker. Then we'd relax with the villagers in the evening; if anything important happened, we'd write it down the next morning. With such a narrow focus, day in and day out, week after week, you get to know people intimately.

So when I arrived in Mexico three years ago I was eager to find some of the real people Lewis had written about—especially the family in his 1963 work, *The Children of Sanchez*—and compare notes. The author's widow, Ruth M. Lewis, did not, however, encourage this. "I am very sorry to disappoint you," she wrote from Illinois, "but it will be impossible for me to help you contact the children of Sanchez, for obvious ethical and professional reasons. The village of Tepoztlán is, of course, available to one and all." The ethical and professional reasons were not obvious to me. Redfield and Foster used real names in their village books; so did I. I habitually gave my villagers their choice and invariably they wanted their own names and photographs used.

Mrs. Lewis's letter went on: "I was in Mexico last month after an absence of four years and found it quite changed. The standard of living, but especially the mode of dress and use of leisure, have become quite Americanized and middle-class. In the Sanchez family, the grandchildren dress better, eat better, have more schooling than their parents. I would have to be there longer to see if the changes go deeper. Other than the use of birth control (after having five or six children) I suspect that values and behavior are pretty much the same. The village, too, has this puzzling mixture of change and continuity, and it takes a lot of patient digging to sort them out."

(Redfield's daughter, Lisa Peattie, a professor at MIT, was to be more forthcoming. After I met her at Harvard in 1980, she wrote me a very frank letter describing her father's sequestered and Victorian childhood—Redfield's wealthy family, who lived on a country estate, did not let him attend school until he was age 12.) Dr. Peattie wrote, "I always thought that one reason Tepoztlán felt to him such an Eden was that it was his first experience with ordinary people leading their ordinary lives, and it was where he discovered that such lives had beauty."

As it happened in 1977, a Hollywood film company was shooting a movie of *The Children of Sanchez* at Mexico City's Churubusco Studios. I was able to meet Anthony Quinn, who was playing Sanchez. Quinn seemed just right for the part. He was in his fifties, had fathered ten children, was Mexican-American, grew up in poverty and had strong feelings about family life. "In all humility," Quinn told me, "I don't see anybody else who, at this moment, is better suited to play Jesús Sanchez." One of Quinn's own sons, Duncan, was playing Sanchez's son, Roberto, in the film and they were spending a lot of time in the slums "trying to get the feeling of what it must be like to be poor in Mexico City today." Quinn said he was also drawing upon the "social theater" of his own youth, when "I suffered a great deal." My impression of Quinn, given the need to adapt the story to his strong personality, was that he might give a more sympathetic and honest portrayal of a poor Mexican than Oscar Lewis did, although I haven't yet had a chance to see the film.

Quinn had met the real Sanchez but didn't know where to find him.

He suggested meeting Mexican playwright Vicente Lenero, who had adapted the book to the stage in 1972. Lenero recalled that the family had attended the premiere; he could not remember Sanchez's real name but thought he worked at Mexico City's Cafe de Tacuba, a famous gathering place for intellectuals.

Oscar Lewis describes meeting Sanchez for the first time, in October 1956: "The father, Jesús Sanchez, walked in brusquely, carrying a sack of food supplies over his shoulder. He was a short, stocky, energetic man, with Indian features, dressed in blue denim overalls and a straw hat, a cross between a peasant and factory worker." He had then been "food buyer and kitchen manager" at the "middle class Gloria Restaurant" for almost thirty years and was forty-eight years old. On June 1, 1977, I watched a short, stocky, energetic man with Indian features, blue denim overalls, a straw hat and the look of a peasant-factory worker, approaching brusquely up Tacuba Avenue. Incredibly, just as if he stepped from Lewis's pages, he was carrying a sack over his shoulder. Mustering what tourist Spanish I could, I hailed him, *"Perdón, pero Usted era Jesús Sanchez?"*

Indeed he was. His real name was Santos Hernandez Rivera and after almost fifty years he was still the food buyer and kitchen manager of the Cafe de Tacuba. He lived in Casa Blanca *vecindad,* or slum tenement, the fictionalized "Casa Grande." It was in the poor Tepito section, where he invited me for a visit. His four children, in keeping with the Mexican custom of using both parents' family names, all had the last name of Hernandez Ramirez. Cristina (Consuelo) was married with two children and lived in Nuevo Laredo, Tamaulipas, on the Texas border. Berta (Marta) lived with her husband in Acapulco; her father said she had "nine or ten kids—you know, it's cheaper by the dozen." As for Pedro (Roberto), he sold clothing and furniture from his house and worked in a car factory "whenever they call him" and Luis (Manuel) "also sells things from his house." Hernandez said his family originally had wanted anonymity because "we didn't know how Señor Lewis was going to use those interviews." But in the seventeen years since the book had been published, Sanchez and his four children had only received $200 apiece from Lewis and his widow and were still very poor.

In his introduction to *The Children of Sanchez,* Lewis made it a point to say that his subjects had not been paid but that it was "their sense of friendship that led them to tell me their life stories." Hernandez challenged this; he said each of his children got "fifty to a hundred dollars" from Lewis from time to time for participating in the tape-recording sessions at his home. Hernandez spoke respectfully of Lewis, describing him as *simpático,* very correct, very hardworking." He said his family met Lewis after Cristina was engaged as his secretary (Lewis wrote that he first met them in their *vecindad*). Hernandez said he felt Lewis tried to get the truth but that "the children were too young to know what to say, to know how to answer his questions. They made up whatever came into their minds." The four children ranged in age from eighteen to twenty-five when Lewis began interviewing them. He continued on and off, for the next seven years.

Hernandez said he had read "parts, but not the whole book," though as *Los hijos de Sanchez,* after being initially banned, it was a best seller in Mexico.

"Was it true?" I asked.

He grinned. "Five percent. Well, not even half of it was true."

"What, specifically, was not true?"

"He wrote that Cristina was a prostitute." I had to go back and look through the book to see what he meant; apparently Hernandez was referring to Consuelo's account of being seduced while trying to break into the Mexican film industry. Hernandez did say that Roberto's prison history and escape, which I found hardest to swallow, was largely true. Hernandez, of course, had a highly prejudiced point of view; Lewis portrayed him as a harsh, authoritarian father who showed little affection for his children. Playwright Lenero, who did make a careful study of Mexico City slum life while writing the stageplay—but, curiously, did not bother to look up the family itself—contended to me, "Everything in the book was true." Life in Tepito, he said, throwing up his hands, was "Oof!—*terrible!*"

Lewis himself wrote in the introduction to *The Children of Sanchez,* "The lives of the poor are not dull." Rather, he said, they lived in "a world of violence and death, of suffering and deprivation, of infidelity and broken homes, of delinquency, corruption and police brutality, and of the cruelty of the poor to the poor." The Lewis books are strange, moving tragedies, but after retracing his steps in Mexico City and Tepoztlán, I think there can be no question that Redfield was right: Oscar Lewis looked for suffering.

But when it comes to villages we must look to the human whole. Looking back, it is interesting to see how much the Redfield-Lewis debate, aside from stimulating each man to his best thinking, firmly launched American anthropology into the study of villages. Anthropology, when Redfield went to Tepoztlán in 1926, was very new. Its founder, E. B. Tylor, wrote about religion, language and culture in general, in what was then usually called ethnography. Tylor studied culture but not cultures and society, and in Europe even today the study of rural people tends toward *volkskunde,* or folklore and the study of folk life. I studied it in 1958–59 at the University of Innsbruck in the Tyrol; we tramped about the remoter Alpine valleys of the Austrian and Italian Tyrol, as Herr Doktor Professor Ilg lectured to us about the architecture of the centuries-old wooden chalets, the endless baroque churches, Illyrian and Roman ruins, and such legends as how the Emperor Maximilian was rescued in a snowstorm by an angel, or the wicked Frau Hitt, a Tyrolese queen who was turned to stone after refusing to give a starving beggar woman some bread. It was fun, sleeping in barns, living on salted cheese, peasant bread and homemade wine, singing German hiking songs as we strode past glaciers, icy streams and misty gorges (like Hannibal and the Trapp family, we crossed the Alps on foot), but we did not learn much about how the mountain people actually lived. In contrast to the European focus, anthropology in America emphasized the study of primitive tribal life.

In the early nineteenth century, villages were lived in and written about, but mostly by missionaries who dedicated long years of their lives to saving the "heathen." Exotic peoples, ever since Marco Polo, had also been described by explorers, by members of natural history expeditions and by journalists. In the nineteenth century their chroniclers included Captain Cook and that intrepid discoverer of darkest Africa, Sir Henry Stanley. It was not until mid-century that scholarly studies began to appear. One by Lewis H. Morgan on the Iroquois Indians came out in 1851 and another by Franz Boas on the Eskimos in 1888. Boas, originally a biologist, and Morgan, a lawyer, did not call themselves anthropologists, but they taught the first students who did— Boas as the first professor of anthropology at Columbia University in 1899. So when we talk about anthropology we are talking about a twentieth-century social science, a very young one.

The research model for social anthropology was not established until 1922 when A. R. Radcliffe-Brown published *The Andaman Islanders* and B. Malinowski *The Argonauts of the Western Pacific.*

These two works set the conceptual model that American anthropology has followed ever since: a man or woman goes to a small and self-contained remote community and comes back to report a culture as a unique whole, and as a whole that can be understood as a system of functionally interrelated parts. Margaret Mead, until the end of her life, applied what she called the "disciplined use of the primitive society as a conceptual model" even when she was analyzing the cultural character of whole modern nations such as Russia or everything from Samoan sex to nuclear war, or from teenage problems to the need to keep grandma at home. Even today, when most non-anthropologists think of anthropologists, they think of somebody living for years on end in some godforsaken place with the primitive Zuñi, Canadian Kwakiutl or the Melanesian Dobu. (When I told Edward Lansdale, a friend from Vietnam days, that I was going off to live in villages, he joked, "You'll end up getting all peculiar and squatting on the floor like anthropologists do." This is the layman's false image.)

In actuality, American anthropology plunged immediately from its first studies of North American aboriginal tribes and South Sea islanders into Latin American—and particularly Mexican—villages, there to study peasants. Redfield went to Tepoztlán just four years after Radcliffe-Brown and Malinowski established the model for research: studies of primitive, isolated tribes. Redfield's work led anthropology in a completely new direction. Villages were not like tribes; they had a relationship with cities and were dependent upon cities for their laws, religion and other aspects of their culture. A. L. Kroeber in 1948 gave them a still generally accepted definition as "part-societies in part-cultures."

There were a lot of peasant villagers. As Oscar Lewis wrote in his introduction to *Five Families* in 1959: "This book has grown out of my conviction that anthropologists have a new function in the modern world: to serve as students and reporters of the great mass of peasants and urban dwellers of the underdeveloped countries who constitute almost 80 per cent of the world's population." Today this would be a bit too high; villagers probably make up about two-thirds of the people alive; if you count those uprooted temporarily or permanently in cities but who retain their village ties and culture, and add the much smaller number of truly citified urban masses, you might push it up to 75 per cent.

The word "peasant" gave everybody trouble from the start; you'll notice I tend to feel more comfortable with "villagers." Both Redfield and Lewis, as did most of the early anthropologists, used "folk" in their first books, later replacing it with the more precise "peasant." The word has a hint of the derogatory about it because all over the world, at all periods of history, terms applied to village people by city people have tended to imply contempt or condescension, if often mixed with a certain admiration for the simple life. So while a peasant may be uncouth and boorish, he is also artless, unsophisticated and rustic; if we have "hick" and "hayseed," we also have "folksy."

I tend to use peasant and villager interchangeably. This is handy but not quite correct; we can define a peasant precisely as anyone who makes a living and has a way of life through cultivation of the land, producing food largely for his own family's subsistence. As Aristotle observed, the way one obtains one's food determines a person's mode of life; hence peasants tend to possess a common mode of life or culture. They do not carry on agriculture for reinvestment and as a business for profit, looking upon land as capital and commodity. Such people are farmers, not peasants. Charan, for example, is still a villager, but a farmer and no longer a peasant. The truest peasants can be found in regions with ancient civilizations, such as Shahhat in Egypt or Husen in Java. They cultivate their land largely for subsistence and as part of an age-old and traditional way of life. It was my impression in a 1980 visit to China that a good many of the Chinese remain peasants. (Aristotle again: long-ingrained habits tend to survive revolutions.) I think it was in this cultural sense that Mao Tsetung was speaking when he told Nixon, "I have only been able to change a few places in the vicinity of Peking."

My own most rewarding village studies have been in Egypt, India and Indonesia—for good reason, I think. These villages have had constant contact for thousands of years with their urban centers of intellectual thought. Such villagers possess a sure sense of cultural identity; this makes it easier to live among them and write about them than it is with partly Westernized people such as, for example, the Filipinos or Mexicans with their Latin culture and their imitator's complex of admiration and contempt.

Hunters, herders and fishermen are harder to fit in. I have included Bedouin shepherds in my work. Yet these nomadic sheep-herding pastoralists are neither peasants nor villagers. They preserve many of the customs of man the hunter, including unity under the authority of a chieftain who daily decides where to seek pasture and pitch tents. Great importance is placed on courage, the male prowess of the warrior and certain kinds of violence and predatory behavior.

Fishermen, in contrast, do live in villages and share many peasant values, as we found in Grand Gaube. Sub-Saharan Africans, like the Nubas, are in various stages of moving out of tribalism; many exist, as Kuwa did, on cattle raising and primitive slash-and-burn cultivation. Again, many common peasant characteristics are seen.

In Latin America, very generally speaking, we find two kinds of villagers. The first, as in Guapira, are descendants of transplanted European peasantry or Africans brought as slaves to work plantation agriculture in the sixteenth to nineteenth centuries, or—perhaps most common in Brazil—a mixture of both. In Mexico we find the other kind of Latin American villagers: Indian peoples influenced by pre-Columbian civilization and later Spanish culture who are still in an incompletely developed relationship with their urban centers of intellectual thought. Huecorio's people, with their mestizo-Indian blood and traditions going back many centuries and their dual culture, part-modern, part-primitive, are much closer to being peasants than the frontiersmen of northeastern Brazil or the tribal Indians of, say, the western highlands of Guatemala.

Still, as formative as Latin America's village society remains, it has given us our first and broadest views of peasant culture. As Robert Redfield observed of the 1930s and 1940s, "It was by moving out of aboriginal North America into the study of contemporary village life in Middle and South America that American anthropologists came first and in large numbers to undertake the study of peasants. . . . In Latin America, anthropology has moved from tribe to peasantry."

Berkeley's George M. Foster, the only one of the three early pioneers in Mexico still surviving in 1981, has made, in Tzintzuntzan village in the central highlands (just a few miles down the shores of Lake Patzcuaro from Huecorio) what must be the longest—thirty-six years—continuous study of a village ever done. Foster first went to Mexico to collect material for his book *Empire's Children; The People of Tzintzuntzan*, published in 1948, and has since returned to the village each summer. This continuity—Redfield and Lewis spent remarkably short periods in the villages they wrote about—gives special weight to Foster's theories of the "limited good," the belief in villages that all good things in life are limited so that one person's success is at the expense of others (although it is fading away today as villages modernize, he says); and the importance of bilateral kinship or contractual ties in villages, based upon friendship, reciprocity bonds, patron-client ties and fictive kinship, such as the Latin American *compadrazgo* godparenthood institution. Surprisingly, since his own portraits of village life are cheerful and humorous, Foster sides with Lewis in his dispute with Redfield on the character of villages, linking my work to the debate. He has written:

> Peasant life has its satisfying side, but frequently it also has its darker side, as Richard Critchfield's *Shahhat* makes clear; gossip, witchcraft, fear or envy, distrust of neighbors, family quarrels, and the like. Today, to say such a thing is no longer viewed as equivalent to an attack on motherhood, as it was when Lewis first took issue with Redfield; we now realize that such behavior, in the context of poverty and the limited opportunity of traditional peasant life, is highly adaptive. Under similar conditions, we would all do the same thing.

Despite the sound of this, I think it was Lewis, not Redfield, who most distorted reality, possibly in the bad luck of choosing Tepoztlán—an unusually grim, brooding village—in the first place. The one Lewis book on India seems positively cheerful.

After Mexico, India next caught the anthropologists' attention, with the rest of Asia and Africa soon following as jet travel and America's post-World War II imperial age made the world a much smaller place. A great many village studies were published, leading Redfield to conclude that, unlike primitive tribes, peasants had a culture that was much the same the world over. Oscar Handlin, in his marvelous study of nineteenth-century migration to North America, *The Uprooted,* wrote that "from the westernmost reaches of Europe, in Ireland, to Russia in the east, the peasant masses had attained an imperturbable sameness." Malcolm Darling in his study of India's Punjabis found their way of life had "an underlying unity which makes peasants everywhere akin." René Porak concluded from his work in French villages that peasants everywhere were "a psycho-physiological race." Others found common peasant values in Bulgarian, Irish, Canadian and Egyptian villages. In the mid-1940s E. K. L. Francis argued, from an analysis of Hesiod's *Works and Days,* about Greek Boeotian villagers in the sixth century B.C., that village culture not only had universality in space, but also in time.

Finally, in 1956, Robert Redfield, in a book, *Peasant Society and Culture,* suggested that all peasants, past and present, have shared a similar view of what he called, still emphasizing enjoyment, "the good life." Redfield found that all villages had a common "reverent attitude toward the land," believed that agricultural work was good and commerce not so good and emphasized productive industry as a prime value. With characteristic modesty, Redfield wrote, "This may not be good science, but it is a way to get people thinking." To support his argument, Redfield compared three peasant societies: the Mayan Indians of Yucatan he himself had lived among, nineteenth-century English villagers and Hesiod's ancient Greeks. Redfield found life and culture in these villages so alike he speculated that if a villager from any of these three widely separated societies could have been transported to any one of the others and known the language "he would very quickly have come to feel at home." This would be, Redfield argued, "because the fundamental orientations of life would be unchanged."

Redfield perceived the resemblances and natural unity in world peasant culture. He also grasped that this perception would have to work itself down to "precise words and procedures" if it was to yield generally accepted proof. He also foresaw that the coming anthropological frontier would be the urbanizing villager, but he wondered whether American anthropology was yet ready for "further complexity." As with Tepoztlán, the pioneer village study, Redfield blazed a trail for others to follow. (For my own summary of characteristics most villages the world over seem to have in common, see the Postscript.)

Again, among those who did was Oscar Lewis. In 1961, Lewis put forward his "culture of poverty" hypothesis. Poverty, Lewis argued, was not simply being poor. It also created its own culture with "a distinct structure, a rationale and defense mechanisms without which the poor could hardly carry on." Lewis applied it to all those "at the very bottom," including "the poorest workers, the poorest peasants, plantation laborers . . . and the lumpen proletariat." He eventually listed seventy traits which identified anyone who was part of the "culture of poverty." Some of these traits simply characterize all poor people. Some shed light on village life such as his "strong present-time orientation and the tendency to spontaneously enjoy the moment without much regard for the consequences." But others, such as the "belief in male superiority which reaches its crystallization in *machismo* or the cult of masculinity" apply in a relative sense only to Latin societies and to the Mediterranean and Moslem Middle Eastern worlds. And a few, such as "frequent use of physical violence in the training of children and wife beating" were just plain silly, having little or no application in Asia, where the vast majority of the world's poorest people live.

Typically, Lewis tried to be too "scientific" and bit off more than he could chew. The "culture of poverty" notion did have a lively, if brief, impact on American politics in the Sixties. Lewis wrote, "It is easier to eliminate poverty itself than the culture of poverty," which "affects participation in the larger culture." When the Office of Economic Opportunity was set up in Washington to wage President Lyndon Johnson's "war on poverty," its policy makers said it was not enough to help the poor with money, i.e., welfare, but that to escape from the "culture of poverty" they had to be organized to fight for their rights, or what became officially known as "maximum feasible participation." The result, all too often, was to federally fund inner-city black gangs who terrorized respectable black families as the gangs took on city hall in a power struggle, neglecting real black needs for jobs, housing and an end to discrimination in private business.

I was covering the White House for the Washington *Star* when President Nixon brought in Daniel P. Moynihan as his urban affairs adviser with the task of defusing, if not dismantling, OEO and framing a welfare reform proposal to take its place. Moynihan, who had been poor himself, did not believe in Lewis's "culture of poverty" theory. He said the poor were just like anybody else; they just had less money. His solution was a negative income tax. To Moynihan, America's greatest domestic problem was the social isolation of the Negro, caused by a whole series of economic developments, such as the mechanization of cotton production, postwar veterans' housing loans, cheap new methods of home construction, the Interstate Highway System and the Aid to Dependent Children provisions in the welfare laws. Their cumulative unintentional result was urban decay, rising crime and family breakdown for the blacks, increasingly isolated in the inner cities of the North and West. Moynihan's solution was to try to help black families disperse into the larger white population through a guaranteed minimum income.

Years later, when Moynihan was our ambassador to the United Nations and was becoming a television celebrity by raising hell with the Third World, I met him for a drink in the Security Council delegates' lounge and asked him if he still felt the same way about the "culture of poverty." His views had softened. "The only thing wrong about the work of Oscar Lewis," he said, "is that he died before he could finish it." When I argued that his demands for the poor nations to behave the same as the rich were too influenced by his sour experience as ambassador to Indira Gandhi's India, and that he should have spent more time out in the villages, Moynihan retorted, "It was one way of looking at a country and the way I looked." A lively argument followed, moving toward its climax. As we came out into United Nations Plaza, Moynihan shouted his vexation at the Third World: "We've taken enough of their bombast and bullshit, and we're not going to take it anymore!"

*

Times change, and I think we've constantly got to be prepared to change our own perceptions with them, even if it goes against what we've thought—or written about—in the past. I was dismayed in 1977 to meet Dr. Foster in Berkeley and hear him say, "Peasant studies today have come to an end." Foster said that from about 1950 to the early 1970s, village studies had dominated American anthropology. "It was an enormously productive period," he said. Theories had emerged to explain peasant social structure, economics, behavior, personality, all aspects of village life. Now, he went on, anthropologists were turning their attention away from peasants "as a field of study," and toward linguistics, Lévi-Strauss, formalism and symbolism, urbanization, religion and economics.

I believe this is a mistake. American anthropology's best work has been to describe life in real, concrete villages or tribes. When it tries to conceptualize or theorize too much, treating village life as if it were an unchanging, fixed state, it moves away from reality and truth. Social sciences, as I shall argue in Chapter 20, do not work in the same way as the physical sciences.

I have read Lévi-Strauss and find his work absorbing but very hard to follow and, as yet, of little practical application to village reporting. The influential French anthropologist's theoretical idea of "structuralism" is adapted to human behavior from linguistics; it argues that universals in culture exist, but as cognitive models of reality, or "structures," not as concrete manifestations of reality. According to Lévi-Strauss, universals of culture have meaning in terms of the way humans perceive and conceptualize, not in manifest fact. For example, if he compared life in a number of villages, he would compare the patterning of relations that link sets of human behavior. He would not simply list evident habits, attitudes and customs villagers have in common, as a newspaper reporter like myself will naturally do.

Foster's comment also reinforces my belief that the villages are a proper province, not of anthropology alone, but also of journalism. What are the precise differences? We are both, of course, investigating the human whole. Anthropology, as Foster's words suggest, has developed from the study of small, isolated and primitive tribes to the study of just about everything human. Both the anthropologist and the journalist today are engaged in attempts to characterize a person, a village, a city, a people, a nation, or even a civilization. Most anthropologists, at least until recently, have done their field work in villages, or in the urban neighborhoods that are their counterpart. A reporter does much the same. When I go to a village I start with its ecological and economic system, or agriculture: the plowing, sowing, weeding, harvesting and threshing of the crops. In time, this look at agriculture leads naturally to an understanding of systems of marketing or converting crops to food for the family. From here, one moves into social life and religion and the way people think and feel. So far the reporter's investigation is the same as the anthropologist's. Like the anthropologist, I study the larger civilization in which a village finds itself, its history, religion, philosophy, art, literature and present-day politics and economics. If possible—a switch from anthropology—I try to interview the nation's political leader. Why? Because I want to fit the villager I'm writing about into a larger, more topical frame of reference; I'm doing a kind of news story.

Such a story can be about social upheaval (the Hindu caste system versus modern farm science, as in India), or urban migration (Husen in Java) or criminal alienation (Barek in Morocco). Politics is the stuff of journalism, but it is commonly just a surface reflection of these other things. (India's agricultural revolution has started to decide its national politics.) In Shush-Daniel, you got an inkling of how settled agriculture, irrigation and our first cities came about, or from the Dinkas and Bedouins how men lived before we had anything called agriculture. A village stay can be aimed to learn more about some big global issue (overpopulation in Grand Gaube, the Green Revolution in Ghungrali). So one difference between journalism and anthropology is motive; the reporter tries to capture that changing moment in time as a way of telling about an event or situation. In newsroom lingo, I write "situationers."

Another departure from anthropology is that the reporter is engaged in what might be called portraiture; he's trying to draw a picture of something. So do novelists, critics, historians and biographers. What they all have in common is that, unlike the social scientists, they rely mostly on their intuition and impressions to convey this picture to readers. Often they're most convincing when they're most personal. Anthropologists, of course, are not mere statisticians, nor are the characterizations of a reporter all that imprecise; factual accuracy matters to both. But when I sit down to write about a village, I choose certain facts, details and dialogue for emphasis and modify and rearrange them so as to satisfy my own intuitive sense that the portrait is as close to reality as I can make it.

This is not social science and not anthropology. An anthropologist comes to a village with a mind trained in social theory; he usually starts out with a conceptual model to guide his choice and arrangement of the facts. Drawing upon his training, he is likely to use technical procedures, such as scientifically accepted psychological tests. He may use questionnaires to gather statistics from a broad sampling of villagers. Whatever his specific technique, it will be something "scientific," "theoretical" or "scholarly." He gets just as close to reality as the reporter does and the difference is one of degree; most anthropologists mix some art with their science. The power of Lewis's later work owed much to his artistry; though his subjects gave the answers, he asked the questions. Yet even Lewis ultimately remained the detached social scientist; his subjects stayed, no matter how much they told him or how diligently he recorded them, his "informants." Their life stories were taken down in their own words because their own words were part of the data. It was this emphasis on the verbal that made so much of Lewis's work so literary, even poetic. But, unlike the reporter, he was not trying to create a portrait in his own words.

Redfield once observed that all observation of human culture lies in a borderland between science and art. He was much more prepared than many social scientists to give non-anthropologists their due, and in his work quoted all kinds of people. "For," he wrote, "understanding is increased and the needs of mankind are met by any and all honest descriptions, responsible to the facts and intellectually defensible . . . Understanding, and her apotheosis, wisdom, are the true gods within the temple; science is not, she is only a handmaiden and serves many others." The common aim is to produce, being honest and keeping to the facts, as true a portrait or as scientifically acceptable a study as the reporter or anthropologist can perceive and write. We need both; but I feel readers need to know how their aims, methods and results differ. When a small minority's culture breaks down, as it has for some black teenagers in the inner cities of our country, then everybody else has to live with some fear of random violence; if millions upon millions of villagers' cultures broke down, that violence would be general, not random. Crisis is the reporter's job, but so is understanding what makes one.

Jets, computers, telecommunications and automation have terrifically speeded things up and made us all much too exclusively city-oriented. As Philip Foise, then foreign editor of the Washington *Post,* cautioned me when I first set out to report villages in 1969, "Remember, cities are where the governments, wealth, power and armies are." (Today you might add TV satellites and direct-dial telephones, too.) All the world's cities are plugged into the same global electronic network; even someone as utterly obscure as Ayatollah Khomeini was in 1978 can be thrust overnight into instant international living room stardom. But twenty-two years of reporting the Third World, twelve of them from villages, have persuaded at least this writer that cities are not necessarily where our real history is being made. In these days of crisis journalism, a lot is going on out there we don't hear anything about.

A century ago we'd be informed about the doings of remote peoples from explorers and missionaries. Now TV crews go everywhere, popping up in Antarctica today, Zambia tomorrow; this is a mixed blessing. With its size trivialization—we are likely to consider the events represented by flickering, noisy images on a piece of furniture to be less important and minor in value—it reduces the Watusi to the dimensions of Kermit and Miss Piggy. Its competition has forced the press to print shorter stories with more snap—often follow-ups of last night's TV news. A vacuum has been created. If the ordinary villagers or slum dwellers are not on a rampage of revolting or rioting, or dying of

famine, they stay out of sight and out of mind. We rarely get a satisfying explanation of why they revolt, riot or starve. On to the next fast
turn-on. At the height of the Iran crisis, when we were being nightly
bombarded with shots of blindfolded Americans, screaming mobs and
strange old men in robes and turbans, I complained about the lack of
interpretation and insight to Walter Cronkite. Cronkite replied that
"no matter what the provocation, the news must remain neutral."

He went on:

> It is not our responsibility to uphold any position, moral, politi-
> cal, religious or what-not. Indeed, our responsibility is just the
> opposite; to present all sides of every issue with as much imparti-
> ality as a human being can muster (even when, in a case such as
> this one, that quality is sorely strained).

The problem comes when a Khomeini, like North Vietnamese
leader Le Duan or the Buddhist monk Tri Quang in Vietnam before
him, is deliberately staging a psychodrama for American TV. The old
journalism-school ideal of "objectivity" loses its meaning when camera
crews, hungry for visual drama, are up against cleverly conceived and
carefully orchestrated stage-managing. Neither CBS nor the other networks could handle this in Vietnam, nor could they in Iran. Stage a
Buddhist monk's "self-immolation" or a flag-burning Tehran mob and
the cameras compulsively crank away. Edward R. Murrow or Eric
Sevareid, though you didn't have to agree with them, at least put
things in a civilized frame of reference. Inadequately explained shock
spectacles in the living room simply jar our nervous systems and feed
our anxieties. Cumulatively, they stand in the way of finding plain old
commonsense solutions to what needs to be done.

This is especially true when it comes to the world's peasant masses,
that silent majority who outnumber us in the West more than three to
one. There are no big names in villages, and exotic foreign settings
leave many people cold. We Americans are one of the few peoples
who never had a peasant tradition of our own we might draw upon;
books about villages are rare in American literature. Pearl Buck's *The
Good Earth* is a notable exception, but it's about China.

*

In closing this chapter on American anthropology and villages, let
me add a footnote to the Redfield-Lewis debate on village character.

Is it pleasant or awful? Lewis kept criticizing Redfield while appropriating his ideas, sometimes with acknowledgment, sometimes not. A striking example of the latter appears in the preface to *Pedro Martinez*, Lewis's full-length portrait of a villager in Tepoztlán, published in 1964. Lewis is as combative as ever, saying, "There is a tendency among all of us, even anthropologists, to idealize the past—and think of Mexican villages as relatively stable, well-ordered, smoothly functioning and harmonious communities." It's the old argument, and to Lewis, Tepoztlán is still a hotbed of meanies—uncongenial, unhappy and cursed by "an undercurrent of fear and hostility." He does grant that Martinez himself (whom I discovered was named Juan Rodriquez in real life; he died in 1973 at age 84) had remained "first and foremost a peasant," sharing "many classic peasant values." Lewis then lists them:

> a love of the land, a reverence for nature, belief in the intrinsic good of agricultural labor, and a restraint on individual self-seeking in favor of family and community. Like most peasants, Pedro is also authoritarian, fatalistic, suspicious, concrete-minded, and ambivalent in his attitudes toward city people.

Compare this with Redfield's final summary paragraph on the universal peasant culture in *Peasant Society and Culture*, published eight years before:

> an intense attachment to native soil; a reverent disposition toward habitat and ancestral ways; a restraint on individual self-seeking in favor of family and community; a certain suspiciousness, mixed with appreciation of town life . . .

A few pages earlier, Redfield had used the phrase, "the idea that agricultural work is good." With the natural modesty and honesty that were so much a part of his writing, Redfield had added: "The characterization is no doubt too vague and impressionistic to serve the methods of more scientific kinds of inquiry." It was as far as Redfield would ever get in developing his idea that all peasants share some common culture, not a culture of "suffering" alone, but a culture of "enjoyment" as well. The fact that Lewis borrowed Redfield's ideas in this key passage suggests that he felt his old adversary's view of "classic peasant values" was sounder than he would admit.

Perhaps one should not make too much of it, though it struck me as fundamental. Redfield was the teacher, the conceptualizer, the pioneer, the idea man. Lewis was the student, the ardent collector of data, details, facts, statistics, dialogue and autobiographical interviews, whose portraits of suffering, while they may have distorted peasant culture, created an unusual new form of literature. Each man's portrayal of villagers and the poor, taken by itself, seems incomplete, perhaps because so many of their books were written in the heat of perhaps the greatest and certainly most prolonged controversy in American anthropology. Their work should be read together. The villagers may be no more stable and happy than we are; they are certainly no less so, which is what matters to them and (eventually) to us.

Both the Book of Genesis and modern archaeology agree that our first civilization was Sumer, the Biblical Shinar, in the land between the Tigris and Euphrates rivers, or Mesopotamia. When I was first in Khuzestan, in 1971, newly excavated hydrological and aerial surveys less than a hundred miles to the east were providing fresh evidence that irrigation was probably invented here, on the Sushiana plain just below the Zagros foothills, making the migration to settle arid Mesopotamia proper possible.

At the same time, a decade ago, archaeologists in Egypt were uncovering evidence that man first cultivated wheat along the Nile as early as 13,000 B.C. It is quite possible that the first villages were in Egypt. This would be logical, as it was from the African jungles that man first left the apes to walk erect on the plains, between four million and eight million years ago. Human thought processes developed about three million years ago. Not until about a hundred thousand years ago, however, did the skull of *Homo sapiens* reach its current size.

Agricultural scientists currently identify at least eight geographical "centers of origin" for domesticated plants. There is evidence that maize and beans were grown in Mexico and Peru by 6000 B.C. and rice near Non Nok Tha in Thailand by 4000 B.C. or earlier. Stored paddy rice and bone plowshares have been excavated at Hemudu in China's Zhejiang province. At Pan-p'o, north of the Tsinling Mountains near Sian, there is ample evidence the early Chinese ate millet, gathered wild plant food, hunted, raised pigs and grew cabbage and by 4000 B.C. had invented the pottery wheel, domesticated cattle and made rice the staple crop. While much remains to be discovered, according to what is so far known, man's Neolithic period outside the Middle East came relatively late.

We do know that men along the Nile pursued a nomadic animal husbandry and primitive hoe cultivation, possibly as early as seventeen thousand years ago, and that the Nile Valley remained wet and marshy until about seven thousand years back. This cattle-centered way of life still goes on among the Dinka, Nuer and Shilluk tribes of Sudan's great Sudd swamp, the last of the Nile Valley still to dry out, which I visited in 1978. Here, in a malaria-infested, fly-plagued, forty-thousand-square-mile swamp—a godforsaken desolation of water, silence, bite-crazy mosquitoes and forlorn little clumps of round grass huts—you can get a good impression of what life must have been like for Neolithic man. The Dinkas, purple-black, often seven feet tall, thin as rails, with long skinny necks and small heads, wear their contentment right up front; they're about the grinningest, laughingest lot I've ever seen. One speculates it must have taken unavoidable necessity—the drying up of the Nile Valley north of the Sudd—to get such people to give up the old free, nomadic life, settle down and invent irrigation.

At the other end of the Fertile Crescent, up on the Central Asian Plateau, we think man first became a shaper of the animal and vegetable life around him, rather than just a predator upon it, about 11,000 to 9000 B.C. Here, north of the Zagros and Anatolia mountains, wild wheat, barley, sheep and goats can still be found. Today almost everybody agrees that agriculture, both here and along the Nile, was not invented by man, the hunter, but by Neolithic woman, the collector. Men did not farm until draft animals were used in the fields (which may be why, in present-day black Africa, wherever hoe cultivation still goes on, women do most of the farming). With the retreat of the glaciers and the progressive drying up of the Central Asian Plateau, animals gradually descended into newly formed grasslands and down onto the Mesopotamian plain, and men followed them. Once on the plain, man diverged into two distinct cultures (symbolized in Genesis by Abel and Cain): hunters, who found field labor little to their liking and adopted instead the arts of the herdsmen (Abraham among them), and the first settled farmers, whose food surpluses made possible the first towns and then the rise of urban civilization, first in Sumer and soon afterward in Egypt. About fifteen million herdsmen still survive from Mongolia to Mauritania.

Archaeological digs in southwestern Iran show the first villages on the eastern edge of the Mesopotamian plain were extremely stable social units, surviving pretty much unchanged for the span of four thousand years, about 8000 to 4000 B.C. The invention of irrigation, probably by the pre-Elamite peoples around what would become ancient Susa, quickly shattered this stability, leading, in a relatively short space of time, to the settlement of the land between the Tigris and the

Euphrates. Or, as the Bible quite accurately tells it, "And as men migrated in the east, they found a plain in the land of Shinar and settled there." And history began. Irrigation, soon followed by the introduction of the plow, led to a surplus food supply, the emergence of towns and cities, a rapid expansion of population and—in Elam—an actual decline in the absolute number of villages. For intercity warfare began almost along with the first Mesopotamian temple communities, as did the construction of defensive walls, the abandonment of small outlying villages, migration to ever-larger urban centers and the rise of soldiers, organized armies, generals and, at last, kings and sovereign states.

Gradually small, family-size farms of free men living in peaceful anarchy were replaced by larger estates, farmed with the economies of scale by serfs and, later, slaves captured in war. Like the first temple cities, most of history's greatest civilizations—pharaonic Egypt, China and Japan under the seventh century T'ang dynasty and the Fujiwara clan, Mexico under the Mayas and Aztecs, France under Louis XIV, on up to Stalinist Russia and Maoist China—practiced something close to modern state socialism, with heavy taxation of the food-producing villages. All civilizations depend upon a big enough food supply through agriculture and the domestication of animals; each has had a large enough population to form a city, social differentiation, some form of government, a calendar, basic mathematical knowledge and written records. Common symptoms of declining civilizations have been overpopulation, environmental decay, status systems, overproduction of luxury goods, wildly fluctuating money, growing arbitrariness of government and more knowledge than the means to assimilate it.

American scholars have never completely agreed about just who, at any given period of history, was a peasant. As I mentioned in the last chapter, the most widely accepted definition is A. L. Kroeber's:

> Peasants are definitely rural—yet live in relation to market towns; they form a class segment to a larger population which contains urban centers, sometimes metropolitan capitals. They constitute part-societies in part-cultures.

Robert Redfield agreed; he contended a peasant could not exist without some relationship to the city his food surplus created; hence, before the rise of Sumer and like civilizations, Redfield argued, a peasant was not a peasant but a "primitive cultivator." Other social scientists said it was not a city but a state that was decisive in whether a man was a peasant or not. Indeed, you don't get very far into such academic hair-splitting before villagers start sounding like bees and ants, social insects whose institutional life follows unvarying scientific laws.

To me what counts to a villager is his civilization. Cities and states are ephemeral political phenomena in the lives of civilizations; they come and go, live short lives and experience sudden deaths. Villages last. Berat and Shush-Daniel have been continuously inhabited for at least six thousand years. No city or state has come close. Western civilization may well be alive in its villages long after the United States has gone off the map like the Austro-Hungarian Empire. Most nation-states today are not whole societies, but arbitrarily detached fragments of them: look at Africa, the Indian subcontinent or North America. Will and Ariel Durant have reminded us that all of the elements of civilization now exist in almost all of the world's two million villages: the making of fire and light, the wheel and other basic tools; language, writing, art; agriculture, the family and parental care; social organization, morality and charity. Of all man's social institutions, villages have the most staying power. Like William Faulkner's blacks, they endure.

*

The economic basis of village life is agriculture. There are three basic types:

Slash-and-burn, where virgin land is cleared of grass, bush or forest, a hoe is used and fields are planted until yields decrease. It rarely supports more than 150–250 persons per square mile; as with the Nubas, whoever engages in it is likely to do lots of walking. It can be destructive by removing natural vegetation and has played a role in many disastrous floods in India, Nepal, Pakistan, the Philippines and elsewhere in recent years and in the movement of the Sahara southward in the African Sahel, which in Kuwa's Neetil village has moved, in terms of drifting sand dunes, right up to the village huts.

Dry-land, rain-fed is based upon the plow. The plow was first invented in the irrigated agriculture of Egypt and Mesopotamia around 3500 B.C. Gradually it evolved into the heavy mold-board plow which made dry-land, rain-fed cultivation on a large scale feasible, eventually leading to the rise of Europe and North America. Land can be cultivated either continuously or left to fallow one to three years. In pre-industrial Europe, it was never able to support more than 30 to 100 persons per square mile. If holdings are too small, dry-land agriculture is extremely hard to modernize.

Irrigated is found either in arid zones which receive less than ten inches of rainfall per year, as in the Nile Valley, the Punjab Plain and the Indus Valley, or in tropical alluvial fans where water-seeking crops such as rice are grown, as in the Gangetic Plain, the lower Yangtze Valley or the Red River and Mekong deltas, as well as most of the rest of Southeast Asia. If irrigated rice is grown, you can produce more food with more labor; this leads to extremely dense populations; in Sumer in 2500 B.C., irrigated agriculture supported about 50 persons per square mile with wheat, barley and lentils. Today, with rice, it supports about 1,800 in Java and Bangladesh, 1,980 in China's Yangtze and Yellow River basins; with wheat and other crops, 2,300 in Egypt's Nile Delta and—the world record—again with rice, close to 5,000 per square mile in a few areas of north-central Java. (Java is the world's most crowded island.) The maximum urban density I have come across is in Cairo's Bab al-Sharia district near the downtown railway station, where in 1980 there were just over 200,000 per square mile. Calcutta and Jakarta have about 80,000, as did New York before it began to lose population.

Whichever agriculture he practices—slash-and-burn; dry-land, rainfed; or irrigated—the villager tries to use as best he can his limited resources of land, labor, water and sun and what technology he may know. His land is shrinking. In 1960 he had, on the average, about six and a half acres on which to feed and clothe his own family of six and produce a surplus to feed just over two and a half city people too. By 1985, this average acreage may be down to five.

The villager will try to pass his land on to his children, either leaving it to the eldest son or, as is more common, dividing it among them all. As this fragments the ever-smaller holdings, he will try to encourage most of his sons to go into other occupations or give his daughter a money dowry instead. If all else fails, he will send them or allow them to go, as Husen's father did, to the city.

Village life is based upon living in groups. Cultivation often needs hands outside the family for planting, weeding and harvesting. The village ethic of mutual help takes many forms, such as the voluntary labor exchange of *gotungroyung* in Java. In India many goods and services had traditionally flowed through the caste-based *jajmani* system, which today, as we saw in Ghungrali, is breaking down. Mutual dependency and help in most villages still survives and is validated by long-standing custom. It is very probably the origin of our Golden Rule; help others to get their harvest in as you would have them help get yours in. Of necessity, villagers live as members of groups, if not, as it sometimes seemed in Shahhat's Berat village, a crowd. As Henry Habib Ayrout noted of Egypt's *fellaheen*, "The village or quarter, not the house, makes up the entity, a community more important in many ways than the family or clan."

Once outside the village, as when marketing, other custom prevails. Most villagers then make decisions, just as we do, in terms of money values. They will drive hard bargains; prices will respond to supply and demand and are decided by haggling. Yet even in the market most villagers like to find regular patrons among the town merchants, who may give them credit so they can avoid paying high interest to a moneylender. Villagers save by working for others to incur future obligations from them; often they hide money at home. Mutual gift giving can be another form of saving. Such credit and savings systems, while very modest, have been the main economic institutions of most of mankind right down through history.

When a villager grows a crop, he will first feed his family, usually with grain such as wheat, rice, maize or sorghum. He must also grow enough to sell to earn money for (1) seeds, livestock feed and replacement tools; (2) religious ceremonies such as marriages, funerals and festivals; and (3) taxes or rent. Land ownership, if he is a tenant, can be feudal, where lords or their heirs exercise power over both peasants and land; prebendal, where land or income from it is granted to officials by the state; mercantile, when land is viewed as the private property of its owner, absentee or not, to be bought and sold for profit; or administrative, as in Russia or China, where the land belongs to the state. I've also come across two other forms of administrative ownership: the Egyptian government retains partial control over land redistributed under Nasser, telling owners or their heirs what and when to plant, and Mexico's post-revolutionary *ejido* land can pass from father to son, but, at least in theory, cannot be sold, rented or given to others to work.

Villagers tend to live in extended families, with several generations and the wives and children of the sons sharing the same household. One finds nuclear, or conjugal, households in villages, but usually only if family members are individually-paid daily wage laborers, such as Poondi's sons or Mukhtar in Ghungrali; in a frontier society such as Guapira village in Brazil; or when a villager modernizes and becomes a farmer so that he, his wife and their children, with machinery, can either farm for themselves or hire labor, as we find here in America.

Like most of us, villagers live under pressure, from the weather, from friction within large, gossipy households, from prying neighbors, from the state demanding larger surpluses or conscripting sons, even from fluctuations in Chicago's world grain market. Pressures affect villagers unevenly (locusts or hailstorms destroy one man's crop and not his neighbor's; one man has fewer children and more land, another only daughters), but scarcity of land and the city's demand for food are the two most common pressures.

Yet on a day-to-day basis, there is little stress in village life. Whenever I come home, it takes a few days to get used to all the noise (all those electronic voices coming at you), the fast speeds of cars and how busy and punctual everyone is. Stress, an inescapable aspect of modern city living, can lead to high blood pressure, heart attacks and nervous breakdowns, but it can also be beneficial. Nothing compares to an American city's efficiency and organization (try making a phone call in Cairo, mailing a letter in Delhi or finding a cop in Manila). The flights to catch, cars to drive, traffic rules to obey, elevators to summon, television to watch, latest global events to follow, goods to buy, deals to make, appointments to keep on time all produce stress but are central to our country's vitality. Our mentality is to *do,* a villager's is often just to *be.*

True, most stress comes from interpersonal relations. "Hell," as Jean-Paul Sartre said, "is other people." Well, maybe. What strain and anxiety there is in villages tends to come from personality conflicts. But fun is other people, too; villagers are fascinated by each other's doing; it's their chief form of entertainment. In a village there's little competition, and nobody has to come to terms with diminished career expectations or learn to live with their limitations. It takes opportunity to cause striving.

Daily routines vary from one village to another and within a village depending upon the season. I try to time my visits to coincide with harvests, when villages are liveliest and the fields are full of people.

There are a few constants. Villagers tend to rise with the sun and go to bed an hour or two after it sets—except for the Javanese, who, with their all-night shadow plays and folk dramas, do with less sleep than anybody I ever saw. For Husen, three or four hours is plenty. Somehow, even if there's electricity, village life is not conducive to reading; I usually read three or four books a week, but almost never open one in a village.

Invariably, the first person in a household to stir in the morning is a woman, who usually gets up about four A.M. to wash, make a fire to boil water for tea or coffee, and to milk the cows or buffalo. Moslem men, if devout, will rise at four too, to say the first of five daily prayers, kneeling in the direction of Mecca; Husen's father did. In Ghungrali we'd be rocked out of our beds at four by the amplified cacophony of a few pious old men praying over the Sikh temple's loudspeaker. This, for most people, was the signal to wrap up in a blanket, huddled and anonymous, and make their way to the fields under cover of darkness to, as the Punjabis said, "answer the call of nature." Then back to bed for a couple more hours of sleep until sunrise. Except during threshing, when you take your cots right to the fields, most village men get up about six or seven, as do women of leisure like Surjit or Ommohamed, once they have a daughter-in-law in the house to do the early chores.

If the family has cows, buffalo, donkeys or other animals, somebody, usually a young man, cuts fodder, in Egypt twice a day, in Punjab and Morocco just in the evening. Aside from harvesting with a sickle, it was my favorite work, especially in Punjab, where you rode back to the village each night, half dozing and tired of bone, on a cartload of freshly cut clover. The rest of the day can be sowing, weeding, harvesting or threshing or, once a week, going to market day in a nearby town (though Berat's was just on the bank of the Nile) or, in slack times, just sitting around. In most countries men tend to work in the fields the entire day, though in Java always and in Upper Egypt in the summer, everything stops at eleven or twelve and doesn't resume until late afternoon. I used to wonder why one often saw around noon so many men sitting around idle in villages; often it's because they've already put in five or six hours of field work.

Only the African Nuba women actually cultivate the land from start to finish, including breaking up the soil with hoes. But, as I've mentioned, in Java women do most of the rice transplanting, weeding and harvesting and in Mexico women winnowed wheat, in Egypt shucked maize and in the Philippines helped thresh rice by dancing on it with their bare feet (this was fun; if enough people pitched in, it was a bit like a disco). And in all villages, very poor women and children are the gleaners. The hardest lot fell to the northeastern Brazilian women; in Guapira they and their children worked three or four days a week peeling, crushing and cooking into edible flour the poisonous (prussic acid) local cassava root. It was no wonder girls like Carolina fled to the city.

Most of the time village women stay at home, preparing meals, washing clothes and dishes, mending, sewing, perhaps weaving cloth, blankets or rugs, caring for the children, raising chickens or a few sheep and goats, sometimes, as in Berat or Neetil, fetching water on their heads in earthen jugs or tins, or going to a village merchant to buy on credit a few matches or some salt, tea, sugar or other essential. Once a week the women go to the weekly market to stock up on provisions and buy clothing or shoes. Yet village women, who tend to be much less sequestered than women in Third World towns, are very social; Ommohamed was forever riding off on Shahhat's donkey to attend a funeral, help deliver a baby, arrange a marriage or consult her favorite sorceress. In the Catholic villages of Guapira, Grand Gaube, Huecorio and Tulungatung, women seemed to spend as much time running to the village church as their husbands did getting drunk at the tavern.

Meals are customarily three times a day, with the noon one brought to the fields. Whether it's all the physical exercise in the open air or just good food, I found village meals delicious if monotonous. Some sample menus: Mauritius, fried rice and fish, washed down with rum; Punjab, hot chapattis, potato-pea curry, sour milk, yogurt, a piece of raw brown sugar and milky tea (Indian food, especially, is much better in villages because everything is fresh); Java, boiled rice, green vegetable soup, shrimp wafers, sliced cucumbers, spice paste, sugary coffee and bananas, papayas or mangos (east of India, only babies drink milk; adults of the Mongoloid races lack the enzymes to comfortably digest it); Brazil, beef, macaroni and *farinha*, the utterly tasteless, sawdust-like cassava flour no Brazilian can do without (don't be surprised in a Brazilian restaurant to be served meat, rice, macaroni and potatoes on the same plate; Brazilians eat few vegetables and salads are a rarity); Iran, beef stew, rice with raisins, greasy kabob (you squeezed orange juice on it); Morocco, *couscous* and *tajim* (beef stew; sadly, the Moroccans use almost no seasoning). By far the best food is in village Egypt, especially if cooked by Ommohamed (a sample menu was given in Chapter 13). The worst fare was the Nuba's sorghum mush with okra, though Vietnam's *nuoc mam,* or fermented fish sauce, or Tibetan tea, made with rancid butter, are definitely acquired tastes. A mistaken notion is that "two-thirds of the world goes to bed hungry every night," if by that is meant the gnawing sensation of an empty stomach. Most villagers manage to stuff down large amounts of bulk and fiber, whether rice or unleavened bread, or cassava, millet or sorghum for the poorest; it was usually about twice as much as I could eat. The Egyptians, an exception, ate quickly and moderately, but they had the tastiest, most nutritious diet. When we talk of hunger we are really talking about malnutrition or protein deficiency, not literally unfilled bellies, as in a famine.

What really makes village living so easy and pleasant is its sense of time; time seems to expand so that each day seems much longer. The only sound you may hear all day is the call of birds, a donkey's bray or other human voices. You mostly walk or bicycle wherever you're going, and you seldom go far. You tend to lose track of what time of day it is or even what day of the week it is; each day is very much like the next. (You always get up and go to bed at the same time, cut fodder, eat the same food at the same times and have the comfortable feeling that not much is going to happen; I suppose this is why you get such a consuming interest in gossip and the other villagers' affairs.) Only in Christian villages is Sunday a day of rest; in Moslem villages the pious go to the mosque on Fridays at noon, but otherwise it's an ordinary workday. In towns throughout the world, however, whether Moslem, Hindu or whatever, merchants and government offices tend to observe Sunday, as they do Christmas; stripped of all religious significance, it has become a universal city holiday.

Far from our kind of stress, for long stretches of time in a village you may do nothing whatsoever, just sit. The Egyptian *fellaheen* even have a word for it, *kaif,* a mental state where you do nothing, say nothing, think nothing. It's very relaxing. When stress comes to a village, it mostly comes from a city. When you start waking up without looking at your watch to see if you've had eight hours' sleep, you know you're in a village.

A villager's basic dilemma today is the same as it has always been:

he has created the food surplus on which the city depends. He has to balance his family's needs with the need for money for tools, religious contributions and rent or taxes, the three ways the city has to draw off his surplus. In the extreme attempt of our times, Maoist China in the 1950s tried to maximize the surplus that went to the state by limiting food through common mess halls, using tools in common and doing away with religion. It failed to work. Poor and powerless as he is, a villager is resilient. He can always eat everything he grows and cut off the surplus to the city or state. In bad times, even if the city sends troops to commandeer his crops, he is likely to be better off.

*

One way to interpret man's history on earth is in terms of the progression of agricultural technology; such historians as William H. McNeill, author of *The Rise of the West,* have done so. The decline and disappearance of the early Mesopotamian and Indus civilizations followed the soil salinity that comes from steady irrigation without sufficient drainage. Egypt was saved from this curse until modern times by the leaching effect of the Nile's annual flood. Since the Nile Delta shifted from flood to perennial irrigation a century ago after barrages were built just north of Cairo, and Upper Egypt shifted in the 1960s after construction of the High Dam at Aswan, salinity has become Egypt's main agricultural problem.

In Europe the disintegration of the traditional village began with the introduction of heavy mold-board plows and the manorial system of farming these made possible, starting in A.D. 1000. It was hastened during the Middle Ages when calculations of price and profit in the medieval towns began to introduce modifications in crop rotation and methods of cultivation. The death blow to peasant agriculture came in the eighteenth and nineteenth centuries with the gradual introduction of modern farm technology and the treatment of land, rent and labor as commercially negotiable property. We saw this process, dramatically speeded up, in Ghungrali. As mounting debt blanketed Europe, 50 million peasants migrated to North America in the century after 1820; their descendants make up the majority of us today.

After England briefly held the technological lead, another revolution followed in the United States from 1890 to the 1950s. The creation of land grant colleges and a countrywide agricultural extension service led to a great accumulation of basic scientific research. A tremendous upsurge in American farm production resulted, first from farming virgin lands on the Great Plains, but, starting in the 1930s, from newly developed seeds, irrigation, electrification, mechanization and the massive application of oil-based chemical fertilizer.

Today modern agriculture is characterized by year-round cultivation, crop rotation (first introduced in Flanders around 1600), heavy use of fertilizer (manure was first used in Europe around 1400, chemical fertilizer in 1761), plant and animal breeding, the introduction of new crops from other parts of the world, and the use of machinery, such as the cast-iron swing plow, threshing machines, reapers, machine drills and combines. The machines were first used with horses, then with steam and eventually were powered by combustion engines. Such agriculture is no longer undertaken primarily to feed a village family, but as a business enterprise for reinvestment and profit. Most crops are produced for sale, not home consumption. In modern agriculture we also find a large amount of specialization, as in dairy farming or specialized horticulture to produce vegetables, fruit, seeds or flowers.

An American farmer today feeds sixty-six persons: 2.7 percent of the U.S. population grow such a surplus that they can feed the rest of the country and much of the world's city people too. This is cause for alarm; since 1935, when the new farm technology really began to take hold, the number of farms in the United States has dropped from 6.8 million to 2.4 million; what small family-size farms are left are being steadily swallowed up as their owners are forced to sell out. A third of the remaining farms take in 90 percent of all cash receipts. The number of farms grossing at least $100,000 a year rose from 23,000 in 1960 to 162,000 in 1977. We support land reform in the Third World; we may need it worse than they do. The cultural implications of this wholesale shift to fewer, larger farms do not seem to have yet sunk in.

In a cover story in its November 6, 1978 issue, "The New American Farmer," *Time* magazine cheerfully ran the headline, "As a bin-busting harvest rolls in, the rule is: Get big or get out." The article told how one Pat Benedict, described as typifying the new breed of computerized Iowa farmer, starts his day:

> Benedict makes a quick trip by pickup truck around his 3,500 acres of wheat and sugar beets. At each of many stops he whips

out a pocket calculator and does some rapid figuring before giving the hired hands orders on, say, exactly how much pesticide to spray on each field. By 8 A.M. he is heading home to start the most important part of his day: several hours spent at a roll-top desk in his small study. There Benedict goes over computer print-outs analyzing his plantings acre by acre . . .

In a generally admiring piece, *Time*'s writers breezily noted, almost in passing: "Small farmers, who do not have the technical expertise, are rapidly leaving the land." No further mention of who these "small farmers" are. Nor do we hear again about those "hired hands." And nowhere is there mention of history's lesson that all civilizations, including the Greco-Roman, without exception, once they moved too far into large-scale estate agriculture and away from family-size farms, began a fatal, irreversible decline. In other times, this has always been a leisurely process, usually taking centuries. But for us, culturally speaking, if so many millions continue to be forced off the land, what takes over, from traditional rural America's church, family, pioneer spirit and small-town togetherness? The decaying cities? The probably-failed experiment of suburbia?

Whatever happens, as we've seen, agricultural technology and the wealth that goes with it have been steadily on the move, starting in the Fertile Crescent six thousand years ago (the invention of irrigation), moving to Europe a thousand years ago (the heavy mold-board plow), briefly to England, then to America about eighty years ago, but with the big change coming just forty-five years ago (new seeds, irrigation, mechanization and the massive use of fertilizer, much of it energy-intensive). In Chapter 22, with the help of Nobel laureate Norman Borlaug, I'll discuss the present epochal movement of this technology, mostly in the past fifteen years, this time outward from America to the world's peasant societies, especially China and India (tropical grain, irrigation, electrification and multiple cropping).

The future will not wait, but before moving into it here, let's just take a last brief look at the past, the far, far distant past, just as agriculture and villages began. The Dinka tribesmen of Sudan's great Sudd swamp, I've mentioned, are among the few human relics left of how we lived before technology made the rise of urban civilization possible. In recent years, jets, dry-weather roads, river steamers and helicopters have suddenly begun to open up this region; when a new

350-kilometer Jonglei Canal is finished within the next decade, the Sudd's long isolation will be gone forever.

It is amazing just how long, starting with Egypt under the pharaohs, this huge and primeval swamp—Africa's biggest—managed to hold back the outside world. A vast, 12,000-square-mile sea of papyrus ferns, reeds and rotting ooze, the Sudd inundates the surrounding marshlands in the May–November rainy season to cover an area the size of Florida. It stopped every attempt to penetrate central Africa down the Nile from Nero's centurions to the nineteenth century, when intrepid British Victorians finally broke through in their search for the Nile's source. Many Europeans died in the Sudd—the name means blockage in Arabic—and most felt like Sir Samuel Baker, who crossed the swamp in 1863–64 and wrote that in "these vast marshes the feeling of melancholy is beyond description. The White Nile is a veritable Styx." Alan Moorehead, who crossed the Sudd by meandering steamer in the late 1950s, while writing his marvelous Nile histories, found it "claustrophobic and sinister." Only British anthropologist E. E. Evans-Pritchard, who in the 1930s was the first to study the migratory life of the Sudd's Nilotic tribes, found the Sudd had an "austere, monotonous charm." At that time the Nuers, whom Evans-Pritchard studied, like the Dinkas, practiced the system of dry-season cattle grazing and wet-season hoe cultivation believed to have prevailed in Neolithic times along the entire Nile Valley.

By 1978 I found the wet-season settlements away from the swamp on slightly higher ground were already going modern: clothes were worn, schools were opening, wells were being dug and traders, tailors and butchers were starting to appear. Even cattle, once only milked (and eaten if they died), were being sold; money values were beginning to take hold.

It was out at the dry-season cattle camps that one could get a last glimpse of a way of life that probably has outlasted any other. It was still a world of naked tribesmen, cattle, water, swamp and silence. Dr. William Payne, a United Nations cattle expert working in the Sudd, told me that even this must be transformed—and soon. "What we have to do is modernize the tribesmen's cattle-based system, not change it. The outside world with its money economy has them surrounded. If they stay as they are, they'll be crushed."

Param cattle camp, with about four thousand cattle, scattered grass huts and high grass windscreens by the fires, seemed to be set in utter desolation on a perfectly flat, swampy plain. To Yul, a twenty-seven-year-old Dinka I met, it was the finest place imaginable. Barefoot, naked, ebony black, long-limbed and seemingly as tall as Wilt Chamberlain, Yul possessed an unshakeable sense of pride and confidence. Despite his naturally good Dinka manners, he could scarcely conceal his contempt for anyone who owned no cows. Cattle are a Dinka's most cherished possession. A rich tribesman may have a thousand; even the poorest has thirty or forty. At Param camp, where Yul's tribe migrates from December to May, his cows were the first thing he looked at when he awoke and the last thing just before he slept.

He watched with pleasure when they were milked by girls or children and spent his days taking them to pasture and water. He composed songs about them, drank their milk and blood, slept on their hides, warmed himself by burning their dung and used the ashes as insect repellent, as hair dressing and to clean his teeth. Yul knew each beast of his herd and the herds of his neighbors, their colors and horn shapes, the quality of their milk, their ancestry, progeny and history. He talked of little else.

Mornings and evenings, there were dancing and drums in the camp and sometimes Yul got a small boy to lead his favorite ox around the camp, its horns decorated with tassels and its neck with bells. Then he leapt and sang:

> Friend, great ox of the spreading horns,
> Which ever bellows amid the herd.
> When I go to court a winsome girl
> I am not a man she will refuse.

The Dinkas love parables. Yul even had one on the wisdom of accepting the new money economy. "An old man warned his son, just before the floods came ten years ago, 'My son, high waters are coming and all the cattle will die. It is better to put them in a box.' The son refused and the father sold his cows, put the money in a box, and went to live in the swamp, eating water lilies and fish. After four years when the floods went away, he bought a new herd of cows and told his son, who had lost everything, 'Look, I kept my cattle in a box. Where are yours? You'd better come work with me and I'll pay you a little money.'"

The moral, Yul explained, was: "Before we didn't want to sell our cows. We only wanted to take the milk. Now people know more. A cow can be caught by a snake and die. Money cannot die." There was a charming wonder about the way the Dinkas perceived their world. Yul told me that if a man fell from his dugout canoe in the Sudd he could be captured by a crocodile who bound him, carried him around on his back, fed him fish and turned him into a crocodile too. The Dinkas are such a humorous lot, you never know when they're snowing you.

At one time, Yul said, the Sudd was a fine country for wild animals: thousands of elephants, giraffes and rhinoceroses roamed the flood plains. In 1978, many had already been driven off or killed, though back at Yul's high-ground village hippopotamuses still trampled vegetable patches at night. For Dinkas like Yul, life is an unending long walk between savannah and swamp, parched or flooded land. Summer floods and mosquitoes force the tribesmen into villages where they grow a little sorghum, beans, maize, peanuts and tobacco (both the men and women smoke pipes). Winter drought forces them back to the cattle camps, anywhere from ten to eighty miles away, to graze their cows, fish, hunt crocodiles with spears and collect honey.

Compared to the Dinkas, Kuwa's Nubas seem very advanced. Dinka chiefs still wear leopard skins and it is only in the last few years that the practice has ended of initiating youths into manhood by six deep knife cuts—right to the bone—across the forehead.

The Dinkas left me feeling that while man changes, he probably loses something with each technological advance. It was tempting in the Sudd to wish the people could stay as they are. But against this impression of cheerful contentment and happy anarchy, the great empty plains, wretched grass hut settlements, diseases and fearful superstitions were facts. Sudan's vice-president while I was there, Abel Alier, himself a Dinka, argued that to want the Sudd's four or five hundred thousand tribesmen to stay unchanged amounted to wanting an illiterate, malnourished and disease-ravaged people to stay as "a sort of human zoo for anthropologists, environmentalists and tourists." And the worst superstitions, like the tribal tattoos and lacerations, are fast fading. Let us hope, as the Dinkas leap from the Neolithic Age into the late twentieth century almost overnight, that the best of early man's culture survives: the pride, the liveliness, the drums, the dancing—and those long, long walks through seemingly boundless empty space.

A villager who goes to the city travels through both space and time. Villages with age-old customs survive; cities of that kind are almost extinct. By this I mean the kind of city originally created by village food surpluses. Sociologist Gideon Sjoberg once described such a "preindustrial city," which I'll briefly paraphrase and summarize here:

It is a marketing and handicraft center, with political, religious and educational roles. Its size is limited by the local food surplus, available human and animal transport and storage facilities. Streets are passageways for people and animals. Houses are low and congested, with bad sanitation. There is rigid ethnic and social segregation. Particular trades, such as goldsmiths, money lenders, butchers or tailors, have their own streets. "Outcaste" groups live in the outskirts. The center is not a "business district," but a mosque, temple, cathedral, palace or fortress.

Power comes from human and animal energy. Artisans make and sell their wares at home; middlemen are few. Each occupation, from merchant to servant, has its "guild." Fixed prices are rare; haggling to settle bargains the rule. Adulteration and spoilage are common. There is no system of accounting or credit.

At the top of the social structure is a literati, literate elite, which both controls and depends upon the masses. Its position, property and prestige are legitimized by sacred scripture. Social mobility is rare. Slaves, beggars and other outcastes, including traveling merchants, itinerant entertainers or foreigners stand outside society. Marriage is a prerequisite to adulthood, arranged by families. Children, especially sons, are so valued that polygamy, concubinage or adoption may be accepted to insure them. Women of the elite stay in their houses, subordinate to males. Lower class women enjoy more freedom and follow peasant custom. Eldest sons are privileged.

Religion permeates daily life, and includes magic, divination, faith healing and exorcism of demons. At public festivals, the literati, through verse and song, interpret the sacred scripture and are given high status. Formal education is restricted to males of this elite; teachers are honored. Students are expected to memorize, not evaluate or initiate. The literati runs the educational, religious and governmental institutions and exacts tribute, preserving law and order with policemen or soldiers. Courts enforce custom and the law of the sacred scripture, there being no other. Speech, dress and bearing convey status distinctions, ethnic origins and occupations.

Any traveler who has been to Kabul, Luxor, Fez or Yogyakarta or the older sections of Cairo or Delhi has observed relics of such cities. Medieval Cairo, with its narrow, crowded lanes, crumbling tenements and Mameluke palaces, its many mosques and thousand minarets, almost perfectly fits. It centers on Al Azhar University, the cultural center of the Moslem world, and Al Husein Mosque, where every Egyptian *fellah* feels compelled to go and pray as soon as he sets foot in Cairo. Scholarly *imams* who interpret the Koran and Sharia law dominate the class structure of a society that seems utterly medieval; there is even a gigantic wall to one side, built by Saladin to keep out the Crusaders.

Few villagers move into medieval Cairo; there is no room. Its artisans work, sell and live in the same ancient tenements generation after generation, preventing invasions of newcomers. This part of the city, little more densely populated than it was in the Middle Ages, has resisted both industrialization and urban migration. The hordes of arriving ex-peasants must go elsewhere.

In 1947, just over a third of Cairo's two million people had been born in villages; in 1981 almost three-fourths of Cairo's eight million people had been. As such scholars as Smith's Janet Abu-Lughod have found, only a minority of the immigrants are bright youths in search of education and opportunity. Most are village Egypt's "have nots." The typical immigrant comes by train, first stays with a relative or friend from his village near the station itself—which explains why nearby Bab al-Sharia district is the world's most densely populated area—and later may find permanent housing in the same or a nearby neighborhood. Cairo has several hundred village benevolent associations; even more important are its eight thousand or so coffee shops, mostly run by ex-villagers who serve the needs of the men from home. The distinct village cultures of Lower and Upper Egypt are reflected in immigration; peasants from the Delta bring their families and, better educated, find a variety of jobs. The male-female ratio is about even. Upper Egyptians go into domestic or other personal services or work in unskilled labor gangs; four of five Upper Egyptian immigrants are male. Both groups, however, try to recreate village life in communities on Cairo's rural-urban fringe, the Lower Egyptians on the city's northern side, the Upper Egyptians on the southern. Many outlying neighborhoods closely resemble villages; streets are seldom used for wheeled traffic but serve as pathways, playgrounds, meeting places and to tether animals.

Housing is much more congested in Cairo than in the villages. Many immigrants seek the top floor or roof of tenements so they can make an earthen, flat-topped village oven to bake bread (and sleep upon on cold nights). As in village huts, a high four-poster bed with wrought-iron frame embellished with gilt remains the main status symbol. Dress changes little; men cling to their *galabias,* the long, loose gowns of the *fellaheen;* women may discard the black veil over their high-necked, long-sleeved gown, though many mosques campaign among the women to keep the veil. Upper Egyptian males, especially, may completely reject urban life, confine their social activities in Cairo to the coffee house frequented by their fellow villagers, and feel that their "real life" begins on visits home. Shahhat, for example, on his few trips to Cairo, practically had to be dragged away from the "Qurna Friendship Club," a dingy coffee house near the railway station where men from Berat village congregated. Even at work immigrants stick together; often gangs of laborers on a construction project are all from the same village. Women attempt, with less success, to recreate their village social life in Cairo; births, deaths, marriages, circumcisions and religious festivals provide countless occasions to visit the homes of fellow village women.

What is true of Cairo is equally true of most big cities in the Third World. Sociologists customarily tell us that large numbers of heterogeneous people in dense, permanent settlements in cities tend to become anonymous, sophisticated, tolerant toward change and dependent upon impersonal relationships. Erich Fromm, David Riesman and so many others have said that the urban outlook, ethos and personality are individualized, depersonalized, atomized, unstable, secularized, blasé, rationalistic, cosmopolitan, highly differentiated, self-critical, time-oriented, subject to sudden shifts in mood and fashion, "other directed," trendy and so on. The consensus of such descriptions and their wide acceptances suggests that there are some general psychological consequences of urbanization in Western cities (and here, from my observations in Manila, Mexico City and Rio de Janeiro, I would include cities with Latin cultures as part of the West).

It is not true of villagers from the Islamic, Hindu or Far Eastern civilizations (again excepting such Westernized hybrids as Hong Kong and Singapore). Nor will it, I suggest, ever be. In cities in countries where an ancient civilization exists and the vast majority of the population remains peasant villagers, we find urban immigrants actively trying to recreate their village's social organization and customs; like the *fellaheen* in Cairo, they consciously cluster together with villagers from home to protect themselves from the shock of anomie.

The reason is cultural, but there is an economic side to it. Very generally speaking, we find two distinct types of cities in the Third World today: the first is a remnant of an ancient preindustrial city earlier described; the second came into being only during the past century or so, as a port of colonial exchange of local natural resources for Western capital and consumer goods. Among such cities are Calcutta, Bombay, Manila, Jakarta, Rio de Janeiro, Bangkok, Hong Kong and Singapore. Jakarta, for example, was just a sleepy port of four hundred thousand people forty years ago, a Dutch colony on the edge of tropical jungle. Today it is a fast-modernizing metropolis with heavy traffic, skyscrapers and six million people. If you look carefully in the oldest sections, you can find the canals, arched bridges and little houses with brown-tiled roofs and diamond-paned windows built to remind the Dutch of homes left behind in Holland.

If we except a few like Rio, Hong Kong and Singapore, even these comparatively "modern" cities are barely part of an urban-industrial system; they do not yet command enough local savings, skills, energy and other resources. Coming more than a hundred years after the industrialization of the West, after a further century of technological advance, their new industries provide much less untrained manual work than ours did at a comparable stage. As a rough rule of thumb, we can say that these industries need an investment of about $2,000 per worker, as opposed to $100 to $200 per worker in the late nineteenth century.

I sometimes read of the "industrializing and urbanizing peasant." In fact, nine times out of ten, the peasant is doing neither. He goes to the city, but he does not find a job in industry nor does his village culture change. Industry has not drawn him in; agriculture has pushed him out. Most ex-peasants, lacking any skill save cultivation, turn to the kind of employment that keeps a man from starving but contributes little or nothing either to their country's development or their own acquisition of skills and confidence: street vending, petty hawking, shoe shining, errand running, labor gangs or, in the tropics, rickshaw pedaling. These villagers live in great new slum areas surrounding established urban cores, crumbling ant heaps of anxious people who manage to survive from day to day by providing each other extremely modest goods and services. Often they confront terrible conditions of housing and a scale of misery far worse than anything they left behind in their villages.

Culturally, they do not find, as their ancestors did, a literati who keeps the sacred scripture. Instead they are likely to discover their intellectual elites are frantically pursuing North American lifestyles; Arnold Toynbee called this *Herodianism,* or adopting the culture of a dominant foreign power so as to live as comfortable a life as possible in an inescapable social environment. Its opposite is *Zealotism,* the impulse to retreat fanatically into one's own traditional culture, as we have seen most spectacularly in Iran. The ever-perceptive Robert Redfield, writing with Milton Singer in 1954, also found that the villager encounters two types of cities, much like the preindustrial city and modern ex-colonial port city earlier mentioned. They called these the city of *orthogenetic transformation,* or the city of moral order, and the city of *heterogenetic transformation,* or the city of technical order. Medieval Cairo, our earlier example, typifies the orthogenetic city; even today it remains a center of culture, political power and administrative control; local religious and moral norms prevail and a literati interprets the sacred scripture.

In the heterogenetic city the local culture has collapsed, all but swamped by Westernization; men are concerned with the market, producing goods, expedient relations between buyer and seller, ruler and ruled, native and foreigner. Priority is given to making money. Common types to be found are businessmen, administrators alien to those they administer and rebels, reformers, plotters and planners of all kinds. Redfield and Singer asked themselves whether heterogenetic cities, such as the great colonial ports (Jakarta, Bombay, Manila), could change their cultural character now that we're in the postcolonial age. They decided, "They are not likely to live down their heterogenetic past, even as centers of nationalism and of movements for revival of local cultures." Despite the pedantic terminology (*ortho* means straight, *hetero* diverse and *genetic* origin), I have found the Redfield-Singer hypothesis a very useful tool in understanding how Third World cities work. For example, heterogenetic cities (Calcutta, Rio de Janeiro, Singapore) have much higher crime rates than more orthogenetic cities (Delhi, Cairo, Beijing). And the two big heterogenetic cities of the Moslem Middle East (Beirut, Tehran) have sustained the worst damage from the revival of fundamentalist Islam. (Khomeini preferred the orthogenetic Qom.)

Redfield also helps us to understand why it matters so much to the villager to have literati in the city to interpret sacred scripture for him; this is his famous concept of the *little tradition* of the village and the *great tradition* of the city. Redfield maintained, rightly, I think, that culture originates in villages and then flows into cities, where it becomes systematized. In his own words:

> In a civilization there is a great tradition of the reflective few, and there is a little tradition of the unreflective many. The great tradition is cultivated in schools and temples; the little tradition works itself out and keeps itself going in the lives of the unlettered in their village communities. The tradition of the philosopher, theologian, and literary man is a tradition consciously cultivated and handed down; that of the little people is for the most part taken for granted and not submitted to much scrutiny or considered refinement or improvement. . . .
>
> The two traditions are interdependent. Great tradition and little tradition have long affected each other and continue to do so. . . . The ethics of the Old Testament arose out of tribal peoples and returned to peasant communities after they had been the subject of thought by philosophers and theologians. . . . Great and little tradition can be thought of as two currents of thought and action, distinguishable, yet ever flowing into and out of each other.

Redfield said the two traditions develop institutions to promote a common understanding as to the meaning and purpose of life, and a sense of belonging together, to all people, rural and urban, of the larger community.

Such institutions, he said, could include sacred scriptures embodying the great tradition, such as the Torah, Bible, Koran, Vedas, Buddhist "Three Baskets" or Confucian thirteen classics, and such literati to interpret them as rabbis, priests, *imama,* or Brahmans. Eminent men, such as Mahatma Gandhi, Nehru, Mao, Chou En-Lai or John Paul II could embody the great tradition and mediate it to the masses (as Anwar Sadat did when he accused Iran's revolutionaries of being un-Islamic). So can physical places such as monuments or sacred or patriotic shrines (the Lincoln Memorial, the black stone of Mecca, Jerusalem). Periodically a cultural gap between village and city will grow if the urban literati transforms the simple values and world views of the villagers to

a degree of generalization, abstraction and complexity incomprehensible to ordinary villagers, and in doing so to leave out much of the concrete local detail of geography and village activity.

To Redfield, this potential village-city cultural gap did not matter as long as both belonged to a common civilization and villager and city man alike shared

a consciousness of a single cultural universe where people hold the same things sacred.

Sometimes, in Redfield's terms, there was a complete village-city break when the villagers found themselves in an urban world where "original modes of thought had authority beyond or in conflict" with their own ways and views of what life should be. At times the little tradition can rebel; the Old Testament prophets, as pastoralist shepherds with stern patriarchal traditions, revolted against urban Mesopotamian culture; to express their extreme anti-urban bias, they made Babylon, Sodom and Gomorrah and other cities their prime symbols of vice and evil. The pendulum swung the other way when early Christianity spread to the Greco-Roman world; villagers, living in the countryside or *pagus,* were simply dismissed as *paganus,* pagans. We find much of this estrangement today; Carolina in Salvador, Shahhat venturing into modern Cairo by the Nile or Barek on the Champs Élysées felt apprehensive, even threatened in a heterogenetic *milieu* in conflict with their own "little tradition" culture.

Indeed, every villager, when he goes to a city, encounters all kinds of basically alien thinking. He meets people with money values geared to a technological-industrial order. He runs into such new sentiments of common cause as nationalism, class consciousness or religious reform; he's faced with such unfamiliar social types as reformers, agitators, nationalist leaders, missionaries or foreigners. For the first time he encounters an unstable future outlook—in his village the future merely repeats the past, though this too is changing—as in reform or revolutionary movements, future myths and future planning. He confronts future views that may be optimistic, pessimistic, radically reformist, escapist, defeatist or apocalyptic. At the same time this villager is forced in the city to struggle hard for a meager wage in congested shantytowns, probably without sewage, clean water, schools, health care or electricity; he also faces crime, outbreaks of disease and feelings of claustrophobia. Once an educated elite would have provided him with explanations and justifications; but the old literati is now likely to be Westernized, not only in terms of material technique (the industrial system) and not merely in externals (stuff like shirts and trousers), but in its social and political institutions: the Western status of women, the Western method of education and the Western machinery of parliamentary government (even the Russians and Chinese make a pretense of it, Marxism-Leninism being a Western export, or what Toynbee called a fanatical Christian heresy which took a leaf from the book but left out the heart).

In a few nations, the villager may be led by a man of real stature, as the Indians were under Jawaharlal Nehru. Nehru, totally Westernized himself, instinctively took pains to conceal it from his people (I was in Nehru's house just after his death and was startled to learn that the last words he wrote, in a notebook in his bedroom, were the famous lines of Robert Frost which begin, "The woods are lovely dark and deep . . . .") But most likely the villager will be led by one of the two-thirds of the world's 159 heads of government who are business leaders or generals unequipped to cope with the problems which face them and whose main concern is not to get murdered in their successor's *coup d'état*. Walter Lippmann, in one of two conversations I had with him, recognized this and told me that the "supreme question before mankind," to which he wouldn't live to know the answer, was whether the men or women who govern "will be able to make themselves willing and able to save themselves."

Villagers need and want governments that can govern in the face of overpopulation and environmental decay. Our Western kind of democratic freedom matters much less. Freedom is perceived by the villager in personal, not abstract, terms, such as the right to share equally in village benefits, maybe to marry whomever he pleases or be protected from arbitrary arrest and beating from the local police. In villages freedom also has another, more cultural, meaning. Almost everywhere, I've found the same pattern over the years: youth makes demands, parents resist; after a period of rebellion, youth surrenders to tradition. This is not always, perhaps, the best thing in terms of personal self-interest, but it keeps the villages going. The freedom that really seems to matter in villages, then—and it does not have to mean craven surrender—is the voluntary limitation of individual choice so that you can live together with other people in a group. Most villagers, as they mature, find themselves doing it; one might call it the freedom to choose self-responsibility.

So our political ideas tend not to have much meaning to the ex-peasant in the city who cannot find an industrial job—the economic means—to Westernize himself and who finds the old literati is too Westernized and estranged from him to help him. Western industrial technology eludes him (he cannot learn manufacturing skills without a job). Furthermore, the West has failed to spread the core of its culture, its Christian religion, even among the otherwise Westernized elite (in the sense, as Roderick MacFarquhar has put it, that the admonitions of the Sermon on the Mount still constitute the standard for the West in a post-religious era); it has converted capitalists and commissars everywhere, but mighty few apostles. With so little offered him in the city, materially or spiritually, the villager naturally retreats back into the familiar fastnesses of his own little-tradition culture. We now find dual societies—a Westernized, secularized elite side by side with villagers who remain villagers in the city—in five of the world's twenty biggest cities (Mexico City, Calcutta, Bombay, Cairo and Jakarta) and partly in five more of them (Shanghai, Beijing, Buenos Aires, São Paulo and Rio de Janeiro). In most of these cities today an actual majority of the population was born in villages. These villagers, in the city or at home, can't escape the West; its medicine put them in the fix they're in and only its grain supplies and contraceptive, agricultural and industrial techniques can get them out of it (hopefully before such bizarre dangers as terrorists getting the nuclear capability to destroy the planet or the bio-physical scientists being able to control behavior come to pass).

So what does the villager do? We sometimes assume that culture is mostly the work of an innovating urban elite. Redfield took pains to refute this; he argued that village culture "does not become inert," but may possess "a greater vitality and disposition to change" than city culture. He emphasized that culture flows back and forth between village and city and said, "Cities themselves are creatures as well as creators of this process." The Western political ideologies of nationalism, socialism, communism, capitalism and democracy have all emerged in cities. No great religion ever has. Abraham was a herdsman, Zoroaster raised cattle, Jesus was a village carpenter's son, Mohammed a shepherd and later a petty trader and Buddha, though a Hindu prince, came from a remote backwater of Nepal. These religions were all formed as little village traditions in revolt against existing city traditions which had somehow failed millions of villagers, just as the Westernization of the great Third World cities so often fails them now. They all emerged in civilizations which, like ours, were *in extremis*. Prophets come from villages.

Bombay has its cages; these tenements—two or three stories high, red-lit, open to the street, with prison-like bars in place of walls—are filled with girls who, in curtained-off beds at the back, may take on twenty or thirty men each night. The girls, in this doomsday vision of sex that is Forest Road, are paid so little they powder their faces with some bright yellowish stuff that makes them look fair in the red light but ghastly by day. Most are very young and tell the same horror tale of deception and bondage; a stranger came to their village, proposed marriage, won the agreement of their usually destitute parents and then, once they reached Bombay, raped them and sold them into the cages. Like the Bengali girls carried off to brothels by Pakistani soldiers during the 1971 war in Bangladesh, they fear that even if they escaped, their families would now reject them. Dacca's liberators found girls, imprisoned at army bases, who were wearing only shorts, their hair clipped, so they could not hang themselves with their saris or the long tresses of their hair. Others bled to death from the way they had been raped. So did some young boys; survivors told of having to suck the penises of Pakistani *jawans*.

Sexual degradation in the urban slums of Asia, Africa and Latin America tends to be pathetic rather than provocative, because of its obvious roots in poverty and the absence of any sense of human esteem. Yet the faces of nervous international tourists can be seen nightly gawking from horse-drawn carriages along Forest Road. What foreigner has not been accosted by pimps or whores along Manila's Roxas Boulevard, Bangkok's Patpong Street or Calcutta's Chowringhee Road? The Singapore-by-night circuit takes in male transvestites on Bogie Street, or, for the venturesome, the tortuous alleys behind the famous Raffles Hotel, where patient queues of Chinese seamen and factory hands file through the corridors of foul brothels, the women in their open doorways and the slowly passing men eyeing each other sullenly and mutely, like zombies. Or there are Cairo's domed and underground *hamams,* as old as *Arabian Nights* and tinted Saladin green, where in the dark recesses, amidst steaming hot water vats and the thump-thump of masseurs, the city's poorest laborers find satisfaction and relief in furtive sodomy. Even the North Vietnamese, in their attempt to bring Saigon's labyrinth of prostitution under control, have discovered that big urban vice networks are extremely complex and hard to uproot.

Thomas Robert Malthus, in his 1798 essay, warned that over-population would face humanity with "misery and vice." The "vice" once seemed Victorian, but in the Third World's shantytowns, *colonias proletarias, gecekondo* districts, *bidonvilles, bustees* and *barriadas,* it flourishes like weeds, along with the spiritual destruction it brings with it. Let us take the example of Jakarta. As was observed in Chapter 14, most of the Javanese who migrate to Jakarta to look for work are nominally Moslem but are equally influenced by Hinduism and pagan animism. In the village they are cultured, artistic and mystical, with a character, as Sir Thomas Stamford Raffles, the British governor of Java, described it in his *History of Java* in 1817, "ever graceful, amiable and ingenuous." Yet it is a culture with pathetically few defenses for surviving in city slums. My first time in Jakarta, in late 1967, the city was just recovering from Indonesia's anti-communist bloodbath of 1965–66; at least a third of a million had died and Sukarno's decline and fall had left the economy in ruins.

Rival gangs of hoodlums, inspired by movies to call themselves the "Alamo Boys" and the "Djanggos," had seized large slum areas as their private fiefdoms. Five thousand girls, almost all of them from Javanese villages, were packed into an abandoned freight yard called Planet, which was just behind Jakarta's main railway station and its central marketplace, Pasar Senen. Planet was the worst—the girls were crowded into concentration-camp-type freight cars—but brothels had sprung up all over Jakarta, usually identifiable by the young men sitting in the entryways, smoking hashish and opium; they also took morphine. In Kramat Tunggak near the harbor, then and today Jakarta's largest center of prostitution, a mile-long street of shops sold little but contraceptives and aphrodisiacs.

In those days women did not walk the streets, as prostitutes sometimes do today, but hundreds of male transvestites, known as *bancis,* did; they were all over the main downtown boulevard of Jalan Thamrin after dark, grotesque and tacky, rather than alluring, in their dresses, heavy makeup and wigs.

In addition to Planet, another prostitution area, Bongkaren, was a vision of hell. I crossed it one morning with Husen, a maze of bamboo and beaten tin shanties, flying dust, heat, garbage dumps swarming with flies, dazed-looking women with unkempt hair wandering around with cooking pots, their bare feet treading on the filth, like survivors of some disaster. We heard angry voices coming from one of the sheds, its walls made of old charcoal baskets, still a grimy black with coal dust. A woman crawled out, shrieking at a man who followed her, "You made me a whore!" She thrust her hands at him; we could glimpse the rash of syphilitic sores. The man first stood dumbly and watched her. Then he pulled off his belt and, in a frenzy of rage and hysteria, began lashing her with it. Those who argue that there is any psychological validity to the theory that out of violation comes adoration should have witnessed such scenes in Jakarta. That was 1967, the city's nadir.

Going back to Jakarta off and on since then, I've found that Planet has disappeared altogether and areas such as Bongkaren have been cleaned up. In 1970 I spent a week in a Kramat Tunggak brothel, interviewing the dozen or so girls who worked there. The house faced the Java Sea across some mud flats and was not unpleasant; there was a porch-like bar in front and six well-furnished, clean and comfortable bedrooms. These were strictly for business. The girls slept on straw mats out in a back shed; they were fed a miserable diet of a little rice and vegetables and most owned only one decent dress, which they had to keep washing and ironing. I soon found that the girls were too young—fifteen to seventeen—and too illiterate and pathetic to have much to tell. Unlike the women in India, most had entered prostitution voluntarily; the most common story was needing support for one or two babies after their husbands or lovers had abandoned them.

I soon struck up a friendship with Aminah, a Sundanese woman of about forty who lived next door. At home in a cotton dress with her hair tied in a bun, Aminah looked demure, middle-aged and respectable. But once or twice a week, she struggled into a corset, curled her hair, painted her face, put on a bright red dress and went out to try to solicit foreign sailors on the waterfront. Aminah's story went back to a decade before when her husband, a shipping clerk, one day brought home a teenage second wife. Aminah threw him out and had since managed to support herself and educate her only son as an engineer. Her specialty was to find bitter sailors who had suffered one of the many bad experiences the waterfront had to offer, and bring them home to mother them with good meals, cold beer, hot baths, instant laundry and shoeshines and her own humorous good nature. She accepted it all except having to go out and solicit, which she hated and feared. I went with her a couple of nights and saw why.

Her main haunt, the Java Bar, was just off the main pier and was run by the Indonesian navy, so once inside you had some protection, though you still had to get home safely. A hatchet-faced Batak woman with a ring of keys chained to her waist let you in and out a padlocked door; the entire front was covered with steel fencing, so you could see the street. The clientele ran to opium-addicted harbor coolies and aging prostitutes with chalkily powdered, corpse-like faces—a stuffed, moth-eaten orangutan on the bar, the only decoration, looked more alive. There were also a few younger prostitutes, foreign sailors who had wandered in, and members of the Djanggo gang. Aminah used to keep up a whispered commentary in English, since few of them knew it:

"Cowboys, hah! The Djanggos are cowboys for money. That big one with the long moustache is Poli. He's jobless. That's his only suit of clothes. He stops people in the street and makes pressure. If they don't give him money, he beats them. Those girls get money for him. All these boys are nothing working, just joking all day and smoking marijuana. Don't speak to the one in the yellow shirt. He takes morphine and carries a razor. The character of these women here, if you have money, they will take it all." (I later interviewed several of the Djanggo gang; like Barek, they seemed desperate for a sense of self-identity. Poli, for instance, told me the bar was too dangerous and I should not return.)

In the mid-1970s, in an attempt to control prostitution, Jakarta's Governor Ali Sadikin set up a legalized complex of just over a hundred new houses, each with a madam and up to fifteen girls. Bars on the front terraces sold beer and soft drinks, but otherwise it resembled a seedy modern suburb. An American anthropologist, Hanna Papanek, volunteered to help as an interpreter—you need a woman with you to really talk to women in much of Asia—and we spent a day with Tarwi, a lovely, sloe-eyed Javanese in her twenties. Tarwi said she had become a *wanita tuna susila,* "woman without morals," when her husband left her in her village with three small children. (Hanna at once demanded to know the phrase for "man without morals"; there was none.)

Tarwi said a factory job, if she could find one, paid a woman the equivalent in Indonesian currency of only two or three dollars a week; a man doing the same work earned at least three times that much. As a prostitute, Tarwi earned an average of ten dollars a night, sleeping with just two or three men, mostly students, businessmen, clerks, tourists or sailors; a foreigner paid fifteen to twenty dollars.

She had a clean room—she did not have to sleep on a floor mat—had a private bath and said she insisted that her customers wear condoms to prevent disease and pregnancy. She visited a doctor three times a week and every Friday got an injection—she did not know of what, to Hanna's horror. Tarwi said women who became careless sometimes fell sick—*broken* was the word she used—and some became sterile. She could go out with the men, but since a friend came back after several days of being abused and beaten she had not left the house with a man. After eight years of school back in her village, she was studying sewing and English at a government "rehabilitation center." Yet the only English she had been taught ran to such phrases as "When did you come to Jakarta?" and "What would you like, sir?" She managed to send home a hundred dollars a month—practically a year's wage in village Java—and planned to someday open a tailoring shop. "I like and I don't like the life," Tarwi told us. "It is nice and not so nice. My parents think I make the money I send as a seamstress. If they knew the truth, they would kill me."

The human offensiveness of prostitution was brought home to Hanna and me in another interview. Some days later, in another part of Jakarta, we met a printer's wife, Karlina; she was Tarwi's age but looked much older. Pale and worn, Karlina had borne five children in that many years but now, like most of the women she knew, took the Pill. Her husband earned twenty-three dollars each month, putting him in what was then the upper third of Jakarta incomes. They lived in a typical two-cubicle bamboo shed, sharing an open well and pit privy with forty people. Karlina said rice prices had quadrupled in recent years; she could afford to cook just one liter a day, plus a little salted fish, a vegetable and coffee, boiling the grounds again and again. She bought drinking water for twelve cents a can from a neighbor with a tap from the city supply, a common practice in Asian city slums. Some neighbor women earned $1.25 a day working sixteen-hour days at a nearby Chinese paper factory. Karlina was saving to pay a two-dollar admission fee and sixty cents monthly charge so that at least one of her children could go to school. Interestingly, she was sending one of the girls, though she had sons who were older. Why?

Karlina replied that her greatest fear was that her daughter would grow up to become a *wanita tuna susila.* In her neighborhood, the poorest were men who went about the streets picking up cigarette butts to sell to a Chinese merchant for reuse. They earned about twenty cents a day. Then came the shoeshine boys at about fifty cents and the pedicab drivers at seventy cents, with construction laborers perhaps getting as much as a dollar. The pimps and prostitutes were earning at least ten times this much. Karlina was poor. Her home had that salty, sour stench you get only with the worst poverty. Older children were patiently removing lice from a baby's hair; the laundry hanging about was threadbare and permanently gray. You wanted to get out no matter what it cost. But it was a matter of intense concern to this woman that her daughter did not choose to escape through prostitution.

In parts of Asia and the Middle East, one also encounters male prostitution; in Manila I interviewed the inhabitants of such a brothel not more than a mile from the presidential palace. The boys, mostly in their late teens, were as abused and mistreated as the girls of Kramat Tunggak. In Jakarta, however, homosexuality took the bizarre form of the transvestite *bancis;* these were hard to interview, as they took on false personalities along with their falsetto voices. Some were said to be educated—students or even professionals, including married men with families—but most were village immigrants who had come to Jakarta looking for a job. In my book, *The Golden Bowl Be Broken,* there is a scene where Husen tries to talk several *bancis* from his village into seeking a man's work. The *bancis* insist that they are women and try to kiss him.

"Why?" Husen protests, dodging away. "You are men. Why do you want to kiss me? You are *sama sama* [the same as] me. If you are girls, okay, I kiss. But you have beards. Your chins are *kasar,* rough." The *bancis* flounce away, indignant, saying, "He is a crazy boy, this Husen!" Husen claimed some of the *bancis* even wore foam-rubber vaginas and turned out the light so their *tuans* (foreign customers) never did know they were really male. The *bancis'* confusion of sexual identification seemed complete. Java has rural theatrical troupes, who go from village to village performing folk dramas; as in Shakespeare, the women's roles are customarily performed by *bancis.* In their wigs, heavy makeup and women's clothing, the *bancis* carry on in a feminine manner even backstage, flirting with the village stagehands. Husen knew several of them; they were farmers and behaved in a masculine fashion back in their villages.

After spending most of the past twenty-one years in the Third World, I would venture to make three observations about homosexuality in villages. First, it has some direct relationship with urbanization. It is more widespread than one might expect in the Third World cities, possibly because so many urban migrant workers leave their wives back in their villages.

Second, with one major exception, it is virtually nonexistent in the vast majority of villages and rarely is it even talked about. In the hundreds of conversations my interpreters and I have noted down, homosexuality was almost never mentioned. Once, in the Punjab during the 1970 harvest, Sindar, the nonstop talker, joked, "Do you know why Dhakel is so tired today? He was raped by all of us last night. He was drunk and couldn't even tell what was happening to him. In the morning he asked, 'Who spilt milk on my pajamas?'" But sexual banter was Sindar's specialty and it was hard to take anything he said seriously.

The major exception is the region of the Mediterranean and the Middle East. Here, where homosexuality does appear in villages—and this is my third observation—it manifests itself as a purely physical act, a way of finding sexual satisfaction and relief similar to masturbation. It is associated in the villagers' minds with manliness and virility. *Fellaheen* in Egypt's Nile Delta might jokingly curse one another as sodomites or catamites, *"Yah khawel!"* and *"Yah elg!"* But in the Delta joking seemed to be as far as it went. Only in Upper Egypt did I experience homosexual advances in a village. It happened so often—more than a dozen times—and from villagers who fit no special category, being married or single, young or middle-aged—I asked my Egyptian interpreter about it. He saw it as an attempted expression of dominance, a way of reducing another male, especially a foreigner, to lesser (female) status. It was all done in an unthreatening pathetic-funny way and no offense was taken. It did arouse my curiosity as to why Upper Egyptians should behave so differently when it came to sex than other villagers.

In Sudan about this time I happened to come across a copy of Fawn M. Brodie's *The Devil Drives: A Life of Sir Richard Burton,* which provided a possible explanation. In this 1967 biography of the famous

English explorer who was one of the first Europeans to visit Mecca and later search for the source of the Nile, Miss Brodie describes how, in the *Terminal Essay* to his translation of *The Arabian Nights,* Burton theorized that what he called a "Sotanical Zone" extended along both the north and south shores of the Mediterranean and into present-day Iran and Pakistan. He also included China, but this can be discounted because, although he knew the other regions well, he had not been there. He excluded black Africa and most of India.

In this zone, Burton wrote, sodomy between males was casually tolerated and treated as a trifling offense. Burton was insatiably curious regarding the erotic and evidently wrote more about homosexuality; what he had to say we shall never know. The day he died in Trieste in 1890, his wife, Isabel, took all his papers and unpublished manuscripts out into their garden and burned them. It was a senselessly destructive act of censorship and made her a pariah in English society.

What the villages in Burton's zone all have in common, at least those in which I have lived, is an unusually strong cult of male dominance and male superiority. Women gain much greater social equality once you move southward from the Pakistani frontier down into India. In black Africa, tribal women possess remarkable independence, although polygamy is practiced. Each wife tills her own fields to feed herself and her children. The women collect roots, herbs and berries; they peddle these at the weekly market, together with baskets, mats and other things they make at home, and keep the money themselves. The same is true in Asia's hill country, where women play an equal economic role.

Burton's zone, except for southernmost Europe, is mainly Moslem. Yet in Islamic law, sodomy between males, like adultery, is punishable by death; in Khomeini's Iran, men have been shot by firing squads or stoned to death for sodomy. My guess, based upon several years of observation in only a few villages in Morocco, Egypt, Iran and Pakistan, tends to confirm Burton's theory; it is that casual male sodomy is tolerated in village societies where tradition puts men in a position of extreme dominance over women while sequestering and "protecting" them, so that there are few heterosexual outlets. When this happens, as in Upper Egypt, a detected adulteress may be stoned to death or otherwise executed in the name of Islam, but the like Koranic penalty against sodomy between males is ignored. This is how I handled it when describing Berat village in my book, *Shahhat:*

The village men took fierce pride in their strength, masculinity and solidarity; the severe penalty given a woman caught in adultery assuaged this pride, as did some men's treatment of their wives, never addressing them as more than *"Yah mara! Woman!"* and forever putting them down. This same pride led to a drive to reduce competing males to lesser status through domination, sadism, and even sodomy; dominance was everything. Sodomy with another male or an animal was treated as a mere peccadillo. . . . The prevalence of sodomy deeply mortified the village women.

It should be emphasized that in all villages marriage is practically a matter of survival, because the basic agricultural economic unit is a man, wife, children and draft animals; procreation and the family are fundamental to any peasant society. This may explain why homosexuality, if it exists at all in a village, is associated with male virility and strength and tends to be regarded as such a trifling matter. In Berat, it was treated in almost the same manner as animality, which also went on. Many of the young men, soon after puberty, had sex with donkeys; both Shahhat and a friend, El Azap, had done so, to "see who was the strongest" as teenagers. They'd been caught at it out in a cane field by some other boys, who years later found it hilarious to recall, much to Shahhat's mortification. Indeed, their sense of humor redeems the Upper Egyptians; they have life to them, no matter what. Most bizarrely, in Guapira village in Northeast Brazil, the priest at the village church one Sunday delivered an angry sermon on the evils of having sex with hens and chickens. I was sure that Sebastion, my interpreter, somehow had gotten it wrong until, after a few rounds of cachaça in the village tavern, the boys sheepishly admitted the practice was not entirely unknown in Guapira. I'll spare you the gory details.

Prostitution, like homosexuality, is conspicuous by its almost total absence from most villages. The one exception is the willing widow, who seems to be a universal village fixture. At least such women, living either with no adult male or a very old one in the house, popped up in almost all the villages, even in Egypt and Punjab. Loud, raucous, easygoing pariahs, they somehow existed beyond the pale of strict village social conventions. They were outcastes, without status, but seemed to be tolerated by other village women as an undesirable but necessary safety valve. Shahhat had his first initiation into sex (the business with the donkeys when he was an adolescent aside) with such a widow. But he had such an exaggerated terror of all illness that when he found out how many other men went to her, he was afraid to go back. Once Charan and I encountered two Harijan widows working in the fields; he exchanged jokes with them and they laughed in a good-humored way. Later Charan told me that in his younger days they had been "useful."

One explanation why prostitution, like homosexuality, is absent in most villages but prevalent in Third World cities is that in a city sexual or any other kind of behavior can be hidden in the protective anonymity of the crowd. Young people are no longer constrained by the surveillance of the village; in rural communities everybody not only knows everybody else, but everybody watches everybody else all the time. What is true of individual urbanizing villagers may be just as true of whole urbanizing societies.

Sex just may be the area of greatest mutual incomprehension between villagers and ourselves in the West. The gap separating their traditional family structures, long-held moral restrictions and old taboos from our relatively new permissiveness is wide. After so many years in villages, I sometimes feel, on visits home, like a cultural Rip Van Winkle, especially among upper-middle class liberals. (Lower middle-class conservatives and the poor don't seem to change all that much; I find the Americans who empathize with villagers most readily are older, low-income blacks.) When I published a magazine article on sex in villages a couple of years ago, both favorable and unfavorable reaction was unexpectedly intense, suggesting how emotionally freighted and psychologically complex the American sexual revolution has become. No other article I've written brought so many requests to reprint it. You could just say everybody's interested in sex. But I suspect there's more to it than that.

People are genuinely seeking decent, useful and happy ways of life that are neither too restrictive nor too permissive; they naturally want to learn how other people handle things, including sex, elsewhere. Our mutual incomprehension with villagers when it comes to sex is rooted, as all culture is, in economics. We're rich and they're poor. We live mostly in cities and suburbs; they live in villages. Our wealth and technology, as discussed in Chapter 1, allow us to live according to individual choice, something brand new in human history.

In villages, people don't have this choice. They belong to small rural groups which live by cultivating land. They're dependent upon each other and mostly human muscle power to grow the crops and feed themselves. Of economic necessity, marriage, the family and property are every village's three basic social institutions. With few exceptions, chastity, early marriage, divorceless monogamy and multiple maternity have been the rule. There's no economic basis for the emergence of anything like a "gay" subculture or the kind of freedom and independence for women that works in our society (where, in the United States, 4 million mechanized farmers manage to feed about 262 million non-farmers who are freed to think about something other than how their next meal can be produced from the land).

Marriage in a village comes soon after puberty, so there is little frustration from the strong restraints placed upon premarital sex. Aristotle, as I'll discuss in Chapter 21, found from his study of both humans and animals that the mode of living of all creatures is determined by how they obtain their food. As we've seen, villagers are likely to tacitly tolerate what they regard as aberrant forms of behavior (the willing widow in most villages, male sodomy in the Mediterranean-Middle Eastern region, animality in some places) whenever frustration might get out of hand, *provided* that there is no serious threat to the fundamental village institutions of marriage and family, upon which their agricultural economy depends. The Nubas' polygamy, like the Tibetans' polyandry, is exceptional and most probably represents some adjustment to a sex ratio imbalance back in their history. (Possibly females once had a much lower life expectancy than males in Africa. For some mysterious reason, considerably more male than female babies are born to Tibetans.) And Java's custom of frequent consecutive marriages and divorces must be unique; Raffles mentions it in his *History of Java,* published in 1817. Husen, who regards himself as conservative and conventional, has now been married four successive times; one man in his village—the record-holder—had been married and divorced twenty-one times. Yet Husen's parents and perhaps a majority of married couples in Pilangsari had practiced divorceless monogamy and it was considered socially more desirable. Husen recently wrote me that he hopes his present marriage lasts until "we are grandmother and grandfather." The Javanese were aware that frequent divorce led to emotional insecurity; there was a great fear of aging, especially among women, and most Javanese, male or female, dye their hair rather than let it turn gray.

In the Punjab, where village divorce is almost unheard of and women are most secluded, I found the most sexual repression. Hindu India, especially the northwest, was long ruled by Moslem Moghuls, whose nobles had a nasty habit of abducting pretty village girls for their harems; the sequestering of women may originate from that or there may be deeper reasons. Only in Ghungrali, of all the villages, was I not allowed by custom to speak with women younger than I was, though in the case of Charan's beautiful daughter, Rani, whom I have known since she was a little girl, I ignore tradition. Punjabis live in extended families and tend to sleep on string cots all crowded together in a courtyard or in a room or two. Married couples may be given their own room, if one exists. But generally there is so little privacy, studies have shown, that most husbands and wives tend not to have sexual relations more than two or three times a month (compared to two or three times a week in village Java). Often this is accomplished in the fields after a wife is seen taking food to her husband's well house at noon; the neighbors, in a general tacit understanding, keep away. It is one way to escape the wife's ubiquitous mother-in-law, often a despot until the wife has grown, married sons and daughters-in-law of her own.

In conversation, especially working in the fields, Indians tend to talk about sex the most, the Javanese least. Rare among villagers, the Javanese enjoy the crudest barnyard humor. The Punjabis almost never mention bodily functions and it is bad taste to refer to one's predawn sorties into the wheat fields to, as the Punjabis say, "answer the call of nature." Again in Java, nakedness, as, for example, bathing in a canal, is regarded as perfectly natural. (Although in my monthlong village stay in Bali I found it embarrassing that the whole lot of us—men, women and children—took a communal bath in the river each evening. It was embarrassing not because I was prudish, but because a middle-aged American among the lissome, svelte Balinese looks like a penguin.) In India exposing one's body, except among the very poor, is never done.

One reason for so much violence in the Punjab—drunken swordfights were not uncommon in Ghungrali—may be that so much sexual repression produces aggression and hostility that needs to be worked off some way. The sexually active Javanese are remarkably serene. I felt the greatest tension in Upper Egypt, where a combination of male license and sensuality combined with the threat of brutal

Islamic punishment against a woman detected "sinning" gave daily life an odd sense of suspense; you never knew when all hell would break loose. This double standard, combined with the need to bear sons to justify themselves, puts great pressure on Egyptian women. Even in Java, where village women almost do have equal rights, we saw how Husen was coerced by his parents to divorce Karniti, whom he loved, after one male baby died and she suffered several miscarriages. As I mentioned Husen's alternative was to face banishment from the village and the family land, his only security and psychological buttress. Karniti in this case had the last laugh, as in her subsequent marriage she bore two healthy children, one of them a son. If she and Husen remarry—and anything is possible in multi-divorce Java—her position with his critical parents would be much strengthened.

Even in a village culture with a strong cult of male superiority, a woman can exercise much power—through her adult sons. Ommohamed certainly tries—not always successfully—to dominate Shahhat and rule the roost. In Upper Egypt, despite the extreme emphasis upon male dominance, the love of a son for his mother, even when he is grown up and married, is the most conspicuous emotional attachment. If a son is lacking in respect to his mother, the whole village is shocked; behind the mud walls of home, she is mistress of his household until her dying day. Indeed, a man gives heavy weight to his mother's feelings in his choice of a bride. Shahhat told me before his marriage last year, "I know that the girl is not beautiful or anything like that. But she works hard, will not fight with my mother and will be good for the house." (Actually, they did fight, and Shahhat and his wife, who is pretty, moved out to a nearby house. In his letters, Shahhat writes about "the woman, my wife," but always refers to Ommohamed by name.)

Indeed, it's remarkable that Egyptian village women exercise as much freedom as they do. It has not been many years since Al Azhar University in Cairo, the world's leading Islamic university, published an interpretation of the Koran flatly stating that the "right of protecting and managing the affairs of woman is derived from the fact that man is superior to woman by nature . . . and more powerful and capable of confronting the struggle of life than woman." Allah has not shown favoritism to one sex over another, the scholars hastened to add, but merely made "one to excel the other." The idea of male supremacy, reinforced by the husband's right to divorce his wife at will, giving him enormous power over her, is deeply rooted in the Moslem psyche. In 1980 I found myself the unwelcome target of denunciation by Cairo's *Ikhwan al-Muslimin* or Moslem Brotherhood, an extremist movement, which objected, among other things, to my portrayal in *Shahhat* of the village women's struggle for emancipation; interestingly, the pro-Sadat journals and Cairo's Westernized liberals came to the book's defense. The truth is that Egypt's feminist revolution is not only waged by Sadat's wife Jihan and its professional women, but by women out in the villages every day of their lives.

In Surjit's story in Chapter 11, we saw how another gritty, hard-headed woman managed to lift her family out of poverty, transforming her farm from a pathetic subsistence clearing in the jungle into a prosperous commercial enterprise. It was not easy, since she did not have direct access to modern agricultural technology as the Punjabi men did. Nor could she herself engage in heavy field labor; she had to depend upon driving such physically strong males as Buldev. Surjit cooked, washed and did all the woman's traditional chores; she was almost obsessively conscious of her village neighbors' potential censure and once, when she was serving meat, told me, "Ah, the neighbors are looking across the field. I don't want them to cast their evil eyes on this pork we are going to eat. How jealous they will be!" I chose this episode in her struggle, a few days in 1970, to illustrate how, though she would eventually win entrée into the larger world of state politics and the university-educated, she would do it, as with Buldev, through the manipulation of men, particularly her sons. It was a fierce struggle and, if Surjit emerged a rather hard woman, one could see why.

The most difficult role is given to the young unmarried village girl; it is even worse if she is pretty. She grows up in a sexually charged atmosphere; on most matters of sex, married women in the village tend to speak among themselves as frankly and unblushingly as do the men, often discussing the most detailed physical intimacies of their married life with each other. A young girl grows up learning everything but experiencing nothing. She may be subject to constant flirtation and the lewdest of advances and is the target of continual village gossip, yet she is expected to be a chaste virgin until her wedding day or face severe punishment.

As I hope to have suggested, villagers tend to be prudent in their sexual behavior. I'd like to explode the old myth, often heard from some taxi driver or somebody down the bar, that poor people have more babies because they can't afford any other entertainment. It is true that the poor two-thirds of us produce a mere one-fifth of our food but four of every five babies. But sexuality and fertility are not the same. Sexually permissive Sweden had a yearly population growth rate in 1977 of 0.1 percent, the United States 0.6 percent. In countries where it is still stuck around 3 percent—Togo, Sudan, Oman, Bangladesh, Laos and Pakistan—the only real common denominator is that the majority of the people are extremely poor. Fertility and sex are not closely related; fertility and poverty are. This is particularly true where poverty, and the illiteracy that goes with it, coincide with a culture which places great value on male dominance, as in some Moslem societies, or, as in Latin America, on *machismo,* a variation of the same thing.

The conventional wisdom is that pronatalist attitudes in countries with high growth rates are because of the poor peasants' desire to have many sons to relieve them of hard physical labor, help protect their household from thieves or feuding neighbors and provide for them in old age (or middle age, as it usually works out). I think these are all true, but would argue that male-female equality matters more. I was amazed some years ago when I interviewed women in northern Thailand's opium-growing Golden Triangle and discovered that they thought the dumbest thing imaginable was to want more than two children. These women simply couldn't believe that women elsewhere might want four, five or six children. What made them so different? I found two reasons. First, it turned out that many of their husbands were addicted to opium and the wives, by custom, did most of the physical labor in the poppy fields and handled the money. The men were dependent on them and there was no question of male superiority. Second, the Thai government had recently introduced free, compulsory primary education in this region. The women, explaining that it still took money to clothe and supply the schoolchildren, felt it was more in their long-term economic interest to be able to afford to educate two children than to have more sons and daughters to help them with the field work. For the women it was both a matter of the freedom to choose and the availability of education—and the opportunity it represented—so that they could make the right choice.

Without getting too pedagogic and messagy, I think it can be argued that the questionable assumption of male superiority is a big—perhaps *the* big—obstacle to village development. Or, put another way, much more attention should be given to the rights and education of women, especially to ways they can improve their incomes. The notion that males are inherently superior and that females are inferior and ineffectual when it comes to earning a living is closely tied to poverty. As I hope to have shown, it is also related to the slide into prostitution, homosexuality or other forms of sexual behavior that occur when villagers are forced to migrate to cities. Sex in the city has a lot to do with what people said and did back home.

In *Rosemary's Baby,* the young expectant mother, at last convinced that a witches' coven has designs on her unborn child, seeks help from a doctor. In his waiting room she picks up a copy of *Time.* It is the one with the famous cover, "Is God Dead?"

In the decade since the death of God was announced, the Devil continues to be reported alive and well. This appears to be one more sign of the end of the eighteenth- to twentieth-century era of humanist optimism. There seems to be a new realism about man and his ultimate chance of perfectability. Whether people believe in a personalized Satan sabotaging both man's and God's work, or merely suspect that there exist mysterious but hostile forces in an otherwise Godless and Devilless world, this new realism is a great change.

It brings us much closer to the mentality of villagers. Ever since the day Francis Bacon proclaimed science as the religion of modern man, the gradual "death of God" as an external deity has created a widening psychological gap between the traditional-minded two-thirds of the world and the modern, scientific-minded third. Villagers continue to explain natural phenomena in terms of the supernatural, just as everyone did before the birth of science. In the West, Freud, Marx and Darwin relegated such beliefs to the junk heap of superstition. Yet, as Ernest Renan observed, religion and its supernatural supports may be necessary to morality—that is, a natural ethic may be too weak to withstand the savagery that lurks below our civilization and emerges in our dreams, crimes and wars.

In all history, with the exception of the modern West, some supernatural belief has been seemingly indispensable. It begins to look as though we find it indispensable too. The commercialized revival of interest in Satanism has continued. Soon after *The Exorcist* packed movie houses in 1974, an opinion poll reported that the American belief in the existence of Satan had risen from 37 percent to 48 percent in the ten years since 1964. Two years earlier Pope Paul had declared that the Devil actually existed as a "live, spiritual, perverted and perverting being, the hidden enemy who sows errors and misfortunes in human history."

Much of the interest in demonology is just the latest trendiness; those with the show biz instinct jump in to make the most of it. But such films and books might have only average box-office appeal if they did not have a substratum of real *Angst* to work on. This is also reflected in the fascination with psychic myths, mythical figures, parapsychology and the search for new forms of spiritual experience, for a new release from an existence walled in by birth and death. Sometimes it can go terribly wrong, as it did in the horror of Jonestown. An easy and popular reaction to Jonestown was to ask, "Is Satan alive after all?" If Satan is, in some sense, not dead, the implication is that God is not either.

In villages, some supernatural hope may be the only alternative to despair. Political leaders grasp this. Anwar Sadat told me in 1976, "Egypt must return to its Moslem cultural heritage. I don't want our younger generation to be a lost generation, as in your country." In all village religions, since God must be good, evil is explained by the existence of Satan, demons, black magic or other hostile forces. To live in villages, even temporarily, is to suspend one's disbelief in the supernatural; indeed, seemingly supernatural occurrences are part of everyday life. Supernatural comforts are usually valued as more precious than medicine, especially by the unhappy, suffering, bereaved, sick and old. Religion's supernatural supports help parents and teachers discipline the young, confer meaning and dignity upon the lives of the lowliest, and encourage stability by transforming village rules of conduct into solemn relationships with God.

Indeed, one might say that the great divide in the world today is not so much between the rich and the poor—or between the educated, healthier and wealthier and the illiterate, malnourished and impoverished—as between those who think that humans can shape their own destiny and those who still believe that one's fate is decided by outside forces.

Village religion is still highly propitiatory; the gods are to be served and appeased. All religion, of course, began as the propitiatory worship of hidden forces in the earth, rivers, oceans, winds and sky, which early man feared and could not understand. Only when priests emerged to use these fears and rituals to support morality, order and laws did the state emerge. An illustration of this was provided in the

Nuba tribal religion and Sultan Ahmed's use of it. All early societies told their people that the local code of morals and laws was dictated by the gods (Thoth gave them to Menes in Egypt, Shamash to Hammurabi in Babylonia, Yahveh to Moses for the Jews). Will Durant has written, "As long as there is poverty there will be gods." Villagers universally still show a desire for a religion rich in miracle, mystery, myth and the supernatural.

Be he Christian, Moslem, Hindu, Buddhist or animist, a villager believes in a very personal God to whom everything matters, from the control of the universe to the most trivial affairs of his own personal life. In Hinduism this may extend to the smallest form of life, even insects, for the Hindu belief in the transmigration of souls—not to be confused with reincarnation, which refers only to humans—allows for the rebirth of the human soul in the body of anything that lives. When I lived in India, my servants refused to kill ants or mosquitoes. (They brainwashed me, too; it was years before I could swat a fly without feeling guilty.) Yet even Hinduism, with its confusing pantheon of gods, has only one, Brahma, who controls the universe.

Our revival of interest in the supernatural has so far taken a negative direction. That is, it has emerged as an eruption of unease about evil and how it works. It is unlikely the old optimism can be recaptured when for thirty-six years people have had to get used to the idea that they might be blown up at any time. But the rediscovery of belief in Satan is probably a very healthy thing. If people really believe in evil as a force in the world, they will eventually have to accept good as something equally objective. Villagers do. Evil is seen as the work of hidden demons or the solicitations of Satan, good as the work of God. This gives them a perception of man's condition totally unlike our own: life might seem unrelenting and absurd, but things are what they are—predestined as part of God's plan. Man has no choice but to make the best of them.

*

Contemporary authorities on the supernatural, or what we like to call "psychic phenomena," tend to group them into three categories: (1) extrasensory perception (ESP), when information is transmitted through channels outside known sensory means; (2) psychokinesis, when something is physically affected without use of any conventional known force; and (3) survival phenomena. In the villages, I have witnessed what could conceivably be interpreted as instances of all three:

Precognition. The prediction of future events that cannot be inferred from present knowledge appears in the Bible in the Witch of Endor's prophecy, Joseph's interpretation of the pharaoh's dream and Daniel's interpretation of the handwriting on the wall. In December 1961, in Nagpur, India, a widely acclaimed fortune-teller, Dadi Balsara, correctly named the five most important dates of my past, giving the exact years, months and even days. He then asked whether his horoscope-and-palm reading was on target. When I replied, "Wow, yes," he predicted for the future—quite accurately, as it turned out over the next twenty years—seven global journeys (all the village work counts as one), when they would be, which years would be professionally auspicious and what kind of work I would be doing. He also predicted death on September 8, 1988, from something like gastroenteritis, but charitably held out hope that I might squeak through and live another twenty years. It was a written prophecy in Balsara's hand. I still have it. Such stupefying displays of retrocognition and precognition are fairly commonplace in India; few Indians marry or enter into business deals without consulting a fortune-teller. Sigmund Freud suggested one possible explanation. Such uncanny intuition, said Freud, might be picked up through thought transference; the subject then consciously or unconsciously conducts himself so as to fulfill the prophecy. I'd never thought of writing a book in 1961; well, hardly ever. Suddenly, there in a remote town in the heart of India, amid smoking oil lamps and the smell of incense, a voice was saying, "You will turn to be a writer of books and earn name and fame for yourself." (Wham, hey diddle diddle, there's a bright golden haze on the meadow!) Then I thought to ask, what kind of fame? It turned out not to be the big-time super-star variety, but "definitely more than provincial" and "your name will be known across the seas." (Pretty vague, that.) Yet I suppose I ran out and bought an Olivetti portable right there. What Freud's theory doesn't explain is how Balsara got so many exact dates right. (I hope he got one wrong.)

Telepathy and clairvoyance. One afternoon in March 1974, as Kuwa, his son Ali and I were walking through the bush in the Nuba Mountains, Kuwa complained of feeling ill and we stopped to rest in a clearing; he seemed quite agitated, looked ghastly and kept mumbling to himself. Soon he recovered. As we went on our way, he told me to be sure to go into the town of Dilling the next day because a telegram was waiting for me at the post office. I just assumed somebody'd told him and he'd only then remembered to mention it. I walked to Dilling in the morning and, sure enough, there was a telegram. Then the clerk said, "You must be psychic. It just arrived an hour ago from Khartoum." It came from friends in Cairo. How could Kuwa have known about it the day before? I asked him about it as soon as I got back to Neetil village. Kuwa was not surprised. He explained that what we mistook for illness had been a trance. Most likely, he said, his *kudjur,* Neetil, the ancestral spirit which sometimes possessed him, had spoken of the telegram. Kuwa said he received such messages from his *kudjur* even in waking consciousness, but most commonly in dreams or in a trance.

Psychokinesis. One form is psychic healing. Kuwa had *ju-ju* to protect a man from a gun or a knife, to bring back fading virility or to cure all kinds of illnesses. Once I saw him put an empty hollow gourd on a sick man's bare stomach and pull out roots, sticks and a live toad; it could have been sleight-of-hand. In Java, Husen had an even more bizarre story of psychic healing. In the early 1960s, long before I knew him, Husen almost died of yaws. Large boils formed all over his body (yaws is a skin infection linked to malnutrition and has since been eradicated in Indonesia). In the Jakarta slum where Husen lived, a man named Tjarti was said to have cursed Husen for refusing to marry his daughter. Husen almost died. His family took him back to Pilangsari village and one night a neighbor, Suleiman, secretly came to Husen's bedside. Villagers in Java do not admit to possessing the powers of a *dukun* or sorcerer (a *dukun* also can be just a midwife). "I want to try and help you if I can," Suleiman told Husen. He brought a glass of river water, spat into it and recited from the Koran. He told Husen, "If you recover, tell no one about this. It is not I but Allah who will make you well. I am only His instrument, an ignorant peasant. Please, take this water, drink. If you are good at heart, you will get well. And if another has put a magic curse upon you, the curse will go back to him, he who made you suffer." In time Husen recovered. When he went back to Jakarta he learned that Tjarti had died of yaws. Husen swears this story is true.

Once, in Shahhat's village of Berat in Upper Egypt, I did put psychic healing to something of an improvised, spontaneous test. Shahhat had gone about in a vile temper for days, fighting with everybody, and his mother, Ommohamed, decided someone had put a curse on him. I accompanied her to her favorite sorceress, who burnt incense, recited the usual Koranic verses and told her to look behind a certain loose brick by the front door. I rushed home before anybody else could get there, pulled out the brick and—sure enough!—there was a tiny piece of paper folded into triangles. When we unfolded it, we found it was covered with illegible writing in red, blood-colored ink. Ommohamed said it was a magic incantation. She washed away the ink, dried the paper and had Shahhat burn it. He was cured, his good humor restored.

Ommohamed swore by her sorceress, a blind woman known as Sheikha Daiyi. Once, when the family buffalo stopped giving milk and everyone said it was a victim of the Evil Eye, most of the neighbors advised cutting off a piece of the suspected culprit's tunic or getting him to urinate on the buffalo. But Ommohamed instead went to the sorceress, who did her stuff. The buffalo began giving fresh milk again the next day, though it could have just recovered from whatever ailed it.

Episodes involving the supernatural occurred almost every day in Berat. Babies did not die from disease, but were "strangled by Satan." If Shahhat felt lust for a certain village girl, he would say she had probably paid Sheikha Daiyi to make a magic amulet containing the sulphur of matches and thorns—causing a burning and pricking in his chest. Shahhat had an eerie power over scorpions, whose stings can be fatal in Egypt. If he found one in the field, he would put it on his arm and let it crawl around to show that it would not sting him. At the risk of losing all credibility, I must report that once, when he extended his hand toward a gecko lizard and whispered, "Allahu Akbar!" (God is most Great!) I saw the lizard leap some twenty feet or so into his outstretched palm—or it certainly looked like it did. When I exclaimed in astonishment, Shahhat, who had not known I was in the deserted café, looked secretive and sly. It was in the restaurant-lobby of a deserted—except for us—Arab village hotel. Shahhat had thought he was alone. He said I should not have witnessed the lizard leap, as he had been given such power by a sorcerer on condition that it stay secret.

Although Egyptians are devout Moslems, some of their supernatural beliefs are pharaonic or Christian. Barren village women will drink water from the ancient sacred wells within the ruined temples of

Seti I or Ramses III. And a Coptic Christian priest's magic is thought to be unusually powerful, especially if used to curse an enemy.

The Moslem belief in good and evil *djinn* is sanctioned in the Koran. Shahhat claims that once, when he was a teenager, he was tormented many nights by an evil *djinn* who appeared in his dreams. She became so insatiable in her sexual demands that Shahhat lost weight; when the *djinn* demanded Shahhat marry her, Ommohamed went to Sheikha Daiyi. The sorceress told her that when the *djinn* returned, Shahhat must cry *"Allahu Akbar!"* and hold up some iron, as the *djinn* had a great fear of that metal. Shahhat did so, exorcising the *djinn* from his dreams. But it reappeared, twice attacking him in the road at night, once appearing as "a black horned demon with an ugly face which laughed and turned somersaults" and again in the form of a whirlwind, which whipped Shahhat off his donkey, nearly suffocated him and left him lying unconscious. Or so Shahhat and his mother tell the tale.

All villagers believe in some kind of ghosts. In Pilangsari at night, if we heard weird noises like "knick knack knick knack" coming from the garden, Husen's mother would say something like, "A ghost. In town a small baby has died every day this week. One can hear so many ghosts of children calling in the night." I thought this more humorous than spooky, especially after Husen's parents said they feared to have me use the privy at night in case I might sit on one of the invisible *tinul,* or ghost children (I was more worried about spiders). Husen himself avoided certain haunted trees after dark. He once cut down a perfectly good shade tree by his house after the neighbors complained that it had an evil spirit in it. Once, when I was staying with Husen and Karniti in a Jakarta slum, a would-be rapist broke in. I was in bed, ill with fever, in the next bamboo cubicle. When I heard Karniti scream, I shouted and the attacker was frightened off. The episode took place during the night when a blacksmith who lived next door, Muri, had left a small stone idol with us. Muri was a *dukun,* or secret sorcerer, said to possess occult powers. He was forever fasting and going without sleep, supposedly to strengthen these powers. That night Muri brought in the idol, called a *djimat* in Java, and asked if he could leave it with me. He and Husen wanted to play cards across the road and the people in his house complained that whenever he went out and locked his room, the idol started making loud rapping noises. After the attacker broke in, Karniti, who was naturally terrified, described him as tall, with a moustache and wearing black. He sounded human to me, but all the neighbors were convinced, because Muri's *djimat* was in the house, that one of Satan's demons had tried to rape Karniti.

Husen, who stayed up all that night, sitting beside Karniti with a hammer in his hand, was as superstitious as the rest. He told a story about how, late one night in Jakarta many years ago, when he was pedaling a *betjak*, he was hailed by a beautiful girl. After silently directing him from one dark street to another, the girl suddenly vanished as they were passing a graveyard. Husen's friends told him that she must have been a *kuntil anak*, or the ghost of a prostitute. They said if he had pulled out a hair from her head, he would have become rich. For years afterward, if a pretty girl rode in his *betjak* late at night, Husen would carefully pull out one hair. If the girl screamed, he would apologize, "Oh, very, very sorry, Miss. Your hair was flying in the wind and it caught when my hand holds the handle." Even so, he kept trying in hope of striking it rich.

Another form of psychokinesis is an apparition of the living. A description of this was offered one time in Ghungrali village in the Punjab. One noon, as we rested during the wheat harvest, the village chief attacked the idea of life after death. "It doesn't exist," he said. "People used to say there couldn't be chickens without a hen sitting on them, so there must be a God. But now we have electric incubators. Man is a seed, a fetus, a child, a man, and in the end he dies. And nothing happens. They have just cleverly cooked up these things like heaven and hell."

An old Harijan harvesting with us, Chanan Singh, a saintly man whom I much admired, objected. He said, "There can't be anything after death and yet there are many mysteries. One night some years ago, when my wife was alive, I was lying awake. It was a cold night, but for some reason I had brought my *charpoy* outside to sleep under the stars. My wife told me, 'It's cold. Bolt the door from the outside or it flies open.' I told her, 'All right. I'm here if you need me.' I slept and then I awoke. I got up again and looked at the stars. Then I felt something and I looked around and saw my wife. I didn't speak to her. But she appeared to be standing by my bedside, looking down. I kept looking at her and wondering how she had come out. Then she went away and I went back to sleep. The next morning, the door was still bolted from outside. My wife told me, 'I was inside all night. I never asked

you to open the door.' And after some days she died. I have no superstitions or anything. But I can't explain it. She was alive then. It was
no dream. I saw her."

Survival phenomena in villages most commonly take the form of
seeming spirit possession, as in the case of Kuwa's *kudjur,* his ancestor, Neetil; or Shahhat and his evil *djinn;* or Tonio in the Philippines
with the ghost that made him lose his mind and run amok. Poltergeists
also have a lively history in most of the villages. Typically, Tonio told
me, "At night in my parents' house you can sometimes hear different
sounds on the roof, like somebody throwing sand or rocks or walking.
Sometimes you can hear voices calling you." In my tree house in
Tulungatung, I was also plagued by nocturnal knockings and creak-
ings and what seemed to be sudden drops in temperature to a cold
chill. It became scary enough so that I arranged for a village family to
come and sleep in the other bedroom at night. With their arrival, the
strange noises and temperatures abruptly ended.

Perhaps the most frightening survival phenomenon is an apparition
of the dead. Once I saw a ghost. It happened in 1963 in eastern
Nepal, along the route of what was later to become a Chinese-built
highway from Katmandu to Lhasa. I was then the New Delhi correspondent of the Washington *Star* and wanted to be the first American
to travel this route as far as the Tibetan border and to photograph
some of the hundreds of Chinese and thousands of Nepalese working
along the site. Unfortunately, the road mostly moved through low-ly-
ing valleys and jungle, gaining high mountain altitudes only near the
border.

The incident took place in a village called Balafi, located eighty kilometers from Katmandu, which was then a four- or five-day trek. The
villagers in this area were very poor—short, stunted tribesmen who
wore only loincloths and dirty rags. Worse, the village huts were
infested with a vermin called *urus,* little spider-like creatures which
came out of the walls by the hundreds each night and invaded your
sleeping bag. After a couple of sleepless, panicky nights fighting them
off, I was determined not to sleep in one of the village huts. Some Chinese engineers were living there, in a villa they had sprayed with
DDT, but they refused to let an American enter their compound. As it
got dark, in desperation I took my Tamang porter and went to sleep in
a pavilion in the village graveyard, putting candles in each corner so

it did not seem too spooky. The Tamang, who did not like this a bit, curled up in an inner corner with a cloth pulled over his head.

I laid my sleeping bag out on the pavilion's broad stone steps; it was great under the stars and well away from the village huts and the *urus*. I awoke around midnight. The candles had gone out, but there was moonlight. Down the slope to the left of the pavilion was a deep gorge crossed by one of those perilous rope bridges so peculiar to the Himalayas. I saw a figure in loose white garments standing there. Slowly, as I watched, he crossed the bridge, climbed up a rocky slope toward the pavilion, and for a moment came and stood quite near. He looked Tibetan and he was weeping. I asked him in English what was wrong. But he did not reply; in a moment he turned and went away.

The next morning I asked the Tamang to find out from the villagers who it was. They seemed to anticipate the question and gathered around us, all talking at once with excitement. They claimed that I'd seen the ghost of a Tibetan merchant who, on his way to Katmandu, had fallen from the rope bridge to his death just weeks before. Several villagers said they also had seen the ghost; all locked themselves in their houses with shuttered windows and bolted doors after dark. When I went to sleep in the graveyard, they thought I must be crazy. Well, to this day I know that, man or apparition, there was *somebody* out there and I talked to him.

Fifteen years later, in Tashi Palkhiel, Ngodup decided that I had seen a *Dre*. I described the creature's clothing. Ngodup said it must have been a Tibetan *chuba*, a loose tunic belted at the waist that is sometimes white. After hearing my story, Ngodup wanted to visit Balafi, now a four or five hours' bus ride from Katmandu. We went, but in the bright sunlight of day the pavilion in its graveyard and the old rope bridge looked harmless, especially as traffic was moving along the new highway just down the hill. But I did not want to spend the night there, nor did Ngodup—nor, if you go to Balafi, will you.

*

In the modern West, the denigration of magic as a means of reinforcing religion has made the existence of the supernatural a cause for controversy. No other branch of scientific investigation has encountered such contempt and hatred as research into psychic phenomena. One thinks of Hans Castorp's revulsed "Forgive me!" in *The Magic Mountain*'s seance scene, which is certainly one of the most terrifying in all literature; the phantasm of Castorp's dead cousin, the honorable soldier, is hideous and grotesque. Thomas Mann made the seance his metaphor for the ultimate decay of Western civilization. The reason for such hostility is obvious: to admit to the existence of something outside the areas of normal perception is to go against common sense, to overthrow "natural laws," to have one's hold on reality undermined.

Yet, at the risk of sounding kooky, I cannot be honest about life in villages without reporting that instances of paranormal phenomena do actually seem to happen. And rather often. One's attitude quite naturally becomes one of cautious acceptance. The apparent existence of the inexplicable does not flout "natural laws," so much as it suggests that that code of laws may not be as all embracing as we think it is. One should be skeptical, but not too skeptical; as Goethe said, "incredulity can become like an inverted superstition." The supernatural has always been with us. It appeared in all its forms from the early civilizations and tribal societies through classic Greece and Rome, the early Christian period, the Middle Ages, the Renaissance saints and their miracles, to the eighteenth century and such modern psychic phenomena as poltergeists, rapping noises, precognition and extrasensory powers, such as telepathy.

To admit that, in the Biblical phrase, "there are great and hidden things we do not know," is not to suggest that we ought to find out. While many scientists seem willing to consider a *rapprochement,* the village experience has reinforced my personal belief that there is no possibility of harmony between religion, with all its supernatural trappings, and science. An exception, perhaps, is the scientists' recognition that they have found no substitute for the moral function of religion, nor a satisfactory explanation for the existence of good and evil.

Some scientists, of course, dispute this. Edward O. Wilson, in his *On Human Nature,* for one, tells us that religious belief has simply been "incorporated into the brain by thousands of generations of genetic evolution." He offers scientific materialism as man's post-religious mythology, saying, "Man's destiny is to know, if only because societies with knowledge culturally dominate societies that lack it." What he calls "anti-intellectuals," he says, "do not master the differential equations of thermodynamics or the biochemical cures of illness. They stay in thatched huts and die young." Maybe so. But almost all of the great religions have come out of those thatched huts.

Science and religion, and the supernatural that is part of religion, I feel, do not mix. Freud, Jung and William James, all unquestioned modern scientists, were fascinated by the supernatural. So was Aristotle, the father of science, who believed in precognition through dreams —a belief he passed on to Alexander the Great. But all of these scientific-minded men recognized the careful distinction between the supernatural and the natural. There is no litmus test for good and evil. To accept a new realism about man and his imperfectability and the existence of mysterious good and hostile forces, whether personalized God or Satan, is also to accept their essential unprovability. It is enough that, as in villages, the role of the supernatural is to support religion and morality, which embody the rules any society lives by as it tries to persuade its members to behave in a manner consistent to its order, security and growth.

Psyche is the Greek word for soul. Nowadays we are told that the word "mind" will do as well. But the soul, or spirit, not the mind, has always been the repository of man's oldest, most universal and most enduring strengths—love, honor, pride, pity, compassion and sacrifice. Out of these comes man's unique claim to transcend his biological limitations: his religion.

Every villager today faces the enormous compulsion of working out new meaning to his life. This is true whether he stays home in his village, where there may be too many people for the land and food supply, or goes to a city, where he can earn enough to eat but may face far more terrible conditions. His old view of things is losing its coherence. He must ask himself the ultimate question of all metaphysics: If the world and life have a meaning, what can it be? And how will the world have to look to correspond to it?

The answer, historically, has been supplied by a prophet. Typically, the prophet presents a unified view of the world derived from a consciously integrated and meaningful attitude toward life. To a prophet, both the life of a human being and the world have a coherent meaning. The conduct of an individual must be oriented to this meaning if he or she is to find salvation, for only in relation to this meaning does life obtain a unified and significant pattern. This is why prophets arise during times when, for large numbers of men and women, life seems to have lost its meaning. This applies to a good many people, both in the villages and in the West, right now—but as I have said, prophets come from villages.

Prophets are almost never priests, but rise from humble people, usually peasants. Priests serve to preserve a sacred tradition; Pope John Paul II, for instance, with all his humanity, wit, virility, sympathy, strength, energy and fatherliness, is a powerful world leader whose magnetism can do enormous good. John Paul has much of a prophet's charisma; like a magician, he exerts his power simply by virtue of his personal gifts, healing and counseling. But the Vatican has rarely and then only reluctantly been the instrument of change, and John Paul's conservatism suggests he belongs to the priestly tradition of preservation.

A true prophet goes much further, either trying to radically renew an older religion or claiming to bring a completely new deliverance. Max Weber identified two kinds of prophets, the "ethical prophet," such as Abraham, Jesus or Mohammed, who has emerged only in the

Middle East and demands obedience to a personal god, and the "exemplary prophet," best represented by Gautama Buddha and most characteristic of Asia, who directs himself to the self-interest of those who crave salvation, recommending to them the same path he has found himself.

In 1946 Arnold Toynbee wrote of the world's villagers:

> This neolithic peasant is the last and mightiest sleeper, before herself, whom the West has waked. . . . and though today there are still some fifteen hundred million not yet awakened peasants—about three-quarters of the living generation of mankind—in India, China, Indochina, Indonesia, Dar-al-Islam and Eastern Europe, their awakening is now only a matter of time, and, when it has been accomplished, numbers will begin to tell.

These words were written just after the Second World War ended and before Eastern Europe went communist, the Chinese and Indochinese revolutions succeeded, attempts at such revolutions in India and Indonesia failed and global wealth shifted toward the largely Moslem oil producers. Yet even in 1946 Toynbee could see that the gravitational pull of sheer population would draw the center of human affairs eastward to some point equidistant from Europe-North America and India-China. Ever since the first three volumes of Toynbee's *A Study of History* came out in 1934, arguments have raged about it. It filled twelve volumes all told; by the last, which appeared in 1961, Toynbee had tried to trace a grand pattern in human history, from the obscure beginnings of settled society in the later Stone Age down to the present day. He decided that the smallest intelligible unit fit for historical study was what he called a "civilization." He identified first twenty-one of these and eventually thirty-one at the very least. Five of Toynbee's civilizations are still current: the Western, Byzantine (Russian), Islamic, Hindu and Far Eastern. (He called smaller groups like modern Parsees or Jews "fossilized relics" of older civilizations.) In my own work in the Third World I've found six major variations of village culture, which also might be called civilizations: Christian, Islamic, Hindu, Malay-Javanese, African tribal and post-Confucian. These cultures affect how people think and act much more than mere nationality does.

Toynbee was looking for similarities between civilizations and for the reasons why they rose and fell; he emerged with a doctrine that was reasonably consistent. His work followed by a generation Oswald Spengler's *Decline of the West,* which argued that civilizations—like the seasons—rose and fell in conformity to a fixed timetable. Spengler offered no explanation of this; it was simply a law of nature. Toynbee generally agreed, but went on to suggest the possibility, based upon his study of the rise of Christianity in the decaying Greco-Roman civilization, that new forms of the great Eastern religions might rise again to defeat the technologically superior West on a spiritual plane.

Toynbee felt that the West's decline was by no means predestined and that the West could save itself if, in politics, it established a constitutional cooperative system of world government; in economics, it found working compromises between free enterprise and socialism; and, in the life of the spirit, it put the secular superstructure back onto religious foundations. Toynbee's central point was that, in the five centuries since Columbus reached America by sea and Vasco da Gama reached India from Portugal, the West had unified the earth as never before with its technology, but had failed to spread its religion. He believed that the majority of mankind was suffering from the same spiritual starvation that led to the rise of Christianity amid the disintegrating Greco-Roman civilization. Toynbee asked, "Is something like this historic denouement of the Greco-Roman story going to be written into the unfinished history of the world's encounter with the West? We cannot say, since we cannot foretell the future. We can only see that something which has actually happened once, in another episode of history, must at least be one of the possibilities that lie ahead of us."

In the years since, many such warnings have been raised. Reinhold Niebuhr speculated, "Modern technical civilization may perish because it falsely worshipped technical advance as a final good." Much more recently, Pope John Paul II has attacked "the frenzy of consumerism, exhausting and joyless" and has warned of the dangers of giving "full rein to the instincts of self-interest, sex and power." He urged instead: "We must find a simple way of living." Almost echoing Toynbee, the Pope said, "A critical analysis of our modern civilization shows that in the last hundred years it has contributed as never before to the development of material goods, but that it has also given rise to a series of attitudes in which sensitivity to the spiritual dimension of human existence is diminished." In 1976, Norman Macrae, *The Economist*'s deputy editor, warned that a weakening of our mechanisms for living together, our government and our business corporations suggested that "there is a danger that the Americans, with all their power for dynamism and good, may be about to desert what should be their manifest and now rather easy destiny of leading the rest of us towards a decent world society and an abundant cheap lunch. If they do, the leadership of the world may be yielded from American to less sophisticated hands at a perilous moment."

In 1980, British sinologist Roderick MacFarquhar, also writing in *The Economist,* suggested what that new leadership might be:

> In Tokyo last autumn, a Chinese vice-premier reportedly told his Japanese hosts: "Add your 100m to our 900m and we have a wonderful force that none can ignore or obstruct." A piece of wishful rhetoric? Perhaps. Calculated to revive Kaiser Bill's nightmare of the "yellow peril"? Possibly. A foretaste of the greatest threat to western supremacy since the industrial revolution? Definitely.

In a remarkably perceptive analysis, "The Post-Confucian Challenge," MacFarquhar noted that for the two hundred years since the Industrial Revolution, the West has dominated the world. Today, he argued, that dominance is threatened, not just by the Russians, who are partly heirs to the Western tradition, nor by the Arabs, whose stranglehold will last just so long as their oil, but more fundamentally by the East Asian heirs to Confucianism—China, Japan, Korea, Taiwan, Hong Kong, Singapore and, to some degree, Vietnam. Militarily, MacFarquhar wrote, the challenge began with the Japanese-Russian War of 1905 and continued with World War II, followed by conflicts involving the Chinese, Koreans and Vietnamese since then. Politically, the main challenge has come from Maoist China; economically, from Japan, followed by South Korea, Taiwan, Singapore and Hong Kong. Just what is meant by Confucian culture and how does it differ from ours? The difference emerged most clearly to me in a South Korean village, Cho Dong Kok, where I spent five weeks in April and May 1980.

*

At Panmunjom, on the edge of the Demilitarized Zone, the fixed, staring eyes of the North Korean border guards, like the cold spring wind sweeping down from Siberia, send a chill down your spine. Cho Dong Kok was just sixty miles south of Panmunjom, and some mornings children brought in propaganda pamphlets from the fields, floated down by balloons at night. Some in English said, "Americans you will die." The village was also not much more than two hundred miles north of the South Korean city of Kwangju, at that time torn by a bloody insurrection that everyone feared would spread. A Peace Corpsman, a young Texan treating lepers in their bleak, windswept colony down the valley, came one day to warn, "If anything happens, just head south to the nearest American base."

Yet the village was extremely peaceful, fitting Korea's famous name as "the land of the morning calm." Against the backdrop of blood and tension, I was learning that the ideals of individual perfection and a harmonious social order which Confucius inculcated in the East Asian mind are as relevant today as they were nearly 2,500 years ago. Daily life in Cho Dong Kok was shaped by ethical standards set down by Confucius in China in 500 B.C. and deeply rooted from the long Confucian rule of Korea's Yi Dynasty (1382 to 1910), a period of extraordinary stability which, except for the eighteen years of Park Chung Hee's government, was afterward followed by almost continuous strife.

Nesting swallows, for Korean peasants as for Macbeth, are a happy omen. In what was aptly named the Valley of the Swallows, the tiny birds were just migrating back, darting in and out of almost every farmhouse to remake last year's nests under the ceiling beams. The valley's rice fields, like most of South Korea's 5.75 million acres of cultivated land, nestled among pine-forested hills, which cover 70 percent of all land on the mountainous Korean peninsula. This rugged terrain helps explain why Korean peasants have preserved such a distinctly rural and traditional mentality, shaped by Confucianism and even older shamanistic beliefs. Confucianism is an agnostic philosophy and, as I've mentioned, villagers universally have a need for belief in magic, demons, evil spirits and exorcism. In Cho Dong Kok two elderly witches, *mudangs,* still got paid to wield their supernatural powers to protect families from evil spirits, a practice that was old in Korea three thousand years ago.

Seoul, just a ninety-minute bus ride away, has in fifteen to twenty years become a great modern city of skyscrapers, subways and 8 million people. In Seoul, as in Kwangju and other cities, turmoil among students, workers and other discontented members of South Korea's new industrial society were challenging the soldiers, businessmen and technocrats who were trying to pick up the reins after the October 1979 assassination of President Park. It is worth remembering that, until recently, Koreans had never been urbanized, and so few rules of urban conduct exist for non-rural life. When the Korean War broke out in 1950, 80 percent of Koreans lived in villages; today only 29 percent do, or 11 million of the 38 million South Koreans. Twenty-five years ago, farm households formed two-thirds of the total; this has dropped to one-third, though the number of farms has declined very little, which suggests that the younger generation in the cities keeps its village ties. Much of the farming is now done by women or older men, such as one used to see strolling about in white pajamas and black horsehair hats (the hats have disappeared completely).

Indeed, the first Asian village I ever saw was near Pusan in 1953. Our Army Engineers unit had arrived from Japan by plane late at night; in the dark we had been moved by truck to the small airstrip we were to maintain. I'll never forget coming out of a tent that first morning and seeing, spread out beyond the barbed wire fencing, a green valley of startling beauty and serenity. The villages were all thatched, the people very poor; barefoot men trudged along, bent over by the weight of huge loads on their A-frames. It was spring rice transplanting time, and the fields were filled with straw-hatted figures, moving steadily down each paddy, thrusting clumps of seedlings into the soft mud. The stone-strewn fields, orchards and vineyards, the chorus of frogs and cicadas at night, the shaded greens and blues of distant mountains, pinewoods, paddy and barley for a year framed our world. Returning in 1980 was to find that smokestacks, factories and bustling commercial streets had obliterated all traces of the valley's old rural scene; it had happened very quickly.

So the mind of almost every Korean over forty, and a good many of the younger people, too, has been formed by a village. Confucian thought still governs how most villagers think and act, from the basic adage that "filial piety is the basis of all conduct" to notions of hierarchy and harmony, communal obligations and subordination of son to father, younger brother to elder brother, wife to husband and subject to state. I arrived assuming almost everybody had opposed Park's dictatorial rule; I discovered instead that in Cho Dong Kok he was generally respected.

For good reason. During the 1970s, average family income in South Korean villages rose from about $800 to just under $3,000 a year. Today everybody gets plenty to eat, even in what used to be the pre-harvest hungry season. All village children go to primary school; 90 percent go on to high school and a few pass the examinations to join 278,000 students in colleges and universities. If sick, a villager takes antibiotics or sees a doctor. Almost every household has a TV set. Every village is electrified; every villager is literate; no place in the country is more than a day's bus or train journey away and the older folks charter buses for sight-seeing tours. Daily field wages of eight to ten dollars, plus meals, rice liquor and cigarettes, are as good as, or better, than an unskilled worker gets in the towns. Almost every farmer has a cow or an ox, but nearly 200,000 power tillers are hauling, plowing, harrowing and harvesting four times faster. In 1980 men and women were being trained to operate newly introduced Japanese power rice transplanters. Family-owned irrigation pumps have replaced traditional water wheels. Rice seedlings and vegetables are now grown in cold-resistant vinyl greenhouses.

This startling ten-year agriculture transformation comes mostly from South Korea's successful adoption in the 1970s of new dwarf high-yield rice varieties. In 1977 South Korea broke the world's highest-average-yield-per-hectare record with 4.9 tons of milled rice. Its farm science establishment, dominated by American-educated Ph.D.'s, invites comparison with Japan's. This technology, plus a doubling of the subsidized rice price since 1970, a spread of industry to the countryside (villagers get an average 20 percent of their income off the farm), and a fast expansion of transportation and the urban market, has made all the difference.

The government likes to give credit also to its Saemaul (New Community) movement, launched by Park in 1970. Villagers were exhorted with a Confucian-style slogan—"self-help, cooperation and diligence"—to build roads, bridges and wells, and, most spectacularly, to replace their old thatched roofs with brightly painted tile or metal ones, completely changing the appearance of the countryside. At first there was some coercion from over-zealous local officials—laggards might come back to find their home open to the sky. Today, however, the Saemaul movement is generally praised—even by the student dissidents—for showing that once villagers get capital, technology and access to markets, a government drive to get local officials to work better can do wonders.

Despite all this, South Korea's 36,000 villages remain as deeply

Confucian as ever. There are a few changes: young men and women can sit together (Confucius wanted them separated after age seven); a once-outcaste butcher's son can aspire to college. General literacy, fairly equitable landholdings and income and lively village politics make a South Korean village as free and open as any in Asia. Yet the village *yangban,* or old landlord-official class, whose landholdings were brought down to average size in 1949–53 land reform, still sacrifice present comfort to educate their children for government service, whereas the seemingly more prosperous former commoners, *sangmin,* are more likely to invest in better food, houses and farm machinery.

Spring comes with the swallows. In the last two weeks of May, just as the civil fighting in Kwangju reached its peak, most students and workers returned to their labor-short native villages for a few days to help with the rice transplanting, which, together with the harvest, is the peak work season of the year. It was a time of angry generational clashes. Kim Hwan Yun, the sixty-eight-year-old peasant with whom I stayed, anxiously told his son, home from Seoul University, "If you young people make more noise, another tragedy will come. It's not good for us."

The son bowed his head respectfully, but his talk to me had been full of stirring all-night rallies and torch-lit "marches for democracy," burning effigies and battling black-clad riot police with their tear gas and Darth Vader masks. Now he earnestly declared to his father, "My classmates and I have vowed to be the first to sacrifice ourselves if North Korea attacks."

Exasperated, Kim exploded, "Have I not tied my empty belt and boldly given money to send you to the university? I'm literate. I have a classical education. But I was for President Park and what he stood for."

It was evident that the freedom the son wanted—and was prepared to take to the streets and fight to get—was our Western concept of the right of the individual to decide and choose and act for himself. It went against the father's deeply ingrained Confucian belief in the subordination of the individual, whether to parents or to the state. Park was respected because he worked through this Confucian culture, a philosophic justification of government by a benevolent bureaucracy under a virtuous ruler. The Park regime emphasized the idea that the state and family are mirror images, the government's benevolent rule reciprocated by the obedience of the subjects in the same way that father rules son. In a book published in 1979, Park wrote that

> just as a home is a small collective body, so the state is a larger community. . . . A society that puts the national interest above the interests of the individual develops faster than one which does not.

Virtue, as a Confucian classic explains it, ensures harmony between man and nature and ensures obedience within a stratified society:

> Possessing virtue will give the ruler the people. Possessing the people will give him the territory. Possessing the territory will give him its wealth. Possessing the wealth, he will have the resources for expenditure. Virtue is the root, wealth is the result.

The ultimate guarantee of harmony was the justness of the ruler, which permitted him to enjoy the "mandate of heaven." Korean dissidents maintained that the Park regime merely used Confucian precepts to mask a dictatorship. They argued that Confucius gave the people the right, even the obligation, to rise up against a tyrant—but Park's record, in the villagers' eyes, didn't support this. In the cities, the Park regime was often heavy-handed and repressive, but few villagers experienced this repression directly. Most Korean dissidents under Park were in some way Westernized (Christians, university students, the urban middle class). The freedoms they held precious did not have the same appeal to Confucian-minded villagers, where the idea of individual choice is alien and unfamiliar, subtly threatening the basic village ethic of filial piety itself.

Of course, the Confucian system is no more immune to the ambitions and ruthlessness of man than any other political philosophy. Many Confucian emperors of China and Korea were models of brutality rather than benevolence. Some months after my stay in South Korea in 1980, General Chun Doo Hwan, a relatively obscure young soldier, became president; he assumed dictatorial powers, imposed rigid censorship and tightened the army's grip on the South Korean people much more than even Park had done. He even defied international opinion by sentencing to death the country's leading opposition politician. Most liberals were silenced, fired from their jobs or sent to jail. This violated the crucial ethical basis of Confucianism, yet Confucians among the intellectuals could still be found to say that the threat from North Korea, the enormous power of the army and the lack of experience of Western-style democracy all meant that South Korea could not afford open elections.

Whatever happened in Seoul and the cities, the ambivalence of the South Korean villagers about democratic values seemed certain to remain. In terms of these villagers, an essential aspect of the Confucian system is that a morally motivated bureaucracy act as a transmission-belt between ruler and subject. In an interview in April 1980, before General Chun seized power, Jae-Chang Lee, the Saemaul movement's national director, told me he credited the advance of the villages in large part to Confucianism. He said, "It brings cohesion to our way and view of life. Korean ethics are according to Confucian ideals of virtue." Dr. In Hwan Kim, who ran South Korea's impressive agricultural research and extension system, said in an interview that Confucian emphasis on applied learning had greatly eased the spread of new technology.

MacFarquhar, whom I met in London in 1979, has described the post-Confucian characteristics as

self-confidence, social cohesion, subordination of the individual, education for action, bureaucratic tradition and moralizing certitude,

which he called "a potent combination for development purposes."

The very name of Cho Dong Kok village meant "Place of the Confucian School." It had closed down in the early 1970s, but Kim had received a classical education there; he argued that Confucianism remains the longest-lasting and most influential philosophy ever devised. Certainly the first is true. The aphorisms of K'ung-fu-tzu, an obscure and frustrated official and extraordinary teacher (circa 551–479 B.C.) were set down by his disciples a generation before Socrates; they became the official ideology of China under the Han dynasty two centuries before Christ. Confucianism is agnostic in the sense that it lacks a personal god or belief in an after-life and it has no priests nor churches, always working through education and example. Yet its ideal of the superior man of the golden mean instills authentic religious feelings of an omnipresent spiritual heaven. Confucius has been called "China's greatest gift to mankind." During the Chinese revolution, his philosophy has been kept tenaciously alive in the villages of South Korea and Taiwan. It is, of course, a way of thinking very different from our own, but Confucius still calls millions of East Asian villagers, through the teachings that bear his name, to seek after harmony and righteousness. This makes him a prophet, as much as any other, for the spiritual yearning of our time.

As MacFarquhar wrote:

Confucianism is as important to the rise of the east-Asian hypergrowth economies as the conjunction of Protestantism and the rise of capitalism in the west. The tenets of Confucianism still provide the inner compass to most east Asians in the post-Confucian age, just as the admonitions of the Sermon on the Mount still constitute the standard for the west in a post-religious era.

When we turn from Confucianism and East Asia to the geographically more far-flung but less populous Islamic world, the cultural challenge to the West is equally evident. Toynbee felt that the extinction of race consciousness between Moslems was one of the outstanding moral achievements of Islam; he suggested that if the growing gap between the poor black, brown and yellow races of the earth's south and the rich white races of its north ever precipitated a race war, Islam might rise again. In its Arab homeland, Islam, its only weapon oil, is facing the West with its back to the wall, as it did during the Crusades. The difference is that today the world's 750 million Moslems live in sixty countries from Morocco to Indonesia, from Turkey to Tanzania; only one Moslem in five is Arab (there are more Moslems in either Russia or China). Islam is the most egalitarian religion, a rankless army in which all are warriors for the faith.

When it comes to villages, Islam does seem to possess the most vital spiritual force of any contemporary religion, that inward power which alone creates and sustains the outward manifestations of civilization. Christian, Hindu, African tribal and Confucian societies have gone communist, but, if we discount the little Marxist anarchy of South Yemen, no truly Islamic society yet has. The real confrontation between Marx and Mecca is in Afghanistan, where one interpretation of the Russian occupation can be seen as a heavy-handed and self-defeating attempt to stop the Islamic counter-reformation at its borders. In 1971 I spent some days in a remote Afghan mountain village—I'd picked the wrong time of year and was forced to go when the village got buried in snow—and was impressed by the fiercest faith in rewards in paradise I'd seen anywhere. Even then the Afghans hated the Russians with a passion for being infidels who disbelieved in God.

In all the Moslem villages I've stayed in—Romanni, Shush-Daniel, Berat and Sirs el Layyan (nominally Moslem Pilangsari was something else), a simple belief was shared: The prophets of Israel were all right and Jesus was God's last and greatest prophet before Mohammed. (The six prophets of Islam are Adam, Noah, Abraham, Moses, Jesus and Mohammed.) The Moslem quarrel has never been with Jesus of Nazareth but with the Christian Church—Roman Catholic, Protestant, Greek and Russian Orthodox—for capitulating to pagan Greek polytheism and idolatry. From the betrayal of the One True God, or *Allah,* these villagers believe, Islam retrieved the pure religion of Abraham—and in Islam's survival lies the hope of mankind. This faith—and one can hardly exaggerate its hold on villagers like Shahhat, Hadj, Karim or Fatih—is quite unlike the eroded belief one finds in so many Christian villages, affected as they are by the West's post-religious phase. Only Ngodup, with his Tibetan Buddhism, or old Sultan Ahmed, with his tribal gods, were as deeply religious. Islam's great weakness, in terms of development, is its medieval attitude toward women. In a Moslem village, women are accorded a respected place, but it is definitely subordinate to that of men. This varies. In Egypt's Delta the *fellaheen* see nothing wrong in women working in the fields; the Upper Egyptians find it shameful. There are strong objections to birth control in Bangladesh, but virtually none in Morocco or Iran. Most Moslem male villagers are uneasy with Koranic injunctions on divorce (all a husband has to say is "I divorce thee" three times and that's it), which they would make as difficult as possible. Polygamy (a Moslem can take four wives), they point out, is impossibly expensive except for an unusually rich villager. Amputation for repeated theft should never happen, they say, because in an Islamic village nobody steals (and theft *is* pretty rare). Under Koranic conditions, which include four eyewitnesses, adultery can almost never be proven.

Yet, more fundamentally, almost no male Moslem villager is willing to agree that women should have the rights, especially to equal work and education, that they must have if half of every Moslem village's people are not to be denied their chance to be fully productive. This straightjacket of female subordination strangles advance across West Asia as far as the upper Gangetic plain, reappearing only in Bangladesh. Mind you, I'm not saying that the post-Confucian societies like Japan, Korea and Taiwan are stampeding to pass Equal Rights Amendments, but they have moved way beyond the point where an inferior position for women in work and education drags a whole society down. In all villages, women not only keep the households running, they teach their children how to live. If women are kept too subordinate, their ignorance passes from generation to generation, preventing cultural adjustment to necessary changes.

Moslem women tend to be more conservative than men for this reason. It was Shahhat's mother who demanded that the most medieval Koranic precepts remain binding. Yet all Moslems, men and women, tend to take the basic admonitions of the Koran seriously, even literally, and try to obey them. Among these admonitions is the affirmation that Islam is a total way of life; Islam claims authority over every little thing you do. Moslem villages can really go one of two ways. They can partly deny the laws of Islam and opt for a more modern, more secular way of life, educating the girls as well as the boys, using the Pill and the IUD so they can afford to educate them, and can apply this education to modernizing their farming methods or other means of livelihood. Or they can persist with the more difficult—and probably, in the end, futile—task of remaining a true Islamic society. This creates unusual stress and spiritual confusion for Moslem villagers. When the process of Westernization accelerates too dizzyingly as in Iran, a fanatic retreat to the certainty of Islam can follow. Unlike the post-Confucian challenge, the Islamic revival, without reformation from within, seems fated, one might say doomed, to be a force of reaction.

*

The Hindu, Malay and African religions seem too rooted in race and region to have much universal application. Aside from the post-Confucian and Islamic challenges to the West's cultural domination, there remains the possibility of a new faith arising, just as Christianity did during the Greco-Roman civilization's decline. What Spengler saw simply as the operation of a law of nature and Toynbee sought to explain in terms of spiritual failure, Will and Ariel Durant have given an economic explanation. The Durants have argued that all civilizations begin with agriculture, prosper with commerce and industry, luxuriate with finance, and then, cut off from the old agricultural moral code and its work ethic, begin to decline. (This is why I make so much of the disappearance of the American small farmer.)

One benefit of village living is that it is much easier in a village than in a city to observe what is unique and peculiar about any society's culture. (All cities are too Westernized for this to be done easily.) In the Christian villages observed—Huecorio, Guapira, Grand Gaube and Tulungatung—religious faith tended to be vitiated by European priests tainted with colonialism (all but Huecorio had them) and by the unprecedented materialism, secular belief and scientific doubt of Christian Euro-America. All four were Roman Catholic and, in terms of villagers, Pope John Paul II is quite right to cling to doctrinal conservatism (but not birth control) even if it appalls Western liberal, urban Catholics. The Reformation and the emergence of the ascetic Protestant ethic greatly reduced Christianity's appeal to villagers.

As William McNeill masterfully put it in a memorable passage in his 1962 book, *The Rise of the West:*

The Protestant reformers set out to achieve a radical sanctification of all human endeavor before God, but, in fact, after a lapse of a couple of generations, provoked in parts of Europe a disciplined application to the business of making money such as the world had scarcely seen before.

Protestant peasant villages are rare. Where one does find Protestants in the Third World—usually in cities—they tend, like agnostics, to be groping for many of the old traditional values, such as family and self-responsibility, in today's permissive fog. Indeed, the closest thing to the old-fashioned Protestant work ethic seems strongest in the post-Confucian villages, particularly in China. In most villages the work ethic, and the value given industry, is secular and distinct from religion. Only Protestant Christianity and Confucianism created religious or philosophical motivations for seeking salvation primarily through hard work and a more rational control of life. As Max Weber has argued, a work ethic linked to salvation was never true of the "nonintellectual classes of Asia" with their "magical religiosity"; and even in Korea we found ancient Mongol beliefs in witches and evil spirits persisting in villages.

Yet the world-affirmation of Protestantism, which led to the Industrial Revolution and the West's world domination the past two hundred years, stands in direct contradiction to the figure at the core of our civ-

ilization, the historical Jesus of Nazareth. Perhaps, if we wish to spec-
ulate about what kind of new spiritual challenge to the West could
arise from the villages, it is to Jesus we should look—for he was a villager, with all that implies about his way and view of life. He rejected
the world totally in a way found elsewhere only in Buddhism. He was
a "magician" who believed in Satan and exorcised demons. He
preached that the kingdom of God was at hand. As Weber described
his message, it was "a nonintellectual's proclamation directly to nonin-
tellectuals, to the 'poor in spirit.'" He was a prophet who came from
the villages to speak to villagers. In terms of his culture, his closeness
to nature, his belief in magic and the supernatural and his hopes for
miraculous deliverance, this historical man had very much in common
with the villagers I have been writing about and very little in common
with us. As a university-educated, urbanized Protestant of the affluent
West, this writer had to spend years in villages to realize just what an
antithesis of our own contemporary culture the man who is at its very
core really was.

Jesus was a man of the village "little tradition" rising in revolt
against the existing Greco-Roman and Judaistic "great traditions" of
his time because they had failed him and his people, just as our Western culture is spiritually failing the villagers now. He lived at a time
when all sorts of new religions or religious reforms were rising in remote settings on the fringes of the empire, which is again happening
now. What happened with the message of Jesus is an oft-repeated historical pattern: a religion originates with peasant villagers, then, once
it is taken up by educated urban elites, villagers tend to be seen as
religiously suspect. This has happened in Christianity, Hinduism, Buddhism, Judaism and Islam. For a time in the nineteenth century,
thanks largely to such Russian writers as Tolstoy, Turgenev and Chekhov, there was a religious glorification of the villager, whose piety was
given a special worth—but this was a temporary exception.

In most of history, the peasant villager has been given no special
religious merit; in Hinduism, for instance, peasants are at the bottom
of the caste system, just above untouchables but below priests, soldiers
and merchants. The same thing happened with Christianity. It was
very quickly transformed—even by the Gospel authors, especially
Luke and John, and the apostle Paul—from Jesus's simple message
into a complex urban religion stated in terms of sophisticated Greek
philosophy. Very early it became the religion not of the villagers but

of the urban middle class. It is only in this century, beginning with works like Albert Schweitzer's *In Quest of the Historical Jesus,* that modern Biblical scholars have been able to tell us what the actual man said and did. Christianity continued to evolve because the urban middle class is naturally inclined to a rational, ethical, world-affirming religion that tells it honesty is the best policy and faithful work will be justly compensated. The reforms demanded of John Paul today on priestly celibacy, the ordination of women, abortion and the right to practice birth control are reflections of social change among the Western urban middle class, but not among Catholic villagers.

All great religions, including Christianity, have had to develop a dual character to accommodate the magical religiosity of villagers with the more intellectual and philosophical emphasis the educated city people want. Mohammed felt it necessary to transform the ancient pagan Arab pilgrimage rites into the Moslem *hajj* to Mecca; he also sanctioned the widespread Middle East village belief in good and evil *djinn.* Islam has even been forced to condone, in some regions, idolatry in the cults of local Moslem saints, just as Roman Catholicism has had to do in Latin American villages (for example, that St. George of Carolina's mother). Village Hinduism is polytheistic, magical and unphilosophical, whereas the higher forms of India's religion are theistic and ethical. In philosophical Taoism, the emphasis is on the subordination of man to nature; in village Taoism, as one finds in Taiwan, it is on the acquisition of human morality through magic, another direct contradiction.

In villages, magic and miraculous deliverance are universal qualities of religion; in every instance they have been replaced or rationalized by philosophy once the religion has been taken up by urban intellectuals. If we are to understand the present peasant awakening and the kind of Eastern spiritual challenge Toynbee considered possible, we need to take a good look at village religion. Since Christianity is most familiar, let us take that.

Biblical scholars tell us the most factual—one might venture to say journalistic—account of what Jesus said and did is to be found in the Book of Mark. Mark was the only Gospel author who was not a sophisticated intellectual; his is a perfectly straightforward story, without Luke's poetry and appeal to Gentiles and women, John's Greek philosophy, nor Matthew's strong Judaism. He was literate but not literary and, as far as we know, took down the words and deeds of Jesus from Peter in Rome not more than thirty or forty years after Jesus's death. There is no evident theological bias (the post-Crucifixion passages were added by later theologians and must be discounted). In the Near East, even today, there is a strong tradition of memorization. Egyptian *fellaheen* like Shahhat memorize much of the Koran as children. Some of them memorize the whole thing, which is about the length of the entire New Testament. Quite a few remember long stretches as middle-aged men. Egyptians have an extraordinary capacity for retention because often the Koran is the only thing they ever learn. Peter's recollection of what he recounted to Mark was probably just as good, or better.

Keeping strictly to Mark's account, it soon becomes evident that Jesus was a man of village culture. We know that he was a carpenter's son and, in the custom of the times, probably worked at carpentry himself until his thirtieth year. His neighbors in Nazareth were peasant cultivators or sheep herders; as a young man, he must have helped out during the harvests and at other times of labor-intensive work as all able-bodied village youths do today. As a carpenter he would also have made plowshares, hoe and sickle handles, hay forks and other tools; he had to know how they worked.

Jesus used the metaphor of the village; nobody but somebody who had actually cultivated grain would say:

. . . . there went a sower to sow; and it came to pass, as he sowed, that some fell by the wayside, and the fowls of the air came and devoured it up. And some fell on stony ground, where it had not much earth; and immediately it sprang up, because it had no depth of earth. But when the sun was up, it was scorched; and because it had no root, it withered away. And some fell among thorns, and the thorns grew up and choked it, and it yielded no fruit. And other fell on good ground, and did yield fruit that sprang up and increased; and brought forth, some thirty, some sixty, and some a hundred.

Take away the poetry and this is exactly how peasants in the Near East talk today. One has to have a lot of experience sowing to create this kind of metaphor; no city person can, or not without a lot of research. Those yields are telling.

When I spent some weeks with Bedouin shepherds in southwestern Iran in 1971, the metaphor of the Twenty-Third Psalm took on concrete meaning for the first time. Yahkoub really did run about in long flowing robes, carrying a rod and staff for practical uses. (The rod was to lead the sheep; he sometimes threw it at them. The staff was for walking and for use as a weapon against hyenas.) We led the herd of some four hundred sheep to whatever pastures of sparse green grass we could find on the otherwise barren desert. To water the herd, we had to move it down the Karun River's banks until we reached the "still waters" of a shallow place where the current was not too strong; the sheep could drink without danger of drowning. And in the desert hills there were ravines where the sun never penetrated; some had caves, filled with sheep bones, the lairs of hyenas who dragged their prey back for the kill. What more fitting image for the valley of the shadow of death? Imagery drawn from the ordinary daily life of the herdsman is found throughout the Old Testament.

With Jesus it is the universe of the settled peasant villager. Only a villager would try to convey meaning through "first the blade, then the ear, after that the full corn in the ear." I've mentioned that metaphor is a form of memory. Take "Like a grain of mustard seed" which "becometh greater than all herbs, and shooteth out great branches; so that the fowls of the air may lodge under the shadow of it." This is the remembered observation of a villager. So is the parable of the tenant who tries to seize the rented vineyard from the landlord, the kind of episode we often heard about and talked about in Upper Egypt's Berat village. As I've said, my method of work is to rely upon stenographically recorded dialogue of villagers while they work in the fields. To reread Mark a couple of years ago was to experience a revelation: Jesus spoke just as many of my villagers did, making the same observations from village life and sometimes using the same phrasing.

The meals of loaves and fishes, the dogs under the table eating fallen bread crumbs, shooing the curious children away, the need to show respect for parents—how true they ring in villages today. Once Shahhat, returning from the fields hungry, actually cursed a barren fig tree, a very human act of Jesus which has long puzzled theologians. And try to lead a stubborn camel through a narrow gate, much less the Biblical needle's eye, and you will see what an apt metaphor this is. Even the cry from the cross, "My God, my God, why hast thou forsaken me?" finds contemporary echoes in the despair of villagers badly treated by fate despite the utmost faith and piety.

Typical of the villager, Jesus did not want to remove even a letter of existing law. Conservative, tradition-minded, he did not intend to found a new religion. Scholars assume that Jesus was literate; the Dead Sea Scrolls suggest he may have read some of them at the Essenes' library. Yet he was lowly and unlearned, as villagers most often are even when they can read. Jesus ignored nearby centers of contemporary Hellenistic culture, just as a modern villager ignores Western art, music, literature and film in a heterogenetic city; it is alien to his life. Jesus was not as strict on ritual as were the Hellenized, urbanized Jews; peasants engaged in cultivation and animal husbandry could not completely stick to it anyway. Like all villagers today (except the Javanese), he was much stricter than city intellectuals when it came to adultery and divorce.

What made Jesus a prophet was his awareness that, though he was a humble villager, he possessed a healing power and speaking ability with his fellow peasants that far surpassed those of the sophisticated urban elite. Importantly, his magic power did not work in respect to his own family, his village neighbors, the wealthy or highborn, or city scholars. It depended on faith. He found such faith among peasants, fishermen, tax collectors, prostitutes and all sorts of simple people, even Roman soldiers. *Jesus Christ Superstar* caught this in a terrific scene when Jesus is besieged by a mob of such people, who call out in frenzy, "See my face, it's a mass of blood!" "See my feet, I can hardly walk!" "I believe you can make me whole!" "See my purse, I'm a poor, poor man!" Then they turn aggressive, almost screaming at him, "Will you help, will you heal me, Christ? Will you love, will you *pay* me, Christ?" There are too many of them; Jesus is overwhelmed. It is electrifying theater because it plays on our subconscious fears of riotous, poor masses. But these are the people who then and now have had faith in village magic. As I mentioned in the last chapter, not only does belief in the supernatural widely exist in villages today; supernatural phenomena seem to happen.

That Jesus was culturally a villager can be argued in many ways. His extreme present-time orientation—let man pray for his daily bread and be unconcerned for tomorrow—represents a universal village spontaneity and fatalism. Another characteristic peasant trait is his strong rejection of scholarly arrogance. Most villagers I have known are sensitive about their ignorance; they esteem learning, but will reveal a strain of anti-intellectualism if they feel someone is looking down on them. The peasant ethic of mutual help, mentioned in Chapter 16, pervades the teachings of Jesus. Villagers almost invariably believe that preoccupation with wealth destroys the sense of brotherhood; the richest villagers are always Basant Singhs. It is this notion that is at the heart of the matter when Jesus tells the rich young man to give away his worldly goods. Jesus merely carried this common village trait further. The village ethic is to help your neighbor in expectation of a like response; that way you both get your harvests in.

The agricultural moral code, universal in all villages, is, however, much closer to the stern Ten Commandments than the loving Sermon on the Mount. Jesus completely transcended village culture when he taught unconditional forgiveness, unconditional charity, unconditional love even for enemies and unconditional suffering of injustice without requiting evil with force. These lift his ethics far above any to be found in any other great religion. Jesus demanded an ethical heroism possibly beyond human nature, certainly beyond us with our ethical fabric torn to shreds in recent years. But his teaching that God alone will punish and reward in an implied equalization in heaven is again a universal village belief, no matter what the local religion—as is the idea that to be rich in this life endangers one's prospects in the next. Jesus placed moral incentives above material ones, yet he was just the opposite of the revolutionary; there was no merit in deeds for which early compensation was expected. On the contrary, what Jesus held most decisive for salvation was an absolute indifference to the world and its concerns. The kingdom of God was at hand. Of what value was money or material goods or state power? Render unto Caesar that which is Caesar's. One simple commandment mattered—to love God and one's fellow men—and this was to be judged solely by its faithful demonstration.

*

The words and deeds of this simple man, who lived as a humble villager until the age of thirty, went about preaching to his fellow villagers, and was executed by Roman soldiers at thirty-four—his story, told by a man who was very possibly an eyewitness, and set down for us thirty or forty years later—exemplifies the kind of prophet we might expect to arise in our spiritually similar times. Doubtless his life, at the time it happened, would be equally obscure. It would not get on the evening news. This obscurity, and Jesus's village origins, were not coincidental but necessary. His culture could not have been formed in a city. We can find no such village cultural influences in the works of Confucius, Plato or Socrates, urban philosophers; nor in Shankara, Ramanuja, Luther, Calvin or Wesley, urban religious reformers. It is only if we make a supreme effort of the imagination and strip away all the intellectual accretions to Christianity from Hellenization, the Renaissance, the Reformation, yes, and the two extremely world-affirming creeds of ascetic Protestantism and Marxism-Leninism-Maoism, that we get down to the world-negating spiritual core of what this actual historical person had to tell us. This villager would almost certainly be physically indistinguishable in his dusty robes, black beard, swarthy and weathered face from millions of Middle Eastern peasants today; his mind would be formed, just as theirs still are, by fatalism, spontaneity, belief in magic, demons and exorcism, and rejection of worldly goods won at the cost of one's neighbors.

If we make this leap of imagination, I think, we arrive not too far from the kind of spiritual challenge Toynbee had in mind. Such a message is what tens of millions of villagers are longing to hear. For them the spheres of reason, order and justice are terribly limited and no progress in our science and technology has yet convinced them otherwise. Man is alone and it is a short way to the grave. Blind fate, the solicitations of Satan and his demons or the hot fury of his own blood awaits every man in ambush at the crossroads. There is no use asking for rational explanations. Things are what they are, unrelenting and absurd. It is a terrible insight into man's condition and something we rarely have to face so nakedly. Yet, in the very excess of his deprivation lies the villager's claim to dignity. His only hope may be for miraculous deliverance, some incomprehensible repose. He longs, just as a village carpenter's son in a remote corner of Syria did two thousand years ago, for a resurrection of the spirit and for a better life, if not in this world, then the next.

Nothing quite prepares you for Calcutta.

In the half-hour drive from Dum Dum Airport to downtown Chowringhee Road it is all there: the multitude of people hanging from trams and buses, pulling rickshaws, pushing carts, carrying enormous loads on their heads; the meandering, skeletal, white sacred cows; urchins rummaging through garbage heaps; old women drying cow-dung cakes for cooking fuel; peeling walls plastered with revolutionary graffiti; mud-and-wattle huts giving way to crumbled, pestilential tenements and palaces; the stench, filth and unutterable squalor.

Through the haze of dirt and smoke and traffic fumes the very city seems made of dust, the people of dust moving—Calcutta, the hell on earth of degradation and destruction, Kipling's "city of dreadful night," the ultimate vision of the urban apocalypse.

Yet even before your jet lands you sense you are moving into the big time. Few cities convey such an instant impression of urbanity; few await you with an air of such tragic distinction. Sprawling vast, gray and smoky on the banks of the muddy Hooghly, the westernmost tributary of the sacred Ganges, Calcutta is so lost in everything big and crowded and old, so scarred with struggle and violence and hazed with apprehension, that when you land you feel as if you are setting foot in some ultimate moment of history. It is like arriving in Carthage or Babylon or Ur.

Soon you have to put on a wool sweater in the frigidly air-conditioned, depressing gloom of the cavernous old Grand Hotel. But outside on Chowringhee Road it is as dank and steamy as any tropical rain forest. On top of blistering heat that melts the tar of the pavement, there is almost 100 percent humidity in this city of eight million people, packed eighty thousand to the square mile. Here, in the late afternoon, for the price of a two-cent cup of sweet, milky tea at a Rajput *chai wallah*'s stand under a banyan tree, you can sit and watch all India parade by: giant, heavy-shouldered Tibetans; Moslem women shrouded head to toe in suffocating black; flocks of chattering Hindu families; tall Sikhs, whiskered and turbaned; an elegant matron, her sari all swirls of pale blue silk, stepping from her chauffeured Mercedes into Prince's restaurant for tea, perhaps coming from the races at the Royal Calcutta Turf Club. Everywhere are the dark-skinned village migrants from Bihar and Orissa who serve as the city's coolies, rickshaw pullers and freight carriers—short, muscular men with rags tied around their heads to keep sweat from dripping into their eyes. Most are shaven-headed, with only a single lock of coarse black hair at the crown; this is for Yama, the god of death, to seize when he is ready to release their spirit from the wonders and horrors of this incarnation.

Calcutta—the capital of the British Indian Empire until the bloody mutiny of 1857 forced a shift to Delhi—remains the most English of Indian cities, a peculiar mixture of grand facade and squalor, imperial bigness, muddle and disorder. The nightmare vision comes when roaming the streets after dark, a frightening mélange of naked light-bulbs, surging bodies, dense humidity, heat, smells—and beggars, many of them deliberately maimed children. Above the electronically amplified Hindi movie songs, there is the rattle of trams, the eerie jingle of rickshaw bells, the haunting clomp-clomp of horses' hooves. An ancient carriage, ruinous and neglected, passes by and you catch a glimpse of tattered horse plumes and a skeletal driver in scarecrow rags.

If a single night's walk can produce panic and despair, so can the statistics: they say 80 percent of Calcutta's families live in single rooms; for two hundred thousand more, the pavement is home. As many as three hundred persons share a single water tap; a fourth of the city's food is eaten by rats. When the rich emerge on Chowringhee, beggars swarm around them like flies; they are dismissed without being seen, with an automatic flick of the wrist. The cars of the rich speed through the streets, horns blasting to clear the crowds; if anyone is hit, mobs can pull the occupants to pieces. In the twenty-two years since I first visited Calcutta in 1959, I have written many predictions that the city would ultimately collapse in a plague of disease, a reversion to savagery, a nightmare of knives and tearing claws.

So, revisiting a certain kiosk on the Maidan not far from the Grand Hotel in 1979 became something of an anxious quest. Here, twenty years before, there had been a shoeshine man, Ahmed, who spoke English as the result of being "adopted" by some American G.I.'s stationed in Calcutta during World War II. He had invited me for tea at

the kiosk, where he shined shoes. A monsoon storm broke, and about
a dozen of us ended up spending an hour or two talking together. All
of them were either shoeshine men, beggars or pickpockets. Chowringhee Road was their universe. A meal was served in a big tiffin can.
It was rice and curry mixed together—leftovers scraped off the plates
at a nearby government canteen by some enterprising Bengali. One
portion cost about five cents. It was dumped in a big pile on a newspaper and everyone squatted around in a circle, avidly eating with his
fingers. Each day was much the same for these men. They bathed in
the morning in a fishpond on the Maidan, sat in the kiosk all day waiting for customers, and slept there on torn straw mats at night.

Most of them were peasants from Orissa and Bihar. They were
cheerful, remarkably so, with shy, diffident manners and big grins,
bobbing their heads from side to side when they spoke. The occasion
was made memorable by Calcutta's worst cyclone in many years.
Within days, floods and rice riots followed and the city was threatened
by total breakdown. Whole shantytowns collapsed, tens of thousands
were left homeless and the official death toll was soon in the thousands. Normal life in Calcutta stopped. The only transportation
through the flooded streets was rickshaws, the pullers running barefoot
in water up to their knees. The airport closed down, stranding all travelers, including myself.

One day, as I fought down feelings of panic on my way to the hotel,
a squall hit. Wading through the mucky water, I came to the kiosk
where the men were huddling and shivering in a little group in the
center as the rain whipped in and lashed them from all sides. They
must have been there the several days of the storm. I suppose they had
nowhere else to go. A baby whimpered in its father's arms. Everyone
was wet through; their eyes seemed darkened by hunger or exhaustion.
With the streets awash, few of them would have had any way to make
money. Some of the faces looked baleful and, fearing to be set upon
for money, I started toward the other side of the road. Then someone
called out.

It was Ahmed, the shoeshine man. When I turned back and the
others recognized me, they cried out in dismay that "sahib" was wet.
Someone ran to fetch a box to sit upon. In a minute someone else
came running, somehow producing a cup of tea. To my dying day, I
shall never forget their faces: wet, trembling, sick, half numb and
shivering with cold and lack of food, and yet eager, cheerful, trium-

phantly alive. I had to quickly turn away and hurry off into the rain, so they could not see my face. I did not go back.

Now, twenty years later, the old kiosk was once more in view. Sure enough, there were shoeshine men and beggars sitting inside. No one looked in the least familiar. Then an older man with a lined face and shaved gray hair turned my way. I thought it could not be, then saw it was, Ahmed.

He didn't know me at first. Then, as we started to talk, the flash of recognition came. He seized my hands and began laughing and laughing.

His laughter kept tumbling out, unstoppable, and in that moment I realized that so many of us were wrong about so many things in the Third World, and that Calcutta will somehow always survive.

*

It was only much later, rereading the French philosopher Henri Bergson on the island of Mauritius, that I began to understand. I had studied the work of Bergson (1859–1941), years before at the University of Vienna, but its true meaning had not sunk in. Bergson argued that intellect only catches the fixed states, not the flux, of reality. When it comes to change, he said, introspective intuition gets you closer to truth than external sense can. That is, when you test both by matter-of-fact experience over a period of time, the findings of intuition tend to be more illuminating and correct. Calcutta's statistics were as bad as they ever were, nor was what you saw much different. What I had badly underestimated was its people. I had treated Calcutta as a solid object, like a biologist dissecting a frog.

Now I could see the wisdom of Bergson's insight. Life is not a fixed state. So how do we catch the flow? Bergson tells us how. He says to stop thinking and instead gaze inward upon that one thing we know best—ourselves. What do we see? Mind, not matter; time, not space; action, not passivity; choice, not mechanism. We see life in its subtle flow, not in fixed states or in devitalized and separate parts. This direct perception, this simple and steady looking upon, is intuition. Not any mystic process, as we sometimes think, but the most direct examination of the world around us possible to the human mind.

Factual evidence is better, no doubt, than hearsay, but, when it comes to human life, how weak it is compared to the direct perception of life itself. Bergson argued that we must get as close as possible to the original and sound its depths and feel the pulse of its spirit, and when we did, this direct perception, through intuition, would bring us much closer to the truth of things.

Bergson used a remarkable image:

> The animal takes its stand on the plant, man bestrides animality, and the whole of humanity, in space and time, is one immense galloping army beside and before and behind each one of us in an overwhelming charge to beat down every resistance and clear the most formidable obstacles.

History *is* the actions of men, no matter if we seem to be losing our emotional belief in the proposition. I knew I had a false picture of villages before I went to them: collections of mud huts, dust, flies, misery, apathy, resignation, their inhabitants mere objects, statistics, things to be manipulated. Now, with the help of Ahmed, the Calcutta shoeshine man, I began to see the villagers in a new way, possessed of what Bergson called *élan vital*—the vital urge that makes us act and grow and change and survive.

*

I felt that somehow I had to exorcise some of the old faith in science. In the villages I had found that documentary evidence was not reliable because families and petty officials often distorted the facts of any given situation to evade social, legal, tax or other implications. Oral evidence was better, but not much better; in a village, accounts of any event by two persons or by one person from one visit to the next had often differed in significant details. If one stayed in a village long enough, the truth came out, but it took time. There was also the problem of language. I used an interpreter for dialogue and interviews, but this was not enough. Modern linguists have shown that in ordinary, nontechnical talk you can say just about anything in a few hundred words. What I did was master eighteen basic verbs and a vocabulary of a couple of hundred more words, in Spanish, Portuguese, Russian, French, German, Arabic, Urdu, Hindi and Indonesian. It meant being fluent in no language but having a small ability to communicate in most of those you really had to have. The trouble with a "scientific" approach to villages is that it treated them as fixed states, as if their people were sticks and stones and their communities a stream of radiation or a constellation of protons and electrons. This was a false path. Any science, natural or social, is an extension of the ordinary senses (sight, hearing, smell and so on) albeit using exotic techniques. The proof of the physical sciences is in the eating; we swoop Voyager I past Saturn or predict the existence of a star. Physical or natural science works because the scientific establishment agrees upon what has already passed scientific scrutiny and then they go from there. This agreement about many things frees scientists to engage in rash, if understated, speculation at new frontiers of knowledge. Nine-tenths of this speculation may turn out to be wrong; but the one-tenth that survives wows us all. Theories are a vital part of what scientists agree on. They are a kind of map by which the physicist can plan the next stage of his journey. The status of any given theory, at any given time, depends largely on its ability to produce creative results, accounting for what is known and predicting what new facts will be discovered. Tomorrow today's theory will be replaced by a better one.

But when we turn to the social sciences—and social scientists are just as obsessed with theories as are physicists—we find almost nothing that is generally accepted as having passed scientific scrutiny. There is nothing much to build upon in terms of added speculation. Life, especially human life, is too diverse to fit easily into nice and tidy theories.

This is why I believe the real challenge to behavioral science comes from writers of fiction, who, with their sensible ears and discriminating eyes, articulate the universal elements in human lives and teach us more about mankind than any formal theory.

For example, perhaps no one shed more light on the way villagers actually behave than Anton Chekhov, particularly in his stories, "The Steppe" and "The Peasants," two of his finest. He pictures a life in which there is want, ennui and hopelessness; his villagers can be coarse, drunken and brutal, as some villagers are. Others possess "a quietness of soul," a sense of joy in nature and a deep and lyrical feeling for the land that can also be true of villagers. Chekhov had the compassion and candor, the genuine fondness for the calm of the Russian countryside and the hard-won skeptical independence of judgment to intuitively catch the atmosphere of village life; his stories can have the impact of direct experience. There is some of this in Tolstoy and Turgenev, but in my opinion Chekhov was the master when it came to villages; reading his work, I experience frequent flashes of recognition. I also agree, from my own experience, with his distrust of the dogmatic and his view that the political left, rather than the right, is likely to be more partisan and intolerant toward something it disagrees with. He was also pro-technology, feeling that steam and electricity were the most sensible ways to show sympathy for the poor.

Chekhov, as Avrahm Yarmolinsky has described him, saw himself in "the modest role of a reporter, a witness." He aimed at honest objectivity yet, unlike the work of so many modern social scientists, his village stories were endowed with a moral certainty, a clear vision of good and evil. There is an entry in one of Chekhov's notebooks, "Man will become better when you show him what he is like."

Interestingly, the father of science himself, Aristotle, gives us more insight into the way villages actually work than anyone I can think of; I would have been lost without his common sense, clear thought and precise expression. Although he lived 2,300 years ago, Aristotle remains amazingly contemporary. He saw plainly that man's culture is decided by how he gets his food, ". . . for of beasts, some are gregarious, and others solitary—they live in the way which is best adapted to obtain the food of their choice." Change agriculture and you change culture. Aristotle also gives the best explanation for fertility declines, saying that the more highly developed any species or individual becomes, the smaller will be the number of his offspring. He believed in birth control, through late marriage (twenty for girls, thirty-seven for males) and abortion ("but let abortion be procured before sense and life have begun").

The best of Aristotle is, of course, his golden mean—right is what works best. His idea that true happiness comes as a pleasure of the mind in pursuit of truth is also contemporary. In John Fowles' novel, *Daniel Martin,* there is a striking modern echo:

> To hell with cultural fashion; to hell with elitist guilt; to hell with existentialist nausea; and above all, to hell with the imagined that does not say, not only in, but behind the images, the real.

Aristotle knew people. To him the power of habit, or "second nature," was enough to defeat revolutions. Man could change, but only by changing his environment, which in turn would change him; "we cannot directly will to be different than we are." He believed that marriage, family and property were the fundamental human institutions. He had few illusions about human nature: "Man, if perfected, is the best of all animals; but when isolated, he is the worst of all." Politically, Aristotle was the Great Conservative. Revolution was almost never the answer; while it might do some good, the cost was much evil. "Young men are easily deceived, for they are quick to hope." Communism broke down because of man's natural inequality; it provided no adequate incentive to those of superior ability. Aristotle believed that the stimulus of gain was needed for hard work, just as the stimulus of private ownership was needed for industry, husbandry and care. He wrote: "That which is common to the greatest number has the least attention bestowed upon it. Everyone thinks chiefly of his own, hardly ever of the public interest," and "There is always a difficulty in living together and having things in common, but especially in having common property." Helping the naturally weak and lazy with state subsidies, he said, was "like pouring water in a leaking cask."

Aristotle's ideal state, unlike Plato's, combined aristocracy with democracy under a constitutional government. "Rule by the poor" had advantages because "the people, though individually they may be worse judges than those who have special knowledge, are collectively as good," and "the many are more incorruptible than the few." Democracy's main weakness, he said, "arises out of the notion that those who are equal in respect to the law are equal in all respects; because men are equally free they claimed to be absolutely equal." Aristotle was against everything that went against the laws of nature, especially human nature; it would not work.

*

The wisdom of great men like Aristotle, Bergson and Chekhov, like a poor Calcuttan's laughter, can help to free our minds of cant so we can look at things as they really are. Such freedom is never complete. We are all slaves of our own historical and geographical backgrounds. For instance, I am a middle-class, middle-aged (forty-nine), Midwestern American of semirural origins—my father was a country doctor in North Dakota. After years as a student in America and Europe, a soldier in Korea and a teacher in India, I have spent most of my adult life as a newspaper reporter, over twenty years of this in Asia, Africa and Latin America. Evidently, my nationality, social milieu, professional experience and age, between them, will have a lot to do with the way I look at villages.

Just about the only personal advantage I can claim is the reporter's training. This gives me an awareness from my work that my fleeting and fragmentary visions of the kaleidoscopic, fast-moving passing scene are no more than caricatures; the true picture of anything remains unknown to us. What I can offer you with my individual human camera is at best shots in the dark.

You might ask, Why write about villages? To search for an answer, my mind goes back forty years or so to summer afternoons on the North Dakota plains. I see a boy on a bicycle riding along dusty roads in a landscape as flat and empty as the Russian steppe. Wheat fields stretched to every horizon. You can go on and on in North Dakota and never see where this horizon begins or where it ends. What trees there were—elms and poplars—were planted in straight, homely rows as windbreaks. The white clapboard homesteads were few and bleak; sometimes there might be a grain elevator way off in the distance. Wind howled through the telephone wires; it never seemed to stop.

Some summers we went to my mother's native village in Iowa's Grant Wood country—all rolling hills, cornfields, woods, limestone bluffs and meandering rivers. Here, among Methodists and Quakers of English stock, life was gentler; you mowed hay, put up bales in the barn, helped to get the cattle in, sat in cool dark rooms in big white frame houses with enormous lawns, memorizing Longfellow and Whittier and listening to the aunts play Chopin and Rachmaninoff, or you snuck off to the creek to swim and read contraband crime novels. The main event was Sunday church, where the congregation sang "Blessed Be the Tie That Binds" after every service.

But the North Dakota plains were home. Just about everyone but us was Scandinavian, morose and stolid Swedes and Norwegians, first- or second-generation immigrants, children of Grieg and Ibsen. When my father went to see patients in the winter blizzards the old Norwegian who drove his sled knew almost no English. Just as in Iowa, there was a thick, gloomy Protestant austerity, but harsher and more cheerless. Yet there was an elemental earth spirit on that raw, wind-chilled prairie, an intuitive sense of closeness to land and air that somehow balanced the human gloom. You grew to love those open spaces with their flat, empty horizons, which promised a whole world of foreign ports, primitive jungles and great rivers, all the marvels of the seven seas just waiting to be explored as soon as you grew up.

My parents were born the year of Queen Victoria's Golden Jubilee; my mother was fourteen the year Victoria died and as I write this she is nearing ninety-three and still living; she remains a Victorian yet. She was forty-three the year I was born, the last of five children. Her grandmother's grandfather, Brigadier General Joseph Reed, was George Washington's secretary at Valley Forge (where Nathaniel Critchfield, on my father's side, was a lowly private). My origin, then, was the small towns that grew out of America's post-frontier rural society; little church-going communities, large families, dominant fathers and children who grew up self-reliant by performing useful chores from toddlerhood, all in an atmosphere of gossipy neighborliness. With all its restraints and restrictions, everybody knowing everybody else, it brought some material well-being, some sense of individual achievement and a strong social support system of family and friends; it still may be the most civilized living pattern yet seen.

My father died just before World War II and for a time we were very poor. My mother managed to feed us as a seamstress, later as a policewoman; we let rooms, slept in the attic, survived on a staple diet of stale bread fetched once a week from a bakery in a laundry sack and, when a kindly neighborhood grocer gave us "bones for the dog" it was not unknown that they went into soup. We survived almost ten years on the low-protein, high-carbohydrate food most villagers still eat—so bread and potatoes, no money and crowded households are hard for me to readily equate with misery; these were happy years. We all read like mad, for one thing: Dickens, Jane Austen, the Brontës, Tolstoy, Dostoevsky, Chekhov, Shakespeare, Mark Twain, Sinclair Lewis, Booth Tarkington, Edna Ferber, Thornton Wilder, Hemingway, Faulkner, J. D. Salinger—everybody from Thomas Mann to Laura Hope Crewes. Books went in and out of that house in shopping bags; I never again had the same fierce hunger to know about the outside world as in those North Dakota years. Somehow it all fit together with croquet on the lawn, sneaking ice from the ice man's truck, making leaf houses, snowball fights, hide-'n'-seek and kick-the-can, and, later on, the Boy Scouts, stealing apples in season, football on the vacant lot, *The Shadow, Snow White* and Miss Schleuter's civics class. (She was a noble tyrant who, because I was a wild boy frequently threatened with being expelled, made me sit at a special desk in front; I can hear her now, sternly saying, "No man can serve two masters" or "You can lead a horse to water but you can't make him drink.")

Then came the great good luck to come of age just as America's post-World War II imperial era began. Real per capita income in the

United States has quadrupled since 1947, when I was sixteen. Without this extraordinary burst of American wealth and technology (especially jets), I would not be a reporter who writes about villages.

Books still matter. But, like many people who travel a lot, I have mostly backslid to detective novels and spy thrillers. What a person reads most of the time should be as worth mentioning as what he reads almost none of the time. Agatha Christie was once asked if, like Tolstoy and most great novelists, she put real people in her books. She replied, "For me, it is quite impossible to write about anyone I know, or have ever spoken to, or indeed heard about. For some reason, it kills them for me stone dead." This unreality, together with a mastery of plot, nostalgia, the dream of gracious living and cozy old-fashioned values makes for perfect escapism in some sleazy Asian hotel or African jungle guesthouse. Harder to explain is the even greater appeal, I find, of the how-it-really-is thrillers of John Le Carré, Eric Ambler, Maj Sjowall-Per Wahloo or Nicholas Freeling. Maybe it's because their message, cleverly encoded, is so close to Mack the Knife's funny-cynical, "In real life the messenger seldom arrives, and if you kick a man he kicks you back again; therefore never be too eager to combat injustice." I find great literature, far from escapism, can provide a total turn-on; rereading Dostoevsky's *The Possessed* not long ago revived unwelcome memories of the Leninist nightmare of internal subversion in the 1960s in Saigon as nothing else had.

One last autobiographical footnote: In the summer of 1950, when I was nineteen, my family, whose fortunes had improved, took me on a tour of Europe—Paris, Salzburg, Wolfgangsee, Cortina, Venice. We swam on the Lido and climbed the Zugspitze, and ended the two most idyllic months I ever spent on the almost-island of Sirmione on northern Italy's Lake Garda. Sirmione in those days had a grand hotel, a fishing village, a thirteenth-century castle and, at the tip of the peninsula where cliffs plunged down to the lake, the ruined villa of Julius Caesar's political adversary and favorite poet, Catullus. One evening at sunset, as my mother, sister and I strolled through the villa's ancient garden and a late, flat sun came through the olive trees, it came to me, with the sudden shock of recognition, that my universe had culturally exploded. It was both liberating and sad; I saw all at once that I had left home forever, that life would be a grand adventure, but far too short, and that whatever one, anyone, did, in the end one would be alone. It got dark, we walked back to the village and had cocktails in the hotel's oleander garden; now, looking back, it seems that that moment in Sirmione, like those empty prairies and terrible Calcutta in its monsoon floods a decade later, came to shape a sort of odyssey. Just as I set out to go to the villages in 1969, I came across these words by Barbara Ward: The post-colonial world, she wrote, was changing so fast it was like "a new political country, unexplored, ominous, planetary in scope, and, conceivably, bordering on the end of time."

A journey into the unknown. There would be no setting up of masts, no spreading of sails, no north wind to blow us to the Happy Isles. Just the old "Fasten your seat belts" and a wearying repetition of zooming into the thin blue air at some incomprehensible speed and height, whiskey clutched anxiously in hand. So it had been ten years before, so it now went for ten years more, a monotonous procession of identical concrete-and-glass air terminals and identical concrete-and-glass hotels, proof that our Western technology has triumphed everywhere. But, as every traveler knows, it goes down just so far and stops.

And there the village world begins. Homer's Oxen of the Sun, Scylla and Charybdis, the land of Lotus Eaters, the Laestrygonian giants, Cyclops, Poseidon, Calypso, Circe and the Sirens' Song are legends, not to be recaptured. Yet maybe some very small analogy exists, if just in spirit. Ulysses, in his ten-year journey around the Mediterranean, was on his own; he looked for knowledge, but wasn't sure just what about. He wanted to find out about the world of his time. Tennyson, in his Victorian way, had Ulysses yearning "to follow knowledge like a sinking star." ("Much have I seen and known; cities of men and manners, climates, councils, governments. . . .") But I like Stephen Dedalus's beery declamation in a Dublin bar: "Every day is many days, day after day. We walk through ourselves, meeting robbers, ghosts, giants, old men, young men, wives, widows, brothers-in-love. But always meeting ourselves. . . ."

Eureka! Buck Mulligan cried. *Eureka!*

CHINA: REVOLUTION, RED AND GREEN

Political states come and go. Villages last—and, in them, age-old civilizations. From the bits and pieces a traveler can see, this is true of post-Mao China. What I was looking for, on a journey to Beijing, Shanghai and the countryside in 1980, was whether, in the Chinese villages, Aristotle's fundamental human institutions of marriage, family and property had survived the twenty-seven tumultuous years of Mao Tse-tung's rule. They have.

Moments for private talks are few, but when they come, ordinary Chinese confide their troubles with astonishing frankness. If there was one common theme it was to stress their human individuality. As one young villager expressed it, "A few years ago we were told not to believe in human nature. But that's wrong. All human beings, in all time, all over the world, are alike. We share a common humanity." One youth would tell you he was forced to join the cultural revolution as a Red Guard but swore he never destroyed anything nor hurt anybody. Another said it was one thing to volunteer and quite another to be conscripted. It added up to a single common message a new generation wants to get across to the outside world: think of us as individual Chinese who have kept faithful to ourselves, not as one billion ideological robots.

Since the communist revolution of 1949, China has managed to feed a people whose numbers doubled in thirty years to one billion, almost a fourth of the world's people, and on just 7 percent of the world's cultivated land. During those thirty years, the amount of staple food per person rose about 50 percent, from 205 kilograms to 309 kilograms (though some put it lower, at 286 kilograms). In 1949–79, Chinese grain production grew from 180 million tons to 315 million tons, even though until 1960 China had never used chemical fertilizer. It has since built fourteen large and 1,200 small fertilizer plants and, though organic matter still accounts for two-thirds of China's fertilizer, increased use of oil- and coal-based nitrogen led to an amazing 50 percent rise in China's wheat production in 1977–79, from an annual 41 million tons to 60.5 million tons.

Harijans eating noon meal at Charan's house in Ghungrali village, the Punjab, India. Mukhtar is at far right; the others are Poondi's sons.

Gungrali's last bullock-cart race: Dhakel's father, Sarban, is second from left.

Charan.

Two shots of tiger man in India, in a Carnival-like rite to spring.

Charan threshing
in Ghungrali village,
the Punjab.

Charan under the banyan tree (1980).

The author in his first village study—India, 1959

Author interviewing Prime Minister Morarji Desai in 1979.

Author harvesting with Charan and Mazhbis in Ghungrali, 1970.

Dhakel (1970).

Basant Singh.

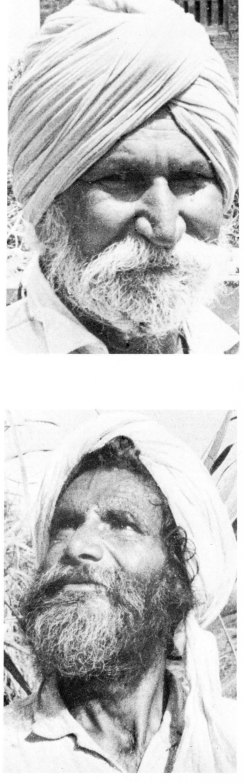

Poondi.

Saroop.

Pritam.

Buldev.

Nobel laureate Norman E. Borlaug, who traveled widely in rural China in 1974, 1977 and 1980, predicted after his third trip that China will become the world's largest grain producer, surpassing the United States, in 1981 or 1982. Borlaug and Gurdev Khush, chief plant breeder at the International Rice Research Institute in the Philippines, who was also in China in 1980, told me that with increased fertilizer China can quite easily boost its present wheat, maize and rice yields 50 percent to feed a population now projected to reach 1.2 billion in the year 2000 and ultimately level off at 1.5 billion. This should give China a sound agricultural base for fairly rapid industrialization.

Yet Mao Tse-tung's legacy to Chinese agriculture is very mixed. Most scientists agree that Mao's 1958–60 Great Leap Forward and the 1966–70 cultural revolution set back biological science and its application to agriculture at least a generation. That is, what China has done is not so impressive as what it might have done and what it is probably now likely to do. After seeing China, one can understand why it is now turning to Western science and technology in an attempt to snatch economic success out of so many partly wasted years. It is in our interest that China succeed. For its traditional culture—subtle, human, Confucian, supremely civilized, as I was happy to discover for myself—is still triumphantly alive in the Chinese villages.

Eight out of ten Chinese are still villagers; China has about one-third of the earth's total village inhabitants. Its high technological aspirations are based on a grasp of the fact that the main difference between the world's villagers and the West is technology and the wealth that goes with it. By technology is meant man's power over nature (but not his own human nature). From the day man followed his cattle into the Fertile Crescent and invented the sail, the wheel, the plow, irrigation and so on, nothing really big happened—aside from the invention of gunpowder and the Gutenberg printing press—until about 1800. During those six or seven thousand years of relative technological stagnation, average annual incomes globally, per head, were about $100 to $200. The man of A.D. 1800 used much the same energy resources as the man of 1800 B.C. (animal power, wind, water and sun); he could travel much the same tiny maximum distance per day; he used much the same materials for tools (iron and wood) and fuel (firewood, and forage for draft animals); and had much the same life expectancy (to his late thirties or early forties). Although the average villager in the world in 1981 could expect to live to age fifty-six and earn $500–$600 a year (in China sixty-four and $460), his tools and fuel were still much the same.

For those of us in the West, though, after 1800 everything suddenly went whoosh. Today, thanks to technology, in Norman Macrae's reckoning, world population has increased sixfold; real gross world product has risen eightyfold; the distance a person can travel in a day has increased between a hundredfold and a thousandfold; the killing area of the most effective megadeath weapon a millionfold or more; the amount of energy that can be released from a pound of matter over fifty millionfold; and the range and volume of information technology (computers, telecommunications) several billionfold. Man's control over matter and energy has gone up at such accelerating speed and his ability to process and distribute his knowledge has grown so fast, a very sudden closing of the 1800–1981 technological gap is now possible.

As of right now, though, the village two-thirds of the planet, including that large chunk of it in China, is still pretty much stuck with 1800 technology, with four exceptions. Medical science, in the form of vaccines, antibiotics and other drugs, has reached most villages; more babies and old people survive because of them, until recently doubling village populations every thirty years (it's now up to thirty-four). Contraception—mostly the Pill and intrauterine devices, both invented in the 1950s—have reached most villages and become generally used in the past five years; two-child families are a new village norm and China is pushing a one-child family. Farm science, mostly American, really began spreading to the villages on a big scale after breakthroughs in tropical plant genetics in the mid-1960s. Transistors reached most villages in the early 1970s and television sets have spread to villages in China, India, Indonesia, Egypt and elsewhere in the past three or four years. So while modern medicine got a head start, a race is now on for birth control, farm science and information to catch up. Half the world will stay on a margin of hunger until they do and that half world, if desperation drives it to a return to revolutionary politics, could blow us up.

*

Villages played a key role in the Chinese revolution. As in all major revolutions of this century—in Russia, Mexico, Indochina, Algeria,

Egypt, Cuba, Iran and other African and Latin American states—what happened was a local reaction to much bigger social dislocations. In every case revolution was set in motion by population pressure, the commercialization of traditional village labor, land and rent, and the erosion or collapse of traditional authority, which was replaced by modern businessmen, labor bosses, technocrats or soldiers.

No cultural system is ever static, but usually there is time to make adjustment to change. If change comes too fast, a system can grow incoherent; those caught up in it find that their inherited solutions to problems, the old design for living, no longer work; their universe becomes, much as it was to the Brazilian villagers during *Carnaval*, incomprehensible. An uprising can then, without conscious intent, bring an entire society to a state of collapse, as we have seen in Iran and nearly saw in Korea. In his *Peasant Wars of the Twentieth Century*, which came out in 1968, the same time as my own study of the Vietnam war, *The Long Charade*, anthropologist Eric Wolf traced the pattern in a number of modern revolutions. First, population pressure put a serious strain on village life. Then, as land, rent and labor came to be treated as commercially negotiable (as we saw in the Punjab), market behavior no longer depended upon village subsistence; rather the villager's need to eat became subsidiary to the market as the city turned against the village. In Mexico, Cuba and Algeria, there was outright seizure or coercive purchase of land; in China and Indochina, a shift in the manner of payment of rent from a share of the crop to money led to widespread transfer of ownership from the poorer to the richer peasants. Commercialization threatened peasant access to communal lands in Mexico, Algeria and Vietnam, to unclaimed land in Mexico and Cuba, to public granaries in Algeria and China, and upset the balance between nomadic herdsmen and settled villagers in Algeria. This happened just as some villagers were migrating in large numbers to the cities, yet keeping their village ties.

Wolf noted, and most authorities agree, that peasant villagers are not good revolutionaries but rather natural anarchists. The universal peasant ideal is a village free from officials, army recruiters, policemen, tax collectors and all other representatives of the city-based government. No Marxist-Leninist movement has won peasant support without the populist slogan of "Land to the Tillers," but this land is always seized back again once state power is in the revolutionary leadership's hands. Accordingly, the slogan is a fraud.

When things come apart in a village society, the peasant first looks to supernatural deliverance, or in Wolf's words:

> . . . the vision of a mahdi who would deliver the world from tyranny, of a Son of Heaven who would truly embody the mandate of Heaven . . . Under conditions of modern dislocation, the disordered present is all too frequently experienced as world order reversed, and hence evil. . . . The true order is yet to come, whether through miraculous intervention, through rebellion, or both. Peasant anarchism and an apocalyptic vision of the world, together, provide the ideological fuel that drives the rebellious peasantry.

Robert Redfield held the view, which I share, that historically—with the possible exception of the Russian revolution—peasant revolts always aimed not at overthrowing governments but at reducing or abolishing oppressive dues and services exacted by landlords. Redfield believed—as do I—that most villagers take social stratification for granted and only resent abuses of power. Oscar Lewis, forever in opposition, held a peculiar belief that revolutions benefited peasants by freeing them from their shackling underdog psychology. Most revolutionaries have not put much faith in mobilizing the peasants; Frantz Fanon complained they hung on "like grim death" to their "unchanging way of life" and at best would burst out in "religious fanaticism or tribal wars."

Karl Marx had an almost pathological loathing of peasant villagers, which he described as "a class that represents the barbarism within civilization" whose behavior was "an undecipherable hieroglyphic to the understanding of the civilized." To Marx the peasant was "clumsily cunning, knavishly naïve, doltishly sublime, a calculated superstition, a pathetic burlesque, a cleverly stupid anachronism." The peasant was, in short, anathema. He was reactionary. His small-scale capitalism had no place in socialist society. Like grains of sand, peasants were impossible to organize into revolutionary movements.

Marx even praised the hated West for forcing peasants off the land and into factories. He envisaged a new communist society that would transform peasants into landless rural proletarians whose culture and way of life were to be reshaped to eliminate the differences between village and city. Small family farms would be replaced by big cooperatives worked by brigades of workers with machinery. David Mitrany has described how European peasants became aware of Marxist doctrine and were almost universally hostile to communist movements. Marx's aim was to eliminate peasants. It is fascinating how Thomas Jefferson took the extreme opposite position; in the justly famous passage from his 1787 book, *Notes on the State of Virginia,* Jefferson praised the superiority of village life, uncorrupted by the evils of the city:

> Those who labor in the earth are the chosen people of God, if ever he had a chosen people, whose breasts he has made his peculiar deposit for substantial and genuine virtue . . . While we have land to labour then, let us never wish to see our citizens occupied at a work bench. . . . The mobs of great cities add just so much to the support of pure government, as sores do to the strength of the human body.

Lenin was more expedient. To him the necessity to seize state power overrode any of Marx's theoretical objections to bringing the peasants in as partners of the revolution. Lenin's basic principle was to "exploit internal contradictions in the enemy camp"; he saw that in Eastern Europe and Asia, where most poor people were peasants, there could be no revolution without their temporary support. They were to be eliminated as a social and economic class later. Lenin took Marx's theory of internal proletarian revolution and transformed it into a global class warfare between the West and the East, most of whose people were, of course, peasant villagers.

If we want to understand what happened to us in Vietnam, it is not to Marx that we must look, but to Lenin. Lenin's technique was to win over the peasants by promising them land. Landlords and traditional elites were to be identified with feudal exploitation and foreign imperialism. The appeal was to the peasant's land hunger and resentment of outside or Western domination—both yesterday and today powerful peasant feelings; the technique was used very effectively in Vietnam. This served to conceal the basic, irreconcilable differences between communists and peasant villagers. In Leninist strategy, once state power is achieved, the peasants are betrayed. Then the Marxist-Leninist program to eliminate them as a class is put into operation. First, land reform, a calculated deception to win peasant support to eliminate landlords, is carried out and the promise of "Land to the Tillers" is fulfilled. Second, agricultural cooperatives are formed on an ever-larger scale. Third, land is taken away from all peasants to become the property of the state. Fourth, peasants are forced to work harder for less return to generate surpluses for rapid industrialization. It is only then that the peasants realize that their former allies have deceived them all along; they have been used as instruments to seize power and modernize the state. Their own identity is now to be submerged into a single class of urban workers and landless rural proletarians.

Does it work? No, not in the long run. The whole story of Russian and Chinese agriculture during the past sixty years has been one long losing battle to make human nature fit the peculiar ideas of Marx, Lenin and Mao. But it has taken the Green Revolution to successfully challenge the red one.

In Russia itself the communist experiment has ended up with today's *sovkhozes,* huge mechanized farms worked by squads of men and women who have no other tie to the land; there are also *kholkhozes,* collective grain farms. But state and collective farm members (as well as many urban workers) now work some 32 million private plots, which produce about one-third of the Soviet Union's meat, milk, eggs and potatoes.

Just over 300 million acres planted in grain has not been enough to feed 266 million Russians. Over $500 billion has been pumped into Soviet agriculture during the past fifteen years. It remains an unpredictable mess. What ails Russian farming? True, nature has not been particularly helpful. Large areas of Russia are subject to five-yearly cycles of frost and drought. There's low rainfall and a short growing season. These won't change even if, miraculously, Russian farming becomes more efficient. Russia's shortage of adequately watered, warm and fertile land also makes it unable to adopt much of the new tropical agricultural science.

Yet the Russians have done well in electronics, physics and the exploration of space, all physical sciences. Why, then, are they so backward in agriculture? The answer partly lies in the bizarre history of T. D. Lysenko, a quack agronomist and charlatan who was allowed absolute dictatorship and control over research in biology from 1936 to 1964; the destructive effect on Soviet agriculture is still being felt.

Lysenko denounced Mendel's universally recognized chromosome theory of heredity and the theory of mutation and instead came up with something he called "vernalization," an agronomic practice to obtain winter crops from summer planting. The success and spread of vernalization followed Stalin's famous, "Bravo, Lysenko, bravo!" and Soviet biology and agriculture went off the rails for thirty years. Until 1936, Russian agricultural science was well advanced, especially in soil science and plant physiology. Nikolay Ivanovich Vavilov, at the time the world's outstanding plant breeder and applied geneticist, famous for his discovery of the centers of origin of crop plants, mentioned in Chapter 16, rebutted Lysenko, was arrested by the NKVD and sentenced to death for "sabotaging agriculture"; he later died in the Gulag.

Lysenko's quack dogmas and new varieties of wheat and other crops turned out to be worthless, yet he was not fired as top Soviet geneticist until February 1965. Dr. Borlaug, on a visit to Russia in 1970, found that while Lysenko was discredited, his influence had never entirely vanished. (A personal footnote: I. A. Benediktov, the Russian minister of agriculture who, in 1948, officially outlawed all agricultural research "not in the spirit of Lysenko," was the ambassador to India and a member of the Soviet Communist Party's Central Committee at the time of Khrushchev's ouster in 1964. When Benediktov returned to New Delhi from Moscow he briefed Krishna Menon; one of my former journalism students happened to be in the room. He later filled me in, saying Benediktov told Menon that Khrushchev was partly ousted for his agricultural failures, but also because he had failed to bring China into COMECON, the Soviet-bloc common market. What the Russians feared most, Benediktov was quoted to have said, was a Chinese rapprochement with the United States.)

It now seems incredible that a country capable of developing a nuclear potential rivaling that of the United States could have entrusted Russian agriculture for three decades to an obvious quack. Yet the notion that villagers can be transformed into a rural proletariat may turn out to be just as unworkable. Experience in China, Iran, Sudan and Egypt, as well as in Russia, continues to prove that large corporate farming simply doesn't produce as well as the small family-size farm. (We may learn the same lesson.) Young Americans who have lived on Soviet collective farms in late-1970s exchange programs have been amazed to see workers leave their tractors promptly at five o'clock no matter what; planting might be weeks behind or a harvest threatened by a storm. Their mentality was of factory workers leaving their shifts, not farmers. As long as they got paid, so what? Then, too, the long

Lysenko years must have been demoralizing. The Russian rural population must have realized they were being left way behind. Today they are just about the poorest white people on earth in relation to their rather high level of education.

So many grandiose schemes, imposed by bureaucrats from above, have gone wrong, from Khrushchev's mid-1950s "virgin lands" scheme and his early 1960s attempt to plant millions of acres of Iowa-bred hybrid maize (the Russian growing season was too short) to a more recent effort to reverse the flow of rivers to the Arctic for irrigation. In 1960 Russia fed itself. Then in 1972 Moscow decided to buy feed abroad rather than slaughter cattle; grain imports have steadily risen, up from 9 million tons a year in the mid-1970s to around 30 million tons in 1980. As Russia's oil reserves run dry (and with them the means to pay for grain, computers and technology for agriculture, oil extraction and consumer products), Russia enters the 1980s facing many choices. They include, grimly, what *The Economist* calls "a Soviet *Drang nach Suden* through the Middle East, and nuclear world war." (A danger if it begins to look as if foreign subversion and military conquest is all the Russians are good at.) Or—the happy alternative—tacit abandonment of the whole sixty-four-year-old Leninist dream of world revolutionary conquest and a Chinese-style dash for scientific and economic freedom.

As early as five years after the Russian revolution, Maxim Gorky was bemoaning that the new collective farm workers had become "a half-savage, stupid, heavy people." Gorky asked, "Where is the good-natured, thoughtful Russian peasant, indefatigable searcher after truth and justice, who was so convincingly and beautifully depicted in the world of nineteenth-century literature?" The authors of that literature could have told him. Chekhov had no faith whatsoever in political doctrine or systems or in the Russian intelligentsia, proletariat or even in the peasants *en masse,* though he shared the populists' belief in the essential moral soundness, indeed superiority, of peasants. Of all Tolstoy's characters, it is the illiterate peasant, Platon Karatayev—pious, resigned, patient, laughing, talking in proverbs—who best exemplified the author's own overwhelming love of life and feeling that everything close to nature was good. Both Chekhov and Tolstoy put their trust in the individual; a man's own conscience was the best arbiter of right and wrong.

The most damning criticism of Mao Tse-tung, as visits to Chinese villages have brought home to me, was his attempt to deny this individuality to the ordinary, lowly, anonymous Chinese peasants. One must hasten to say that the best of Maoism may survive. Mao was an unusual leader for our age in that he actually carried out a philosophy that, broadly, aimed to eradicate the mood of privileged acquisitiveness, which he thought had degraded China in the past (and is the curse among elites in most poor countries today). Certainly, life in Canton is more pleasant than in Calcutta. The mood Mao created may have the virtue of being one of those uplifting happenings that create real contentment, élan and pride among some of the people. But a younger generation bitterly resents the regimentation and all denial of their individual human nature. This was what struck me most in China. None of the standard books I had read—Han Suyin, Edgar Snow, John King Fairbank—in any way prepared me for it.

Mao tried to carry Marxism-Leninism to its logical conclusion. In 1949, when the communists seized power, China was torn by warlords, foreign invasion, civil war and general chaos; the villagers suffered from high rates of tenancy, high rents, high interest rates and extremely small, fragmented holdings. Methods of cultivation had scarcely changed in two thousand years. What savings there were went for expensive religious rites or were siphoned off by the landlord-official class. Initially, Mao followed the classic Leninist model, promising "Land to the Tillers," exploiting anti-Japanese hatreds, eliminating "feudal landlords" through execution or sending them to be "reformed through labor" and distributing land, a process mostly completed by late 1952. Gradually land, tools and animals were placed in collective village pools and by 1958 almost all of China's peasants had been organized into cooperatives of about 164 families each. That year the Great Leap Forward was launched to put all China's peasants into 26,000 "people's communes" with an average size of 24,000 people. China was to pass from the socialist to the communist stage of society and achieve utopia. As with the 1966–67 Great Proletarian Cultural Revolution, with its concept of perpetual or constant struggle, Mao saw that revolutions must keep moving forward or, as in Russia, reaction sets in.

The human ant heaps that resulted and Beijing's claims of fantastic rises in agriculture and industry shocked the world, but it was soon evident that the Great Leap Forward was a colossal failure. Too much labor was shifted away from agriculture, the confiscation of private plots led to a steep fall in food production, there was little material incentive to work, and the mess halls, the disruption of family life, the long hours of labor and the regimentation of every waking hour made commune life a nightmare and badly demoralized the Chinese people.

In retrospect, Mao's failure seems fundamental; China may have to continue its steady retreat back to the family-size farm of individual entrepreneurs if it is to feed itself. After 1960 the peasant was given back his own house and yard, his kitchen utensils, his animals and his private garden plot. The communal mess halls closed in 1961. Peasants were again allowed to sell their pigs, chickens and garden produce for profit. At present China has 50,000 communes, relics of Maoism, which are usually communities of over 10,000 each, often based upon an old small market town and the cluster of traditional villages around it. In 1980 the Chinese press debated whether communes were too big and unwieldy; it was said that commune managers get too remote from the problems they are solving. Officials have admitted that the central problem of collectivized farming is to link the interest of the individual with that of the collectives. Also under consideration was a plan to raise the privately cultivated garden plots from a present 7 percent to 10 percent of China's total cropped land.

Today the traditional Chinese village, officially known as a "production brigade," has been restored as the basic work, planning, organizing, accounting and *de facto* ownership unit. Likewise, the family has survived Mao's unsuccessful experiments to create a familyless communism. The old clans and landed gentry no longer exist, but leadership has returned to the villages and the families that make up the villages. One finds 80 percent to 90 percent of most villages are made up of descendants of the age-old inhabitants. The village, notwithstanding twenty-seven years of Maoist experiment, has resumed its traditional role. It may be that post-Maoist China will adopt a new synthesis between the old acquisitiveness and its Maoist antithesis. Much depends upon China's Green Revolution. For as Dr. Borlaug contends, China may be carrying out the most spectacular modernization of peasant agriculture ever.

*

When we use the phrase "Green Revolution," we tend to have two different meanings in mind. In the narrowest sense, we are talking about a purely scientific phenomenon: a breakthrough in plant genetics which allows man to breed and grow artificially short, stiff-stemmed tropical wheat, rice and other grain which can take large amounts of nitrogen fertilizer (up to 120–180 pounds per acre) and water, and support heavy grainheads without falling over. This increased tolerance for fertilizer, combined with a quick maturation period—often only 120 days compared to 180 with other species—makes the new seeds two or three times more productive through multiple cropping, provided they get the fresh water and nitrogen. Thirty years of patient research—in Japan, the American Pacific Northwest, Mexico and the Philippines—went into producing the seeds. They take hold best in areas where there is an advanced, homogeneous farming population culturally prepared for change, some degree of capital, careful water control (which may require irrigation) and adequate farm prices. Policies such as land reform and minimum farm-wage laws are needed to ensure that higher incomes are adequately shared. Experience shows that transfer of this technology without social leveling can be politically explosive. The first great breakthrough is familiar: India, Pakistan and Mexico almost doubled wheat production, enabling average annual harvests for all the poor countries to rise from 49 million tons in 1961–65 to 75 million in 1971–75, a jump of 50 percent.

*

"It's new but terrific," the bearded young French economist told me as we sipped *café espresso* under Rome's blue September sky. "In four years thirty-four million acres planted in the new seeds in Asia alone. Incredible. Malthus may have been right, but the crisis in our time will be the social consequences of growing more and more food, not mass starvation."

His British colleague agreed. "It could be an agricultural revolution of even greater magnitude than transformed Europe at the end of the eighteenth century. But the social dislocation will be enormous."

This was in 1969; I was just starting out to report villages and I remember gazing down, as they spoke, from the rooftop *terrazza* of Mussolini's old colonial ministry, which houses the U.N.'s Food and Agricultural Organization. You could look directly across the Via de le Terme di Caracalla to that supreme assembly of Roman ruins: the Palatine Hill, the Circus Maximus, the Coliseum, the Forum. Oddly enough, the FAO, which had then just completed a master plan to avert world famine between 1970 and 1985, is situated in the very heart of ancient Rome. One was reminded by the ruined splendor how one of the Romans' failures was their disinterest in the world around them. They failed to learn anything about the ordinary people of India, China, Persia, Scythia, the Huns, the Africans, the Scandinavians, or Buddha or Zoroaster, or the mysteries of the Western seas. It was a social atmosphere that made such indifference possible, an attitude one writer called the "mindless conservatism of the affluent." She was comparing it to the "baleful anarchism of the dispossessed." She was Barbara Ward and she was writing about us.

It was an apocalyptic time. The year before, C. P. Snow had prophesied that within ten years:

> . . . many millions of people in the poor countries are going to starve to death before our eyes. . . . we shall see them doing so upon our television sets.

The title of a serious book warned of *Famine 1975.* In *The Population Bomb,* Paul Ehrlich had declared:

> The battle to feed humanity is over. In the 1970s, the world will undergo famine—hundreds of millions of people are going to starve to death.

Yet here, barring some local famines due to drought in the Sahel, Ethiopia and some parts of India (and due to war in Cambodia), we all are. For what the FAO economists were talking about in Rome twelve years ago, now known as the Green Revolution, has spread since then to over 130 million acres and has become something we can now define in very sweeping historical terms indeed. Earlier I mentioned that it had a second meaning; in 1981 I would define this as the transfer of scientific technology to grow food that is likely to eventually rank with the invention of agriculture itself by Neolithic woman, the invention of irrigation in the Fertile Crescent that led to the rise of civilization, the invention of the heavy mold-board plow and the manorial farming it made possible that led to the rise of Europe, and the American revolution of the past century, but especially since about 1935, in new seeds, irrigation, electrification, mechanization and chemical fertilizer. It's a way of helping all those Chinese and Indian and other villagers still stuck with 1800 technology to catch up on two hundred years' lost time. Indeed, the present North-South, rich-poor gap between the industrialized nations and the peasant societies is mainly a gap in agricultural technology. Close this gap, as the Green Revolution is starting to quickly do, and a momentous shift in world power and wealth is certain to follow.

My guess is that while historians will properly credit the scientific achievements of Dr. Borlaug and others, they may put equal importance on the Iowa plant breeder's tenacity. (Lord Snow, more astute as an observer of human nature than as a prophet, said in one of his novels that tenacity is the single most important human quality when it comes to success.) In several days of long talks in 1977 and 1980 at the International Maize and Wheat Improvement Center in El Batan, Mexico, Dr. Borlaug told the story of how the Green Revolution got started and how "finally, scientific agriculture is respected in Asia."

I came down to Mexico in 1944. Our main task in those days was to try and grow wheat from the Yaqui Valley in twenty-eight degrees latitude near sea level up to Toluca at 8,400-feet elevation and eighteen degrees latitude. Which meant it had to be nonsensitive to the length of day and resistant to many forms of disease. I got tired of hearing that Mexican wheat varieties didn't need fertilizer. Like hell they didn't. We found yields could be doubled in many places just by using the right kind and the right amount of fertilizer.

Right from the start we learned how easily farmers lose faith in science, especially traditional villagers used to age-old ways of doing things. In Sonora I was trying to get chemical fertilizer accepted by farmers who'd never used it when a shyster salesman sold the farmers the wrong kind for the soil. Oh, my God, I thought, the whole fertilizer program will be set back five years. I tried to find the fertilizer man but he'd skipped out. Acceptance of modern methods all hung by a thread there, something that was going to happen again and again. Some little slip and it looks like science is a disaster.

Anyway, when things worked out in Mexico and it came time to turn over this program, I wanted to take a crack at soybeans in the tropics. But the Rockefeller Foundation said no, stick with wheat. When we got to Asia, the first thing we had to do was get a new attitude among the young scientists. They all had advanced degrees from the United States and Europe, ran around in white coats in laboratories, living in a very sophisticated, isolated scientific world, chasing their academic butterflies. We had to teach those kids to make science and technology work so we could expand food production. We had to teach them that there could be dignity in human sweat even if you were a Ph.D.

We trained our first group in Mexico; there were a few Pakistanis and Egyptians but no Indians. So in 1961 we went out to the main research station near Delhi and got them to plant just three or four rows of dwarf wheat. "Do you think these seeds can be transferred to our climate?" they wanted to know. "I can tell you in a couple of weeks," I said, "because some of my Egyptian and Pakistani trainees took some seeds home."

I went to Pakistan and was met by some senior scientists. We looked at all the plots. What they showed us was all the conventional stuff. Finally I asked, "How are the Mexican seeds doing?" "They don't adapt here," one of the senior men said. "Have you planted and fertilized them decently?" I asked. They assured me they had. Then that night the two Pakistani trainees who had been in Mexico sidled up to me and said they wanted to show me something at daylight. Hell, I was up before daylight and waiting for a knock on the door. One of the boys told me, "They wouldn't let us plant the Mexican seed right and fertilize it." The boys had taken some of the seed to a plot the senior men didn't know anything about and secretly grown some. And it looked marvelous.

In Egypt it was much the same story. The senior men refused to cooperate but our trainees raised the Mexican wheat on their own. When I saw the dwarf varieties were doing fine in the tropics, I told those senior scientists, "Why don't you get on this train? It's about to leave. If you hurry you can jump on the caboose. You can be the big heroes." You know what they told me? "What if something goes wrong? It's my family and my living, Dr. Borlaug. You'll go away. I have to live here." I just kept on, "And I don't mean just catch the train. From now on, we've got to get together. No more chasing academic butterflies, research papers, white coats in laboratories or anything that doesn't fill people's bellies." Well, it worked.

About this time, according to Montague Yudelman, who, when I interviewed him in 1980, was the World Bank's chief of agricultural development, the Rockefeller Foundation itself was split over whether to continue its support of Borlaug's high-yield grain research, a faction of "sociologists" opposing the "technicians." (This division, between those who measure the effect of what is done and those who actually do it, a reflection of the broader division between social and natural scientists, still characterizes the development community.) Yudelman was hired, as an agricultural economist, to make a case on behalf of the "sociologist" faction against further funding. He told me, "Thank God I failed." But back to Borlaug's narrative:

In the winter of 1961–62 we planted a hundred kilos of four different dwarf wheats at the Delhi research station. Then we had to fight India's extension service. How did you get the seed off the station? So we told the extension people we needed to do some "micro-plot" testing on the farmers' fields. It was a subterfuge. I got all the research scientists in India and Pakistan to plant these micro-plots in the 1962–63 season. Then, three years later, we got Pakistan's directors of research and extension and their soil fertility man—he was a big roadblock because he was against chemical fertilizer—to come to Mexico and we put them in the hands of Mexican farmers. At the end, the head of Pakistan's research, I. Narvez, said, "We'll put it out in nine hundred farms." And India's M. S. Swaminathan, one of the world's best wheat scientists, agreed for India. India took two hundred and fifty tons of seed and Pakistan three hundred and fifty.

That was in 1965. We planned to send the seeds on some freighter out of L.A. Then the Watts riot broke out and the trucks couldn't get to the pier. We finally got the ship loaded. But then it turned out the Pakistani check for about $100,000 to pay the Mexican government for the seeds had been incorrectly endorsed and it bounced. There was the government of Mexico demanding immediate payment. The seed was on the way. Mexico was yelling that it wasn't being paid. Then India and Pakistan went to war. I called M. K. B. Bucha, President Ayub Khan's minister of agriculture, in Rawalpindi and he said, "Don't worry about the money. It's been deposited. And besides, if you think you've got problems, I've got problems. Bombs are falling in my backyard."

The Rockefeller Foundation kept calling from New York, demanding to know why we hadn't paid the Mexican government. I stopped taking calls and told my secretary, "I won't talk to anybody from New York." Then Pakistan was afraid India would confiscate the seed, as the freighter was scheduled to call at Bombay. So we cabled the ship and they unloaded Pakistan's seeds in Singapore for trans-shipment. I flew out to Pakistan and found after the seed arrived that we were getting only 20 percent to 30 percent germination. I thought the whole thing was destroyed. I told them, "Double the seed rate, put on more fertilizer and hang the expense!" I tried to call Glenn Anderson, a Canadian and our most experienced wheat man in India, but because of the war I had to go through Mexico City. The seed looked miserable. Later we found it was damaged in the warehouse in Mexico from over-fumigation. The germination rate for some of the seed was as low as 20 percent. I told both the Indians and the Pakistanis, "You send top officials to supervise the inspection of the fields and the bagging and loading of the seeds. We can't afford to have anything else go wrong." On the basis of what turned out to be a fantastic harvest despite everything, India ordered 18,000 tons of Mexican seed for its 1966 planting and a year later Pakistan ordered 32,000 tons.

In the twelve years since Dr. Borlaug received the Nobel Peace Prize, he has traveled the world as both founder and prophet of the Green Revolution. In an age when we seem to be losing our faith in the proposition that history is the actions of men, the plant breeder who grew up on a small Cresco, Iowa, farm in the heart of the Bible Belt seems an old-fashioned figure, almost a personification of the Protestant work ethic. In his odyssey, he has found this ethic strongest in China, which he has visited several times, most recently in 1980. He believes that Mao Tse-tung developed the best philosophy and system to modernize agriculture of any contemporary peasant society, though he readily admits the human cost may have been terrible, saying, "Nobody knows how many people were sacrificed during the revolution."

Above all, Borlaug said, Mao gave top priority to agriculture. He gave this example:

In 1960 virtually no chemical fertilizer was used in China. They composted animal and human waste to maintain the organic structure of the soil. In China they developed coal mines and used the coal for cooking fuel in villages. India has the coal, but it's never been exploited. Instead the Indians cook with cow dung, which is why India has such poor soil compared to China. Then in 1960, China began setting up chemical nitrogen fertilizer plants, using coal as a base. During my first trip to China, they had 1,200 or more small factories scattered about the country, I suppose because it simplified distribution and transport. By 1974 China was the world's biggest importer of nitrogen fertilizer too. What happened then was that most of it was coming from Japan and when oil imports to Japan fell after the first oil price rise, Japan abruptly cut way back on fertilizer production, producing just enough to supply its own farmers. Within six weeks China decided to build twelve 1,000-ton-per-day capacity anhydrous ammonia fertilizer plants. They hired the top people in the world to build them, Americans, Dutch, French and Japanese. Now they've added two more and they're doubling the size of the 1,200 small plants too. It represents the largest investment in chemical fertilizer within a short time the world has yet seen.

You can see the priority China gives agriculture in other ways. But this speaks loudly. The pressures of population can destroy the Chinese system just like any other. Right now it looks good. There's still great unharnessed irrigation capacity along the upper reaches of the Yellow and especially the Yangtze rivers. And the Chinese can do amazing things with hand labor. A lot of China's production increases are coming in multiple cropping, especially triple cropping south of the Yangtze. Two crops of rice and one of spring wheat. Between the Yangtze and the Yellow you've always got rice and wheat, or corn and wheat, two crops a year. Only northern China, what used to be Manchuria, has a one-crop wheat or soybean system. Now the Chinese are starting to interplant, first two rows of maize in the wheat and then, when the wheat ripens, two more rows are planted on the edges. The Chinese have great potential in multiple cropping, as do the Indians. I have great admiration for Chinese wheat, maize and rice and expect China, as it applies more chemical fertilizer, to become the world's biggest grain producer in the next year or two.

China began testing the dwarf wheats in 1965, but they had to cross the Mexican short-stemmed varieties with Korean cold weather wheat and their own indigenous landrace strains. This breeding program took until the mid-1970s, and then China's Green Revolution was on.

Dr. Borlaug even admired China's practice of sending city intellectuals out to live in villages (which several told me they hated). He said:

It's something we're beginning to need in the United States. All my best senior staff members grew up on farms; they know what it is to work in the rain and dust and have mud under their fingernails. But only four percent of Americans now live on farms. Our greatest problem is recruiting agronomists and plant breeders with actual farming backgrounds. We get all these young men with Ph.D. degrees and I have to baptize them in the dust, mud and sweat before they are any good.

I sometimes worry about American civilization. This revolution in social values that is going on. If it defeats our will to work, if our work ethic goes, what sort of a society will we have? In China, everybody's working and they look contented. I've never seen a hungry person in China.

China leads the developing countries in adopting Western farm science, Dr. Borlaug feels, followed by India, Argentina, Egypt and Pakistan. He estimates that only 30 percent of this science's potential is yet being realized in the villages and blames incompetent leadership, low investment, poor extension, city-biased price policies, the American practice of "dumping" wheat in bumper crop years and a general incomprehension of the complexities of scientific agriculture among politicians and intellectuals.

Political leaders first of all want to stay in power. As the late Zulfikar Ali Bhutto told me in 1974, "I know I should raise Pakistan's wheat prices so our farmers grow more. But if wheat goes up, everything goes up. I have to think about the political repercussions in the cities." Or, unlike Mao, they want to give first priority to industry. Nehru told me in an interview just before he died, "Everything depends on steel." Seventeen years later India had the world's tenth biggest industry but no mass market in its stagnating villages, or as

Morarji Desai put it in a 1978 interview when he was prime minister, "To whom are you going to sell? Who is going to buy?"

In the 1964 interview, Nehru said, "India must favor the have-nots above all else. The mass of people must rise." But it took intense pressure from President Lyndon B. Johnson to get India to plant Dr. Borlaug's wheat so they could. Johnson knew little about India, but he had the sound instincts and practicality of a once dirt-poor Texan who had seen the Pedernales River Electric Cooperative transform a barren frontier into prosperous ranch land. In 1965, as famine followed the India-Pakistan war, Johnson sent his secretary of agriculture, Orville Freeman, to Rome to secretly meet India's agriculture minister, C. Subramaniam. As Freeman described it to me some years later, "I was to tell Subramaniam the President had just one question to put to him and that was, 'Does India want to feed its people?' If the answer was yes, wheat would be coming, but only on a short-tether basis in return for doing what Johnson felt must be done if India was to grow enough food." Lester Brown, now president of Washington's Worldwatch Institute, was then on Freeman's staff and administered what became known as Johnson's "short-tether policy." It forced Delhi to make the right policy decisions to launch the Green Revolution and left Brown with a lasting conviction that American food aid should be tied to agricultural reform and investment by recipient governments. Brown was the first to propose, a few years ago, that the United States and Canada form a joint commission to work out such a policy toward needy Third World food importers. Johnson later used the same kind of pressure on Indira Gandhi, when she became prime minister (though America shipped a fifth of its wheat harvest two years in a row to India to avert what was a very near brush with disaster) and, in Egypt, with Gamal Abdel Nasser. Nasser balked and as long as he lived Egypt never got another grain of American wheat.

Without the scientific breakthroughs of the Green Revolution, it seems safe to say, China would not have reopened its doors, and its ears, in almost headlong haste, to the West and its technology. At last all of Asia is involved in the formidable task of adapting Western ideas to the problems of the East and is producing some agricultural miracles in the process, such as helping to double world grain output during the past thirty years. Future miracles will depend upon both wise politics and continued scientific advance. Wet-rice technology is not too far behind that for irrigated arid land, where the first big gains came. The big challenge is to find new crops and techniques for the small dry-land, rain-fed subsistence holding, which has stubbornly resisted modernization. The political challenges are to devise a more equitable distribution of wealth within villages, countries and regions, and for diplomacy to work out better regional groupings. As Dr. Borlaug points out, the task has only begun.

In the meantime, we must be prepared for the occasional years of bad weather, whether floods, drought or poor monsoons, when the cry will surely be raised again that the world can't feed itself. We must also expect a steady output of gloom and doom from pessimists who say that the limits of usable cropland have been reached (where?), that use of fertilizer is about to tail off (what evidence?), that the world's fish catch, after more than doubling in the twenty years to 1970, has since stagnated (perhaps just as well) and that forests are being pushed beyond their capacity (so we plant more trees). I say such pessimists badly underestimate the common sense, inventive ingenuity and, above all, tenacity of scientists like Borlaug and villagers like Charan, Husen or Shahhat.

In 1978, the U.S. Census Bureau reported a "perceptible decline" in the rate of world population growth over the previous decade. Most demographers now agree that the rate of increase has peaked; the question is mainly how fast the rate will drop. This drop has been notable in Asia (probably 2.4 percent annual growth in the 1960s, 1.8 percent by the late 1970s), dramatic in the small middle-income countries (2.8 percent to 1.4 percent) and marked in the industrialized countries (1.1 percent to 0.5 percent). The world's rate of natural yearly increase by mid-1980 was 1.7 percent. Estimates for world population in the year 2000 have fallen since the early 1970s from 6½ billion or so to under 6 billion—equivalent to wiping India off the map. At the same time, world food output continued to grow slightly faster than population—about 20 percent gross, 4½ percent per head, worldwide from 1970–72 to 1976–78. (Only in Africa did it fall, 7 percent). Even in sub-Saharan Africa there can be rapid advance, once enough males culturally adapt to the role of settled small farmer. The hope lies in growing hybrid maize right across Central Africa and developing such big rivers as the Zambesi, Congo, Senegal, Niger and Volta—just as the Mekong, Brahmaputra, Ganges, Indus, Yangtze and Yellow hold the greatest promise for Asia.

The world is still a long way from zero growth; we gain 80 million people every year and the planet is currently projected not to ultimately stabilize until it has just under 10 billion people. China is pushing 1 billion and India-Pakistan-Bangladesh aren't far behind—but the 1980s could be the decade when Malthus is finally laid to rest. The good reverend was mistaken in his calculations in 1798 because he went by the contemporary technology of 1800 man. So, it appears, were his successors, whose apocalyptic forecasts a decade ago were based upon 1960s technology (the Green Revolution didn't really get going until after 1967). The demographic sky may not be too sunny, but it's not falling.

What happens now depends on us. In the closing chapter I'll go into why, after revisiting most of the villages in this book in 1978–80, I believe that a great change is taking place—a fundamental change in the way people think and behave. Here technology's claims are illusory; for, like logic, though technology can increase our power over nature, it cannot provide the key to human freedom (whatever the social scientists may say) and therefore to human nature. Human beings can be rapacious and selfish. They are also capable of great nobility—and they can be very patient. In China, it is human nature, in the form of the individualist temper of its ordinary men and women, which has outlasted and thereby defeated the rigidly totalitarian system Mao tried to impose.

*

Early one morning in Beijing, in June 1980, I was taking a walk in that immense concrete esplanade that is known as People's Square. In the east the sky was just growing light, yet already a crowd of Chinese were filing in and out of Mao Tse-tung's tomb. The enormous square, with the obelisk of the Monument to the Heroes of the People in the center, T'ien-an-men Gate and the yellow roofs of the Forbidden City at one end and huge ugly buildings in Stalino-Fascist architecture on both sides, made you feel you were in the most totalitarian country you'd ever been in. "Chairman Mao's Thoughts Forever!" proclaimed red Chinese characters from one gray facade, answered by another's "Without the People There Is Nothing." In a society where "political attitudes" and "class origins" had long decided one's wages and a man or woman worked where he or she was born at a job the government chose, until and unless the government told him or her to do something or go somewhere else, *1984* did not seem far away. The setting took you back to those films of the 1960s when Mao and Marshal Lin Piao stood on T'ien-an-men Gate and pledged a global victory of revolutionary forces to all those millions of red book-waving Red Guards. Then, at the height of the Cultural Revolution, it really did seem possible that someday, in Lin Piao's words, the poor "countryside of the world" could isolate and eventually capture the "cities" of the industrialized West.

Now, fifteen years later, with only the people at the tomb and a few cyclists and horse carts on the roads, the emptiness was ghostly, a theater whose audience had gone home. A young Chinese came up, one of the students who are forever trying out their English; he'd just viewed the old Chairman's embalmed body inside the tomb. "Did he look lifelike?" I asked. The student shrugged and replied, "When you're dead, you're dead."

Within a few months, Mao's pictures and all the slogans praising or quoting him would vanish from People's Square; even the tomb would be closed. At the time, an American diplomatic acquaintance told me over drinks in the Peking Hotel bar (a refuge for resident foreigners, who, unlike the frantically busy travelers, can suffer a sense of cultural isolation), "You're lucky to be here when official policy happens to coincide with people's real feelings." Yet even without what chance confidences came along, it was plain in the Chinese villages that all of the essential elements of their civilization still robustly exist behind the courtyard walls: marriage, family and property, Confucian respect for parents, reverence for ancestral land, the universal agricultural moral code. Filial piety seemed as strong as ever, but when I called it "Confucian," a communist party cadre hastened to say it was mere "social morality."

The Chinese have always had a natural faculty for organizing small, happy, private family islands: step inside the mud walls of a household and you'll find carefully tended fruit trees, flowers and a vegetable patch (although the tiny garden plots where produce can be grown for sale at weekly markets are usually detached), chickens, maybe sheep and always a pig (indeed, a pig under a roof is the Chinese ideograph for "home"). After the drab world outside, a peasant house seems bright and cheerful; gaudy red and yellow quilts on wooden beds (heated by flues in winter), snapshots of grandma, grandpa and the children, a porcelain vase or two and calendars with pictures of pretty girls. The country liquor you get offered is the same familiar deadly brew you get in Neetil or Ghungrali.

Chinese villagers (unlike city workers), own their own houses, get no pensions (urban factory workers retire in their fifties), look after the old folks at home and do not follow Beijing's western calendar; sowing and harvesting are still governed, as in centuries past, by such events of the Chinese lunar year as the Clear and Bright Festival or the Winter Solstice. Tradition survives. In Japan swallows no longer nest in village houses as they once did, because people don't like the mess. In China, as in Korea, they still do.

Families make up a village, and a village, in all the ways that count, owns the tools and does the farming and has *de facto* ownership of the land. New principles of "The more you work the more you get" and "Same work, same pay" go a long way to satisfy Aristotle's requirement of the stimulus of gain. What's still missing, as the neglected state of all public property in China shows, including the commune barns and machinery, is the stimulus of private ownership so people will take care of things. Also, the communes' bureaucratic *apparat* tends to stifle initiative; the lower- and middle-level party cadres I interviewed seemed more resistant to innovation than either the villagers or the post-Mao Chinese leaders themselves.

There is some talk that the communes, as economic units, might wither away. The Chinese argue against any major redistribution of land back to individual tillers, not on ideological grounds but on practical ones. They say China's experience in the early 1950s, when families were given land, proved that those with more and better labor power prospered faster; the claim is made that variations between individual families meant that overall village productivity was not so high. Maybe so. But the greatest incentive to produce more food in villages the world over has always been private ownership of land. Besides, commune managers do seem more like remote bureaucrats than farmers. Once, when I joined some men and women harvesting barley, one commune manager tried his hand with a sickle too; it was evident that he'd lost the knack.

Yet Mao's agricultural system did work some wonders. Bone-poor as China remains, it is a universe away from the pre-1949 China of warlords, foreign invasions and civil wars. As in Korea in the 1950s, there was no compelling reason why China should not have stayed hungry and chaotic forever. Every new generation, as we know so well in America, takes the gains won by its father's generation as the starting point for its own expectations. It is the older Chinese who knows that, unlike his father or grandfather, he is in no danger of dying of starvation in a ditch; that if he is suddenly seized by pain he'll get at least rudimentary medical help; and that his children and grandchildren, for the first time in peasant China's history, are assured of all being able to go to school.

The only person in China I heard praise Mao was such a man, an elderly peasant named Chang whose home I visited in Nan Gao village north of Beijing. Mao's picture, in June 1980, was still everywhere and a volume of his *Thoughts* was on most bookshelves, but nobody in the cities so much as mentioned his name. (If you went to People's Square, you had to go there yourself.) You heard a lot more about Dr. Sun Yat-sen or the terrible old Dragon Empress, Tz'u-hsi.

Chang, nearly seventy, told how he was conscripted three times at gunpoint into warlord armies. He always escaped; village men who didn't never came back. "Without the revolution and without Chairman Mao," he said, "I would have been dead years ago." The old man, white-haired, stooped, with muscles knotted as ropes, was as original and independent as any Chinese I met. He seemed genuinely grateful, but then he could afford magnanimity. He and the patient Chinese peasant genius have buried twenty other dynasties. Now, in their gentle village way, they are burying Maoism too.

You might call it, yes, a great cultural revolution. But it's the real kind of revolution, when common sense tells enough people they've got to change their ways and they have the technological means to do it. Unexpectedly, and most desirably, as the villages move into the last twenty years of this century, in most of them food production is rising and human fertility is falling. Contraception and scientific farming are producing, at last, a change in the general human condition.

As is evident in Cho Dong Kok and the Chinese villages, followed by Ghungrali, Bhadson and Pilangsari, this commonsense revolution is taking root most successfully in post-Confucian societies, with villages influenced by Hindu or Malay civilizations not far behind. It is coming more slowly, if Tulungatung, Guapira, Huecorio, Shush-Daniel and Berat are indicative, in villages where Christianity or Islam hold sway, and, in Neetil's case, slowest of all in sub-Sahara Africa. But add up the populations of China, India-Pakistan-Bangladesh and Indonesia, and you've got practically half of the 4.5 billion people alive right there. China alone has just about as many people as the eighty-seven nations of Africa, Latin America *and* North America put together. The Vatican's opposition to contraception and the rise of Moslem fundamentalist groups all through the Islamic world have helped to freeze attitudes in these hold-out regions.

Clearly, the fundamental cause of the social and psychological turbulence in each of the villages in this book comes from the steady, continued and as yet unpredictable working out of the world's post-1800 technological revolution. The wide range of adaptation we have observed is closely tied to the six major variations of the universal village culture. These I define as the Confucian, Hindu, Malay-Javanese, Islamic, Roman Catholic and tribal African. The more socially cohesive, hierarchical, self-confident and agnostic cultures are finding it easier to adapt to contraception and modern farm science than the less tightly knit, less secure and more deeply religious ones.

Elsewhere—above all in Asia, where the vast majority of the world's villagers live—I think we can say four changes are happening at once.

First, contraception is being widely practiced. In places as scattered as China, India's Kerala and Karnataka states, Sri Lanka, and Java and Bali in Indonesia, annual population growth rates have plummeted from 2½ percent–3 percent in the early Sixties to 1 percent–1½ percent now—mostly in the five years 1975 to 1980. Elsewhere, though less spectacularly, fertility has been declining for the first time in the modern era. As Sir Maurice Kendall, head of the World Fertility Survey, has observed, "Something mysterious is happening in much of the world to make women have fewer children."

Second, modern scientific farming methods—high-yield, fertilizer-intensive, fast-maturing crops, year-round irrigation and multiple cropping—are spreading quickly. Good harvests have eased food shortages. Even in two of Asia's poorest regions, both with some of the lowest incomes and densest populations on earth, rice production continues to rise—in Java by 4 percent a year, in Bangladesh, except for the occasional bad monsoon, by 5 percent.

Third, great swollen cities are disgorging some of their inhabitants. In a turnabout of the long march out of the countryside and into the cities, armies of ex-peasants are leaving the Asian cities to return to their villages, which can once more feed them. The vast exodus from village to city is ending, probably has ended already. Cities like Bombay and Jakarta appear to be experiencing reverse migration, though it may take some time until we have the figures to prove it. At present, 61 percent of the world's people are villagers. (In Asia 73 percent, in Africa 75 percent and in Latin America 39 percent, compared to the industrialized countries' 32 percent, a ratio which perhaps can be held. These figures do not include villagers who live and work in cities but keep their village ties and culture; they would push the percentages way up.)

Fourth, the national economies of what have been largely peasant societies, again especially in Asia, are starting to reflect the change. The competitiveness of fast-industrializing countries like South Korea or Taiwan is already causing concern to the developed nations. Successive oil shocks have put the world's money system under great strain and sent debts soaring. Yet if present pragmatic policies succeed in transforming China and India over the next several decades, the West may be challenged to maintain the leadership it won two hundred years ago by harnessing technology first.

Paradoxically, the unsettling effects of rapid population growth may

have been the catalyst which broke down the ingrained cultural attitudes of the villages, long-settled communities of one or two thousand
people living off the land. When village populations started doubling
every thirty years or so, their inherited age-old design for living began
to lose coherence, causing mass migration to the cities, as with Carolina, Aurelio or Husen; cultural breakdown, as with Kuwa; psychological turbulence, as with Shahhat; social alienation and crime, as
with Barek; rising violence, as affected Tonio and Rashid; or even political upheaval, as with the Vietnamese, or more recently, the Iranians
and Koreans.

But the villages could not, by themselves, come to grips with population growth, because the necessary contraceptives, high-yield grain
and farm science and modern communications were not available to
them until the late 1960s. Villagers do culturally adjust to change if
they have the time and technology, as we have seen with Fatih, comparing him to Shahhat. They can do so while preserving what is most
valuable in their traditional culture, as Ngodup or Husen have done.

It seems to have been in the decade of the 1970s that the villages
managed to come to grips with the problem, the past five or six years
probably being decisive. China, for example, did not get significant
amounts of the new seeds until 1973–74, quietly bringing them in from
Australia and Pakistan. In Java, as we've seen, older villagers such as
Husen's parents bitterly resisted contraception and scientific rice cultivation as recently as 1973; now they take both for granted. Some
villagers, like the post-Confucian Chinese, Koreans or Japanese,
with their practicality and superb self-confidence, or the Javanese,
with their special gift for graceful survival, have made the adjustment with relative ease so far; others, such as the Punjabis, have done
so with bitterness and some violence, as modern farming confronts a
caste system it has made archaic.

East Asia—China, Japan, Korea, Taiwan—now leads in transforming village agriculture through irrigation, new crops and cropping systems, pest control, waste recycling and ingenious new machinery.
Modern science gives resource-richer India, if it can overcome its
managerial weaknesses, an even greater farming potential. As we have
seen, modern farming is rapidly moving from northwestern India into
the Gangetic plain toward Bengal. But while, of all our villagers,
Charan has been getting richer faster, making the shift from subsistence agriculture into modern commercial farming in little more than a

decade, Punjabi ideas of male superiority have kept fertility from falling much. Instead, the truly spectacular falls in birth rates in India are moving up from the often poorer south. In India's poorest and more densely populated but best educated and most matriarchal state, Kerala, birth rates quite suddenly dropped by 25 percent, just as they did in largely Buddhist, poverty-ridden Sri Lanka.

My conclusion is that the woman's role in society is the key to population control and, beyond that, to all village development, because women as the custodians of culture and the teachers of the children make the crucial adjustment to change. In the post-Confucian societies, where economic advance is fastest, women enjoy equality in education and work, although they are subordinate to fathers, older brothers and husbands in a delicately balanced hierarchical relationship where they, too, have distinctly defined rights which must be respected and observed by men. In the *Angst*-ridden Islamic world, where village women enjoy relatively little equality in the home, school, field or marketplace, few nations have really joined in the new trend. Yet women, even in Moslem villages, are stirring. In both Berat and Sirs el Layyan something of a pharaonic-spirited women's movement seems to have surfaced among the Ommohameds and Batahs as they wage their own small personal daily wars for greater rights and equality. The same pattern of rising productivity and falling fertility is coming in Egypt, if more slowly.

In tribal Africa, where women often do enjoy near-equal economic rights and do so much of the cultivation, the big need is for the spread of education (without, as could happen, a change in male attitudes). In Java and Bali, where the new rice has given Indonesia some of the highest per-acre yields in tropical Asia, a fall in annual population growth from 2.5 percent to 1.4 percent in the single decade of the 1970s, made possible by the mobilization of village women, seems likely to revolutionize the Indonesian male's perception of a woman's role. Now they know where to go to get things done.

The same thing happened years ago in China, Korea and Taiwan, where women now do 40 percent to 60 percent of the farming, increasingly with machinery; the East Asian advances are slowly moving to India, too. Interestingly, some Chinese women have started complaining that they do more than their share of farming; few are in the army, the quickest path to advancement in China. Yet the tragic sight of an old woman in the Forbidden City, hobbling painfully along on her once-bound feet, brought home to me just how far the Chinese women have come. One sees changes everywhere. One of the most exciting aspects of the cultural adjustment now underway is the growing recognition that, along with more investment in irrigation and for education in sophisticated science and technology, more rights and education for women are now what is really going to matter.

None of this cultural adjustment would have been possible without the technology and wealth needed to bring it about. Years of patient research went into producing Mexican-bred wheat and Philippine-bred rice. The Rockefeller and Ford foundations, along with many individual scientists and technicians and their institutions, deserve credit for patiently slogging away, despite all the pessimism of economic technocrats addicted to doom-laden computer forecasts. Anthropologists, the people who have gone to villages the most and stayed the longest, guessed what was happening, as I've tried to suggest, because they had learned that village cultures will adjust given time—but too many of their findings were buried in scholarly journals or in university libraries. Then, a huge global network of family planning clinics and contraceptive depots, as well as agricultural universities and research institutions (fifty-one in India alone) had to be set up, mostly from scratch. Insects adapt too, and new resistant crop varieties now have to be bred as fast as new biotypes and viruses come along.

During the 1970s more than one hundred and thirty developing countries joined in a new international network linking thirteen agricultural research centers, eight of them set up since 1971. They now pool knowledge and genetic material on all kinds of crops—wheat, maize, rice, sorghum, millet, cassava, potatoes, groundnuts, vegetables, legumes, tubers and others. New findings are exchanged on livestock breeding, plant and animal diseases and farming systems. This new global scientific network cuts across all political boundaries and ideologies; scientists and trainees come from China, Russia, the United States, India, Pakistan, Cuba, Vietnam, Turkey, African and European countries, every nationality you can name. China's increasingly active role since the late 1970s, and its contributions of samples of basic genetic diversity developed only in China, now allows completion at last of the world's major plant germ-plasm collections.

Curiously, most criticism of the Green Revolution in 1980 and 1981 came from neo-Marxists in the West, who do not appear to welcome agricultural change which makes the future possibilities of revolution more remote. (After I was booed and hissed by some members of a faculty audience when I was giving a seminar at Harvard in 1980, it was explained to me that these were neo-Marxists; a majority of the academics present were supportive and applauded.) Criticism no longer comes from the communist governments themselves (though Russia and Vietnam, unlike China or Cuba, are slack about sharing their genetic materials).

Earlier controversy included charges that the new dwarf grain benefited big farmers more than small farmers, reduced rural employment and, where grain replaced legumes, diminished local diets; much was also made of the high-yield varieties' dependence upon irrigation, pesticide and larger amounts of fertilizer. The Consultative Group on International Agricultural Research, formed in 1978 to run the new centers from an office in the World Bank, in 1980 presented a heavily documented case that the new varieties increase rural employment, that the incomes of big and small farmers increase proportionately, that neither farm size nor land tenure need prevent adoption of the new crops and that low income consumers benefit most from them and their nutritional impact. It was found, however, that the Green Revolution widens income gaps between regions within a country, depending upon local soil and rainfall.

It has all taken money. Americans have had the wealth and technology which, as I discussed in the opening chapter, have given them something unique in human history: the ability to live according to individual choice. Nobody else has ever had this freedom nor thought that perpetually rising living standards were conceivable, let alone a basic right. Few villagers do; their main ambition is still to be assured of survival. But human nature is such that yesterday's luxuries become today's necessities. In the Sixties and Seventies, this produced a new emphasis on hedonism and self-fulfillment, with self-indulgent attitudes toward family and society which were to prove no substitute for the older American values. The weakening of these values—fixed family and community ties and the responsibilities that went with them—perhaps unexpectedly created some rather nasty new city and suburban lifestyles, as alcoholism and drug abuse rose along with crime and more old people got dumped into nursing homes.

As discussed in the chapter on Java, ideas such as "small is beautiful" and "the limits of growth" were often seized upon to support inherently selfish anti-technology, anti-growth attitudes. The same thing happened with a Congressional mandate that American aid only go to help the poorest people in every village. Stephen Rosenfeld of the Washington *Post* explained to me that this mandate was largely the work of the late Hubert Humphrey, until his death the driving force in foreign aid. "These are busy people," Rosenfeld said. "They have to latch onto slogans. Who can object to helping 'the poorest of the poor?'" Rosenfeld felt it was never Humphrey's intention to interpret this law in an anti-technology fashion, as so many academics have done. "Humphrey," he said, "was careless and superficial in some ways but he was not dogmatic. If he were alive today he'd be tampering with the law to make sure the poor countries get the kind of technology they need."

As Dr. Borlaug told me in 1980, "I'm tired of hearing the doomsayers who delight in saying the Green Revolution has only made the rich richer and the poor poorer. It's very discouraging for those of us who have worked in the trenches of this battle to continue to hear this criticism from a group of academics who have never produced a ton of food or ever been hungry in their lives." I agree; a lot of fashionable-sounding slogans have too often been used as an excuse for not giving the right kind of aid—our technology (wealth naturally follows). Such arguments are shoddy and fake. From Vietnam to Iran and Afghanistan, foreign aid was under almost continuous attack, often on the grounds that so rightly infuriate Dr. Borlaug. (In my work I hear it all the time, and it's a false, essentially Marxist argument and a cop-out.) The rich nations never produced the 1 percent of GNP that President Kennedy urged in 1963 be given in aid to the poor countries. The official Organization for Economic Cooperation and Development target is now down to 0.7 percent of a rich country's GNP; actual giving in 1980 was down to 0.34 percent for the average donor and to a niggardly 0.19 percent for the United States (which fell to fifteenth place among seventeen major industrial powers in percentage of GNP devoted to aid).

Why aid at all? There are practical reasons of obligations and self-interest: raw materials, markets and security. This is why foreign aid will continue and grow. Rosenfeld said, "In political terms, there's only one issue: to protect aid from the Know Nothings." This probably makes sense in terms of the way Washington works. But just as war is too serious a business to be left to the generals, so helping the poor of the world is altogether too serious for them—and for us—to leave it to the politicians. My favorite argument on why we should help them is voiced by Hazel, the rabbit in Richard Adams's wonderful *Watership Down*, when he defends his friendship with a mouse. "I can't say I fancy the idea myself," another rabbit tells Hazel. "Those small animals are more to be despised than relied upon, I reckon. What good can they do for us? They can't dig for us, they can't get food for us, they can't fight for us. They'd say they were friendly, no doubt, as long as we were helping them; but that's where it would stop."

"All I'm saying," Hazel replies, "is this. If anyone finds an animal or a bird, that isn't an enemy, in need of help, for goodness' sake don't miss the opportunity. That would be like leaving carrots to rot in the ground."

I'm afraid that, by Hazel's standards, we've let a good many carrots needlessly rot. Somehow, though, foreign aid, both money and technology, has been enough to start the job—and what a job. What really is happening in the villages, let me repeat, is part of a movement of agricultural technology that began in the Fertile Crescent six to seven thousand years ago (the invention of irrigation). It moved on to Europe a thousand years ago (the invention of the mold-board plow and manorial farming), then briefly to England and on to America about eighty years ago (new seeds, irrigation, mechanization and massive use of fertilizer). Now, in the past ten years, this technology has started to move outward to the Third World, especially China, India and Indonesia (tropical grain, irrigation, electrification and multiple cropping). This very fast spread of modern farm science in the 1970s saved India, despite one of its worst droughts in this century, from what could have been a severe famine in 1979–80. (After several years of record wheat crops, India had 22 million tons stockpiled; its wheat production of 34.7 million tons in 1979 was up from 11 million tons in 1967, when the Green Revolution began.) This same farm science enables China to feed 24 percent of the world's people on 7 percent of the world's cropped land.

To stop, or even slow down the provision of money, training and technology, to decline to transfer as best we can our available resources, technique and information, would be like trying to stop the rise of Europe in A.D. 1000. That led to the rise of the West and the global predominance of its secular civilization; what we could be talking about are the stirrings of the rise of the East. We are up against something very, very big.

The United States is still the leading power for dynamism and technological advance on the planet and could rather easily lead the rest of its inhabitants toward a more decent world society and more abundant food. It means sharing our wealth, just a little, and our technology, a whole lot—increasingly, in a spirit of cultural equality. The best aid is the gift of useful knowledge. Western, and most often, American, scientific and technical knowledge is fast changing the villages—but the villages need a lot more.

At this point the reader may ask, this is all very well, but does anyone agree with you? In Washington in 1980, at the end of a three-year journey to revisit most of the villages in preparation to write this book, I talked with a man widely described as the best current authority on the world food problem, the Department of Agriculture's chief economist, Howard W. Hjort. I told him about my conversion to optimism and why.

"You're right," he said.

He explained, "World food demand is rising and there even may be a new world food crisis in a couple of years. But it supports your argument that dramatically more agricultural development, coupled with fertility declines, is taking place. For the new rising demand is because people have better diets and are eating more meat. If we have well-distributed rains and well-distributed food supplies, world food consumption is going to go up very fast."

Hjort said that the big populous countries of southern Asia, such as China and India, together with Western Europe, were rapidly moving toward self-sufficiency. The real rise in demand was coming from the Soviet Union and Eastern Europe (so much for the Soviet way of running agriculture), Japan and the fast-industrializing nations of the Far East like South Korea and Taiwan, and the oil-producing countries of the Middle East. When you shift from bread and rice to beefsteaks, it means you rely upon the highly wasteful system of turning grain into meat through very inefficient livestock converters (the world's pigs eat seven times more primary protein than its North Americans and the world's horses eat more than its Chinese). Just about all there is left of old-fashioned Malthusian demand—sheer population outstripping locally produced food supplies—is in black Africa (where, thanks to political turmoil, food production actually dropped 7 percent in the

1970s) and Latin America (where Roman Catholicism still means close to 3 percent annual population growth rates). Such calamities as Cambodia's are political.

Lester Brown, the most effective researcher and publicist of the changing world food outlook, whose 1960s Green Revolution optimism (in terms of buying time) turned to 1970s limits-to-growth pessimism, told me a year ago, "I realize you emphasize the need to take cultural factors into account. Nonetheless, it is my conclusion that the era of cheap food is past and the real cost of expanding food production will rise, making it extremely difficult to eliminate hunger and malnutrition." Hjort took the same position that rising farm costs would limit food production in the energy-intensive agriculture of the West; but he had a much brighter view when it came to Asia's prospects. He said, "People tend to perceive Asia the way it was a few years ago. But I'm monitoring the world food situation every day. When you talk of a great change, especially in Asia, I can see it's happening.

"A lot of technical assistance goes on and a lot of individuals are out breaking their backs to get some little thing done. But in time these small gains start to add up to something with great momentum. It's the old analogy of the snowball running downhill; it gets bigger and goes faster until you've got an avalanche. Eventually, in birth control or the transfer of scientific farming, you reach a point when it's the thing to do in the interest of your village, of your nation. Once you reach this point, when in every village it's a widely accepted social process, you've got it made. This is what is starting to happen right now."

Hjort warned that if the United States were to meet projected world food demand in 1990 all by itself and if meatier diets, fed by rising incomes, continued to push up this demand so fast, we would have to produce 45% more grain each year than we are producing now. This would be, as Brown has rightly pointed out, too expensive. Possibly, a big technological breakthrough could change things; we may soon learn to enhance photosynthetic efficiency, breed anti-transpirant or drought-resistant plants or new hybrid crops or multiple-birth livestock; we might develop fuel-saving tillage techniques or learn to convert things like cellulose and oil waste into animal feed. Lots can happen in ten years, even an exceptionally poor crop year, when, in Brown's words, "Things could get pretty panicky," or, as Hjort put it,

"Everybody would say the Third World can't feed itself." North America, Argentina, Australia and South Africa have steadily produced more food exports, but so far at an ever-rising cost in energy. For American farmers to try to grow almost half again as much food as they do now by 1990—with present technology—would mean tough choices for taxpayers, consumers, factory hands and all energy users. Somebody would have to go without. I agree with Brown; this will not happen.

But the Asian farmers themselves could do it. It would require less reliance on oil for pumps, machinery and fertilizer, combined with more reliance on better seeds, nitrogen-fixing crops, increased irrigation, multiple cropping and hydroelectric power. (You can produce fertilizer from air if you have enough cheap electricity. Egypt makes all the fertilizer it needs at a huge factory beside the Aswan Dam; it combines the atmosphere's nitrogen with hydrogen to make ammonia, which is added to crushed limestone to give it body. This technique, the Haber Process, was used by the Germans during World War I to make nitrates for explosives. It's extremely energy-intensive, but if India, which has one such factory now, could ever harness the untapped hydroelectric potential of the Himalayas, it could meet all its fertilizer, power and irrigation needs right there.) It would also mean that governments would need to give villagers higher prices for what they produce, enact tough land reform bound to hurt some people, broaden the rights and education of women and have special feeding programs for the poorest. It might mean more inflation and restless (maybe rioting) cities. None easy. But I don't say they might do it; I say they will do it. They'll have to; that's the way history is going.

Otherwise, in bad-weather years, the likely tremendous future food demand would force the United States to choose between feeding the poorest with food aid or taking cash from paying, probably overeating customers (though all the bellyaching from farmers after the 1980 Russian grain sales cutoff, followed by their eventual acceptance of it, shows how common sense and patriotism can win out over "I look out for No. 1" ethics). Or, put another way, a choice would face Americans between higher taxes and more spending on aid, or less food for the hungriest and more political upheaval, especially in African and Latin American nations as yet little affected by technological change. (This is based on the assumption that TV news would give us more than shock spectacles so we'd understand that we had a choice.)

The least painful future for everybody is to do what's worked best all along: get more technology out to those villagers. We ought to tie our help to needed reforms so that political leaders feel compelled to do the things they've got to do to make the new technology work: raise farm prices, make land holdings a similar size, educate and liberate women, spread irrigation and up-to-date water management village by village, and make sure everybody can learn the latest techniques and gets the credit so they can try them out. The best kinds of aid are the present global network of agricultural research stations and more higher education in science and technology at American universities for the villagers' children. This way we can increase the material well-being of everyone just as fast as humanly possible (not just the poorest; village social and economic systems don't work that way).

Is our cultural future at stake too? I've been going and coming to and from the Third World for twenty-two years now and growing steadily less concerned about them and more about us. Americans still possess the most vital society on earth, but wealth and technology keep taking us farther away from natural things (all those farmers leaving the land). If there is to be a reruralization of America, as mentioned in Chapter 1—if, in Norman Macrae's words, "America is going to lead the world to a totally new and exciting society"—we need to know more about the villages. We've taken a look at twenty different villages; in each there was some sudden break with the historical past: overpopulation, migration, urbanization, the breakdown of the agricultural moral code, social alienation and crime, the decline of nomadism and tribalism, uprooting, peasant revolution, Islam's fundamentalist reaction, the changing women's role, and the spread of Western farm science and contraception, all creating a whole new world out there.

We also looked at some of the anthropologists' ideas on what all villagers have in common, as well as the history of villages and their rivalry with cities; we touched on sexual behavior, religion and its supernatural supports and why the Green Revolution is going over better than the Marxist-Leninist kind. And we had Arnold Toynbee's 1946 prophecy that the villagers, once awakened, might spiritually challenge the materially superior West, and speculation, based upon the village culture of the historical Jesus, on what kind of challenge we might expect.

Today, four decades later, it is evident that Toynbee was right that

THE GREAT CHANGE   333

the West would awaken the peasant—and he was right that, much to our bafflement and sometimes distress, numbers are starting to tell as the huge populations of the Third World continue to grow. When Toynbee wrote, however, the world was a different place. The West was offering peasant villages just two basic ways to modernize: one capitalist, the other communist. The choice presented was industrialization-urbanization, or Marxist-Leninist revolution followed by a state-run, state-owned society. Both, I believe, have failed the villager —the first because capitalism has not been able to supply enough jobs and incomes in the Third World cities. This has to be hedged a bit because eight countries in east Asia—South Korea, Taiwan, Hong Kong, Singapore, Thailand, Burma, the Philippines and Malaysia—during the late 1970s achieved something near to or above the 7 percent annual economic growth rate that doubles real GNP in a decade. (Brazil and Mexico made rapid strides in manufacturing too.) But their combined populations are but a fifth of the Indian subcontinent's and Indonesia's together. Communism's failure is its denial to villagers of privately owned land and hence sufficient incentives; it goes against basic human nature. Historians, I hope, will someday look back and say that Marxism-Leninism began to burn itself out, at least in Asia, the day Chou En-lai or whoever it was placed his first order for Dr. Borlaug's seeds. This victory was not won on the battlefields of Indochina, but that's part of it; who would wish Cambodia's fate on his own country? We may have won in Vietnam after all.

What Toynbee did not foresee, because technology did not advance enough to make this possible until the 1960s, was that the West would come up with a third way to modernize: the rapid transfer of farm science, made possible by new discoveries in tropical plant genetics, to bring about the kind of agricultural revolution on which its own wealth and industrial power was originally based. Even then it might not have got going so soon had not men like Dr. Borlaug, with his down-home Iowa farm boy's tenacity, seen to it that the first seeds got planted in India, Pakistan and Egypt. (Those practical Chinese didn't need any nudging.)

If the Green Revolution had not come along precisely when it did, I think it quite possible that Toynbee's prophecy would be a lot closer to fulfillment. Had the villagers become hungry and hopeless enough, we might now be seeing new religions or the revival of existing religions bursting out all over. Confucianism, like Islam, could, if things ever got bad enough, have the same mainspring of spiritual hostility to the West and a determination to supplant it. Like Japanese militarism or Maoism at its peak, this would be on a scale to dwarf the posturing of someone like Ayatollah Khomeini. Khomeini quite shrewdly and accurately interpreted the West's most exploitable weaknesses as spiritual and racial, but he was too vengeful to gain real stature; a true prophet, Moslem or otherwise, derives much of his power from his superior morality. As Anwar Sadat and others pointed out, Khomeini's bloodthirsty utterances often went against the precepts of Islam.

Let us leave the future of the Islamic revival to Moslem scholars and men with answers. My guess, from what we've seen so far, is that it's more a shudder of reaction than the wave of the future. Moslem villagers want decent and useful lives just as much as the rest of us and they're aware now that they'll get them from such things as new seeds, fertilizer, pumps and irrigation and knowing how to use them, and not from a lot of bloody upheaval.

One thing we have going for us is the curious love affair most villagers have with America; they can even be a bit possessive about it. America is becoming everybody's second country. I don't mean America as an imperial political power (little love lost there), nor even entirely the actual land and people. But America as a symbol, an idea, of the good life, of oomph and vitality and freedom and fun. Oddly enough, we have pop culture to thank for this. TV and movies have started to penetrate to most villages in recent years. Our worst export is all the violence they carry; our best ambassador may have been Walt Disney. Pauline Kael caught this phenomenon beautifully. In her essay, "Trash, Art and the Movies," she describes how audiences in remote cultures see things differently than we do:

> They may respond with enthusiasm to the noise and congestion of big-city life which in the film story is meant to show the depths of depersonalization to which we are sinking, but which they find funny or very jolly indeed.

This villagers' America is a splendid mythological land that never was, of star treks, star wars and stardust, where Superman swoops among the skyscrapers, Matt Dillon keeps the peace in a durable Old West with smoking sixguns and star-spangled pop and rock forever fill the air. When Maureen O'Hara told Congress, "John Wayne *is* the

United States of America," in the eyes of villagers, she was perfectly right.

Villager behavior is not always predictable; like ourselves, villagers are riddled with contradictions. (For instance, Shahhat, proudly writing to say that his wife had given him his first child, a son, said he had named the boy El Khomeini, after the old ayatollah.) I have tried to show in this book what I found generic in how they live and think, but imagine an historian looking back on them six hundred years from now. He or she will probably put very different meanings on words than we do. For instance, who would be poor? In a village, to be poor is to go without the necessities, not the comforts. A villager who fills his belly twice a day and has a roof over his head may not *feel* poor (that is, a failure in terms of his culture); almost everybody he knows is in the same fix and, if anybody suffers social isolation in villages, it is the few richer families. Not so in America, where a poor person not only suffers indigence and want in comparison to the majority, but is made to feel crummy.

Historian Barbara Tuchman tells how, researching life in the fourteenth century, she discovered constant contradictions in contemporary accounts. One of her examples: "French peasants were filthy and foul-smelling and lived on bread and onions; French peasants ate pork, game and fowl and enjoyed frequent baths at village bathhouses." Mrs. Tuchman comments, "Contradictions, however, are part of life, not merely a matter of conflicting evidence. . . . Starving peasants in hovels live alongside prosperous peasants in featherbeds."

True six hundred years ago, true now. The frugal Nile Delta *fellaheen* may live on bread and onions, but save to send a younger brother to college. We slept on featherbeds in cold weather in Ghungrali, but on cots in the cattle barn. In Iran, if we bathed at all, we bathed at village bathhouses, but Iranians are not nearly so clean as the Nuba tribesmen or the Javanese, forever popping in and out of their canals. The only "foul-smelling" villagers I ever met were, surprisingly, in France. It was in 1950 and after our car broke down near Nancy and we were obliged to spend the night in a village, we went to the local cinema. Whew! The audience, barefoot and in soiled undershirts, looked like they'd come straight from cleaning their chicken coops, and probably had.

Reporters who write about villagers have their own contradictions. If I stay in this line of work much longer, I'll end up, in Tennyson's words, "at the quiet limit of the world, a white hair'd shadow roaming like a dream" (but swimming at the Intercons and reading *Time* over a steak). People *bleibt immer* people. Samuel Johnson wrote of a visit to Westminster Abbey, "When I read the several dates of some that died yesterday, and some six hundred years ago, I consider that great day when we shall all of us be contemporaries, and make our appearance together." Dr. Johnson evidently had in mind a celestial gathering of suitable English notables, but in terms of villagers, if you go far enough, you can experience that great day right now: visit the Stone Age with the Dinkas in their swamp, experience Old Testament times with the Bedouins, get a whiff of medieval life in the narrow lanes around Cairo's Al Azhar University or see something like Europe's agricultural revolution telescoped in India's Punjab. Some of the villagers I know make Mrs. Tuchman's fourteenth-century types seem ultra-modern.

So to end this book—and, as you see, I'm doing so very reluctantly—when it comes to villages, there is no happy ending. But there is a much happier ending than I ever expected to write when I set out ten years ago. Then, I had a squishy and conventional sense of apocalypse. In those days we in the press were like a Greek chorus intoning doom from the wings, gloomily predicting famine, epidemics, migration, pollution, revolution, wars to seize or hold ever-scarcer resources, forever crying wolf. I've since found that cheery inconsequence wears better. As a reporter, I'm very conscious that the sensational or tragic or catastrophic political and economic events occupy the headlines of our newspapers and the foregrounds of our minds. They loom up all out of proportion when they happen, but are quickly reduced to size with the perspective of time. This is true of most wars, revolutions, massacres, terrorist acts, famines, gluts, slumps or booms. We are only vaguely aware that something might be going on in the villages. One reason I took up this work was curiosity; after all, two-thirds of the people on this planet aren't just sitting on their hands. Now I'm convinced that it is the unconscious, obscure and overpowering drives of millions upon millions of ordinary individual men and women that is the real stuff of history. Modern heads of state, like Tolstoy's king, are history's slaves. It hasn't got much zing, but the biggest story of the late twentieth century could well be the sum of countless small decisions and actions by unnoticed, humble little nobodies out there in their villages.

The things that make good headlines attract our attention precisely because they are on the surface of the stream of life. What happens when you watch a river in flood? Your eyes go to the wreckage—the drowned animals, uprooted trees and demolished houses floating by. Of course, you realize that it is the deeper, slower currents that are deciding things. It is those which will stand out when we look back some day and the sensational surface events are all but forgotten.

The same thing happens when you fly by jet out of Katmandu in Nepal. The nearest view of the Himalayas is not the best one; while you are actually over the mountains you see nothing but peaks, ridges, gullies, crags and a lot of snow. It is not until you have the mountains well behind you and look back as you head out over the Gangetic Plain that they rise up at you in their magnificent order—Annapurna, Machhapuchhare, Everest, Kanchenjunga—peak after peak. It is only then that you can see the panorama of the Himalayas themselves.

With these images in mind, I believe people in the future will be able to see our times in a lot better perspective than we can. What are they likely to see? I think that the way so many of the villagers took to Western farm technology and contraception in the decade of the 1970s, making that big first step toward catching up with our wealth, is going to loom up gigantically.

In September 1978, the World Bank's Robert McNamara predicted that if present rates of economic and population growth continued, a total of 600 million people would be trapped in "absolute poverty" by the year 2000. This he defined as:

> a condition of life so characterized by malnutrition, illiteracy, disease, squalid surroundings, high infant mortality, and low life expectancy as to be beneath any reasonable definition of human decency.

Perhaps. But if those 600 million can adjust their culture and find a design for living that really fits the late twentieth century—which is what we have seen starting to happen in the villages in this book—they will find ways not to go hungry, not to stay ignorant and sick, not to let their babies die or live short, squalid lives. As I wrote in *The Economist* in an article, "A Great Change Has Started," published March 9, 1979, "Times change and men, once they have the technological means and enough years to adjust, change with them."

Which makes me, as we head into the 1980s and 1990s, an optimist, though wary of the ever-lurking sentimentality that goes with that word. "An optimist," says Don Marquis's world-weary cockroach Archy, "is a guy that has never had much experience." Let's hope that this once we can prove Archy wrong.

The years in the villages have been enough to persuade me that a good many of these people are going to make it and that along the way they'll have lots to tell us. Our lives are not meant to be perpetually fun, self-absorbed *Carnavals,* reaching for the fast buck and getting zonked out on consumer goodies; that way, when the party's over, you can end up in the kicked-in-the-ribs purgatory of the emergency room. Nor are they meant to be one long back-breaking drudgery over a hoe or a plow.

Certainly, we, with all our technology, wealth and freedom of individual choice, and they, with their closeness to nature and the self-responsibility that comes with living in groups, can come up with something a little better, a way to live that combines the best of our material goods with their simplicity and truth.

We're not all villagers. But our grandfathers were. And so our grandchildren may become. In this book I've made many us-and-them distinctions. But I'll bet you've discovered little about these villagers that you don't recognize. Go to a village and you can't go too far wrong if you assume that everybody is just like you. For in the largest sense, and in those human qualities that really count, on this rather small planet there is only one big us.

*

So ends this particular journey to the villages, if any journey really ends. Like Emily in *Our Town,* anguished to return from the grave because only she knows how things are going to turn out, we are all travelers, traveling alone. Life is a voyage, not a harbor, *on est tout seul,* and we're "a long way from home." As Emily said, *"Let's look at one another."*

We can't go back; we can remember. And I'll close with a memory of an eight- or ten-year-old boy in Scandinavian North Dakota forty years ago learning by heart some lines in a play he'd seen at the local agricultural college's Little Country Theater. They rang in his mind then; they ring there still. It was at the end of Act Three in Ibsen's *Peer Gynt* (and we really need Grieg's "Ase's Tod" on the soundtrack). Peer is about to set out on what is going to be a lifetime journey to the ends of the earth; he says he must start. "Are you going far?" inquires a village neighbor. "To the seacoast," he replies. "So far?" the neighbor asks in anxious astonishment. "Yes," he says, "and farther still."

POSTSCRIPT:
VILLAGE CHARACTERISTICS

Robert Redfield, the American anthropologist I have quoted so often, in 1954 was the first to suggest that all villages share something of a common culture. In his 1956 book, *Peasant Society and Culture*, Redfield wrote, "Peasant society and culture has something generic about it. It is some kind of arrangement of humanity with some similarities all over the world." Unlike Oscar Lewis, with his seventy-trait "culture of poverty," which applies mostly to the Latin-American urban world, Redfield never developed his idea in any detail. Yet over the years I've found it very useful to keep a list of characteristics I find common to most villages I've visited; it helps as a kind of road map. What might be called "a universal village culture" is set down here for the reader who might want to compare it with villages he knows (or our own society). If traits or phrasing are taken exactly from Redfield or Lewis, I've identified them with an (R) or (L). The rest come from all sorts of sources or are original, drawn from my observations:

Individual: A villager has a lower life expectancy (L); in the poorest villages, men have a higher average age of death than women, who may spend half of their years in the childbearing stage; he or she is present-time oriented, is concrete-minded and has a capacity for spontaneous enjoyment; villagers are fatalistic (L) and plain, straight and conservative, with inherited traditional and materialistic drives; grain (most often wheat, rice, maize, cassava or sorghum) is the staff of life; age is respected, tradition and custom are binding.

Family: The head of a village family—the father or oldest son, or, rarely, a widowed mother, has to provide food, shelter and clothing for all its members; each in turn is obligated to work for the family under the father's direction; this gives his authority an economic basis; the family is of central importance and blood ties and kinship have heavy weight; family life is marked by crowding, gregariousness and lack of privacy (L); a relatively high percentage of spending goes for religious rites, liquor and cigarettes and a low percentage for medicine, education and clothing; most males smoke and so do some older women; the family tends to be mother-centered and emotional ties with parents are much stronger than with siblings; a woman comes into her own as a power in the household as the mother of adult sons.

Sex and Love: The approach to marriage is more practical than romantic and to love is often carnal; sex is freely discussed among villagers of the same gender; early marriage reduces frustration from prohibitions (strictly enforced against women) of premarital sex; virginity of brides is valued; a bride is often chosen for her reputation for industry or for her property, and beautiful or well-educated young women may have trouble finding mates; marriage is a provision for economic welfare and accordingly single people are rare in villages, although a few do exist; love marriages are starting to be accepted, but still with major parental involvement; adultery is harshly punished if detected, but still goes on; there is little or no prostitution or homosexuality; most village marriages are a "dogged partnership" of closely related work life and family life, but deep affection can develop based upon compassion and mutual need.

Land: This was Redfield's strongest area. Most villagers have a love of their native land, a desire to own land, an intense attachment to their ancestral soil, a personal bond to the land, a reverence for nature and toward habitat and ancestral ways (all R); there can be an almost organic relationship between a man and a woman, their labor and the land.

Labor: Hard physical labor is the central fact in every villager's life; from this stems a feeling that agricultural work is good and commerce not so good (R) and that ability at labor reflects maturity and a sense of personal worth (R); though there is great enjoyment at surcease of hard labor (R), morale visibly rises during periods of intense field work such as during harvests, and there is corresponding disorientation and demoralization during periods of prolonged idleness; industry and thrift are seen as prime values, though they are not always practiced; villagers believe the habit of hard work has to be inculcated in youth from childhood (R); children become self-reliant by performing useful chores from toddlerhood; a youth is as prepared to earn his livelihood from the land at fifteen as he is at forty; children are eager to perform work well as proof that they are growing up; there is an exaggerated fear of illness or disability, though not of death, because one falls from status if unable to work; there is a certain suspicion, mixed with appreciation, of town life (R); relationships between parents and children become strained if the children are educated beyond the parents' level and lose, as often happens, these traditional attitudes toward labor and land.

The Agricultural Moral Code: This is one of the most striking aspects of rural group living in a traditional village; except for Java and Sudan (and much of tribal Africa, where polygamy is practiced), village morality strongly encourages monogamous, divorceless, multi-child marriages (even in Moslem societies, where a man in theory can take four wives; I have seldom met a village woman, even the most devout Moslem, who did not violently object if her husband tried to take a second, younger wife); many children were traditionally welcomed as more hands for work, more security in old age and more security against potential enemies, hence birth control was deemed immoral and against "God's will"; in the past few years this attitude has begun to undergo a revolutionary change as the incentives to have fewer children, especially in hopes of educating them, start to take hold; there is tacit recognition that while a villager is rustic, he or she has a superior moral code to people in the cities; the thrifty and hard-working neighbor is praised although not if his or her prosperity is seen to be gained at the expense of others in the village; parents, older brothers and sisters, the elderly (and in post-Confucian villages, the state) are to be honored, respected and obeyed (in the case of sometimes bad advice from the fathers of Husen and Charan, I had a harder time accepting this than their sons did); violence, stealing, falsehoods and covetousness are condemned; the agricultural moral code has much more in common with the stern Ten Commandments than with the loving Sermon on the Mount.

Religion: All villagers tend to be skeptical toward organized religion, be it Christian, Moslem, Hindu, Buddhist or whatever, and toward its priests, *imams,* Brahmans or monks; this is combined with deep personal faith, however; villagers believe in a personal god concerned with their individual welfare, who leads the forces of good in perpetual conflict with the forces of evil; villagers tend to believe that life is, to some degree, predestined or "already written," hence their fatalism; most believe in a system of punishments for sins and rewards for virtues in an afterlife; there is a near-universal belief in heaven and hell; evil is explained as the work of Satan or other devils or demons who seek to make humans lustful and violent; religion tends to be propitiatory, although disaster, when it comes—such as illness, death, floods, droughts, famine or earthquakes—is often accepted philosophically as the lot of all creation.

Supernatural Supports to Religion: This is one of the great psychological divides between villagers and ourselves; they invariably tend to believe in good and evil omens, witchcraft, sorcery, magic, demons, ghosts, the Evil Eye of the envious or merely admiring neighbors, herbal remedies, faith healing and protective amulets and talismans; villagers tend to seek and accept explanations of natural phenomena and human behavior in the supernatural rather than in modern, scientific logic, even when they know better; there is a similar tendency to prefer traditional cures and herbs, especially if there is magic involved, to modern medical practices (injections are much preferred to oral medicine, possibly for this reason); belief in the supernatural, as mentioned in Chapter 19, is reinforced in villages by much more frequent occurrences of apparent psychic phenomena than in the modern West.

World View: A person's universe does not seem to extend beyond the distance he or she is likely to travel, which in some villages may mean only a few miles in any direction; accordingly, a villager's horizons tend to be extremely narrow, usually not much beyond the nearest market town and a few neighboring villages; there is much illiteracy, but even the literate villager rarely reads; I've found remarkably little curiosity about or knowledge of the outside world, even among quite literate villagers, and little interest in newspapers; television has spread to most villages during the past few years, but if it is watched, villagers prefer a fantasy, such as a Kung Fu-type martial adventure, to anything with relevance to their own lives; villagers have little sense of nationalism, but tend to identify themselves with a local region or ethnic group; there is a fear of big cities (villagers may be forced to go to work in cities, but they will try to recreate the village by clustering with people from home); the village remains the fixed point by which a man or woman knows his or her own position in the world and relationship with all humanity; from childhood on, a villager forms an inner picture in his mind of his own place, his relationship with others in the village and the world outside, all securely balanced so that he feels a sense of being bound in a community whose common and familiar tasks and values go on forever; politically, villagers just want to be left alone; they accept outside power and are dependent upon the outside world for priests and religious teachers, schoolteachers, agricultural technicians and agricultural inputs, veterinarians, doctors, medicines and family planning clinics; yet all outside authority is to be avoided if possible and specific abuses are resented; police tend to be respected and obeyed if they maintain law and order; police can be hated if they practice brutality; villagers rarely identify their interests with city people; there are notions that city people are "extravagant," "idle" and "false" (R); the typical villager has almost no concept of world geography and is often unaware of such things as nuclear weapons, man's journeys to the moon, or the world population, food and energy problem.

Village Society: The village is the villager's world and Foster was absolutely right in saying that fear of neighbors' censure or "what will people say" is a much more potent force in holding a village together than government fiat or fear of God; village social pressure creates a powerful desire to conform to established ways; gossip is the chief form of entertainment; vil-

Fatih and his friends harvesting wheat in the Nile Delta; Fatih's home is on the right in the background.

The peasant as true believer—Egypt.

Shahhat, the Nile and Luxor Temple.

Shahhat in his field. In the background, left his village and Ramses III Temple.

Fatih and his family.

The canal path near Shahhat's village.

Dr. Norman Borlaug.

Husen, Jakarta, 1970.

A great change in the human condition is coming because millions of villagers, like these, are adjusting to contraception and modern farm science. Here, a village puppeteer demonstrates the characters of the shadow play, an amalgam of Hindu metaphysics, battles, slapstick comedy and faith tales, which have given the people of Java, which has two-thirds of the people of the world's fifth most populous nation, their unique character. Husen is in the white undershirt. This was taken in 1970.

Karniti harvesting rice in Pilangsari village, Java, Indonesia.

Calcutta: it survives.

lagers are intensely interested in each other, with a corresponding almost total lack of interest in anyone or anything outside the village; neighboring villages invariably have bad reputations; there is usually some system of village communal rights and obligations governing such matters as the grazing of cattle, gathering of fuel, cutting of fodder and building roads or canals. Services provided to one's village neighbors, such as hospitality without cost or loans without interest, are expected to be met in kind; there is some degree of mutual cooperation; it is understood that each villager has a part to play in an organic whole; life is governed in harmony with the weather and seasons, as well as traditional festivals and ceremonies, which are carefully observed; houses tend to be mud-brick, though there is much variation depending upon what building material is locally available (grass huts in Sudan, wooden stilt-houses in the Philippines, masonry cottages with picture windows in Java and so on); villagers live close to their animals and tend to communicate with them in special languages; there is little or no difference in the outward aspect of the houses and clothing of the rich and poor; an unexpected characteristic of most villages is that the richer families tend to work much harder and stay a bit aloof; social life revolves around births, marriages and deaths, the local school and the village church, temple or mosque; there is a pattern of frequent buying of small quantities of essential goods like matches, sugar or tea, on credit from village merchants to whom most are in debt (L); there is borrowing at usurious rates from these richer shopkeepers during emergencies, and banks are little used (L); there may be envy of successful neighbors, who tend to conceal gains if possible; above all, there is a restraint on individual self-seeking in favor of family and village (R); daily social relations are marked with great affability, courtesy and elaborate traditional forms of greeting, which may or may not be sincere; judging by my own experiences, I would say that villagers tend to be extremely hospitable and kind to foreigners after an initial period of reserve and suspicion.

Within village culture there are, of course, infinite exceptions to the rule, and local variations. The Javanese, for instance, have their uniquely high divorce rate and in Latin villages we find *macho* behavior, or what might be called ostentatious virility. There is a similar cult of male superiority in Mediterranean villages and in the Moslem Middle East (but not Moslem India, Bangladesh, Malaysia or Indonesia—the dividing line seems to be the upper Gangetic Plain).

Yet these are the characteristics still to be found in most of the world's two million villages and among perhaps three out of every four people alive today. Many of us over forty have experienced something similar in America's own rural post-frontier village society, which lasted from about

1840 to 1940. History suggests that there may be no adequate substitute for this universal village culture, which, for all its old restraints, religious conventions and patterns of obedience, seems necessary in small communities of people living off the land. It just could be the most harmonious way of life for human beings who choose to live in groups.

NOTES

CHAPTER ONE: Jean Cocteau's classic film, *Orphée Noire* (*Black Orpheus*), shot in Rio, is perhaps the best visual portrayal of the Brazilian *Carnaval*. The *mortalha* worn—the word is Portuguese for shroud—was traditionally white, but now is any color. The references to mulattoes relate to the mixture of races, which is so common that it is said, "In North America anyone with a drop of African blood is black; in Brazil anyone with a drop of European blood is white." The popular song, "Turn Into a Wolfman!" in Portuguese goes, *"Vira, vira, vira, vira, vira, vira Lobishomen!"* just as "Beer, Sweat and Rain!" is *"Chuva, Soar e Cerveja!"* During *Carnaval*, pop songs are often given four-letter lyrics, so that *"Ele esta de olho e na botique dela,"* "He has his eye on her boutique," gets *buceta*, the term for the female sex organ, substituted instead.

The belief in werewolves, spoofed in Salvador, is widespread in rural Bahia. They are said to appear on nights of the full moon during Lent and at the dark of the moon the rest of the year. One night in Guapira—it was the dark of the moon—Benedito, who owned a small tavern out in the fields, said one had been seen in the village. He said, "This is the time of night he's beginning to change. His fangs are starting to grow." I asked what a *lobishomen* looked like. "From the waist up like an animal, part donkey, part wolf." "What does he do?" "Sucks blood." "Oh, come now," I protested, "when did a werewolf attack anybody around here?" "Last month." Just then a guest of wind slammed the tavern door, scaring us out of our wits. Try to find a werewolf's victim and it's always somebody who's just moved away or the brother-in-law of some man in a distant village. Well, they enjoy it.

I have taken the quotation of Woody Allen from *Time*, April 30, 1979, pp. 38–41; Pauline Kael from *Reeling* (Atlantic-Little, Brown); Warner Books edition, 1976, pp. 418–19; George Steiner from *Tolstoy or Dostoyevsky* (Penguin Books, 1967, first published in 1959)—I was one of Steiner's students at the University of Innsbruck while he was writing it; Raymond Chandler from *The Long Goodbye* (Houghton Mifflin, 1953; quotation from Ballantine 1971 edition, p. 224); Christopher Booker from *The Neophiliacs* Fontana/Collins, London, 1969); Chrisopher Lasch from *The Culture of Narcissism* (Norton, 1979); Norman Macrae from

"America's third century," a survey in *The Economist,* October 25, 1975; Margaret Mead from *Village Viability in Contemporary Society,* edited by Priscilla Copeland Reining and Barbara Lenkerd (Westview Press, 1980), pp. 29–31; and Will Durant from *Caesar & Christ: A History of Roman Civilization from Its Beginning to A.D. 337* (*Story of Civilization:* Vol. 3, Simon and Schuster, 1944).

CHAPTER TWO: The French and Arabic phrases used reflect Barek's Casablanca argot in spelling and punctuation. A *douar* is a hamlet in Morocco. The *medina,* an old walled city, is not to be confused with the *casbah,* a center of prostitution.

CHAPTER THREE: On a shelf in the Dilling police station I came upon a report dated 1906, eleven years before the Nimang's last uprising, written by Colonel J. R. O'Connell, the local British military administrator, to his superiors in Khartoum. O'Connell reported that the local Nubas refused to surrender people or cattle collected in tribal raids; he was unexpectedly sympathetic. "To expect a brave, warlike and war-loving people," he wrote, "to give up their old habits and surrender what they regard as their right, much less to give up their property without a struggle, is manifestly to expect the impossible. Vendettas, quarrels over women and cattle, and often pure devilment, must give rise to disturbances from time to time. Moreover, a generation of young men has grown up who have seen no fighting. The young women taunt them with this and say they are not half the men their fathers were. As a result, the youngsters look out for the first opportunity to fight as a means of winning favor in the eyes of the women. I cannot think the worse of them for it. There is much more hope for the future of such a race than for a people who have to accept every change with passive docility."

Then, perhaps feeling he'd gone a bit too far, the British colonel added, "As people get to know the government, they will settle down." Yet, more than seventy years later, some of them still longed—as Kuku, the cattle thief, did—for the extreme, unrestricted freedom of the past, just as those of us who are cowboy-film fans do.

Also, in several conversations with me, Sheikh Idris, the Moslem missionary in Neetil, explained why he felt cultural change must come slowly in tribal Africa. He told me, "In the coming years there will be many changes in the Nuba Mountains. Most of the people, I suppose, will become what is usually called civilized, after the old men like Sultan Ahmed die. The coming generation, the children now entering school, will not hold to the old traditions. They will fade away. But at the same time I cannot predict that the outcome will be in favor of Islam. The struggle is no longer with Christianity, nor even with the ancestral tribal religion and the *kudjurs.* The real danger is that the people will become altogether godless. The Nubas could lose their old culture without truly becoming Moslems either. Then they may lose their belief in any God and have nothing at all.

"There is so much that is good in tribal religion. The Nubas have to care for their neighbors. A man cannot sleep with his neighbor's wife and commit adultery or commit theft or murder, for tribalism teaches that he will be punished with impotency, give birth to deformed children or suffer other evil. So all the people tend to behave well. Tribalism is strongly moral; in it, no one escapes a system of punishments and rewards from the moment he is born until he dies. Though the young men and girls dance all night when the moon is full, it is very rare for a boy to sleep with an unwed girl. Even when they go to follow the cattle in the bush. For to do wrong in the tribal religion is to die before one's time or suffer some other evil fate." These were interesting views coming from a Moslem missionary. He wanted to convert the Nubas to Islam but not change their basic customs; all he really challenged in the tribal religion was the *kudjur's* claim to speak for God.

Readers may be familiar with the Nubas from German photographer Leni Riefenstahl's book, *Die Nuba,* which offers superb if misleading photographs of the Nuba Mountains (she focused on naked and muscular young men, and the exotic). The American edition is *The Last of the Nuba,* Harper & Row, 1973.

CHAPTER FOUR: Some authorities on Tibet have disputed whether anything resembling normal nomadic life has returned. My description is based upon what Ngodup and other Tibetans in Tashi Palkhiel, who are in touch with relatives across the frontier, told me. Similarly, the descriptions of the Tibetan religion are also based upon what Ngodup said; they represent the "little tradition" of the village, not the "great tradition" of Tibetan lamaism as it would be known to scholars.

CHAPTER FIVE: The quotation on the need for land reform in the Philippines is from Gurdev S. Khush, chief plant breeder at the International Rice Research Institute at Los Baños near Manila, in conversation with the writer. "Ilagas," the name of the Christian terrorists in Mindanao, comes from Iloilo Land Grabbing Association after the origin of its initial members.

CHAPTER SIX: Sir Robert Thompson's *Defeating Communist Insurgency* (Praeger, 1966) and Dennis J. Duncanson's *Government and Revolution in Vietnam* (Oxford University Press, 1968) are the best accounts on the nature of political subversion in Vietnam; the published articles and speeches of Le Duan, the Vietnamese communist party leader and Hanoi's chief political strategist, are also indispensable in understanding North Vietnam's strategy.

There has been so much inaccurate reporting about Vietnam that one wonders if historians will ever be able to get it right. For instance, in David Halberstam's *The Powers That Be* (Alfred A. Knopf, 1979), there is a passage on p. 488 which describes Morley Safer's famous CBS film of American Marines setting fire to Vietnamese thatched huts in Cam Ne village near Danang. Halberstam goes on:

> (Years later a reporter named Richard Critchfield of the Washington *Star,* who had done a book on villages in Vietnam, told Safer that the reason Cam Ne was leveled had nothing to do with the Vietcong, but simply the province chief. This potentate was furious with the locals, who had refused to pay their taxes, and he wanted their village punished. The Americans who were to do the punishing were not aware of these facts. Vietnam was like that.)

Vietnam was indeed like that, but here Safer has his villages (or mine) confused. After the CBS telecast created such a stir, I went to Cam Ne and concluded that it had concealed a heavily fortified Viet Cong military post. The business about revenge for nonpayment of taxes must relate to another village altogether. Halberstam writes, "It was awesome, the full force of television, the ability to dramatize, now fastening on one incident, one day in the war, that was going to be shattering to an entire generation of Americans, perhaps to an entire country." All I can say about this nearly forgotten episode is that Safer, in support of his own reporting of the burning of Cam Ne, somehow got it wrong.

My own view about the South Vietnamese villagers, spelled out in great detail in *The Long Charade* (Harcourt, Brace & World, 1968), is that they just wanted to be left alone, did not want the communists or North Vietnamese to take over, but were sometimes deceived (with promises of land), tricked, intimidated or terrorized into collaborating with them. Ultimately, as the destructiveness of the fighting grew so intense, the villagers just wanted the nightmare to stop and wanted to end up on the winning side so they would survive. As it turned out, even the war's end did not end the nightmare, as the mass exodus of the boat people has made plain.

CHAPTER SEVEN: The ongoing feed-the-cities-now-by-importing-food versus invest-in-farm-inputs dilemma makes it important to know how much staple food it takes to keep a person alive (or not rioting in the capital city's streets). To background the Bangladesh episode more fully: In 1972 a United Nations mission led by Robert Chandler, the former director of the International Rice Research Institute in the Philippines, had predicted a shortfall of food in 1973 for Bangladesh of at least 2 million tons. This projection was based on the calculation by nutritionists in Chandler's team that an average Bengali needs 15 ounces of grain per day. Sheikh Mujib—fearing food riots in Dacca—panicked and spent $140 million—over half the country's foreign exchange reserves—to import 1.2 million tons of grain; another like amount was supplied by foreign donors.

By the time of my visit in late 1973, Bangladesh was in serious trouble. Its canal barge system—it has few highways—was tied up making food deliveries. Jute, the country's main export, rotted upcountry or on the Chittagong docks. Jute production itself fell 15 percent, mill workers began striking and many villagers, with no way to sell their jute, began growing rice instead. Mujib found he had no money for inputs to grow this rice, such as fertilizer, diesel oil, pump machinery and spare parts, so yields were very low. He had made a mess of the whole economy.

In *The Economist* of October 13, 1973, I reported that most economists and nutritionists in Bangladesh were saying that the Bengalis actually ate 13 or 14 ounces a day, not 15. Sir Robert Jackson (who was Barbara Ward's husband) and then Under-Secretary-General for the U.N.'s relief operations abroad, protested in a letter to *The Economist,* which was published November 3, that my account was "a false representation of the facts." Sir Robert asserted that the 15-ounce figure was "reasonable" and declared that "this irresponsible article" was "an affront not only to the United Nations, but also to the government of Bangladesh and to the intelligence of the country's farmers."

Finally, in another letter to *The Economist* published January 19, 1974, Toni Hagen, a Swiss most renowned for his photography of the Himalayas, but who had headed U.N. relief operations in Bangladesh, took issue with Sir Robert Jackson and said his own findings in 1972 and 1973 were that 13 ounces of grain per capita a day were adequate and that many Bengalis in 1972 had managed to stay alive on as little as 5 to 8 ounces a day.

The point is not, of course, what is the minimum a person in Bangladesh could survive on during war and famine. Rather it is to know what ordinary city people survive on in ordinary times so that when a political leader such as Sheikh Mujib has to make the calculation on how much to spend on feeding the cities or on investment in agriculture to grow more food, he makes the right calculation. The tragic result of the wrong answer in Bangladesh came in its bloody August 1974 upheaval, less than one year later. The episode was important in that it led several international development institutions, as well as the Ford Foundation in Bangladesh itself, to undertake nutritional studies, not only of what poor people ideally should eat, but what they actually do eat.

CHAPTER EIGHT: The quotation from Robert Redfield is taken from *Tepoztlán—a Mexican Village* (University of Chicago Press, 1930), and those from Oscar Lewis from *Five Families* (Basic Books, 1959) and *Life in a Mexican Village—Tepoztlán Restudied* (University of Illinois Press, 1951.)

CHAPTER NINE: The episode of encountering a shark in the Mauritian lagoon took place, luckily, before *Jaws*. Octave saw the shark first and touched my arm. It looked twice as big as it really was, as most things do underwater, and could not have been but a few yards away. I did the worst thing possible and swam quickly for the boat. Octave managed to divert the shark away from my frantic splashing. Mauritians do not fear sharks as much as they do barracudas. Any sign of a *lichien tazar,* as they called the local dog barracuda, and we'd all scramble back into the boat and sail off.

Prem, or Dhanilal Thug, my interpreter in Grand Gaube in 1969, who eventually became a character in the story, was then twenty-two and jobless. He had spent the previous two years writing almost a hundred letters of application to hospitals in England for an orderly's job, a common occupation of Mauritian immigrants. Prem's parents were ill and three younger brothers and a sister had been withdrawn from school for lack of money. In 1971, he finally received a letter of acceptance from a hospital in Nottingham, but he had to be there right away and lacked the $450 for airfare. I happened to be in Africa at the time, but luckily my mother opened the letter and sent him the money. In 1978, I met Prem for lunch in Wimbledon; he was married, was studying law in London and planned to return to Mauritius eventually and perhaps try to enter the government. He had managed to send all three younger brothers to Paris. As with so many people in the Third World, everything hung on a small amount of money at just the right moment.

The quotation from Mark Twain is taken from *Following the Equator,* published in 1897. Charles Darwin is quoted from *Zoology of the Voyage of the Beagle* (1840). Darwin was the naturalist for a surveying expedition which journeyed to Australasia, including Mauritius, and South America, which provided him with widely scattered evidence of biological evolution.

A peculiar problem in Mauritius, faced nowhere else, was the fishermen's constant use of the words *gogot* and *liki,* the terms for the male and female sexual organs in the local Creole *patois*. My work is based upon stenographically recorded dialogue and while I give myself considerable latitude in what is used to form a story, I do have one self-imposed rule: Never change a word of dialogue. When it comes to translating words or phrases that locally are regarded as obscene, in most villages there's no problem. No reader has ever taken offense at the Punjabis' "I rape your mother" or the Egyptians' "May your house be destroyed" and "You are a dog," fighting words in the villages themselves. In Mauritius, I simply left *gogot* and *liki* in the original Creole, while translating everything else into English. What happened, I was chagrined to learn when I last visited Mauritius, was that its leading Anglo-French newspaper, *L'Express,* had published the fishermen's story in nineteen installments without changing a word; it was the first time that four-letter words had appeared in print in Mauritius. It did clear up a mystery; for years I had been puzzled by several outraged letters from Mauritians, including one from an Australian former rector of its university, denouncing me for obscenity.

Jimmy Carter once stumbled into a rather similar cultural pitfall. In February 1978, when Egyptian President Sadat and his wife, Jihan, visited the White House, both their arrival and departure were televised live in Egypt, the first time this had been done. Now, out in its villages Egypt remains a medievally conservative Moslem country where women only threw off the veil a generation ago. Men habitually embrace, but it is taboo among the *fellaheen* to look too lingeringly at, much less physically touch, another man's wife. Suddenly there was Carter, kissing Jihan Sadat, calling her "beautiful," and, after Sadat first offered his hand, playfully shoving the Egyptian leader forward in an aw-go-on gesture to kiss Rosalynn goodbye. Egyptian television audiences were stupefied. Carter now has an interesting image along the Nile.

CHAPTER TEN: Roman Ghirshman's *Iran,* available from Penguin Books, is the standard history of Persia's rise from early Neolithic times; for many years Ghirshman led the French Archaeological Mission in Iran, which was headquartered in an old desert fortress in Shush-Daniel village. Sir Percy Sykes's *A History of Persia* is also recommended. The best account of the present resurgence of Islamic fundamentalism is G. H. Jansen's *Militant Islam* (Pan, London, 1979). The Biblical quotation describing the throne room of Darius the Great at Susa is from the Book of Esther, Chapter 1:6–7. The name, Elam, first appears in the Book of Genesis as one of the five children of Shem, who, as one of Noah's three sons, survived the Flood in the ark. The reason so little is known about Elam, compared to Sumer, according to Essat O. Negahban, who in 1971 was chairman of Tehran University's archaeological department, is because the French had "a virtual monopoly" over diggings in Iran until World War II. There are few source books on Susa and Elam in English; also still untranslated from the French were some seventy volumes written by the French Archaeological Mission in Iran. Much of Susa remains to be excavated; the foundation stones of Darius' palace were not unearthed until February 1970, just a year before my visit.

At this writing I don't know whether the Iraqi Army invading Iran by-passed or overran Shush village and the Susa ruins in its advance on the nearby Iranian towns of Dezful and Susangerd, nor do I know what has happened to the villagers or the desert Bedouins. Once again, as so often in its history, the Susiana Plain was a bloody battlefield.

The best case to explain why irrigation was probably invented in Elam and not Sumer, the Bible's Shinar, just to the west, was made by Robert M. Adams of the University of Chicago in "Agriculture and Urban Life in Early Southwestern Iran," *Science,* Vol. CXXXVI, 1962, pp. 112–13. In 1970, his findings were being confirmed by scientific hydrological and soil surveys being done for the Khuzestan agricultural development projects. The writer visited three very early village sites on the Susiana Plain; one, at Shoghamish, was more than ten thousand years old and two more, at Jafar Abad and Shush itself, were eight thousand years old. At Jafar Abad one morning the French uncovered burnt grains of eight-thousand-year-old wheat in the excavated fireplace of a village hut; apparently they'd been preserved all this time by the collapse of an earthern roof, possibly during an earthquake.

Mark Twain, after visiting the Holy Sepulchre in Jerusalem, wrote that you came away feeling that Jesus had been crucified by priests and nuns. In Shush, you got the impression that Darius the Great was a Frenchman, somebody grand like Jean Marais in *La Belle et le Bête.* Just as you enter the modest Shush museum, a huge sign reads, *"Je suis Darius, le grand roi, le roi des rois, le rois des pays, le roi sur cette terre, le fils de Hystaspe, l'Achemenide."* For anybody who'd like to try the ancient Elamite version, it goes:

^{m} u ^{m} da-ri-ia-mas-u-ish ^{m} sunki ir-sha-ir-ra ^{m} sunki ^{m} sunki ^{m} sunki da-au-ish-pe-na ^{m} sunki mu-ru-un-hi uk-ku-ra-ir-ra ^{m} mi-ish-da-ash-ba sha-akuri ^{m} ha-ak-ka-man-ru-shi. For that *"^{m}"* sound, just purse your lips and hum.

The Bedouins, who were minority Arabs in southwestern Iran, get their name from the Arabic *bedou,* or "primitive" and "of the desert" and also *beda,* "beginning"—just as *fellah* comes from *falaha,* to dig in the soil. The curse of Assurbanipal is quoted from stone slabs excavated at Nineveh and now in the Louvre, where Barek and I chanced to come across them in 1971.

CHAPTERS ELEVEN AND TWELVE: The traditional Sikh greet-ing, used (even by foreigners) with everyone you meet in the village, *"Sat Sri Akal!"* literally translates, "God is truth!" Sikhs do not cut their hair or beards (they keep it neat with a comb), carry a *kirpan* or sword (often today a small symbolic one), wear soldiers' boxer undershorts and carry their guru's charm, an iron bracelet, on their wrists. They tend to become farmers, soldiers, athletes or mechanics and are India's most nerveless taxi drivers. Since they are not noted as intellectuals but as men of action, there is a whole lore of Sikh or *Sardarji* jokes in Hindu India. The best account of what happened in the Punjabi villages during the 1947 partition is in Khushwant Singh's novel, *Train to Pakistan.*

The Sikhs are famous drinkers, but drinking is common to all villages: *cachaça* in Guapira, tequila in Huecorio, *tuba* (coconut wine) in Tulungatung, beer in Pilangsari and Vietnam, rum in Grand Gaube, *chang* (from barley or maize) among the Tibetans and home brew (watch out it doesn't blind you) in Neetil and Ghungrali. Surprisingly, the same potent stuff was also widely drunk in rural China, where it was bottled and sold at the local communes; both in taste and effect (wham) it was the same deadly stuff. Even in sternly Moslem Iran the evening came, at last, when, with smirks and secrecy, the doors and windows were secured and out came the bottle, along with oranges to kill the smell of alcohol on the breath in case, going home, you ran into an ayatollah.

A scholarly account of the *jajmani* system appears in Oscar Lewis's *Village Life in Northern India* (University of Illinois Press, 1958). Morarji Desai is quoted from an interview with me when Desai was prime minister on March 13, 1978.

CHAPTER THIRTEEN: In both my Egyptian village studies I have relied very much upon the classic *The Manners and Customs of the Modern Egyptians* by Edward William Lane (Ward Lock, London, 1890). Although first published in 1836, Lane's book has a depth, as Alan Moorehead put it, "that reaches back in time." Henry Habib Ayrout's *The Fellaheen,* first published in Cairo in 1938 but revised many times (the 1961 edition is best), is also indispensable. The best account of pharaonic Egypt is still probably James Henry Breasted's *A History of Egypt,* first published by Charles Scribner's Sons in 1905 but revised and reprinted in many editions. Interestingly, Breasted was in charge of restoring Medinet Habu, the enormous mortuary temple of Ramses III, which is just across the road from Shahhat's village of Berat. Vivian Gornick is quoted from "Metaphor for Egypt," her review of *Shahhat* in *The New York Times Book Review,* January 14, 1979.

Anwar Sadat is quoted from an interview June 10, 1976, which took place at the Egyptian president's Mediterranean beach house just outside Alexandria and lasted several hours. Sadat talked mostly about Egypt's villages and agriculture. Asked how he envisaged the long-term future of

Egypt, Sadat said, "Agro-industrial complexes. This is the future of Egypt. By the year 2000, I aim to first put new reclaimed desert land into agro-industrial complexes and then, bit by bit, the entire Nile Valley." He said he hoped to gradually shift the valley out of grain production and into high-value cash crops for export. The World Bank has since opposed the desert strategy and urged Sadat to concentrate investment instead in the Nile Valley and Delta, where improving existing cultivation and irrigation systems, it is argued, would bring quicker returns. I liked Sadat at once; this was long before he established himself as one of the world's favorite people. Few Egyptians in positions of power, or for that matter, few people who run things anywhere, have Sadat's village roots and grasp of how villagers feel and act. As he himself told me, "I am a *fellah.*"

CHAPTER FOURTEEN: The best introduction to Java's unique culture is Clifford Geertz's *The Religion of Java* (The Free Press, 1960). Geertz's later work, *Agricultural Involution: The Processes of Ecological Change in Indonesia* (University of California Press, 1963) is harder to follow, but useful in showing that, the more intensively rice is cultivated, the larger is the crop. E. F. Schumacher is quoted from *Small Is Beautiful* (Blond and Briggs, London, 1973). *The Limits to Growth,* coauthored by Donella H. Meadows, Dennis L. Meadows, Jorgen Randers and William W. Behrens III, was first published by Universe Books, 1972. I was quoted for providing "a specific example of the social side effects of the Green Revolution in an area where land is unequally distributed." It was in Pakistan in 1970; I'd interviewed a landowner with a 1,500-acre wheat farm who said that he'd cleared a profit of more than $100,000 on his previous harvest. At that time a Pakistani landless laborer made only about $100 a year. It was, of course, an extreme example.

For the information on Java's village industry, the writer is indebted to Ann Soetoro, an American social scientist married to an Indonesian; I found her to be the most authoritative source in a field where contradictory data abounds. My report prepared for the U. S. Agency for International Development Mission to Indonesia, *Village Java 1979,* which ran to 260,000 words in seventeen sections, is presently available in the AID library in Jakarta. It became so controversial, after questions were raised by Senator Daniel Inouye and others in Washington, that AID restricted all but the final summary section to its staff only.

One of the questions I am often asked about village living concerns bathing and toilet facilities. Since they reached their nadir in the Jakarta slum of Simprug, where I spent some months in 1970 living with Husen and Karniti in their two-cubicle rented shack, this may be the best place to discuss them. Simprug itself was fashionable. American Embassy diplomats had comfortable walled villas there. But our shantytown was hidden from their view by a market street and was down in a swampy, mosquito-infested, hellish hollow. Our Javanese neighbors all used a communal wooden privy, built high over a canal on stilts; you climbed up on a ladder. Privacy was sketchy but adequate as long as you were Javanese, because nobody looked. Not so for me; every time I climbed that goddamn ladder, a crowd would collect on the canal bank to watch. In desperation I took to rising each day, showering and shaving, gulping down a cup of tea, running for the bus and riding a mile downtown to the swanky Hotel Indonesia and making a rush for the men's room. The doormen got to thinking I was some eccentric *tuan* who stayed there.

It was *the* big problem everywhere. One of the crucial technological gaps between villagers and ourselves is the use of toilets—and toilet paper; two-thirds of mankind still just splashes on water. I did find toilet paper in Chinese village privies, although possibly put there with "our visiting foreign friends" in mind. Egypt has a particularly exotic kind of toilet where you turn a handle and a jet of cold water gets squirted up at you from inside the toilet—quite a surprise if you're not expecting it.

As mentioned in Chapter 16, in Ghungrali you got up at 4 A.M. to the sound of first prayers over the village temple loudspeaker. Then, huddled anonymously in a blanket, covering head and all, you walked about a quarter of a mile to a wheat field with a conveniently located irrigation ditch. Then you returned to the barn, still bundled up and greeting no one whom you might pass, and slept for a couple of hours more until Charan's old father woke up and began harumphing and fussing for his morning tea. Punjabi farmers, no matter how many tractors and combines they buy, rarely install an indoor toilet unless their children go to college and come home and demand it. Every visit to Ghungrali I have kept hoping that Charan has finally broken down and installed some modern plumbing; so far it's always been back to the predawn sorties. Only in three of the village houses where I've stayed was there anything resembling a bathroom. In Iran it was across an open courtyard and the lady of the house, whose unveiled face I never did see, was forever going by, head averted, as we met in wordless encounters going to and from. In Pilangsari, after a few ventures running to the Cimanuk River, I'd make Husen rig up a temporary privy of dug-out pit, bamboo and palm. In most villages the routine was to wander off, flashlight in hand, looking for an appropriate bush or a clump of trees, need overcoming fear of snakes, spiders and rats. The where-to-go dilemma occurs in all villages, the biggest cultural problem for your host as much as for you, only for him it's the where-will-*he*-go dilemma.

CHAPTER FIFTEEN: No one can safely write about villages without some familiarity with the works of Robert Redfield, whose disarming style

and penetrating thinking contrast with what is found in many anthropological works; I have read and taken quotations or described his ideas
from *Tepoztlán—A Mexican Village;* his introduction to the work of a student, Horace Miner, in *St. Denis, a French Canadian Parish* (University
of Chicago Press, 1939); *The Folk Culture of Yucatan* (University of
Chicago Press, 1941); *A Village That Chose Progress: Chan Kom Revisited* (University of Chicago Press, 1950); *The Primitive World and its
Transformations* (Cornell University Press, 1953); *The Little Community: Viewpoints for the Study of a Human Whole* (University of Chicago
Press, 1955); and, finally, his very short but most important book, *Peasant
Society and Culture* (University of Chicago Press, 1956). His response to
the criticism of Oscar Lewis, which runs through his last three books, was
first made in 1952 when, in a lecture at Cornell University, he accused
Lewis of lacking "humanity" and of taking "his own values" to Tepoztlán.

The work of Oscar Lewis is, of course, much more familiar. Quotations
have been taken from the previously mentioned *Life in a Mexican Village
—Tepoztlán Restudied; Five Families: Mexican Case Studies in the Culture of Poverty; The Children of Sanchez; Autobiography of a Mexican Family* (Random House, 1963); *The Study of Slum Culture—
Backgrounds for La Vida* (Random House, 1968); and *Pedro Martinez:
A Mexican Peasant and His Family* (Random House, 1964), from which
came (pp. xxx–xxxii) the quotation on classic peasant values. The best
criticism of Lewis's "culture of poverty" hypothesis can be found in *The
Culture of Poverty: A Critique,* edited by Eleanor Burke Leacock (Simon & Schuster, 1971) and Charles A. Valentine's *Culture and Poverty:
Critique and Counter-Proposals* (University of Chicago Press, 1968).

The third and only survivor in 1981 of the three American anthropologists who pioneered village studies in Mexico, Dr. George M. Foster of
the University of California, has been prolific, but is best known for his
original study, *Empire's Children: The People of Tzintzuntzan* (Imprenta
Nuevo Mundo, Mexico City, 1948). Confirmation of Foster's findings on
Tarascan Indian culture is found in Ralph L. Beale's *Chevan: A Sierra
Tarascan Village* (Smithsonian Institution, Institute of Social Anthropology, 1946). Beale's book includes a good deal on Mexican witchcraft,
which I found bore startling resemblances to sorcery in Egypt. Foster's
comments on the Redfield-Lewis debate are taken from his foreword to my
Shahhat: an Egyptian (Syracuse University Press, 1979; Avon Books
edition, 1980).

Mrs. Ruth Lewis is quoted from a 1977 letter to the author. She was
then completing a series of books based on her husband's last, and evidently harrowing, project in Castro's Cuba in 1969–70. Reviewing the first
to be published, *Four Men: Living the Revolution—An Oral History of*

Contemporary Cuba (University of Illinois Press, 1977), John Womack, Jr., wrote in *The New York Review of Books* that the literary quality was so similar to the earlier Lewis books "admirers of Oscar Lewis may suspect that the art in the earlier books could have come in good part from his wife." My own feeling is that Mrs. Lewis, a psychologist, who did many of the family psychological tests in Tepoztlán for her husband, may have influenced him to go so deeply into family life. Family life has a way of being more tragic than social life, which in villages has more elements of comedy. Mrs. Lewis did give the Cuban portraits happy endings, something Lewis himself did not do in his Mexican or Puerto Rican studies.

Ruth Lewis did supply me with the name of a friend in Tepoztlán, Sarah Rojas. But when I visited her, Mrs. Rojas told me Sanchez was dead and that she had gone to his funeral in Mexico City. After repeated visits—I began to feel like Lew Archer—this turned out to be some other man.

Dr. Foster, in a 1980 conversation with the writer, commented, "Oscar Lewis was an artist, not a social scientist, in his later work." Lewis spent relatively little time in villages. He was in Tepoztlán for a year in 1943–44, made several shorter revisits, and spent some time in an Indian village on the outskirts of Delhi when he was a Ford Foundation consultant from October 1952 to June 1953, although most of his research, as he points out, was done by a team of Indian students. The book that resulted, *Village Life in Northern India* (University of Illinois Press, 1958), was much more sympathetic to the villagers than his Mexico studies. In his youth he had spent time with Blackfoot Indians. In Puerto Rico and Cuba, though, he focused, as he came to in Mexico, upon city slum dwellers with Latin cultures, the prime area of his interest and insights.

Margaret Mead is quoted from the earlier-mentioned *Village Viability in Contemporary Society;* Foster's concepts of "limited good" and "contractual ties" have been taken from chapters on each of them in *Peasant Society; A Reader,* edited by Jack M. Potter, May N. Diaz and George M. Foster (Little, Brown, 1967). Among sources cited in support of Redfield's concept of a universal peasant view of what constitutes "a good life" were Oscar Handlin, *The Uprooted* (Little, Brown, 1951), p. 7; Malcolm Darling, *Rusticus Loquitur: The Old Light and the New in a Punjab Village* (Oxford University Press, 1930), p. *x;* René Porak, *Un village de France: Psycho-physiologie du paysan* (G. Doin & Cie, Paris, 1943); Irwin T. Sanders, *Balkan Village* (University of Kentucky Press, 1949), p. 147; J. Weuleresse, *Paysans de Syrie et du Proche-Orient* (Paris, 1946), p. 173; Ayrout's *The Fellaheen;* Hamed Ammar, *Growing Up in an Egyptian Village, Silwa, Province of Aswan* (Routledge & Kegan Paul, Ltd., London, 1954), pp. 35–39; and E. K. L. Francis, "The Personality Type of the Peasant According to Hesiod's *Works and Days:* A

Culture Case Study," *Rural Sociology*, X, No. 3, September 1945, p. 278.

The best analysis of what went wrong with the Johnson administration's "war on poverty" was in "The Neurotic Trillionaire," a survey of America written for *The Economist* by its deputy editor, Norman Macrae, in 1969. Remarkably, since it reflected like thinking, Daniel P. Moynihan had not seen the article until I showed it to him. Moynihan landed his White House job after his book, *Maximum Feasible Misunderstanding*—the title is a play on the OEO principle of "maximum feasible participation"—caught Richard Nixon's eye. After I wrote a story reporting that Moynihan's proposed reforms were aimed to help black families "disperse" into the larger society, Moynihan phoned and said, "My God, don't use that word, 'disperse.' It sounds like concentration camps."

CHAPTER SIXTEEN: Richard and Mary Leakey, Donald Johanson, Timothy White and others continue to shed more light on man's emergence from his immediate primate family. Information on Neolithic man in Central Asia was supplied by Louis Dupree, who has done archaeological studies in northern Afghanistan. Quotations are taken from the Book of Genesis, 11:2; A. L. Kroeber's *Anthropology* (Harcourt, Brace, 1948); Redfield's *The Little Community: Peasants* by Eric Wolf (Prentice-Hall, 1966); *The Lessons of History* (Simon & Schuster, 1978), by Will and Ariel Durant; Ayrout's *The Fellaheen;* and William McNeill's *The Rise of the West* (New American Library, 1964), the authoritative account of the role of agricultural change in history. The *Time* cover story, "The New U.S. Farmer," appeared November 6, 1978.

Since so many varied kinds of diet were mentioned in this chapter, readers may want to know if illness was a problem. I feared it would be; in 1960–62, while teaching journalism at the University of Nagpur in India, I had amoebic dysentery twice, bacillary dysentery, trachoma and pyelonephritis, and some years later I had hepatitis in Laos. So when I set out to live in villages, I feared the worst. As it happened, in eleven years of village stays, I was seriously ill only twice and both times I was not in villages. In Khartoum I contracted hepatitis a second time from an infected needle while undergoing a series of anti-rabies injections in a British-run clinic. In 1979, in Jakarta, where I was given what seemed a most luxurious American Embassy apartment, I came down with amoebic dysentery. Perhaps I've just been lucky, but I've never been really ill from anything I could blame on the villages.

You are cautioned never to drink unboiled water in the Third World; harvesting wheat in hot, arid climates as in the Punjab or Upper Egypt, you'd soon dehydrate if you didn't. While working in the fields I drank large amounts of well water, carried out in pails and drunk from a common dipper. In Egypt I soon grew accustomed to sharing tea glasses, cigarettes, spoons and even Ommohamed's water pipe with other family members. Husen once even offered me his toothbrush.

In all the villages, a good interpreter could make all the difference. You have to be extremely fluent in a language to note down dialogue as it is spoken. I found it made little difference in the villages whether I knew the local language, as I did in India, or not a word when I arrived, as in Egypt. You just plunge in and almost always you'll find an army veteran, a schoolteacher, a student or even a habitual moviegoer who will know some English. The only country where this didn't happen was Brazil; almost nobody speaks anything but Portuguese in this extremely insular land; I had to drop everything and study it for six weeks.

Ideally, an interpreter is one of the villagers. In my experience, city-bred journalists, professors, students or even professional interpreters tend not to work out too well; they often have hangups about village life and lack sufficient empathy. Sherif, who came with me when I lived with the Bedouins, had picked up some English while working for an American construction crew. My two best interpreters were self-educated. Krishanjit Singh, a Punjabi Sikh aspiring novelist, had managed to survive by translating the works of Tolstoy, Dickens and Henry James and had a splendid ear for dialogue. Nubi el Hagag, who worked in a surveyor's office in Luxor, could translate Arabic, so Egyptians tell me, without losing its essential flavor. He'd picked up his English as a youth, guiding tourists.

CHAPTER SEVENTEEN: The writer has condensed and paraphrased Gideon Sjoberg's description of "the pre-industrial city" from his "The Pre-industrial City," *The American Journal of Sociology,* Vol. LX, No. 5, March 1955, pp. 438–45. Janet Abu-Lughod was the first, as far as I know, to call attention to the way peasants keep their village culture in a city in "Migrant Adjustments to City Life: The Egyptian Case," *The American Journal of Sociology,* Vol. 27, No. 1, July 1961, pp. 22–32.

Arnold Toynbee's concepts of "Herodianism" and "Zealotism" are from his *A Study of History* (Oxford University Press, 12 volumes, 1934–61). Redfield's theory of "orthogenetic and heterogenetic transformation" was put forward in an article co-authored with Milton B. Singer, "The cultural role of cities," *Economic Development and Social Change,* Vol. 3, 1954. Redfield's perhaps most famous concept of "little tradition and great tradition" is taken from his *Peasant Society and Culture.*

CHAPTER EIGHTEEN: The Javanese word, *banci,* was formerly spelled *bantji,* just as *becak* was *betjak.* (Because so many Javanese, including Husen, still use the old *betjak,* I've not used the new form in the text. Many, if not most, Indonesians still use the old spelling in their own names.) The old Dutch spelling, abandoned in the 1970s, came closer to the true pronunciation. It should also be noted that the western third of Java, known as Sunda (as in the Sunda Straits), is inhabited by a people who, with a slightly different culture and language, prefer to be called Sundanese, not Javanese. Reference also has been made to Bali, where the writer spent a month in a village in 1973; I concluded that while Bali remains one of the most hauntingly beautiful islands on earth, Java's culture is more profound. Thomas Robert Malthus is quoted from his 1798 treatise, *An Essay on the Principle of Population,* and the *Al Azhar* Koranic interpretation I have taken from "The Feminist Revolution of Jihan Sadat," by Susan and Martin Tolchin, *The New York Times Magazine,* March 16, 1980.

CHAPTER NINETEEN: For the analysis that the rediscovery of belief in Satan may lead people to accept good as something equally objective, and his ready agreement to use it here, I am indebted to Brian Beedham, Foreign Editor of *The Economist.*

Balsara, Nagpur's gifted soothsayer, first came to my attention in the early 1960s when he told the fortune of Yuri Gagarin, the first man in space, during a visit by the astronaut to New Delhi. Nikita Khrushchev was so impressed by what Balsara told Gagarin, he invited Balsara to Moscow. Although Balsara did the horoscopes and palm readings of many eminent Indians, Jawaharlal Nehru steadfastly refused him, on the grounds that all pretense at precognition was "nonsense."

CHAPTER TWENTY: Max Weber in *The Sociology of Religion* (originally published in Germany in 1922 as *"Religionssoziologie"* from *Wirtschaft und Gesellschaft*) gives the best account of the villager's historical role in religion that I was able to find. Quotations are taken from the 1964 Beacon Press edition, pp. 46–59 and 80–85. Quotations have also been taken from Arnold Toynbee's *Civilization on Trial* (Oxford University Press, 1946), Reinhold Niebuhr's *The Nature and Destiny of Man* (Charles Scribner's Sons, 1953), D. Howard Smith's *Confucius* (Paladin, London, 1974), McNeill's *The Rise of the West,* the Gospel of St. Mark and Pauline Kael's *Reeling.* Macrae is again quoted from *The Economist,* this time from a survey, "America's third century," October 25, 1975. Roderick MacFarquhar's penetrating analysis of the cultural role Confucianism is playing in East Asia's economic rise appears in "The post-Confucian challenge," *The Economist,* February 9, 1980, pp. 67–72. Will and Ariel Durant's theory on the rise and fall of civilizations has been taken from their *The Lessons of History.*

CHAPTER TWENTY-ONE: Henri Bergson is quoted from *L'Évolution créatrice,* originally published in Paris in 1907 and translated as *Crea-*

tive Evolution in 1911 (the quotation is taken from p. 271). The thinking of Aristotle is drawn from his *Organon, Ethics, Politics, Aesthetics, Metaphysics* and *Poetics*. John Fowles is quoted from *Daniel Martin* (Little, 1977), which has superb descriptions of Upper Egypt and the Nile. Quotations have also been taken from Agatha Christie's introduction to *The Body in the Library* (William Collins, London, 1942) and from James Joyce's *Ulysses,* originally published in Paris in 1922, from the 1977 Penguin Books edition, p. 213.

CHAPTER TWENTY-TWO: The best account of villager participation in Marxist-Leninist revolutions, from the anthropologist's point of view, can be found in Eric R. Wolf's *Peasant Wars of the Twentieth Century* (Faber and Faber, London, 1971) and his "On Peasant Rebellions," *International Social Science Journal,* Vol. 21, 1969. In his *Peasant Society and Culture,* Redfield wrote, "In every part of the world, generally speaking, peasantry have been a conservative factor in social change, a brake on revolution, a check on that disintegration of local society which often comes with rapid technological change." Oscar Lewis challenged this in *Pedro Martinez,* saying, "It has commonly been held that peasants are essentially a stabilizing and conservative force in human history. The events of our own century, however, throw some doubt on this comfortable stereotype." Again I agree with Redfield.

Frantz Fanon is quoted from *The Wretched of the Earth* (Penguin, 1967, original French publication in 1961), David Mitrany from *Marx Against the Peasant* (University of North Carolina Press, 1951), Thomas Jefferson from his *Notes on the State of Virginia* (1787) and Maxim Gorky from *On the Russian Peasantry* (Ladyzhnikov, Moscow, 1922). The quotations from Marx and Lenin have been taken from their collected works. The figure of $500 billion invested in agriculture by the Russians since 1965 (converted from 340 billion rubles) is from *The Economist,* December 29, 1979, p. 31. It is interesting that, according to Leo Tolstoy's biographer, Henri Troyat, the great novelist's most noble character, Platon Karatayev, came into being only in the third draft of Book IV of *War and Peace.*

For the sketchy synopsis of the Chinese revolution I have read and taken information from Jack M. Potter's paper in the previously mentioned *Peasant Society,* Mao Tse-tung's *Selected Works,* Wolf's *Peasants, Red China: An Asian View,* by Sripati Chandra Sekhar (Praeger, 1961), *The Commune in Retreat,* by T. A. Hsia (University of California Press, 1964), *The Tragedy of the Chinese Revolution,* by Harold R. Isaacs (Stanford University Press, 1951), Stanley Karnow's *Mao and China* (Viking, 1972), John King Fairbank's article, "The New China and the American Connection," *Foreign Affairs,* Vol. 51, No. 1, October 1972, and an anthropological view, "Continuities and Discontinuities in China: The Natural Village and the Production Brigade," by Molly G. Schuchat and James D. Jordan, from the previously mentioned *Village Viability in Contemporary Society*. Particularly valuable have been two surveys in *The Economist*, "Three people's China," by Emily MacFarquhar, Brian Beedham and Norman Macrae, December 31, 1977, and "China in the 1980s," by Emily MacFarquhar, Brian Beedham and Alice Barrass, December 29, 1979. As Beedham memorably put it in the second survey, "Leninism fossilizes. Maoism anarchises. Can a communist avoid either, without falling into the other?"

C. P. Snow is quoted from a lecture at Westminster College, Fulton, Missouri, November 12, 1968, and Paul Ehrlich from *The Population Bomb* (Ballantine, 1968).

Norman Borlaug's remarks have been taken from a series of lengthy interviews by the writer in 1977 and 1980 in Mexico. Both times he had just returned from China. I am also indebted to him for keeping me informed, based on his world travels, of agricultural developments in Russia, India, Mexico and elsewhere. A coincidence is that my mother and grandparents lived for several years just a few miles from Borlaug's native town of Cresco, Iowa. He grew up during the Depression on a fifty-six-acre farm, only half of it cropland.

Zulfikar Ali Bhutto has been quoted from a 1974 interview with me. Jawaharlal Nehru's remarks come from the last interview I had with him, in March 1964, just two months before his death. The already gravely ill Indian leader had just come from a rehearsal of a Ramayana ballet and seemed very relaxed; he offered me a cigarette (Nehru smoked, but never in public, so few Indians knew he did) and I noticed as I took it that his hands were paler than mine. I asked what he felt had been his greatest achievement. Nehru replied it was the political liberation of India's women. His greatest fear for the future? "Fascism," he said instantly. "By this I mean revolutionary forces trying to achieve their ends by violent or subversive means. By creating an atmosphere of violence and conflict, such forces may arise from any side. They can be communist, social fascism led by big industrialists or Hindu fascism."

Much of this interview concerned the conflict over the Vale of Kashmir, which Nehru, "facing God," as Chester Bowles put it, tried in his dying months to settle. An account of this, which I wrote for *Reporter* magazine, was later quoted by Gunnar Myrdal in his *Asian Drama* (putting me permanently, it seems, in a bad light with Indira Gandhi, who opposed her father's attempt to reach a compromise Kashmir settlement with Pakistan). Jawaharlal Nehru was all too human, but despite such weaknesses as vanity and little real knowledge of Indian village life, he conveyed an impression of greatness as few men do. Nehru had a deep and authentic belief in democracy; this was perhaps his noblest characteristic.

An interview with Morarji Desai in 1978, when he was Prime Minister, was quite different. Desai, whom I'd been interviewing since the early 1960s, was then eighty-three; I felt a bit like I was being called on the carpet by a crotchety grandfather. When I asked him about the future, he demanded, "Do you want me to be a visionary? Who knows what will happen? Are you sure you will survive the next five minutes? Yet you bother about it?" But when I switched to the past, he snapped, "Why are you interested in postmortem? Why create unnecessary controversies?" When it came to agricultural policy, however, Desai was very sound. I left thinking that he had turned out to be a more decent man and a better Prime Minister of India than I ever would have imagined. Nehru, in his final years, had projected an authoritarian, anti-Moslem image for Desai; when he finally came to power, Desai was neither. So many years were lost when the Indian villagers, especially, could have benefited from his pragmatic leadership. This was one of those episodes in a reporter's career that teach you never to judge people too quickly, if at all.

CHAPTER TWENTY-THREE: Quotations have been taken from Richard Adams's *Watership Down* (Macmillan, 1975), Pauline Kael's *Going Steady* (Warner Books, 1979), Barbara Tuchman's *A Distant Mirror: The Calamitous 14th Century* (Alfred A. Knopf, 1978), Alfred Lord Tennyson's 1860 poem *Tithonus,* Samuel Johnson's paper on Westminster Abbey (*The Spectator,* No. 26, 1711), Tolstoy's *War and Peace* (Vol. II, Book IX, Chapter I), and the line from one of Don Marquis's poems from *The Oxford Book of American Light Verse* (Oxford University Press, 1979). Lines have been quoted from Thornton Wilder's *Our Town,* first performed in 1938, and Henrik Ibsen's *Peer Gynt,* 1887.

The remarks of Howard W. Hjort, the Department of Agriculture's Director of Economics, Policy Analysis and Budget, have been taken from an interview with me in June 1980, although earlier talks in 1979 and 1980 covered much the same ground. Lester Brown is quoted from conversation in June 1980; although Brown and I amicably disagree on many aspects of the world food problem, we have met regularly to exchange ideas since 1968, the year I began to prepare for village reporting.

A question sometimes asked by members of my large, close-knit family is, "Don't you ever get lonely?" It always strikes me oddly, because in villages loneliness, both as an idea and a reality, doesn't exist; solitude becomes a luxury. You do experience, as Margaret Mead understood so well, a varying amount of culture shock. Berat, Huecorio and Grand Gaube all have small country inns. The amenities aren't much better than in the village homes, but it's a real pleasure to treat your culture shock with somebody like Agatha Christie in the evenings—Miss Marple, vicarage, cozy pub and all. In 1971–72, after my first two years of village living, I spent a final year with the Washington *Star,* mostly writing profiles about how Americans live. ("Use the same techniques as you do in villages," my editor told me.) What struck me about the twenty or so families and individuals whom I lived with and wrote about was how much of every day, compared to villagers, they spent physically alone (reading or watching TV). The same was true of an Iowa farmer I once wrote about; between the noise of machinery in the fields and television in the home, there was much less dialogue than in a peasant village.

The full notes from the village stays, including all the dialogue, are available at the Mass Communications History Center at the State Historical Society of Wisconsin, in Madison.

To young reporters, whom I'd like to encourage to try village reporting, my advice is to spend five or six years doing conventional foreign correspondence first, preferably in some crisis spot, to avoid getting hangups about missing out on the big time later on. This done—now voyager.

INDEX

Abadan, Iran, 107
Abel and Cain, 210
Abominable Snowman, 48
Abortion, 290
Abraham (biblical patriarch), 210,
    234, 263, 274
Abu-Lughod, Janet, 226, 361 n
Acapulco, Mexico, 81
Adam (biblical figure), 274
Adams, Richard, 328, 365 n
Adams, Robert M., 354 n
Adi-Buddha (God-like spirit), 47
Aesthetics (Aristotle), 363 n
Aete aboriginals, 51
Afghanistan, 327
    Russian occupation of, 273–74
Agency for International Develop-
    ment (AID), 135, 174, 356 n
Age of Pericles, 99
Agricultural Development Council,
    174
*Agricultural Involution: The
    Processes of Ecological
    Change in Indonesia*
    (Geertz), 356 n
Agricultural moral code, 342–43
Agriculture, 9, 11, 71, 212–24, 290
    dry-land, rain-fed, 212–13
    economy and, 212–19
        daily routine, 215–17
        living in groups, 213–15
        meals, 217–19
        shrinking land, 213
        technology and modernization,
        219–24
    types of agriculture, 212–13
    women, 216–17

hoe cultivation, 209–10
irrigated, 213, 323–24
slash-and-burn, 212
See also Revolutionary change
Ahmed, Sultan, 33, 39–41
Ahmed Ibrahim (magistrate), 37–38
Aid to Dependent Children, 201
Alamo Boys (hoodlum gang), 236
Al Azhar University, 33, 226, 247,
    336
Alcoholic beverages, 154–55, 355 n
Alexander the Great, 99, 107, 262
Alexandria, Egypt, 147
Algerian Revolution, 298, 299
Al Husein Mosque, 226
Ali, Mohammed, 144, 147
Alier, Abel, 224
Allen, Woody, 8, 11, 347 n
All Saints Bay, 4
Ambler, Eric, 294
American Journal of Sociology, The,
    361 n
American Nazi Party, 68
Ammar, Hamed, 359 n
Anatolia Mountains, 210
Andaman Islanders, The (Radcliffe-
    Brown), 195–96
Anderson, Glenn, 312
Angola, 316
Animism, 164, 253
Annapurna Range, 49
Anthony, St., 14
Anthropological Society of Washing-
    ton, 10
Anthropology, 195
    and journalism, 203–5
    and villages, 189–208, 357–60 n

Anthropology (Kroeber), 360 n
Apparition of the dead, 259
Apparition of the living, 255–56
Arabian Nights, The (trans. Burton), 242
Arab-Israel War of 1967, 145
Argentina, 314, 331
Argonauts of the Western Pacific, The (Malinowski), 195–96
Aristotle, 197, 245, 290–91, 319, 363 n
Aro or *Kuni* (intermediaries with God), 32, 41
Asian Drama (Myrdal), 364 n
Assurbanipal, King, 100–1, 354 n
Assyria (ancient), 98
Aswan Dam, 143, 147–48, 219, 331
Atlas Mountains, 18
Austen, Jane, 293
Australia, 314, 323, 331
Austro-Hungarian Empire, 212
Awami League, 73
Ayrout, Henry Habib, 214, 355 n, 359 n, 360 n
Aztec Indians, 78, 79, 82, 211

Bab al-Sharia district (Cairo, Egypt), 213, 226
Babylon (ancient), 98, 99, 231, 253
Back-to-the-country movement (U.S.), 9–10
Bacon, Francis, 251
Baggara (or cattle-raising) Arabs, 38
Bahia State (Brazil), 4, 12–13, 347 n; *See also* Guapira Village; Salvador, Brazil
Bai Dinh district (Vietnam), 63
Baisaki "April 13" (Sikh New Year), 127
Baker, Sir Samuel, 222
Bakhtiari tribe, 104
Baksheesh, 152
Balafi Village, 259–60
Bali, 162, 246, 324, 362 n
Balkan Village (Sanders), 359 n

Balsara, Dadi, 254, 362 n
Baluchi tribe, 123
Bancis (of Java), 240–41, 361–62 n
Bangba Chugdso, Tibet, 42
Bangkok, Thailand, 228, 235
Bangladesh, 71–77, 148, 213, 235, 249, 274, 317, 350–51 n
  dacoits (bandits), 72–74
  food production, 76
  landholdings, 71
  revolutionary change and, 321, 322
  See also names of villages
Barbeiro cockroach, 14
Bargaining, market, 214, 225
Barrass, Alice, 364 n
Bassac River, 65
Batage sticks, 90
Bathing and toilet facilities, 356–57 n
Beagle (ship), 91
Beale, Ralph L., 358 n
Beatles, 9
Bedouins, 100, 101, 102, 108, 279–80, 354 n
Beedham, Brian, 362 n, 364 n
Behrens, William W., III, 356 n
Beijing, *see* Peking, China
Beirut, Lebanon, 230
Bellow, Saul, 92
Benedict, Pat, 220–21
Benediktov, I. A., 303
Berat Village, 145, 150–59, 160–61, 212, 214, 216, 217, 242–43, 256, 274, 280, 321, 324, 365 n
Bergman, Ingmar, 92
Bergson, Henri, 287–88, 291, 362–63 n
Betjak drivers, 162–63, 165, 167, 168–69, 170–71, 173
  Jakarta's ban against, 165–66
Bhadson Village, 113–19, 321
Bhati phantoms, 36–37
Bhutan, 44, 45
Bhutto, Zulfikar Ali, 314, 364 n
Bible, 15, 59, 99, 211, 231, 254, 261
Bihari militiamen, 73
Bihar Village, 285, 286

Binh Thuan Province (Vietnam), 63
Birendra, King, 45
Birth control, 290, 298, 322, 323, 325
Blackfoot Indians, 359 n
Black magic, 252
Black Orpheus (Cocteau), 347 n
Boas, Franz, 195
Boat people, 64, 350 n
Bock, Philip, 80
Boeotian villagers (ancient Greece), 199–200
Bogor, Indonesia, 174
Bojong, Indonesia, 181
Bombay, India, 176, 228, 230, 233, 235, 322
Bongkaren (prostitution area), 236–37
Booker, Christopher, 9, 347 n
Book of Esther, 99
Book of Genesis, 99, 209, 210
Borlaug, Norman E., 133–34, 177, 221, 297, 303, 306, 309, 310, 311–12, 314, 315, 316, 327, 333, 364 n
Bowles, Chester, 364 n
Brahmaputra River, 44, 71, 133, 316
Brandão Vilela, Dom Avelar, Cardinal of Salvador, 6–7
Brazil, 3–15, 46, 134, 172, 198, 217, 299, 347 n
  revolutionary change and, 333
  See also names of villages
Breasted, James Henry, 355 n
Brodie, Fawn M., 241–42
Brontë Sisters, 293
Brown, Lester, 315, 330
Brunei, 51
Bucha, M. K. B., 311
Buck, Pearl, 206
Buddha, 46, 234, 264, 308
Buddhism, 46–47, 179, 231, 253, 274, 277
Buenos Aires, Argentina, 233
Burma, 333
Burton, Mrs. Isabel, 242
Bustamente, Jorge, 83

Butch Cassidy and the Sundance Kid (motion picture), 78

Caesar, Julius, 294
Caesar & Christ: A History of Roman Civilization from Its Beginning to A.D. 337 (Durant), 12, 348 n
Café Bouchaib (Casablanca), 20
Café Brasserie du Maghreb (Casablanca), 20
Cairo, Egypt, 33, 143, 144, 145, 147, 150, 158, 176, 213, 215, 219, 226–27, 229, 230, 232, 233, 235–36, 255, 336
  population, 226
  villagers in, 226–27
Calcutta, India, 176, 213, 228, 230, 233, 235, 284–88, 295, 305
  élan vital, 287–88
  housing, 285
  population, 284
  rickshaw pullers, 285, 286
California Farm Bureau, 103
Calvin, John, 283
Cambodia, 308, 330, 333
Cambyses, King, 100
Cam Ne, Vietnam, 350 n
Canada, 315
Candomblé practices, 12
Can Tho, Vietnam, 65
Canton, China, 305
Carnaval in Brazil, 3–7, 11, 12, 15, 35, 299, 347 n
  compared to Saturnalia (of ancient Rome), 12–13
  sex, 5–6
  songs, 5, 15, 347 n
  trios, 4, 5, 6, 13
Carter, Jimmy, 8, 176, 353 n
Carter, Rosalynn, 353 n
Carthage (ancient), 99
Casablanca, Morocco, 16–17, 20–22, 27–28, 348 n
  douar, 18, 19, 348 n
  medina, 16–17, 18, 348 n

Caste system (India), 120–21,
    125–27, 203, 277
    economic basis (in Ghungrali),
        126–27
    See also names of castes
Castro, Fidel, 358 n
Catullus, 294
Central Asian Plateau, 210
Central Intelligence Agency
    (C.I.A.), 45
Chagas disease, 14
Chamar (leather worker) caste,
    125–26
Chandler, Raymond, 8, 347 n
Chandler, Robert, 350–51 n
Change, see Revolutionary change
Chang Tang Plateau, 42
Charpoys (string cots), 110–11
Chekhov, Anton, 277, 289–90, 291,
    293, 304
Chemical fertilizers, first use of, 220
Cheops Pyramid, 147
Chevan: A Sierra Tarascan Village
    (Beale), 358 n
Child adoption, 225
Children of Sanchez, The: Autobi-
    ography of a Mexican Family
    (Lewis), 191, 192–94, 358 n
China, 105, 134, 197, 211, 213, 214,
    219, 242, 266, 271, 273,
    296–320
    agricultural priorities, 312–14
    communes, 306, 319
    communist revolution, 296, 298,
        305, 363–64 n
    Confucianism, 297
    Cultural Revolution, 305, 318
    Great Leap Forward, 297, 305–6
    Green Revolution, 302, 306–7,
        309–17
    Maoism, 283, 305, 306, 317–20,
        364 n
    population, 296, 317
    "production brigades," 306
    Red Guards, 296, 318
    revolutionary change and, 321,
        322, 323, 324–25, 326, 328,
        329, 333
    wheat production (1977–79), 296
    See also names of cities; villages
Chinese lunar year, 319
Cho Dong Kok Village, 266–67, 272,
    321
Chogha Zanbil, Iran, 100
Chou En-lai, 231, 333
Christie, Agatha, 294, 363 n, 366 n
Chun Doo Hwan, General, 271, 272
Cimanuk River, 164, 357 n
Citadel, 147
Cities, villagers and, 225–34, 361 n
    cultural gap, 231–32
    ex-colonial port cities, 229
    freedom, 233
    immigrants (in Cairo), 226–27
    Islamic, Hindu, or Far Eastern
        cities, 228–29
    "little tradition" culture, 230, 232
    orthogenetic and heterogenetic
        transformation, 229–31
    pre-industrial city, 225–26, 228,
        229, 361 n
    urbanization (in the West),
        228–29
Civilization on Trial (Toynbee),
    362 n
Civilizations, decline of, 211
Clairvoyance, 254–55
Climaco, Caesar, 51
Club of Rome, 175
Cocteau, Jean, 347 n
Colbert, Claudette, 100
Collier, Dr. William, 174
Columbus, Christopher, 189, 265
COMECON (Soviet-bloc common
    market), 303
Commune in Retreat, The (Hsia),
    363 n
Communism, 291, 333; See also
    Union of Soviet Socialist Re-
    publics (U.S.S.R.)
Concubinage, 225

Confucianism, 231, 266–72, 273, 276, 297, 321, 333–34
Confucius, 267, 270, 271, 273, 283
Confucius (Smith), 362 n
Cong Hoa Hospital (Saigon), 61, 63
Congo River, 316
Consultative Group on International Agricultural Research, 326
"Continuities and Discontinuities in China: The Natural Village and the Production Brigade" (Schuchat and Jordan), 364 n
Contraception, 290, 298, 322, 323, 325
Cook, Captain James, 195
Cornelius, Wayne, 83
Cortés, Martin, 79
Creation story, 47
Creative Evolution (Bergson), 362–63 n
Creoles, 93, 95
    patois, 89, 352–53 n
Crewes, Laura Hope, 293
Critchfield, Nathaniel, 293
Cronkite, Walter, 206
Crop rotation, first use of, 220
Cuba, 189, 359 n
    revolutionary change and, 325, 326
Cuban Revolution, 299
Cultural Revolution (China), 305, 318
Culture
    compared to lifestyle, 11
    practice of, 10–12
    See also names of cultures; villages
Culture and Poverty: Critique and Counter-Proposals (Valentine), 358 n
Culture of Narcissism, The (Lasch), 347 n
Culture of Poverty, The: A Critique (ed. Leacock), 358 n
"Culture of poverty" hypothesis, 200–1

Dacca, Pakistan, 76–77, 235, 351 n
Dacoits (bandits), 72–74
Daiyi, Sheikha (sorceress), 256, 257
Dalai Lama, 42, 44, 45
Dalang (shadow play), 164–65, 172, 173, 180
Damietta, Egypt, 145
Danang, Vietnam, 66, 69, 350 n
Daniel (prophet), 99, 100
Daniel Martin (Fowles), 290, 363 n
Darius the Great, 98, 99, 107, 353 n, 354 n
Darling, Malcolm, 199, 359 n
Darwin, Charles, 91, 251, 352 n
Dead Sea scrolls, 281
Decline of the West (Spengler), 265
Defeating Communist Insurgency (Thompson), 349 n
Delhi, India, 215, 226, 230, 285, 311
De Mille, Cecil B., 100
Demonology, 251–52
Desai, Morarji, 133, 135, 315, 347 n, 355 n
Devil Drives, The: A Life of Sir Richard Burton (Brodie), 241–42
Dez Dam, Iran, 103
Dezful, Iran, 97, 99, 354 n
Dharmasala, India, 45
Diaz, May N., 359 n
Dickens, Charles, 293, 361 n
Dilling, Sudan, 29, 32, 33, 37, 38, 348 n
Dinka tribe, 210, 221–24
Disney, Walt, 36, 334
Distant Mirror, A: The Calamitous 14th Century (Tuchman), 365 n
Divorce, 245–46, 247–48, 274, 281
Djanggos (hoodlum gang), 236, 238
Djinn beliefs, 33, 257, 259
Dobu people, 196
Dolpo, Nepal, 43, 44, 48
Dorpatan, Tibetan refugee camp at, 43
Dostoevsky, Fyodor, 293, 294
Douar, 18, 19, 348 n

Dres (or ghosts of men), 48
Drinking, *see* Alcoholic beverages
Dry-land, rain-fed agriculture, 212–13
Dsalung (lamasery), 42
Duan, Le, 69, 206, 349–50 n
Dukun (or sorcerer), 255
Duncanson, Dennis J., 349 n
Dupree, Louis, 360 n
Durant, Will and Ariel, 12, 212, 253, 275–76, 348 n, 360 n, 362 n
Dur Untashi, Iran, 100
Dur Untashi (temple), 99
Dwarf rice crops, 185, 269
Dwarf wheat crops, 119, 121, 123, 133, 177, 309–10, 312, 314

Eastwood, Clint, 52
Economic Development and Social Change (Redfield and Singer), 361 n
Economist, The, 9, 92, 96, 265–66, 304, 337, 348 n, 351 n, 360 n, 362 n, 363 n, 364 n
Egypt, 11, 32, 96, 105, 134, 143–61, 172, 181, 197, 209, 210, 212–13, 214, 216, 217, 218, 219, 222, 242, 247–48, 252, 255–58, 274, 279, 303, 310, 314, 355–56 n, 357 n
   birth control, 158–59
   cultural characteristics and differences (Upper and Lower Egypt), 143–61
   family earnings, 151
   homosexuality, 241
   Islam, 148, 157–58, 160
   migrant labor force, 149
   prostitution, 235–36
   revolutionary change and, 299, 331, 333, 335, 336
   sugar cane crops, 144, 146
   See also Fellaheen; names of cities; villages
Egypt (ancient), 99, 100, 211
Ehrlich, Paul, 308, 364 n

Elam, 353 n
Elamite people, 98, 100, 107, 353 n
"Elective village" proposal, 10
Elizabeth II, Queen, 30, 93
El Kom, Egypt, 150, 154
El-Obeid, Sudan, 29, 32, 39
El robo practice (bride theft), 84
Empire's Children: The People of Tzintzuntzan (Foster), 198, 358 n
Environmentalists, 176
Eskimos, 195
Essay on the Principle of Population, An (Malthus), 362 n
Ethical prophets, 263–64
Ethics (Aristotle), 363 n
Ethiopia, 30
Euphrates River, 209, 211
Evans-Pritchard, E. E., 222
Evil Eye, the, 256
Exemplary prophets, 264
Exorcism, 277
Exorcist, The (motion picture), 251
Expanded Program of Technical Assistance (EPTA), 93
Extended families, 214–15
Extrasensory perception (ESP), 253

Fairbank, John King, 305, 363 n
Family, village characteristics of, 341–42
Fanon, Frantz, 300, 363 n
Fantasia (motion picture), 36
Faulkner, William, 212, 293
Favelados (of Salvador, Brazil), 13–14, 15
Fellaheen, 143–44, 145, 146, 148–49, 152, 155, 214, 218, 228, 274, 279, 335
   gowns of, 227
   population, 144
   See also Egypt
Fellaheen, The (Ayrout), 355 n, 359 n, 360 n
Ferber, Edna, 293

Fertile Crescent, 210, 221, 297, 308, 328
Fez, Morocco, 226
Fishermen, 198
Five Families: Mexican Case Studies in the Culture of Poverty (Lewis), 80, 196, 352 n, 358 n
Foise, Philip, 205
Folk Culture of Yucatan, The (Miner), 358 n
Following the Equator (Twain), 352 n
Food and Agricultural Organization (FAO), 93, 307–8
Ford Foundation, 325, 351 n
Foreign Affairs, 363 n
Forster, E. M., 72
Foster, George M., 190, 191–92, 198, 202, 203, 358 n, 359 n
Four Men: Living the Revolution—An Oral History of Contemporary Cuba (Lewis), 358–59 n
Fowles, John, 290, 363 n
France, 12, 18, 22–27
Francis, E. K. L., 199–200, 359 n
Freeling, Nicholas, 294
Freeman, Orville, 315
French Archaeological Mission (Iran), 353 n
Freud, Sigmund, 251, 254, 262
Fromm, Erich, 227
Frost, David, 97
Frost, Robert, 232
Fujiwara clan, 211

Gadsden Purchase of 1853, 88
Gagarin, Yuri, 362 n
Gama, Vasco da, 265
Gamelan orchestras, 164, 180
Gandhi, Indira, 134–35, 202, 315, 364 n
Gandhi, Mohandas K., 121, 231
Gandhi, Sanjay, 135
Ganges River, 44, 71, 133, 284, 316
Gangetic Plain, 126, 133, 213

Geertz, Clifford, 180, 356 n
George, St., 14, 15, 278
Getulio Vargas Hospital (Salvador, Brazil), 7
Ghirshman, Roman, 353 n
Ghungrali Village, 111, 120–33, 136–42, 214, 219, 321, 357 n
  agricultural modernization, 136
  boycott (winter of 1969–70), 125–28
  dwarf wheat crops, 121, 123
  jajmani system, 126–27
  Jat-Harijan estrangement, 138–40
  massacre of Moslems (1947), 122
  wheat harvest, 130–32, 142
  See also Caste system (India)
Global 2000 Report to the President, The, 176
Goethe, Johann Wolfgang von, 261
Going Steady (Kael), 365 n
Golden Bowl Be Broken, The (Critchfield), 240
Golden Triangle, 249
Good Earth, The (Buck), 206
Gorky, Maxim, 304, 363 n
Gornick, Vivian, 158, 355 n
Gotungroyung, voluntary labor exchange of, 214
Government and Revolution in Vietnam (Duncanson), 349 n
Graham, Katharine, 176
Grand Gaube Village, 89–91, 93, 94, 95, 217, 276, 365 n
"Great Change Has Started, A" (Critchfield), 337
Great Leap Forward program of 1958–60 (China), 297, 305–6
Greece (ancient), 98, 99, 199–200, 261
Greene, Graham, 93
Green Revolution, 112, 120–21, 133–34, 302, 306–7, 309–17, 325–26, 327, 328, 330, 332
  beginning of, 309–11

meaning of, 306–7
scientific breakthroughs, 315–16
Grieg, Edvard, 292, 338
Griffith, D. W., 100
Gross National Product (GNP),
    327, 333
*Growing Up in an Egyptian Village,
    Silwa, Province of Aswan*
    (Ammar), 359 n
Guadalupe-Hidalgo, Treaty of
    (1848), 88
Guapira Village, 13, 14, 15, 198, 217,
    243, 276, 321
Guatemala, 198
Guerrero State (Mexico), 79
Gunung Merapi (volcano), 179
Gurdwara (Sikh temple), 126
Gurkha troops, 45
Guru Granth Sahib (sacred scrip-
    ture), 125
Gurung people, 48

Haber Process, the, 331
Hagag, Nubi el, 361 n
Hagen, Toni, 351 n
Haggling, market, 214, 225
Hajj to Mecca, 278
Halberstam, David, 350 n
Handlin, Oscar, 199, 359 n
Han dynasty (China), 272
Hannibal, 195
Harijan (untouchable) caste,
    120–22, 123, 126–28, 132,
    138–40, 277
  credo of, 121
  discrimination against, 126
Harvard University, 326
Hashish smoking, 49
Hassan, King, 28
Helambu, Nepal, 46
Hemingway, Ernest, 293
Hemudu, China, 209
Herodianism, 229, 361 n
Herodotus, 147
Hesiod, 359 n

Heterogenetic cities, 229–30
Heterogenetic transformation, 229,
    361 n
High Dam at Aswan, *see* Aswan Dam
Hillary, Sir Edmund, 49
Himalaya Mountains, 42, 44, 46,
    48–50, 133, 135, 337
Hindu caste system, *see* Caste system
    (India)
Hinduism, 164, 165, 179, 228, 253,
    273, 277, 278, 321
Hippie communes of 1960s, 9
History of Egypt, A (Breasted),
    355 n
History of Java (Raffles), 236, 245
History of Persia, A (Sykes), 353 n
Hjort, Howard W., 329, 330–31,
    365 n
Hoe cultivation, 209–10
Homer, 295
Homo sapiens, skull size of, 209
Homosexuality, 5, 240–43, 244, 250
Hong Kong, 228, 266, 333
Hooghly River, 284
Hope, Bob, 70
Horticulture, 220
Hsia, T. A., 363 n
Huaztepec Province (Mexico), 79
Huecorio Village, 83–88, 217, 276,
    321, 365 n
  California migrants and, 84–86
  el robo (bride theft) practice, 84
  land and agriculture, 86–87
  nutrition and diet, 87–88
Humphrey, Hubert, 327
Hunters, herders and fishermen,
    197–98
Huong, Tran Van, 183

Ibsen, Henrik, 292, 338–39, 365 n
Idris, Sheikh, 348 n
Ilagas (Christian terrorists), 56, 57
Iloilo Land Grabbing Association,
    349 n
Imams, 226

India, 44, 45, 84, 110–42, 197, 212, 214, 217, 242, 246, 254, 298, 307, 308, 311–12, 314–15, 317, 364 n
  agricultural potential, 134–36
  caste system, 120–21, 125–27, 203, 277
  dwarf wheat crops, 119, 121, 123, 133
  Green Revolution, 112, 120–21, 133–34
  partition of, 122
  prostitution, 235
  revolutionary change and, 321, 322, 323–24, 325, 328, 329, 331, 333
  See also names of cities; villages
India-Pakistan War, 315
Individual, the, village characteristics of, 341
Indonesia, 162–85, 197, 255, 273, 298
  anti-communist bloodbath of 1965–66, 236
  family earnings, 178
  parental wishes in, 166
  pessimism, 177–78
  population, 179, 180
  prostitution, 236–41
  revolutionary change and, 321, 322, 324, 328
  rice crops, 167, 168, 172, 173, 181, 182, 183, 185
  signs of village prosperity, 183–85
  volcanoes, 179
  See also names of cities; villages
Indus River, 44, 316
Industrial Revolution, 266, 276
Indus Valley, 213
In Hwan Kim, Dr., 272
Inouye, Daniel, 356 n
In Quest of the Historical Jesus (Schweitzer), 278
International Bank for Reconstruction and Development (IBRD), see World Bank

International Development Association (IDA), 93
International Labor Organization (ILO), 93
International Maize and Wheat Improvement Center (Mexico), 177, 309
International Rice Research Institute at Los Baños, 55–56, 297, 349 n, 351 n
International Social Science Journal, 363 n
Interstate Highway System, 201
Intolerance (motion picture), 100
Iran, 96–109, 206, 217–18, 242, 274, 279–80, 303, 308, 353–54 n, 355 n
  archaeological digs in, 210–11
  Islam, 96–97, 98
  1971 Persepolis celebrations, 98
  revolutionary change and, 299, 323, 327, 335
  See also Khuzestan Province; names of cities; villages
Iran California Company, 103, 105, 106, 108
Iran (Ghirshman), 353 n
Iran-Iraq War of 1979–80, 97
Iran, Shah of, see Mohammed Reza Shah Pahlavi
Iroquois Indians, 195
Irrigated agriculture, 213
Irrigation, invention of, 210
Isaacs, Harold R., 363 n
Islam, 30, 31, 41, 96–97, 98, 164, 179, 216, 228, 253, 277, 321, 348–49 n
  attitude toward women, 274–75
  extent of, 273
  fundamentalism, 321, 332, 334
  prophets of, 274
  resurgence of, 97
  See also Koran
Italy, 12

Jackson, Sir Robert, 351 n
Jae-Chang Lee, 272
Jafar Abad, Iran, 354 n
Jajmani system, 126–27, 214, 355 n
Jakarta, Indonesia, 135, 162–63,
        165–74, 176, 181, 213, 228,
        230, 233, 255, 322, 356 n
    betjak drivers, 162–63, 165, 167,
        168–69, 170–71, 173
    prostitution, 236–40
Jamasah clan, 156, 157
James, Henry, 361 n
James, William, 262
Jansen, G. H., 353 n
Jansen, Godfrey, 96
Japan, 211, 266, 275, 307, 319, 323,
        329
Jat (landowning) caste, 120–22,
        123, 126–28, 130, 136–40
Java, 135, 148, 179–85, 197, 203,
        213, 214, 216, 217, 245, 246,
        255, 356–57 n
    revolutionary change and, 322,
        323, 324, 326–27, 335
    rice crops, 181–82
    uniqueness of, 179
    See also Indonesia
Java Sea, 162
Jefferson, Thomas, 301
Jerusalem, 231
Jesus, 234, 263, 274, 277, 278–83
Jesus Christ Superstar (motion pic-
        ture), 281
Jews, 264, 277, 281
Johanson, Donald, 360 n
John Paul II, Pope, 88, 231, 263, 265,
        276, 278
Johnson, Lyndon B., 66, 201, 315,
        360 n
Johnson, Samuel, 336, 365 n
Jomoson, Nepal, 46
Jonestown massacre, 252
Jonglei Canal, 222
Jordan, James D., 364 n
Journalism, 203–5
Joyce, James, 363 n

Joypur Village, 72–76
    dacoits (bandits), 72–74
    education and learning, 76
    food production, 76
    landholdings, 71
Ju-ju magic, 30, 32
Jung, Carl G., 262

Kabul, Afghanistan, 226
Kadugli, Sudan, 37
Kael, Pauline, 8, 11, 53, 100, 334,
        347 n, 362 n, 365 n
Kaif (mental state), 218
Kainjinero (poor men), 53
Karjung Mountains, 36
Karma, 46
Karnow, Stanley, 363 n
Karun River, 280
Katmandu, Nepal, 43, 45, 259, 337
Kelud (volcano), 179
Kendall, Sir Maurice, 322
Kennedy, John F., 327
Kenya, 316
Khampa bandits, 42, 49
Khan, Ayub, 311
Khartoum, Sudan, 29, 30, 33, 39,
        348 n
Khartoum University, 38
Khomeini, Ayatollah, 96–97, 205,
        206, 230, 334, 335
Khrushchev, Nikita, 303, 304, 362 n
Khush, Gurdev S., 297, 349 n
Khuzestan Province (Iran), 97–108,
        209
    agribusinesses, 105–8
    ancient history, 98–101, 353–54 n
    Bedouin nomads, 100, 101, 102,
        108
    historical background, 98
    modernization attempts, 102–5
    See also Iran
Kim Hwan Yun, 270
Kim Lien Village, 66–70
Kipling, Rudyard, 284
Kissinger, Henry, 71
Kolak tribe, 37

Koran, 33, 76, 143, 153, 156, 226, 231, 242, 247, 256, 274, 275, 279; *See also* Islam
Korea, 266, 275, 276, 299, 319
  Confucian thought in, 266–72, 273
  family income (South Korea), 268–69
  See also North Korea; South Korea; names of cities; villages
Korean War, 268
Krakatoa (volcano), 179
Kretek cigarettes, 162
Krishanjit, Singh, 361 n
Krishna, Raj, 134, 135
Kristos (bookies), 58
Kroeber, A. L., 196, 211, 360 n
Kudjurs (rainmakers-faith healers), 30–31, 32–33, 348 n
Ku Klux Klan, 68
K'ung-fu-tzu, 272
Kunlun Mountains, 44
Kuntil anak (ghost of a prostitute), 258
Kuttabs (traditional Moslem schools), 150
Kwakiutl people, 196
Kwangju, Korea, 267, 270

Labor, village characteristics of, 342
Lake Pátzcuaro, 83
Lamaism, 45, 46, 349 n
Land, village characteristics of, 342
Landi, Elissa, 100
Lane, Edward William, 355 n
Langtang Valley, 46
Lansdale, Edward, 196
Laos, 249
Lasch, Christopher, 9, 347 n
Leacock, Eleanor Burke, 358 n
Leakey, Richard and Mary, 360 n
Le Carré, John, 294
Le Monde (newspaper), 92
Lenero, Vicente, 193, 194
Lenin, Nikolai, 301, 302
Lenkerd, Barbara, 348 n
Lent, 12

Lepcha sheep, 42
Lessons of History, The (Durant), 360 n, 362 n
Lévi-Strauss, Claude, 202–3
Lewis, Anthony, 176
Lewis, Oscar, 80, 189–90, 191, 192, 193–94, 195, 196, 197, 198, 199, 202, 204, 206–8, 300, 341, 352 n, 355 n, 358 n, 359 n, 363 n
  "culture of poverty" hypothesis, 200–1
Lewis, Ruth M., 191, 192, 358–59 n
Lewis, Sinclair, 293
L'Express (newspaper), 353 n
Lhasa, Tibet, 42, 259
Lichen tazar (dog barracuda), 90, 352 n
Life in a Mexican Village—Tepoztlán Restudied (Lewis), 352 n
Lifestyle, compared to culture, 11
Lilienthal, David E., 102
Limits to Growth, The, 175–76, 177, 356 n
Lingeman, Richard, 9
Lin Piao, Marshal, 318
Lippmann, Walter, 232–33
Little Community, The (Redfield), 360 n
Little Community, The: Viewpoints for the Study of a Human Whole (Miner), 358 n
"Little tradition" culture, 230, 232
Lobishomen, 347 n
Long Charade, The (Critchfield), 68–69, 299, 350 n
Longfellow, Henry Wadsworth, 292
Long Goodbye, The (Chandler), 8, 347 n
Long Phu Village, 62, 63
Los Angeles *Herald-Examiner,* 85
Los Angeles *Times,* 37
Louis XIV, King, 211
Love, village characteristics of, 342; *See also* Sex
Lur tribe, 104

Luther, Martin, 283
Luxor, Egypt, 145, 147, 152, 226
Luzon, Philippines, 51
Lysenko, T. D., 302, 304

Macaulay, Thomas, 77
MacFarquhar, Emily, 364 n
MacFarquhar, Roderick, 233, 266, 272, 273, 362 n
Macho or *machismo*, 53, 58, 59, 82, 86, 160, 201, 249
MacLeish, Archibald, 92
McNamara, Robert, 337
McNeill, William H., 219, 276, 360 n, 362 n
Macrae, Norman, 265–66, 298, 332, 347–48 n, 360 n, 364 n
Madagascar, 94
Magellan, Ferdinand, 51
Magic Mountain, The (Mann), 260–61
Mahabharata (Hindu epic), 165
Maj Sjowall-Per Wahloo, 294
Malaysia, 96, 333
Male prostitution, 240–43
Malinowski, B., 195–96
Malthus, Thomas Robert, 236, 307, 317, 362 n
Manchuria, 313
Manhattan (motion picture), 8
Manila, Philippines, 55–56, 172, 215, 228, 230, 235
Mann, Thomas, 260–61, 293
Manners and Customs of the Modern Egyptians, The (Lane), 355 n
Mao and China (Karnow), 363 n
Maoism, 283, 305, 306, 317–20, 364 n
Mao Tse-tung, 197, 231, 296, 297, 302, 306, 312, 314, 317–20, 363 n
    criticism of, 304–5
Marais, Jean, 354 n
Marcos, Ferdinand, 52, 54, 55, 56, 57–58

Marcos, Imelda, 52, 56
Mardi Gras, 12
Marquis, Don, 338, 365 n
Marx, Karl, 251, 273, 300, 301, 302
Marx Against the Peasant (Mitrany), 363 n
Marxism-Leninism, 232, 283, 299, 301, 305, 332, 333
Mass Communications History Center (State Historical Society of Wisconsin), 366 n
Maulana, 33
Mauritius, 89–95, 352–53 n
    birthrate, 94
    historical background, 92–93
    population, 93–94
    tourism, 94
    See also names of villages
Maximilian, Emperor, 195
Maximum Feasible Misunderstanding (Moynihan), 360 n
Mayan Indians, 82, 189, 200, 211
Mazhbi (barn-cleaning) caste, 125, 126, 131, 140
Mead, Margaret, 10, 190, 196, 348 n, 359 n, 365 n
Meadows, Dennis L., 176, 356 n
Meadows, Donella H., 176, 356 n
Meals, 217–19
Mecca, 231, 273
Medes (ancient), 98
Medina, 16–17, 348 n
Mekong Delta, 62, 213
Mekong River, 44, 316
Mendel, Gregor, 302
Menon, Krishna, 303
Merissa beer, 30, 40
Mesopotamia, 209, 210–11, 212–13, 219, 231
Mestizos, 83–84
Metaphysics, 263; *See also* Spiritual challenge (and meaning of life)
Metaphysics (Aristotle), 363 n
Methodist Church, 292

Mexican-Americans (or Chicanos), 81
Mexican Revolution (1910–1917), 79, 298, 299
Mexico, 78–88, 112, 172, 189, 198, 199, 209, 214, 217, 307, 359 n, 364 n
  agriculture, 82
  dwarf wheat crops, 309–10, 312, 314
  gross national product, 82
  "illegales" in the United States, 81, 82–83
  imports and exports, 88
  mestizos, 83–84
  oil industry, 81, 88
  revolutionary change and, 333
  See also names of cities; villages
Mexico City, 78, 79, 87, 176, 233, 312
Miet Abu el Koum Village, 159
Militant Islam (Jansen), 353 n
Mindanao, 51
Miner, Horace, 358 n
Minh, Ho Chi, 69
Mitrany, David, 300–1, 363 n
Mohammed (prophet), 156, 234, 263, 274, 278
Mohammed Reza Shah Pahlavi, Shah of Iran, 96, 97, 98, 99, 100, 102, 103, 104, 107, 108
Mongol Empire, 98
Mongolia, 210
Montezuma, Emperor, 79
Morgan, Lewis H., 195
Morocco, 11, 16–22, 27–28, 46, 203, 218, 242, 273, 274, 348 n
Moro pirates, 51, 52
Moses (prophet), 274
Moslem Brotherhood (extremist movement), 248
Moslem League, 73
Moslems, see Islam; names of countries
Mount Agung, 179
Mount Sinila, 179

Mouvement Militant Mauricien (MMM), 94–95
Moynihan, Daniel P., 201–2, 360 n
Mughal Empire, 126
Mukhiarmanan (legal transfer of financial responsibility), 111
Mulattoes, 3, 4, 347 n
Murphy, Audie, 57
Murrow, Edward R., 206
Mussolini, Benito, 307
Mustang region (Nepal), 45
Myrdal, Gunnar, 364 n
My Tho Village, 62

Nam O Bridge, 69, 70
Nan Gao Village, 320
Naraghi, Hashem, 103
Narvez, I., 311
Nasser, Gamal Abdel, 143, 315
Nationalism, 232
  ideologies of, 234
Nature and Destiny of Man, The (Niebuhr), 362 n
Naxalites, 73
Neophiliacs, The (Booker), 347 n
Neetil Mountain, 31
Neetil Village, 29–41, 212, 217, 321
  agriculture, 30
  baboon menace, 35
  cattle thefts, 37–38
  conversion to Islam, 30, 31, 41, 348–49 n
  crime of rape, 36
  disease, 32
  drum rhythm and dancing, 34–35
  haunted mountain beliefs, 36–37
  indentured herdsmen, 38–39
  kudjurs (faith healers), 30–31, 32–33, 348 n
  nakedness, 34
  tribalism, 348 n
Nefertiti, Queen, 143
Negahban, Essat O., 353 n
Nehru, Jawaharlal, 134, 135, 231, 232, 314, 315, 362 n, 364–65 n

Neolithic Age, 209, 224, 308, 360 n
Nepal, 42–50, 133, 212, 234, 259, 337
  local border trade, 44
  See also names of villages
"New China and the American Connection, The" (Fairbank), 363 n
New Delhi, India, 133, 259
New York *Times, The,* 158, 355 n, 362 n
Niblock, Tom, 174
Niebuhr, Reinhold, 265, 362 n
Niger River, 316
Nile Delta, 213, 219, 335
Nile River, 143, 146–47, 158, 209, 216, 219, 222, 232
Nile Valley, 145–46, 209–10, 213, 356 n
Nimang (subtribe), 33, 38, 348 n
Nineveh, 100, 354 n
Nixon, Richard, 197, 201, 360 n
Noah (prophet), 274
Non Nok Tha, Thailand, 209
North Korea, 270, 272; *See also* Korea
North Vietnam, 236; *See also* Vietnam
Notes on the State of Virginia (Jefferson), 301, 363 n
Nuba, Die (Riefenstahl), 349 n
Nuba Mountains, 29–31, 32, 38, 39, 254, 348 n
  haunted beliefs, 36–37
Nuba people, 29, 212, 216, 224, 245, 335, 348–49 n
  tribal religion, 253
Nuer tribe, 210

O'Connell, J. R., 348 n
Office of Economic Opportunity, 201
O'Hara, Maureen, 334–35
Oman, 249
Om mani padme hum, utterance of, 47
On Human Nature (Wilson), 261

On the Russian Peasantry (Gorky), 363 n
Organization for Economic Cooperation and Development, 327
Organon (Aristotle), 363 n
Orissa Village, 285, 286
Orozco, José Clemente, 81
Orthogenetic transformation, 229, 361 n
Our Town (Wilder), 365 n
Oxford Book of American Light Verse, The, 365 n

Pahlavi, *see* Mohammed Reza Shah Pahlavi
Pakistan, 96, 111, 122, 212, 242, 249, 307, 311–12, 314, 317, 356 n
  revolutionary change and, 321, 323, 325, 333
  See also names of cities; villages
Pan-p'o, China, 209
Papanek, Hanna, 238
Param cattle camp, 222–23
Park Chung Hee, 267, 268, 269, 270–71
Parsees, 264
Parthians (ancient), 98
"Participant-observer" method, 191
Paul (Apostle), 277
Paul VI, Pope, 251–52
Payne, Dr. William, 222
Paysans de Syrie et du Proche-Orient (Weuleresse), 359 n
Paz, Octavio, 84
Peace Corps, 20, 49, 175
Peasant, defined, 197, 211
"Peasants, The" (Chekhov), 289
Peasants (Wolf), 360 n
Peasant Society and Culture (Miner), 358 n
Peasant Society and Culture (Redfield), 200, 207, 341, 361 n, 363 n
Peasant Society: A Reader (ed. Potter, Diaz and Foster), 359 n, 363 n

Peasant Wars of the Twentieth Century (Wolf), 299, 363 n
Peattie, Dr. Lisa, 192
Pedernales River Electric Cooperative, 315
Pedro Martinez: A Mexican Peasant and His Family (Lewis), 80, 207, 358 n, 363 n
Peer Gynt (Ibsen), 338–39, 365 n
Peking, China, 176–77, 230, 233, 296, 305, 317–18
Persepolis, Iran, 98, 99
Pershing, General John J. "Black Jack," 51
Persia, *see* Iran
Persian Empire, 98
Peru, 209
Philippines, 51–60, 84, 87, 174, 212, 259, 307
    Christian-Moslem tensions, 51, 56
    influence of pop culture in, 52–53
    martial law, 55
    prostitution, 235, 240
    revolutionary change and, 325, 333
    See also names of cities; villages
Pilangsari Village, 163–64, 166–70, 178, 257, 274, 321, 357 n
    brick homes, 172–73
    rice crops, 167, 168, 172, 173
Plants, domestication of, 209
Plato, 7, 283, 291
Podeb lamas, 48
Poetics (Aristotle), 363 n
Pokhara, Nepal, 43
Politics (Aristotle), 363 n
Polo, Marco, 195
Polyandry, 48, 245
Polygamy, 48, 225, 242, 245
Population Bomb, The (Ehrlich), 308, 364 n
Porak, René, 199, 359 n
Port Louis, Mauritius, 93
Portugal, 12
Possessed, The (Dostoevsky), 294
"Post-Confucian Challenge, The" (MacFarquhar), 266

Potala Palace (Lhasa), 45
Potter, Jack M., 359 n, 363 n
Powers That Be, The (Halberstam), 350 n
Precognition, 254, 362 n
Pre-industrial city, concept of, 225–26, 228, 229, 361 n
Premarital sex, 245
President's Council on Environmental Quality, 176
Primitive World and Its Transformations, The (Miner), 358 n
Prison Civile (Casablanca), 20, 26, 28
Profumo, John, 9
Prophets, 263–64, 281, 302; *See also* names of prophets
Prostitution, 14, 235–44, 250, 348 n
    male, 240–42, 250
    willing widow, 243–44
Protestant work ethic, 276, 312
Psychokinesis, 253, 255–60
Puerto Rico, 189, 359 n
Punjab Plain, 123–24, 213
Purim, 99
Pusan, Korea, 268

Qom, Iran, 230
Quakers, 292
Quang, Tri, 206
Quang Ngai, Vietnam, 62
Quinn, Anthony, 192–93
Quinn, Duncan, 192
Qurna Friendship Club (Cairo), 227

Rabat, Morocco, 20
Radcliffe-Brown, A. R., 195–96
Raffles, Sir Thomas Stamford, 236, 245
Rahman, Sheikh Mujibur, 71
Ramadan, Moslem fast of, 151
Ramanuja, 283
Ramgoolam, Seewoosagur, 93
Ramses III, 257, 355 n
Randers, Jorgen, 356 n

Ray, Satyajit, 72
Reagan, Ronald, 185
Recodo Village, 60
Red China: An Asian View (Sekhar), 363 n
Redfield, Robert, 189, 190, 191–92, 194–95, 196, 197, 198, 200, 204–5, 206–8, 211–12, 229–31, 234, 300, 341, 352 n, 357–58 n, 360 n, 361 n, 363 n
Red Guards (China), 296, 318
Red River, 213
Reed, Brigadier General Joseph, 293
Reeling (Kael), 347 n, 362 n
Reformation, 283
Reining, Priscilla Copeland, 348 n
Religion, village characteristics of, 343; *See also* Prophets; Supernatural beliefs; names of religions
Religion of Java, The (Geertz), 356 n
Renaissance, 283
Renan, Ernest, 251
Reporter (magazine), 364 n
Retrocognition, 254
Revolutionary change, 321–39
  agriculture through irrigation, 323–24
  anti-growth attitudes, 326–27
  cause of, 321
  contraception, 322, 323, 325
  failure of communism, 333
  farming methods, 322
  food outlook, 329–30
  Green Revolution, 325–26, 327, 328, 330, 332
  international agriculture, 325–26
  population growth, 322–23
  reverse migration, 322
  U.S. technology, 326–31, 332
  villagers' love affair with America, 334–35
  women's movement, 324
Riefenstahl, Leni, 349 n
Riesman, David, 227

Rio de Janeiro, 4, 12, 228, 230, 233
Rio Grande, 82
Rise of the West, The (McNeill), 219, 276, 360 n, 362 n
Rivera, Diego, 81
Rockefeller Foundation, 309–10, 311, 312, 325
Rojas, Sarah, 359 n
Rolangs (zombie-like humans), 48
Roman Catholic Church, 13, 14, 52, 53, 82, 87, 276, 278, 321, 330
Romanni Village, 17–22, 274
Rome (ancient), 12, 13, 99, 261, 308
Rosemary's Baby (motion picture), 251
Rosenfeld, Stephen, 327–28
Rosetta, Egypt, 145
Royal Calcutta Turf Club, 285
Rural Sociology, 360 n
Russia, *see* Union of Soviet Socialist Republics (U.S.S.R.)
Russian Revolution, 298, 299
Rusticus Loquitur: The Old Light and the New in a Punjab Village (Darling), 359 n

Sadat, Anwar, 144, 158, 159, 231, 248, 252, 334, 353 n, 355–56 n
Sadat, Jihan, 353 n
Sadikin, Governor Ali, 165, 166, 168, 238
Safer, Morley, 350 n
Sahel, Ethiopia, 32, 308
Saigon, South Vietnam, 236
St. Denis, a French Canadian Parish (Miner), 358 n
Saladin, 147, 226
Salinger, J. D., 293
Salvador, Brazil, 3–15, 231
  favelados, 15
  Guapira Village and, 13, 14, 15
  pre-Lenten *Carnaval,* 3–7, 11, 12, 15, 347 n

religion and superstitious beliefs,
14–15
Salween River, 44
Samba (dance), 13
Sanders, Irwin T., 359 n
San Ramon, Philippines, 52
São Paulo, Brazil, 233
Sartre, Jean-Paul, 215
Sassanians (ancient), 98
Saturnalia festival (ancient Rome),
12–13
Savak (Iranian secret police), 107
Schistosomiasis, 14
Schuchat, Molly G., 364 n
Schumacher, E. F., 175, 356 n
Schweitzer, Albert, 278
Science (publication), 354 n
Scythia (ancient), 308
Sega songs, 91, 95
Sekhar, Sripati Chandra, 363 n
Selected Works (Mao Tse-tung),
363 n
Senegal River, 316
Seoul, Korea, 176, 267–68, 272
Seoul University, 270
Sermon on the Mount, 233, 273, 282
Sertão, 4
Seti I, 257
Sevareid, Eric, 206
Sex, 235–50
    conversation, 246
    dances, 35
    divorce, 245–46, 247–48
    fertility, 249
    homosexuality, 5, 240–43, 244, 250
    male superiority, 247–50
    poverty, 235
    premarital, 245
    prostitution, 235–44, 250
    repression, aggression, and hostility,
    246–47
    village characteristics of, 342
    virginity, 248
    week of Carnaval (Salvador, Bra-
    zil), 5–6
    "willing widow," 243–44

Shahhat: an Egyptian (Critchfield),
147, 199, 242–43, 355 n,
358 n
Shakespeare, William, 240, 293
Shamanism, 46, 267
Shanghai, China, 233
Shankara, 283
Sharia law, 226
Shell Mitchell Cotts Company, 103
Shilluk tribe, 210
Shush-Daniel Village, 97–108, 212,
274, 321
    agribusinesses, 105–8
    ancient history, 98–101, 353–54 n
    Bedouin nomads, 100, 101, 102,
    108
    modernization attempts, 102–5
Sikhs, 116, 119, 122, 125, 126, 127,
142, 284, 354–55 n
Sikkim, 44
Simprug, Indonesia, 163, 356–57 n
Singapore, 228, 230, 235, 266, 333
Singer, Milton B., 229–30, 361 n
Singh, Chanan, 258
Singh, Khushwant, 355 n
Sirs El Layyan Village, 145, 150–59,
160–61, 274, 324
Sjoberg, Gideon, 225, 361 n
Slash-and-burn agriculture, 212
Slave trade, 4, 38
Small Is Beautiful (Schumacher),
175, 177, 356 n
Small Town America (Lingeman), 9
Smith, D. Howard, 362 n
Snow, C. P., 308, 309, 364 n
Snow, Edgar, 305
Social anthropology, research model
for, 195–96
Society, village characteristics of,
344–46
Sociology of Religion, The (Weber),
362 n
Socrates, 272, 283
Sodom and Gomorrah, 231
Sodomy, 236, 242
Soetoro, Ann, 356 n

South Africa, 331
South Korea, 322, 323, 324, 329, 333
  agriculture transformation, 269
  dissidents, 271
  See also Korea; North Korea
South Vietnam, 61–70, 349–50 n
  boat people, 64
  Confucian culture, 64
  prostitution, 236
  terrorism, 64, 65, 66, 68
  See also North Vietnam; Vietnam
South Vietnamese Army, 61
South Yemen, 273
Spain, 12
Spectator, The, 365 n
Spengler, Oswald, 265
Sphinx, 147
Spiritual challenge (and meaning of
      life), 263–82, 362 n
  Confucianism, 266–72, 273, 276
  Islamic world, 273–75
  Jesus and, 278–83
  prophets, 263–64, 281
  Protestantism, 276–77, 278
  rejection of scholarly arrogance,
      281–82
  Toynbee and, 264–65, 273, 275,
      278, 283
Sri Lanka, 322, 324
Stalin, Joseph, 303
Stanley, Sir Henry, 195
Steinbeck, John, 105
Steiner, George, 8, 347 n
"Steppe, The" (Chekhov), 289
Sterling, Claire, 176
Stress, 215, 218
Structuralism, 202–3
Study of History, A (Toynbee), 264,
      361 n
Study of Slum Culture, The—
      Backgrounds for La Vida
      (Lewis), 358 n
Subramaniam, C., 315
Sudan, 29–41, 105, 134, 210,
      221–24, 241–42, 249, 303,
      316

agriculture and cattle grazing,
      31–32
  See also names of villages
Sudd swamp (Sudan), 210, 221–24
Suharto, 185
Sukarno, 162, 163
Sulu Island villages, 52
Sulu Sea, 51
Sumer (ancient), 98, 209, 210, 213,
      353 n, 354 n
Sun Yat-sen, Dr., 320
Supernatural beliefs, 251–62
  demonology revival, 251–53
  existence of the inexplicable,
      260–62
  and fate, 252–53
  precognition, 254
  psychokinesis, 255–60
  telepathy and clairvoyance, 254–55
  village characteristics of, 343–44
  See also Religion
Survival phenomena, 253
Susa, city of, see Shush-Daniel
      Village
Susangerd, Iran, 354 n
Sushiana Plain, 98, 209
Sutlej River, 44
Suyin, Han, 305
Swaminathan, M. S., 311
Sykes, Sir Percy, 353 n

Tagore, Rabindranath, 76
Taiwan, 266, 272, 275, 278
  revolutionary change and, 322,
      323, 324, 329, 333
Tamang people, 48
Tamerlane, 98
Tan An, Vietnam, 65
T'ang dynasty, 211
Tantric rituals, 46
Tanzania, 94, 273, 316
Taoism, 278
Tarascan Indians, 83–84
Tarkington, Booth, 293
Tashi Palkhiel Tibetan Camp
      (Nepal), 42–50, 260, 349 n

death customs, 44
  flight to, 42–43
  folk beliefs, 47
  lamaism, 45–46, 349 n
  religious beliefs, 46–47
  yeti beliefs, 48–49
Tehran, Iran, 98, 230
Telepathy, 254–55
Telesphorus, St., 12
Ten Commandments, 282
Tennyson, Alfred Lord, 365 n
Tepoztlán, Mexico, 78–81, 189, 191, 192, 195, 196, 199, 200, 207, 358 n, 359 n
  real estate values, 78–79
Tepoztlán—a Mexican Village (Redfield), 189, 352 n, 358 n
Tepoztlán Restudied (Lewis), 189, 358 n
Thailand, 209, 235, 249, 333
Thompson, Sir Robert, 349 n
Thoughts (Mao Tse-tung), 320
Tibet, 42–43, 44, 47, 48, 49, 50, 245, 259, 349 n
  Chinese rule of, 42–43, 44
  local border trade, 44
  See also Tashi Palkhiel Tibetan Camp (Nepal)
Tibetan Buddhism, 274
Tigris River, 209, 210
Time (magazine), 78, 220–21, 251, 336, 347 n, 360 n
Tithonus (Tennyson), 365 n
Tlaloc (rain god), 79
Togo, 249
Toilet facilities, 356–57 n
Toilet paper, 357 n
Tolchin, Susan and Martin, 362 n
Tolstoy, Leo, 8, 277, 293, 294, 304, 336, 361 n, 363 n, 365 n
Tolstoy or Dostoyevsky (Steiner), 347 n
Torah, 231
Tower of Babel legend, 99

Toynbee, Arnold, 229, 232, 264–65, 273, 275, 278, 283, 332–33, 361 n, 362 n
Tragedy of the Chinese Revolution, The (Isaacs), 363 n
Train to Pakistan (Singh), 355 n
Transvestites, 5, 235, 236, 240
Trapp family, 195
"Trash, Art and the Movies" (Kael), 334
Trio elétrico (truck-mounted rock band), 4–5, 6, 13
Troyat, Henri, 363 n
Trudeau, Garry, 11
Tsangpo River, 42
Tsinling Mountains, 209
Tuchman, Barbara, 335, 365 n
Tulungatung Village, 51–60, 217, 276, 321
  agriculture, 53, 54–55
  Christian-Moslem tensions, 51, 56, 349 n
  cockfights, 53, 58
  education, 52, 53–54
  faith in God, 58–59
  family planning, 59–60
  influence of American pop culture, 52–53, 56
  insect infestation, 54
  thefts, 51, 60
Turgenev, Ivan, 277
Turkey, 96, 273, 325
"Turn, turn, turn, turn, turn, turn into a wolfman!" (*Carnaval* song), 5, 15, 347 n
Twain, Mark, 91, 293, 352 n, 354 n
Twenty-third Psalm, 279–80
Tylor, E. B., 195
Tzintzuntzan Village, 198
Tz'u-hsi, Empress, 320

Uganda, 316
Ulysses (Joyce), 363 n
Union of Soviet Socialist Republics (U.S.S.R.), 105, 211, 214, 273, 325, 326, 329, 331, 364 n

Afghan occupation, 273–74
agriculture, 302–4
grain imports, 304
United Nations (U.N.), 43, 93,
    350–51 n
United Nations Educational,
    Scientific, and Cultural Organ-
    ization (UNESCO), 93, 145
United Nations International Chil-
    dren's Emergency Fund
    (UNICEF), 93
United States Bureau of the Census,
    316
United States Department of Agricul-
    ture, 329, 365 n
United States Department of State,
    176
United States Immigration and Natu-
    ralization Service, 82–83
University of Nagpur, 360 n
Untouchables, see Harijan (untouch-
    able) caste
Uprooted, The (Handlin), 199,
    359 n

Valentine, Charles A., 358 n
Vale of Kashmir, 364 n
Vavilov, Nikolay Ivanovich, 303
Vedas, 231
Victoria, Queen, 292
Viet Cong, 61, 64, 67–70, 350 n
Vietnam, 61–70, 162, 174, 183, 218,
    236, 266, 301, 349–50 n
  boat people, 64
  Confucian culture, 64
  prostitution, 235
  revolutionary change and, 299,
      323, 325, 326, 327, 333
  terrorism, 64, 65, 66, 68
  See also names of cities; villages;
      South Vietnam
Village de France, Un; Psychophysio-
    logie du paysan (Porak),
    359 n
Village Java 1979 (Critchfield),
    356 n

Village Life in Northern India
    (Lewis), 355 n, 359 n
Villages
  agriculture and, 212–24
    daily routine, 215–17
    living in groups, 213–15
    meals, 217–19
    shrinking land, 213
    technology and modernization,
        219–24
    types of agriculture, 212–13
    women, 216–17
  and anthropology, 189–208,
      357–60 n
    Redfield-Lewis debate, 189,
        194–95, 206–8
  characteristics, 341–46
    agricultural moral code, 342–43
    family, 341–42
    individual, 341
    labor, 342
    land, 342
    religion, 343
    sex and love, 342
    society, 344–46
    supernatural supports to religion,
        343–44
    world view, 344
  and city, 225–34, 361 n
    cultural gap, 231–32
    ex-colonial port cities, 229
    freedom, 233
    immigrants (in Cairo), 226–27
    Islamic, Hindu, or Far Eastern
        cities, 228–29
    "little tradition" culture, 230,
        232
    orthogenetic and heterogenetic
        transformation, 229–31
    pre-industrial city, 225–26, 228,
        229, 361 n
    urbanization (in the West),
        228–29
  and culture, 10–12
    economic basis of, 9

debate about character of, 189, 194–95, 206–7
and ideas, 189–339
number of, 10
origin of, 209–12
and people, 3–185
revolutionary change and, 321–39
  agriculture through irrigation, 323–24
  anti-growth attitudes, 326–27
  causes, 321
  contraception, 322, 323, 325
  failure of communism, 333
  farming methods, 322
  food outlook, 329–30
  Green Revolution, 325–26, 327, 328, 330, 332
  international agriculture, 325–26
  population growth, 322–23
  reverse migration, 322
  U.S. technology, 326–31, 332
  villagers' love affair with America, 334–35
  women's movement, 324
sex and, 235–50
  conversation, 246
  divorce, 245–46, 247–48
  fertility, 249
  homosexuality, 240–43, 250
  male superiority, 247–50
  poverty, 235
  premarital sex, 245
  prostitution, 235–44, 250
  repression, aggression, and hostility, 246–47
  virginity, 248
  "willing widow," 243–44
spiritual challenge (and meaning of life), 263–82, 362 n
  Confucianism, 266–72, 273, 276
  Islamic world, 273–75
  Jesus and, 278–83
  prophets, 263–64, 281
  Protestantism and, 276–77, 278
  rejection of scholarly arrogance, 281–82

Toynbee and, 264–65, 273, 275, 278, 283
supernatural beliefs, 251–62
  existence of the inexplicable, 260–62
  and fate, 252–53
  precognition, 254
  psychokinesis, 255–60
  telepathy and clairvoyance, 254–55
Village That Chose Progress, A: Chan Kom Revisited (Miner), 358 n
Village Viability in Contemporary Society (Mead), 348 n, 359 n, 364 n
Virginity, 248
Visayan Islands, 51
Volta River, 316
Voodoo, 12

Wali (subtribe), 38
Walters, Barbara, 97
War and Peace (Tolstoy), 363 n, 365 n
Ward, Barbara, 295, 308, 351 n
Ward, Lyttleton T., Jr., 67–68
Washington, George, 293
Washington Post, 172, 205, 327
Washington Star, 201, 259, 350 n, 366 n
Watership Down (Adams), 328, 365 n
Wayang kulit (shadow play), 164
Wayne, John, 334–35
Weber, Max, 263, 276, 277, 362 n
Werewolf beliefs, 14, 347 n
Wesley, John, 283
Weuleresse, J., 359 n
What Price Glory?, 61
White, Timothy, 360 n
White Revolution (Iran), 104
Wilder, Thornton, 293, 365 n
Wilson, Edward O., 261
Wilson, George, 103, 105
Wolf, Eric R., 299, 300, 360 n, 363 n

Wolfe, Thomas, 11
Womack, John, Jr., 359 n
Works and Days (Hesiod),
    199–200, 359 n
World Bank, 91–92, 93, 182, 311,
    326, 337, 356 n
World Fertility Survey, 322
World Health Organization (WHO),
    93
World view, village characteristics of,
    344
World War I, 331
World War II, 51, 57, 84, 266, 285
Wretched of the Earth, The
    (Fanon), 363 n

Xerxes, 99

Yama (god of death), 285
Yangtze River, 44, 313, 316
Yangtze Valley, 213
Yaqui Valley, 309
Yarmolinsky, Avrahm, 290
Yellow River, 213, 313, 316

Yeti beliefs, 48–49
Yi Dynasty (Korea), 267
Yogyakarta, 226
Yucatan, 189, 200
Yudelman, Montague, 311

Zabeeb (beverage), 154–55
Zagros Mountains, 99, 209, 210
Zaire, 316
Zambesi River, 316
Zamboanga City, Philippines, 51, 52,
    56
Zapatista guerrillas, 79
Zealotism, 229, 361 n
Zero population growth, 316
Zhejiang Province (China), 209
Zhungru, Tibet, 42, 43
Ziggurats, 99
Zomnitz, Claudio, 80
Zoology of the Voyage of the Beagle
    (Darwin), 352 n
Zoroaster, 234, 308
Zuñi Indians, 196